AMERICA'S COLD WAR

AMERICA'S COLD WAR

THE POLITICS OF INSECURITY

Second Edition

Campbell Craig and Fredrik Logevall

The Belknap Press of
Harvard University Press
Cambridge, Massachusetts
London, England

Library of Congress Cataloging-in-Publication Data
Craig, Campbell, 1964–
America's Cold War: The Politics of Insecurity / Campbell Craig and Fredrik Logevall.
p. cm.
Includes bibliographical references and index.
ISBN 978-0-674-03553-9 (cloth : alk. paper)
ISBN 978-0-674-06406-5 (pbk.)
ISBN 978-0-674-24493-1 (pbk.)
1. United States—Foreign relations—1945–1989.   2. United States—Foreign
relations—1989–   3. United States—Politics and government—1945–1989.
4. United States—Politics and government—1989–   5. Cold War—Influence.
I. Logevall, Fredrik, 1963–   II. Title.
E744.C825   2009
909.82—dc22   2009012569

For Sylvie, Elise, Emma, and Joseph

CONTENTS

PREFACE TO THE SECOND EDITION

In the first edition of this book we attempted to make a fresh intervention in the long-running historical debate about U.S. foreign policy during the Cold War. We sought to offer a narrative history of that policymaking but also to put forth a specific—and we believed original—line of argument. In particular, we aimed to show that the vast historiography on the struggle, though extremely valuable in numerous respects, had underplayed the role of domestic politics in the making of U.S. foreign policy after 1945. In our judgment, the desire of American politicians to get and stay in power, to cater to powerful constituencies, among them industries, labor unions, lobby groups, and donors, and to lambast their rivals as weak and naïve, shaped U.S. foreign policymaking during the Cold War in important ways, and indeed helps to explain why the conflict lasted as long as it did.

In making this historical argument, we were also making a larger claim about U.S. foreign relations generally. We suggested that, in the decades after World War II, domestic politics exerted singular influence on foreign policy because of the long geopolitical condition of "free security" (C. Vann Woodward's phrase), which permitted the United States to undertake its foreign policy with less caution and gravity than comparable powerful states elsewhere. The great oceans bracketing the nation, together with the absence of any other great powers in the Western Hemisphere, provided the United States with an easy physical security, especially when contrasted with major powers in Europe and Asia. That meant that the stakes of getting things wrong, of doing something ill-considered, were lower than they were for a nation with powerful rivals just across a border. And that meant in turn that there was far more latitude for politicians to let domestic considerations guide their decisions about foreign policy. The result, we argued, was the "politics of insecurity": a political culture in America in which lawmakers in Washington recognized a powerful incentive to inflate threats, demonize adversaries, and perennially deny that the United States was in fact enviably secure.

This new edition of *America's Cold War* maintains the overarching structure and line of analysis of the first edition. We have, however, altered sections and added material throughout the book to reflect new historical writing, particularly on the latter stages of the Cold War, which has been the subject of abundant new scholarship in recent years. In addition, we have updated our arguments in several places in light of our own writing over the last decade, including on Franklin D. Roosevelt's diplomacy toward the end of World War II, on the intensification and expansion of U.S. foreign policy in the 1950s, on the war in Vietnam, and on the development of the nuclear nonproliferation regime in the late 1960s. Finally, we have rewritten the latter parts of the concluding chapter in light of developments in U.S. foreign policy over the past decade. Despite these changes, however, we have found no reason to revise our larger claim that domestic politics and the salience of free security remain a powerful means of understanding American foreign policy. Indeed, we find ourselves feeling even more confident about this argument in 2020 than we did in 2009.

For their assistance in the preparation of this revised edition, we thank Tomek Maciak and, especially, Karen McCabe.

AMERICA'S COLD WAR

INTRODUCTION

Absence of threat permits policy to become capricious.
—KENNETH WALTZ

On a freezing winter night at Grinnell College—a liberal arts institution in the middle of rural Iowa—a distinguished diplomat and historian, his eightieth birthday just two weeks away, rose to speak on the topic of "American Democracy and Foreign Policy." A crowd of undergraduates and faculty, many of them aware of George F. Kennan's legendary status as "the father of containment," a few of them perhaps not, hurried in to escape the arctic air and filled the pews of the college's dimly lit Herrick Chapel. It was February 1, 1984, the eve of Iowa's famous presidential caucus.

Mindful of the portentous implications of that particular year, Kennan might well have spoken triumphantly of what he and his colleagues had set in motion almost forty years earlier when they took the United States into a Cold War against Stalin's Soviet Union. The predictions in George Orwell's dystopian novel had not come to pass. Rather than yielding to the inexorable march of totalitarianism that Orwell had foretold, the United States bristled with power and confidence, its economy thriving, its democratic institutions intact. "It's morning in America," President Ronald Reagan would exult during his campaign for reelection a few months hence. The Soviet Union, meanwhile, was beset by troubles. While its military power, especially its immense nuclear arsenal, remained formidable, its economy was dysfunctional, its ideology moribund, its imperial rule over eastern Europe brittle and despised. The containment strategy Kennan had helped fashion back in 1946 and 1947 appeared to have worked just as advertised. The great man had reason to be proud.

Instead, he was worried. Worried, he told his audience, about the "extreme militarization not only of our thought but of our lives" during the Cold War. Worried about the growing power of the military-industrial complex, about America's antipathy to diplomacy with adversaries, about the wars fought and weapons bought and crusades undertaken long after containment had apparently been achieved. Worried, above all, about the fact that American foreign policy was becoming more alarmist than ever before, even as the Soviet threat had diminished. "I wonder," Kennan asked, "whether this confusion is not compounded by certain deeply ingrained features of our political system . . . I am thinking first of all about what I might call the domestic self-consciousness of the American statesman. By this I mean his tendency, when speaking or acting on matters of foreign policy, to be more concerned for the domestic political effects of what he is saying or doing than about their actual effects on our relations with other countries . . . Every statesman everywhere has to give *some* heed to domestic opinion in the conduct of his diplomacy. But the tendency seems to be carried to greater extremes here than elsewhere."[1]

Kennan sought to understand the wide gap between the containment strategy he had helped conceive and the Cold War that America had come to wage. It wasn't that he thought the original decision to enter the struggle had been wrong, or the Soviet threat a mirage. He had indeed been among the first analysts in the mid-1940s to call for a policy of containing the USSR. Far earlier than most, he had characterized the Soviet Union as a uniquely cynical and brutal nation whose power must be checked. His vision had won out, as the Truman administration adopted a postwar foreign policy designed to dissuade the Soviet Union from expanding into key regions.[2]

And the policy succeeded beautifully. From the American point of view, containment had largely been achieved by 1949. Western Europe was by then firmly in the American camp, as was Japan, which meant that Kremlin leaders could no longer contemplate a retreat by the United States to its own hemisphere, leaving Eurasia open to their territorial designs. Now it was time to parley. As Kennan later remembered, containment was designed to demonstrate to leaders in Moscow that "they are not going to succeed in extending their rule to further areas by political intrigue and intimidation, that they cannot serve their own interests without dealing with us; and then, when a political balance has been created, to go on to negotiation with Moscow of a general political settlement."[3]

The political balance had been largely achieved by 1949. To the extent it hadn't, the scale tilted toward the United States and the West. But Washington declined to pursue a general political settlement at midcentury, and still had not done so by the time Kennan took the stage at Grinnell College three and a half decades later. The Cold War raged on, and Europe remained divided into armed camps. Since 1950 America had repeatedly projected its military power into far-flung corners of the world, in the name of Cold War imperatives and at huge material and human cost. Despite a thermonuclear standoff predicated on the Orwellian notion of Mutual Assured Destruction, the nation continued to spend billions on new weapons systems. And despite America's great advantage over the USSR in almost every geopolitical arena, Washington politicians and lobbyists warned of present dangers, of windows of vulnerability, of imminent doom.

To Kennan, this state of affairs seemed to suggest something rather radical about America's Cold War: that it had begun for necessary geopolitical reasons and had been waged effectively in its early years, but that it had been protracted for another thirty-five years for reasons largely internal to the United States, rather than in response to external pressures and perils. The Soviet Union, he firmly believed, had long since ceased being a plausible threat to America and its allies. Yet U.S. foreign policy was still dominated by political grandstanding and an alarmist militarism.[4]

Kennan had long since moved out of a policymaking role, and the concerns he expressed in Iowa were shared by few in Reagan's Washington. But the issues he raised—about the connection between the containment strategy as originally conceived and the Cold War the United States was waging in 1984; about the militarization of that strategy and the refusal on principle to negotiate with adversaries; about the power of domestic politics in shaping U.S. foreign policy, which seemed greater than elsewhere—still retain extraordinary historical importance today, three decades after the Cold War wound down and the Soviet Union itself disappeared from the scene. These matters receive close consideration in this political history, by two writers who were college students in 1984 and became professional historians only after the clash of the superpowers had come to an end.[5]

Our principal concern is the United States, the most powerful actor in the global system after 1945. In concentrating on the foreign policy of one nation, we are consciously bucking the historiographical trend toward international history. Though this approach to studying U.S. foreign relations is hardly new—Samuel Flagg Bemis, Ernest R. May, and other giants in the field were writing international history half a century ago and more—only in recent years has it become predominant.[6] Armed in many cases with area-studies expertise and with the requisite foreign language ability, international historians have provided richly textured accounts in which the policymaking of all relevant actors is presented to us simultaneously. And more such work is on the way, as additional archives open up around the world, as greater numbers of historians develop the linguistic skills to work in them, and as more non-American scholars enter the fray.[7]

We find much to admire in this work, and we need no persuading that internationalizing the study of the Cold War can have tremendous explanatory power. But it is not the only approach to the study of post-1945 American foreign policy, or necessarily the most productive. The international history approach cannot easily be used to analyze immense subjects, such as U.S. foreign relations during the whole of the Cold War. Since the United States projected its power to almost every corner of the world from 1945 onward, a true international history of the Cold War, giving full consideration to both the leading and supporting players in this long, complex story, and to its many human and structural dimensions, would be a Herculean undertaking, requiring thousands of pages, so many are the strands that would have to be woven together.[8] Such a history would also rest on documentary materials not yet available, especially from the former Soviet Union.

A more important limitation results from the stated desire among many practitioners of international history to "de-center" the United States in their studies and to "privilege" the foreign.[9] This impulse, though understandable on one level, runs the risk of assigning greater agency to these other actors than they deserve, with the result that the analysis becomes ahistorical. For the fact is that the United States was never, after 1945, merely one power among many. It was always supreme; as such, it had primary responsibility for much that happened during the epoch, both for good and for bad. To say this is not to privilege the United States but simply to recognize the extreme power imbalances obtaining in most places, most of the time, during the Cold War.[10]

For students of decisionmaking, international history can have another distorting effect: it can provide more information about an adversary's or ally's intentions and capabilities than officials possessed at the time. Today, we may know much about North Korea's relations with the Soviet Union and China in June 1950, and about how hard Kim Il Sung had to work to persuade Stalin in particular to approve an invasion across the 38th parallel.[11] U.S. officials at the time, however, though not wholly ignorant of the shifting dynamics of this triangular relationship, could quite understandably conclude that Moscow—emboldened by its new atomic weapon—not only approved but masterminded Kim's action. Similarly, declassified documentation has given us a solid grasp of why Nikita Khrushchev placed nuclear missiles in Cuba in 1962. But John F. Kennedy and his advisers had no such understanding: they had to grope about in the dark, armed with only the sketchiest notion of the mercurial Kremlin leader's motivations.

Why did the United States follow the course it did after 1945? How were the major policy decisions pertaining to the Cold War reached? These "why and how" questions are at the heart of this study. They are America-centered questions, demanding immersion in American sources and knowledge of American institutions, political culture, and social structure. International history has little to offer here, even if foreign archives can sometimes yield fascinating insights into U.S. policymaking.[12] Far from decentering the United States, this book—notwithstanding frequent appearances in its pages by the likes of Stalin, Mao, Churchill, Ho Chi Minh, Gorbachev—places U.S. actors and U.S. actions in the forefront, the better to explain America's external behavior in the decades after World War II, and the better to determine whether that behavior was determined more by foreign or domestic variables.

Our argument, in brief: for much of the Cold War, the domestic variables predominated over the foreign ones. Not completely, of course, and not equally at all times. We attach great importance to the colossal structural changes to the international system wrought by World War II, and to the technological changes that had the effect of shrinking the globe and forcing American statesmen to confront choices and dilemmas they had largely been able to bypass in earlier eras. The spectacular Japanese attack on Pearl Harbor on December 7, 1941, together with Nazi Germany's control over much of Europe, brought home conclusively what alert Americans had already sensed for several years: that the era of "free security" (as the historian C. Vann Woodward referred to it), which dated back as far as the Treaty of Ghent in 1814, was over. No longer could the two oceans—which had served as vast moats—or the European balance of power be counted to keep America safe, as the nation now confronted the possibility that had long tormented its Old World cousins: the specter of national defeat.[13] For the next fifty years, the United States would encounter international dangers and opportunities that were also not of its own political making, the most important of which were the wartime threat of Nazi Germany; the prospect of Soviet preponderance over Eurasia after the war; the possibility of nuclear extermination, especially in the late 1950s and early 1960s; and, in a very different sense, the collapse and dissolution of the USSR in 1989–1991. These were international realities, not socially constructed tropes, and major sections of this book deal with how American leaders responded to each of them, batting, in our judgment, four for four.

Yet, as Kennan asserted and as the following chapters will demonstrate, America's response to these dangers does not comprise the whole of U.S. policymaking during the Cold War. No less a figure than President Dwight D. Eisenhower hinted at this reality in his extraordinary Farewell Address in January 1961, when he referred to the "military-industrial complex" already affecting America's Cold War in myriad and far-reaching ways. Composed of the military establishment, the arms industry, and the congressional backers of these two institutions, this "complex" became a power within itself, a vested interest largely outside the perimeter of democratic control, and arguably the single greatest factor in post-1941 economic life in the United States.[14]

Its tentacles reached into almost every congressional district in the country and distorted electoral politics to a tremendous degree. The preservation of the military-industrial establishment became a kind of national addiction, from which American society could recover only after going through the most severe withdrawal.[15] No one—least of all the powerful committee chairmen whose home districts received hefty defense contracts, and the labor unions and communities who also benefited—was willing to endure such pain. The creation and maintenance of this armed establishment (which had its Soviet counterpart), together with the export of great quantities of arms to other countries, provides a key part of the answer to a question that is likely to loom large in Cold War historiography in the years to come: why did the conflict last so long? A great many powerful people in American society had an unspoken (and often unconscious) need for the Cold War to continue.

The domestic context mattered in another important way, too. More than recent studies acknowledge, party politics and electoral strategizing influenced U.S Cold War policy.[16] In the late 1940s, foreign and domestic anti-communism in American political discourse were consciously meshed, as Republicans hit Democrats with being "soft on communism," with not doing enough to thwart either Soviet aggression abroad or subversive activity at home. Democrats—put on the defensive especially after China's "fall" to communism in 1949—worked hard to demonstrate their anti-communist bona fides, to be just as quick as Republicans to equate superpower diplomacy with appeasement. The range of acceptable political opinion narrowed dramatically, even before the arrival on the national stage of Senator Joseph McCarthy. After his entrance, it constricted still further, as vociferous anti-communism became the default posture of virtually every serious candidate for national office, to a degree unknown in any other Western nation. Any possibility for honest debate or criticism of foreign policy toward the communist world disappeared, as those on the left and center-left who might have articulated an alternative vision lost cultural and political approval. For more than two decades thereafter, campaign attacks from the left on either Democratic or Republican foreign policies were as unsuccessful as they were rare.

The passage of time thus made relatively little difference to how foreign policy choices were discussed. Despite the United States' preponderance of power throughout the Cold War, the proverbial Martian, if it had landed in Washington at any time between 1945 and the early 1980s and had tuned in to U.S. political debate, would have concluded that America was in a life-and-death struggle with an implacable, ruthless, and fundamentally evil foe and that it was on the verge of losing this epic struggle—or, at best, that the two titans were evenly matched. To be sure, the Martian might also have noted that the far right's agitated calls for preventive war against the Soviets received meager support: though partisanship was there from the start in 1945 (the "golden days" of bipartisanship during the early Cold War are more myth than reality), it was tempered by a near-consensus in elite and public opinion that rejected the extremes of isolationism, at one end, and the overt advocacy of total war, at the other. But this did not mean that the middle was really in the center—it always drifted in the direction of alarmism and militarism.[17]

Few Cold War historians would reject the argument that party politics and the pursuit of personal political advantage helped shape U.S. Cold War policy. Some might give it less explanatory power than we do, but most would concede it belongs somewhere in the causal hierarchy. All the more amazing, then, that the literature, especially in recent years, devotes so little attention to the subject. The rise of international history and the move away from America-centric scholarship is one explanation for this phenomenon, but longer-term historiographical trends are also at work. Even the Cold War "revisionists" who burst upon the scene in the late 1950s and emphasized the primacy of domestic forces in the conduct of U.S. foreign policy generally paid little attention to politics.[18] No less than the more orthodox historians they were arguing against, revisionists tended to treat the U.S. government as a monolithic actor, albeit one shaped largely by the economic and ideological interests associated with the U.S. government's capitalist structure. The emphasis was on internal sources of foreign policy, but not on partisan wrangling, election-year maneuvering, interest-group pandering, or other proximate political concerns.[19] Partly, too, the inattention to domestic politics may reflect the heavy reliance by many researchers on official U.S. government documents, which for obvious reasons give few clues that foreign policy choices could be affected by base political motivations. What is lost is the "intermestic" (international-domestic, whereby the two are dynamically intertwined) dimension of policy, which, although much discussed when events are taking place—ask a group of diplomatic historians at a cocktail party whether domestic politics significantly influences present-day American actions overseas and chances are they will answer, with conviction and a knowing smile, that lamentably it does—is too often nowhere to be found in historical scholarship.[20]

The Cold War ended when Ronald Reagan, in the face of staunch opposition from Cold Warriors inside and outside his party, entered high-stakes negotiations with Mikhail Gorbachev (who faced down his own opposition at home) that led to a peaceful resolution of the superpower conflict. But the end was a long time coming, and the question to be asked is whether the price the United States paid for its victory in the Cold War—and a resounding victory it surely was—was remotely necessary. We address that question more fully in our conclusion; here, it may simply be said that we believe the answer is no. America after 1945 always possessed the necessary global power to contain the Soviet Union and seek a larger settlement, and U.S. leaders for the most part knew it. Although threats to the nation's physical security were not non-existent, especially in a nuclear age, they were not as acute as the politicians' rhetoric often proclaimed.

What had been true for most of the nation's history before World War II was also true after: the United States during much of the Cold War was objectively safe from external attack, as safe as any nation could realistically hope to be. Its security was seldom directly imperiled, a reality that shaped U.S. foreign policy in the ways that worried Kennan. From an early point, leaders had the luxury of blurring the distinction between policy and politics, so that governing became less about the common good and more about achieving partisan and personal goals. Policy, in Kenneth Waltz's acute formulation, became capricious.

Indeed, the politicians and operators in Washington who exploited America's Cold War perceived an even deeper reality—that their fundamental interest lay in denying that the United States was secure, no matter what was happening overseas. Talking up the threat, perpetuating the politics of insecurity, became the mission. What unfolded, therefore, especially in the final decade of the Cold War, was a bizarre scene. Even as the Soviet Union declined—rotting internally and alienated from its allies and even from its own citizens—scaremongers in the United States spoke of imminent Soviet superiority, of clear and present dangers. The collapse and death of the USSR, an event we describe in some detail, posed an ironic final challenge to these doomsayers. They lost that battle, but in due course would come storming back.[21]

What follows is a study of American foreign policy during the half-century between the attack on Pearl Harbor in 1941 and the collapse of the Soviet Union in 1991. It is not a study of American domestic politics per se but rather of the shaping of America's Cold War by both international circumstances and internal political interests. What was going on in the halls of Congress and in other domestic entities sometimes mattered little to top-level U.S. policymakers. But at other times it drove their decisions, and it always at least figured in the background, influencing the thinking of U.S. statesmen in ways quite unique to the American experience. To ignore or underplay the intermestic dimension of U.S. policy is, we believe, to misread the nature of the struggle that dominated world politics in the second half of the century.

George Kennan's time on the bridge of the ship of state was brief, and it can be argued that his designation as the "father of containment" is misplaced—that his role in decisionmaking was modest and that at most he gave a name and perhaps a certain conceptual clarity to a foreign policy direction that was already emerging.[22] But Kennan nevertheless seems to us a remarkable figure in post-war American history and will appear with regularity in the following pages. This shy, erudite, introspective man was, like all of us, a flawed figure but one who grasped earlier and more deeply than almost anyone the essential nature of the Cold War.

On that frigid Iowa night in 1984, the aging diplomat concluded his lecture with a plea. He asked for a "greater humility in our national outlook," for a "greater restraint than we have shown in recent decades in involving ourselves in complex situations far from our shores." Americans must bear in mind, he said, "that in the interaction of peoples, just as in the interaction of individuals, the power of example is far greater than the power of precept; and that the example offered to the world at this moment by the United States of America is far from being what it could be and what it ought to be."[23]

I

THE DEMISE OF FREE SECURITY

"The United States," wrote the historian Charles Beard in 1939, "is a continental power separated from Europe by a wide ocean which, despite all changes in warfare, is still a powerful asset of defense." Unlike the degraded nations of Old Europe, America faced no threat to its security, Beard said, no prospect of conquest, and hence no need to go down the path of militarization and war. In 1917 Woodrow Wilson had defied this truth. He had taken the nation to war and expended American lives and treasure in a hopeless attempt to reform European power politics, to blast through, as Beard put it, the "blood rust of fifty centuries." But the American people had wisely rejected Wilson's League of Nations after the war, having no reason to believe that the United States should participate in the welter of European politics when its security was no more threatened in 1920 than it was in 1917. In Beard's formulation, the reality was self-evident: intervention in the Great War was a mistake not to be repeated.[1]

For Beard, free security meant that the nation could avoid the miseries of militarism that beset the European powers. Without great effort, the American people could be spared from debt, confiscatory taxation, political repression, cultural demoralization, the slaughter of entire generations—all of the things that ravaged the warring societies of the Old World, most acutely during the Great War of 1914–1918. With the nation now consolidated, the United States could cultivate a continental civilization built not on cynicism and war but on peace and prosperity.

Why, if it enjoyed this absolute physical security, would the United States ever involve itself in great-power intrigues or major wars? Beard offered two answers. First, it might happen if economic elites thought they could benefit from American adventurism. Overseas military interventions made the economically powerful more so, he maintained, and these elites were sometimes able —such as in 1898 and 1917—to manipulate U.S. political leaders for their own purposes. Second, and no less objectionable to Beard, Americans might involve themselves in the affairs of other nations if they believed, as did some liberal commentators, that the United States had an obligation to solve the world's problems. This, he thought, was naive at best, dangerous at worst. Echoing what he saw as the wisdom of early leaders such as George Washington and John Quincy Adams, Beard regarded America's duty to the world as one of example: America's exceptionalism in rejecting power politics and easy war should be presented to the world as a model, an ideal to pursue. "She goes not abroad, in search of monsters to destroy," as Adams had famously put it in 1821. "She is the well-wisher to the freedom and independence of all. She is the champion and vindicator only of her own."[2]

If U.S. leaders tried to force other states to adopt American institutions, Beard foresaw only trouble. Not only would the United States be pulled into destructive wars, it would also lose its own innocence. It would become the thing it was trying to eliminate. American intervention in the First World War thus epitomized the folly of defying free security. By succumbing to economic interests and at the same time persuading himself that the United States was destined to save the world, Wilson involved his nation in a war for no good purpose.

Beard protested too much. Wilson was a subtler statesman than he perceived. The president believed that the United States must enter the Great War not out of some vague world-saving ideal but because the spreading conflict revealed the bankruptcy of the European power-politics system. If the United States stayed out, the postwar order would continue to be dominated by European states unable to give up their antiquated ideologies of *Realpolitik* and colonialism—a sure recipe for further international conflict and Europe's eventual collapse. Even more ominous, should the European nations totally wipe one another out—and in 1917 that hardly seemed like an impossibility—radical movements, such as Vladimir Lenin's rising Bolshevik party in Russia, could seize power throughout the old world.

Either way, the system of democratic capitalism that Wilson believed represented the most advanced form of political order faced a bleak future. In his view, the world's great powers should create a new kind of international politics—open, demilitarized, orderly. They should strive for freer trade among themselves, respect national self-determination, and abandon the defunct system of colonialism. Above all, they should form a League of Nations in which disputes and conflicts could be worked out through discussion and diplomacy. The transparent international arena that Wilson envisaged would allow nations to air their disputes and avoid the deep misperceptions and secret alliances that had triggered the Great War in the summer of 1914.

Wilson's Bolshevik nightmare was not groundless. By late 1917 the party had seized power in Russia and was calling for a new world order based on the Marxist logic of proletarian liberation. For Lenin, the Great War signaled the impending end of capitalism and the beginning of a global revolution that would sweep away the "imperialist order." Wilson confided to his aide, Colonel Edward House, that he wanted to tell the Bolsheviks to "go to hell," but he accepted House's argument that he had to address Lenin's claim that there was little to distinguish the two warring sides from one another and that socialism represented the future. The result was Wilson's famous Fourteen Points, a moderate call for free trade, decolonization, demilitarization, and open diplomacy. As Beard suggested, this campaign was not altruistic, at least not in its original motivation—a new world order based on these principles would benefit the United States at old Europe's expense. But Wilson believed he could persuade the Europeans to see reason. Follow me, he was telling his exhausted counterparts in London, Paris, and Rome, or the Bolsheviks will prevail.[3]

Wilson's appeal did not impress Lenin, who called for an immediate end to the fighting, the eradication of colonialism, and self-determination for all peoples. But there were similarities in their messages. Both men rejected the old system of diplomacy that had created the conditions for the current war, and both insisted on the need for a new world order no longer dominated by the discredited European powers. But while each professed adherence to democratic principles, they defined democracy quite differently. For Lenin, it meant workers seizing control of capital from its owners and establishing worker-led governments. For Wilson, it meant independent governments operating within capitalist systems and according to republican political practices.

In a sense, this divergence in vision set the scene for a cold war to begin already in 1918. The reason it did not happen then was that old Europe was not quite dead. The great powers rejected Wilson's idealism at the 1919 Paris Peace Conference and rebuilt themselves, or tried to, as they were before, while the laboring masses of Europe ignored Lenin's call for revolution. With their respective demands to overhaul international relations repudiated, both Bolshevik Russia and the United States retreated from the international stage. Faced with a resurgence of European power in the 1920s and 1930s, especially a revanchist Germany, the Bolshevik state, now named the Union of Soviet Socialist Republics (USSR, or Soviet Union) turned inward. Its leaders—the ruthless

Lenin and, beginning in the late 1920s, the even more ruthless Joseph Stalin—downplayed the goal of global revolution and worked to consolidate their hold on national power and to bring about rapid industrial development, the better to prepare the country for future war. The American public, disillusioned by Wilson's failure at the Paris peace talks, also shunned further involvement in European politics and dedicated itself to the reform of its domestic institutions, especially during the Great Depression of the 1930s. America, after all, still enjoyed the luxury of free security.[4]

Return to War

If Charles Beard's reasoning and that of like-minded observers failed to do justice to Wilson's strategy, most Americans nevertheless had little doubt about where they stood on Wilson's legacy, not to mention the question of becoming involved in another war.[5] As late as the fall of 1939, after Germany's invasion of Poland made a new European war inevitable—and several years after Japan had begun its war of conquest against China—a majority of polled Americans continued to believe that the U.S. entry into the Great War had been a grave mistake and that their government should steer clear of participation in the new conflagrations.[6] During the general election campaign a year later, a majority of the candidates running for the Senate and House of Representatives followed this general line, as did the two major presidential candidates, Republican Wendell Willkie and Democrat Franklin Delano Roosevelt, who won an unprecedented third term.

Yet, even as he campaigned, Roosevelt was quietly moving toward an interventionist position. The fall of France to the Germans in June 1940, in a campaign lasting a mere six weeks, made a deep and disturbing impression on him, as it did on many Americans.[7] If the French with their formidable military could not stop the Nazi war machine, who could? But as Beard and other critics of intervention detected, there were base economic interests as well as idealism at play. The United States was lending billions of dollars and selling and leasing goods on a vast scale, mostly to Great Britain—actions that went far to end the economic depression that had beset American society (and much of the world) since the Wall Street crash of 1929. Roosevelt was not above alluding to this economic advantage, as when he informed his audience during a campaign speech in Boston that the increased aid to Great Britain was providing the working class there and around the nation with jobs and affluence not seen since the 1920s.[8] Furthermore, the president regarded the struggle between totalitarian Nazi Germany and the major European democracies, of which only Great Britain was still standing by the middle of 1940, as a contest between liberty and tyranny. For this reason alone, he argued, the United States had a moral interest in supporting Britain. The brutality of Japanese conquests in China and elsewhere concerned him as well, but not to the same degree.[9]

Roosevelt was more skeptical than Wilson had been that the United States could reform Europe by dint of sheer example, and he did not share the former president's deep faith in America's moral purity. Scion of the old Dutch elite in New York and a distant cousin of an earlier president, Theodore Roosevelt, FDR brought to the White House a pragmatism that was forged in his climb to the top of the state's largely working-class Democratic Party, his tragic battle with polio and eventual confinement to a wheelchair, and above all his Herculean struggle to end the Great Depression. But Roosevelt also had his Wilsonian side, which emerged as the European crisis deepened. Little by little, he began to see the new world war as a moral and geostrategic contest in which the United States must become involved. In 1939 and early 1940, Roosevelt seemed genuinely to believe that America could fight tyranny in Europe and Asia merely by providing economic support to nations like China and Great Britain. But following the French collapse in

June, and more definitively following his own reelection in November, the president moved steadily toward the conclusion that the United States had to do more than act as the world's "arsenal of democracy"—it had to enter the war.

FDR had come to understand what Charles Beard did not: that the world, and America's position within it, had changed since 1918. During the Great War the United States was still a militarily weak nation, relatively speaking. It could not plausibly coerce European powers into accepting Wilson's vision of a new world order, even after they had endured four years of devastating trench warfare and slaughter. Wilson had been forced to rely on moral suasion at the Paris Peace Conference—with miserable results. The British and French, though they probably would not have won the war without America's timely entry in 1917, were unwilling to heed his postwar demands and proved largely invulnerable to pressure. The United States, for its part, could also afford to display some degree of intransigency in 1918. It remained as secure from the European powers at the end of the First World War as it had been at the beginning—even more so, given their postwar exhaustion. The idea that America could be threatened by a European state, implausible in 1914, was by 1918 absurd. Disillusioned by the cynical behavior of Britain and France at the peace talks and unthreatened by any overseas power, the Senate (backed by a large chunk of the electorate) decisively rejected American participation in what Wilson viewed as the capstone of his postwar architectural vision, the League of Nations.

Things were much different in 1940. On one hand, the United States was stronger relative to many other nations than it had been a generation earlier, despite years of economic depression and military isolation. If Japan and especially Germany were defeated, the United States would likely emerge from the war as the most powerful nation on earth. The vulnerability of the British empire, combined with France's shattering defeat in the spring and the continuing backwardness of the Soviet Union and China, made it clear to the president that if the United States participated in a war that led to the defeat of Germany and Japan, it would dominate world politics whether it wanted to or not. In such a position, Washington could in all likelihood impose its democratic and capitalist institutions on much of the world, as Wilson had hoped to do, not by pleading with the European powers to accept them for their own good but simply by giving them no choice.

On the other hand, despite its growing strength, the United States was also now more vulnerable than at any time since the War of 1812. Free security was coming to an end. The balance of power in Europe—the political mechanism that had divided America's potential rivals for so long—had failed. By the fall of 1940 Germany controlled much of western and central Europe and had a nonaggression treaty with a wary Soviet Union. Soon Hitler could dominate the whole continent from the Atlantic to the Soviet border, with a completely overmatched Great Britain in no position to stop him. Moreover, advancements in aeronautical technologies had made the world a smaller place. A Nazi Germany that could bombard and potentially obliterate Great Britain's cities and navy could also send aircraft carriers into the Atlantic or operate from bases in Central America, with the aim of bombing American cities. In 1941 this remained a distant but not nonexistent possibility, whereas just a few years earlier it would have been unthinkable.

Did the distant prospect of German attacks on American soil really constitute an existential threat to the United States? Beard thought not, and derided those who imagined "German planes from Bolivia dropping bombs on peaceful people in Keokuk or Kankakee."[10] And even if Germany eventually attempted to bombard such towns, or even larger cities like New York or Philadelphia, this was a far cry from being able to conquer the whole United States. America was a continental nation, and to defeat it a nation like Germany would have to deploy a vast army across the Atlantic and wage a war that could last decades.[11]

What Beard did not know, and indeed what very few Americans knew, was that a new technology was being developed which might make such an invasion unnecessary. During the 1930s, scientists in many countries, including Germany, had begun to conduct research into the possibility of atomic fission. The implications were huge. A nation that could successfully split the atom, these scientists theorized, might be able to use the power released by fission in a weapon of unprecedented destructive capability. And any country wielding monopoly control over such weapons could dispense with the problems of invasion entirely and simply threaten to destroy its enemy's cities, one by one, until the adversary sued for peace. In 1939–40 neither Franklin Roosevelt nor anyone familiar with atomic science could have any confidence that Hitler's Germany would not build such a bomb and threaten to use it against the United States.

Thus, while it is tempting to regard the atomic bomb simply as an American project that propelled the United States to superpower status in the Cold War, such a view would distort history. The Germans had their own scientific experts, and no one could be sure that they would not conquer Britain (which led the world in atomic science research), just as they had already taken France, the Low Countries, and much of Scandinavia. A German scientist understood the stakes: he informed the German war office in April 1939 that the nation able to invent the bomb first would have "an unsurpassable advantage over the others."[12]

When Alexander Sachs, prompted by such leading scientists as Albert Einstein and Leo Szilard, met with the president in the fall of 1939 to urge him to build a bomb, this was the danger he stressed. "Alex," Roosevelt said during their brief White House encounter, "what you are after is to see that the Nazis don't blow us up." "Precisely," Sachs responded. The president's reply was simple:

"This requires action."[13] With that, the Manhattan Project came into being, conceived not in calculated ambition but in genuine fear.

Having issued the order, Roosevelt promptly ignored plans for the atomic bomb, whose production would not move into high gear until 1942. He and other internationalists in Washington were far more concerned with the shifting course of the war and their conflict with isolationists at home than with an exotic new weapon based on advanced scientific theories that only a few people in the world even understood, and which might in the end not amount to anything. What Roosevelt's 1939 decision signified, rather, was his general understanding that military technology was putting an end to free security. An adversary who meant business, as Nazi Germany surely did, could well be acquiring these technologies for itself, and if the United States did not do the same it could face a kind of danger that Americans had never really experienced before. For a U.S. president, these were uncharted waters.

But was the United States really in mortal danger? Many American intellectuals, remembering the inflated rhetoric of 1917 and the ghastly casualty figures of the Great War, refused to believe it. Beard took the lead, demanding in every journal article and book he could publish that the United States stay out of the war, cultivate a peaceful, social democracy at home, and let the woeful Europeans stew in their own problems. Before Pearl Harbor, Beard's position was difficult to refute. The monstrous enormity of Nazi power was not yet obvious, the oceans still seemed to provide physical security, and no one, apart from a few political and scientific leaders, knew anything about any atomic weapon. Perhaps America should stay out of the war.

Reinhold Niebuhr, a Protestant theologian and political philosopher at New York's Union Seminary, worked to develop an answer to Beard. To be sure, America could probably remain physically safe after a Nazi victory in Europe, Niebuhr allowed. But the stakes had become much higher than in 1917. If America stood aside while Hitler seized all of Europe, including Great Britain, the United States would become the last major democratic state on earth. Isolated in a world dominated by fascist totalitarianism, how long would democracy survive under such adverse conditions? Could the United States remain forever a democratic island in a sea of fascism? Recalling the ideas of the turn-of-the-century German sociologist Max Weber, Niebuhr argued during the tense months of 1940 and 1941 that great nations sooner or later face a critical moment when they must choose to contend for great power or decline the chance. If they refuse to contend, they do not necessarily face physical defeat, but they do accept the prospect that their national identity, their civilization, will be influenced or even dominated by the nation to which they defer. For Niebuhr, the civilization at risk was not *American* per se but *democratic*. If the United States did not act and Great Britain went under, democratic civilization could be doomed. Conversely, if America entered the war and defeated German and Japanese fascism, the United States could cooperate with Britain to establish democracy as the dominant form of political order on the planet.[14]

The time, for Niebuhr, was now. He recognized that in 1916, or even 1936, the moment of truth had not yet arrived; but by 1940 it had. Germany's victory in Europe allied with Japan's victory in Asia would mean the demise of the British and French empires, the destruction of liberalism and capitalism everywhere outside the Western hemisphere, and probably the relegation of the United States to a minor, regional power. This was a worst-case scenario, to be sure, and not one that could come true in the short term. Free security would not end abruptly, and as a consequence Roosevelt could face his decision to enter the war gradually. Distance still gave him some time.

America Intervenes

Roosevelt needed the time, because he faced formidable political obstacles to any move to bring the United States into the war on the side of Britain. Foremost among them was the legacy of Wilson's intervention in World War I. Many in middle America and in Congress were so determined to avoid being hoodwinked a second time that they dismissed as overly alarmist Roosevelt's frequent claims of threats to American civilization. There he goes, they said, crying wolf again.[15] Beard and many other antiwar liberals hammered this theme home, their message driving much of liberal political discourse in the United States during 1939 and 1940. Furthermore, many Americans of German or Italian descent opposed a war against those two countries, and many Irish-Americans loathed the prospect of siding with Britain. Italian- and Irish-Americans wielded significant clout in the Democratic Party, as did other liberal antiwar groups.

Finally, Roosevelt struggled to articulate effectively why he believed U.S. intervention might be necessary. Time and again he emphasized that the oceans could no longer protect America, that Germany could project its power into the Western hemisphere, and that the United States faced the danger of isolation in a tyrannical world. The American people, he declared in a typical speech, could not "draw a line of defense around this country and live completely and solely to ourselves."[16] He refused before the November election to suggest that this would eventually require American entry into the war. Rather, during the grim spring and summer of 1940, he stressed America's obligation to serve as the arsenal of democracy, to provide U.S. wealth but not American blood to the enemies of fascism.

Following his reelection, Roosevelt moved more decisively toward intervention, and by the middle of 1941 he was working actively to insinuate the United States into the war. In December 1940 he announced his proposal to lend Great Britain a vast amount of war materiel, knowing full well that this would tie American fortunes much more tightly with those of the British (and then, after June 1941, the USSR)—a reality not lost on the opponents of his Lend-Lease program. In the spring of 1941 he authorized the use of American convoys to protect U.S. and British ships delivering this materiel to the United Kingdom, again fully aware that it would likely lead to hostilities in the Atlantic between the United States Navy and German U-Boats, which were sinking transatlantic ships on almost a daily basis. That summer, after Japanese troops occupied French Indochina, the U.S. government placed an embargo on strategic exports to Japan, including oil. FDR had earlier resisted embargoing oil because he feared (rightly) that Tokyo officials would consider a cutoff to be a life-and-death matter. "The oil gauge and the clock stood side by side," wrote one observer.[17]

Perhaps most important, in August 1941 Roosevelt met with British prime minister Winston Churchill for four days off the coast of Newfoundland. They got on well, swapping stories and enjoying the fact that Churchill's mother hailed from New York. The two leaders issued the Atlantic Charter, an Anglo-American declaration of war aims that bore the hallmarks of Wilsonianism: self-determination, collective security, disarmament, economic cooperation, and freedom of the seas. But the postwar order they envisioned at that moment would be run by the United States and Great Britain, not by a genuinely international body. Churchill, for his part, anxious as always to preserve the empire, sought to downplay the commitments to self-determination and absolute free trade, suggesting that due attention be paid to "existing obligations."[18]

The significance of the meeting and the charter for American foreign policy, however, was undeniable. The Anglo-American partnership emerged stronger than ever, and U.S. intervention in the war more likely. The charter laid out a postwar plan that fit American objectives and played to Americans' idealistic sentiments. No longer did the president speak of the United States acting merely as an arsenal of democracy; he seemed to be making it his business to overcome domestic opposition and get America into the action. And indeed, upon his return to London the prime minister told aides that FDR had promised to "wage war" against Germany and to do "everything" to "look for an 'incident' which would justify him in opening hostilities."[19]

Within days German and American ships came into direct contact in the Atlantic. On September 4 a German submarine launched torpedoes at (but did not hit) the American destroyer *Greer*. Henceforth, Roosevelt said, the U.S. Navy would shoot on sight. He also announced a policy he already had promised Churchill in private: American warships would convoy British merchant ships across the ocean. Thus, the United States entered into an undeclared naval war with Germany. In October, when the destroyer *Reuben James* went down with the loss of more than one hundred American lives, Congress scrapped the cash-and-carry policy and further revised the Neutrality Acts to permit transport of munitions to Britain on armed American merchant ships.

In light of this rising tension in the Atlantic, it is ironic that America's formal entry into the Second World War came by way of Asia. Relations with Japan plummeted further in the fall, as leaders in Tokyo rejected U.S. demands to respect China's sovereignty and territorial integrity—in short, to get out of China. Japanese-American talks continued in November but went nowhere. Suffering under the embargo and certain that war with the United States had become inevitable, the Japanese High Command authorized a daring raid on America's Pacific Fleet moored at Pearl Harbor, on the Hawaiian Island of Oahu near Honolulu. The Japanese struck on the morning of December 7, damaging most of the fleet's battleships and killing or wounding more than 3,000 servicemen.

Roosevelt asked Congress to declare war on Japan, which it did, the determined isolationism of many of its members melting away. Japan's major allies, Italy and Germany, responded by declaring war on the United States four days later. Charles Beard's great fear had been realized: America was once again at war.

The Tide Turns

As war leader, Franklin Roosevelt hoped to defend America's security and elevate the United States to global power. But he had to defeat Germany and Japan first, fighting alongside Grand Alliance partners Britain and the USSR. Dreams of American greatness and a new world order would mean nothing if Germany prevailed, for in that event the Nazi regime, not the United States, would rise to global dominance regardless of whatever happened to Britain.

It is tempting to picture a calculating Roosevelt planning for American postwar supremacy from December 7 onward, with the war a mere means to that end, but this is a hindsighted and misleading view. At the time of Pearl Harbor, Germany was at the very height of its power, having conquered great swaths of the Soviet Union in a matter of months and sitting now on the outskirts of Moscow. It had consolidated control over western Europe and seemed poised, once the Soviets surrendered, to cross the channel into England. Its ally, Japan, had just launched a devastating surprise attack on the American Pacific fleet, sinking much of it, and was readying its forces to sweep over East and Southeast Asia. Singapore fell in February 1942, and by mid-March Malaya, Java, and Borneo were gone too. When the Philippines fell on May 6, the Stars and Stripes, which had flown over the vast archipelago since 1898, was replaced by the Rising Sun.

But if the immediate outlook was grim, the story of U.S. diplomacy during the war, especially as it shaped America's postwar confrontation with the Soviet Union, is nevertheless a story based on the presumption of ultimate victory. Even in the dark weeks after the attack on Pearl Harbor, when Japanese and German might were at their greatest, the vast majority of Americans told pollsters that they expected success to come in the end. This presumption, though grossly premature in December 1941 or March 1942, became reasonable over the following eighteen months. America's defeat of the Japanese navy at the Battle of Midway in June 1942, just weeks after the fall of the Philippines, put an end to any chance of Japan's naval advancement toward the Western hemisphere and, correspondingly, to its ability to stop the U.S. Navy's eventual westward progress toward Asia. Victory in the Pacific was not assured by Midway, but outright defeat looked far less likely.

Even more important, the astonishing success of the Red Army at Stalingrad over the winter of 1942–43 indicated that Germany was probably not going to bring the Soviet Union's forces to their knees, or at least not before allied troops arrived on the continent from the west. Had Germany's armies won the battle of Stalingrad and taken Moscow, Hitler might well have been able to secure terms from a shattered USSR and redeploy his armies to the west, making a German invasion of Britain likely and an Anglo-American invasion of France well-nigh impossible. Now, with Hitler's armies slowed down in Russia and also in North Africa, these fears could in large measure be put to rest.

Lastly, although few at the time were aware of it, British bombardment of German installations, combined with sabotage operations undertaken by local resistance fighters in Norway in 1942 and 1943, badly damaged Germany's program to build an atomic bomb.[20] The ramifications were immense: if these operations had failed and the German project had succeeded, the Berlin government could have threatened to deploy the new weapon against London or even New York, even though its armies were in retreat. British and American officials, being at least vaguely aware of what an atomic bomb could do, might well have been tempted to negotiate a peace with Hitler before suffering such a devastating attack. And they very likely would have done so if the Germans had destroyed even one city. We know now that the German project was actually lagging far behind the Anglo-American one, even before the bombing and sabotage operations had proven successful.[21] But Roosevelt and Churchill could not know it at the time.

With the military outlook much brighter in the early part of 1943, FDR could turn his attention toward fashioning a general American policy for the postwar order. He had no way of foreseeing what the power politics of Europe would look like after the war—this depended on how the Soviet Union fared in its now-offensive war against Germany, and on how the United States and its allies performed in opening a second front on the west. What the president could assume by the time he met with Churchill at Casablanca in early 1943 was that a corner had been turned, that the security of the United States was likely assured. In addition, he could feel considerable confidence that by the end of the war the United States would have established itself as a dominant power in Asia and the Pacific, a leading power on at least some part of the European continent, and a formidable presence elsewhere around the globe. Britain—debt-ridden and war-weary—would probably struggle to restore its empire and its role as leader of the capitalist world. In Casablanca, Roosevelt and his aides commenced the delicate process of taking this leadership role away from Great Britain, an effort that would culminate in the Bretton Woods conference of 1944.

Distant Allies

Three issues of contention divided the United States from Great Britain. To begin with, Winston Churchill consistently refused to accede to the American demand that Britain respect the Atlantic Charter's call for self-determination of all peoples. His principal concern was India, the jewel of the British empire which he had no intention of liberating. Nor did the prime minister express much concern about Stalin's evident desire to dominate eastern Europe, and in particular to deny Poland its right to self-determination.[22] In addition, the United States and Great Britain at the beginning of 1943 remained at odds on the matter of the atomic bomb. Roosevelt and Churchill had initially agreed that the project would remain a joint Anglo-American enterprise. The work was being done in America, but it relied on the historic contributions of British science and the current work of many British physicists. Yet several American officials associated with the Manhattan Project, including both Vannevar Bush and James Conant, Roosevelt's key advisers on the issue, suspected Britain of demanding greater involvement in the project merely for economic purposes, even though this increased the risk of espionage.[23]

Finally, and most important, at least during this part of the war, U.S. and British officials had been at loggerheads concerning the chief wartime objectives in Europe. Many American military officials, including Army Chief of Staff George Marshall, had pressed in the aftermath of Pearl Harbor for an invasion of occupied Europe as soon as possible. Stalin, too, wanted an Anglo-American operation from the west, through France, to relieve his beleaguered troops. Churchill disagreed. He pressed instead for peripheral operations in North Africa and Italy. Roosevelt dithered but eventually took the prime minister's side. His rationale was that U.S. forces were not yet ready for a major campaign and that the American people needed to experience some success in the European war before risking the enormous casualties of a western front invasion.[24]

Thus, while the Soviet Union waged an intense land war against the German *Wehrmacht* along a vast front in eastern Europe, suffering some 10,000 casualties a day, America and Britain were fighting German and Italian forces well away from the center of the action. They were winning battles that certainly dented Nazi power and ultimately drove Italy out of the war, but these operations only put off the inevitable task of confronting German might in western Europe. American critics of this decision saw that Churchill's larger aim in advocating the peripheral strategy was to avoid the collision of arms in northwest Europe that would recall for the British public the interminable and intolerable trench warfare of the previous war. They also suspected that he wanted to secure the Mediterranean basin for the benefit of a postwar British empire.[25]

Roosevelt and Churchill resolved none of these issues at their first summit meeting in Casablanca in January 1943. They were both optimistic the war would ultimately be won. Stalingrad was holding, the Japanese navy was reeling, and it looked as though Anglo-American forces would soon secure most of North Africa. In this hopeful climate, Roosevelt and Churchill took pains to avoid conflict. They secretly approved a plan to launch a second-front invasion of France in 1944, though this was far enough in the future to be altered or abandoned as events dictated—something Stalin, who had been promised a second front in 1942 and then again in 1943, understood all too well. They also agreed, despite Roosevelt's earlier denunciation of the deliberate bombing of urban populations, to step up the strategic air campaign against Germany—which entailed the deliberate bombing of its urban populations.

Finally, they agreed to issue a public declaration that both nations would continue fighting until their adversaries agreed to "unconditional surrender." That statement assured allies such as China and the Free French (the fighting force under General Charles de Gaulle working out of London, in opposition to the collaborationist Vichy government), as well as the Soviet Union, that neither Washington nor London would accept negotiated terms with Germany or Japan, and it ensured that after the war the Japanese and Germans could never claim they could have won it, as many Germans had maintained at the end of World War I.[26] As the historian Gerhard Weinberg has noted, unconditional surrender appealed to Roosevelt above all else because it played to the American public's desire to regard the war as a moral crusade.[27]

During the ten months between Casablanca and the first Big Three conference in Tehran in November 1943, Roosevelt acceded to Churchill more explicitly on all three issues of contention. The president toned down his criticism of British colonialism and accepted Churchill's arguments that working to deny Soviet domination in eastern Europe would be pointless. After a lengthy internal dispute, the president countermanded his atomic advisers and ordered that Britain be included as an equal partner in the Manhattan Project. Finally, and of greatest irritation to many of his military advisers, Roosevelt adhered to his private agreement with Churchill that the second front be postponed until 1944, and ordered his staff to prepare instead to invade Italy. An American officer's assessment of the deliberations at Casablanca was representative of much military thinking during and after the conference: "One might say we came, we listened, and we were conquered."[28]

Roosevelt was certainly not immune to the prime minister's formidable persuasive powers, and his own unwillingness to explain his motivations in any detail adds to the impression that he was indeed "conquered" by his British counterpart—that American foreign policy during the first two years of the war was largely dictated by London. But this assessment underestimates Roosevelt's abilities and his view of the larger picture. The president had two basic objectives with respect to Great Britain during the middle years of the war. Foremost, he sought to keep Anglo-American relations strong and to bolster the British commitment to defeating Germany. Churchill's delay in opening a second front was an irritation, but after the Soviet victory at Stalingrad it was nothing more than that, in the larger strategic frame. Hitler was no longer in a position to defeat the USSR and move his armies to the west, so Washington and London had the luxury of choosing their own time to launch a second front. They knew they could not wait too long, for the Red Army might push farther and farther into Europe, with potentially dire implications for the postwar settlement. But Roosevelt wanted a British ally that would cooperate fully in the battle to liberate western Europe when the timing was most propitious, and by agreeing to the delay, this is what he got.

More broadly, Roosevelt sought to have the United States succeed Great Britain as the leader of the western, capitalist world, and to replace its old imperial system with one based on free trade and decolonization. By giving in to London on issues that did not threaten this objective, and indeed by linking the two nations as closely as possible to one another militarily, the president skillfully put himself in a position to achieve this goal. For once the war moved toward its resolution in Europe, the fact of America's economic and military power would elevate the United States to a position of postwar superiority vis-à-vis Great Britain, irrespective of any concessions or other agreements made between Roosevelt and Churchill in 1942 and 1943. Diplomatic skill, even of the caliber possessed by Churchill, can get a nation only so far. Unlike Woodrow Wilson a quarter century earlier, Roosevelt would be able to insist on his vision of a postwar order from a position of commanding power.[29] In late November 1943, delegations from the United States, the Soviet Union, and Great Britain arrived at the capital of Iran for what turned out to be the most important summit of the war. In four days of meetings, Roosevelt, Churchill, and Stalin debated the second-front question and hashed out the basic outline of a post-war European order. There were secret deals to parcel out spheres of influence in southern and eastern Europe. Military and diplomatic aides coordinated strategies for defeating

Hitler. Stalin, having left the Soviet Union for the first time since taking power almost twenty years earlier, made his acquaintance with the two imperialists from Britain and America.

And in Tehran, Roosevelt personally began to assert U.S. predominance over Great Britain. Churchill, for his part, came to the summit with two broad aims. The first was to maintain British imperial power in the Mediterranean region, and the second was to restore a postwar balance of power. Therefore, he strongly advocated a continuing effort in southeastern Europe, proposing further invasions in the Balkans and even Turkey, where Britain had long wielded influence, even if these operations delayed the main invasion of France. At the same time, he dissented from plans to dismember Germany and France.

Roosevelt would not have it. Rejecting Churchill's peripheral strategy, he assured Stalin of a spring 1944 frontal invasion of France. He accepted Soviet demands for preponderance in the Baltic states and Poland, protesting only that he could not officially accept Soviet domination over the latter for domestic political reasons. He went along with talk of eviscerating France and Germany, even joking, after Stalin cold-bloodedly proposed executing between 50,000 and 100,000 German officers, that it might only be 49,000. FDR frequently ignored Churchill's interventions, and in front of Stalin he even mocked the Englishman as an old-fashioned British imperialist. When the three leaders left Tehran on December 2, Roosevelt and Stalin had agreed on an invasion of France within a few months, a winding down of Mediterranean operations, and a postwar Europe in which the Soviet Union would be the only predominant continental power.[30]

It was a pivotal moment, not least for Anglo-American relations. British foreign policy since the Elizabethan era had been based on a balance of power in Europe, with London always taking care to ally with one side and then another to prevent domination of the continent by any one threatening state. After Tehran, the prospect of having no powerful ally in western Europe would force Britain either to contend by itself with the last remaining European power or to ally itself with the world's other remaining giant across the Atlantic, the United States. Could there be any doubt which side Great Britain would choose? It would join with America in opposition to the Soviet Union, and it would do so in a postwar environment in which there could be no question who the senior partner was.[31]

The basic structure of this relationship was finalized during 1944. The successful D-Day invasion of France on June 6, commanded by General Dwight D. Eisenhower, spelled the beginning of the end for Nazi Germany. Operation Overlord, as the invasion was called, also symbolized the growing inequality of the Anglo-American relationship, since much of the invading force, not to mention almost all of the weapons and materiel, came from the United States.[32] American civilian and military decisionmakers now largely controlled western Europe's liberation from German occupation, and after the war they would determine the region's political fate.

Economically, too, the Americans reigned supreme. A month after the invasion, the Roosevelt administration organized a conference on postwar economic planning in Bretton Woods, New Hampshire, at which American officials set up institutions designed to open up free trade around the world and to promote industrial development in former European colonies. These institutions would be largely funded and controlled by Americans, and they were formulated precisely to establish a new economic order to replace the previous one associated with European imperialism. Moreover, at Bretton Woods the conferees agreed to make the American dollar the standard coinage of world trade, replacing the British pound sterling. By accepting these plans, London quietly transferred the mantle of hegemonic control to the United States.

A low-interest American loan to Great Britain in 1946, made

with the stipulation that the British pound would be made convertible to American dollars throughout the empire, sealed the deal.[33]

Stalin Recalcitrant

For a while, Roosevelt appeared to believe he could duplicate with Moscow the relationship he sought with the British—that he could incorporate the Kremlin into a partnership dominated by the United States, not only during the war but after it. He had always been confident of his ability to handle Russia, ever since his decision, shortly after becoming president in 1933, to extend diplomatic recognition to the Soviet government. (Wilson as well as the Republican presidents of the 1920s had refused to do so.) The bilateral relationship had functioned reasonably well through the 1930s and into 1942. Even when friction arose over the timing of the Anglo-American invasion of France, the president expressed confidence that he and Stalin could keep things on an even keel.

In 1943 and early 1944 the administration explored the possibility of tendering a massive postwar loan to the Soviet Union, which the Russians would use to buy U.S. consumer goods. They would pay the United States back with exports of raw material. Like the later Marshall Plan for western Europe, this plan would likely have had the effect of integrating the USSR into the world economy, effectively forcing it to abandon its autarkic, communist economic system. The idea had considerable appeal in official Washington, where some analysts voiced the hope that Stalin had lost interest in communism during the war—that the wartime impulses of Russian nationalism, together with Moscow's evident need for postwar economic aid, might combine to convince the Kremlin leader to accept a Wilsonian world order and jettison his dreams of socialist revolution. Joseph Davies, whom Roosevelt had appointed as ambassador to the USSR in the late 1930s, regularly advanced this hypothesis, and it was echoed as well by numerous visiting American businessmen, by the current ambassador W. Averell Harriman, and by Roosevelt's trusted advisor Harry Hopkins. Stalin, they suggested, had changed. The Soviet Union had become more pragmatic and nationalist—more like the United States. During the war, the Kremlin had even relaxed its longstanding repression of religion.[34] Perhaps Soviet leaders would accommodate themselves to an American-style global system.

All of this was, of course, a textbook example of wishful thinking. Stalin in this period never seriously entertained the idea of voluntarily abandoning Soviet-style socialism in order to enter a global economy defined by American capitalism.[35] But the larger question remained: even if he rejected participation in an integrated economic order, would—or could—he still cooperate with the United States and other powers to avoid a return to prewar power politics? Stalin might have assumed what any student of international political economy would assert—namely, that the two decisions went hand in hand: by rejecting economic integration into the capitalist world, the Soviet Union had effectively chosen as well to oppose the U.S. politically.[36] Roosevelt appeared to resist this linkage, repeatedly and publicly expressing the hope until his death in April 1945 that the two powers could cooperate after the war. He could not know exactly what Stalin intended, and he retained his characteristic optimism that things would somehow work out.

Three actions taken by the Soviet Union during 1944 and early 1945, however, tempered the president's optimism about postwar cooperation. The first occurred at the Bretton Woods conference in 1944. The Soviets indicated clearly that they were not interested in cooperating to establish an integrated global economy based on the American dollar. U.S. negotiators conspicuously sought to secure the Soviet Union's involvement, by offering it a vast postwar loan in exchange for its participation in the World Bank and the International Monetary Fund—two new institutions introduced at

Bretton Woods. The USSR's clear rejection of this bribe, as the Soviets must have regarded it, indicated that the optimists in Washington were, at least on economic issues, clearly wrong.[37] The USSR would remain a communist state, and by necessity therefore an autarkic one, relying upon its own economic devices rather than trading freely with the world's capitalists, led by the United States.[38]

Stalin also revealed in 1944 that he was uninterested in paying even superficial heed to the idea of self-determination, at least with respect to eastern European nations along the Soviet Union's western border. Eastern Europe had been the launching pad for Hitler's invasion in 1941, and the resulting war had cost the lives of millions of Soviet citizens and caused massive physical destruction. Henceforth, it would be imperative to have friendly—which was to say socialist and subordinate—regimes in the Baltic states of Estonia, Latvia, and Lithuania, in Romania and Bulgaria, and, most vitally, in Poland. Stalin sought to achieve this goal irrespective of the opinion of the Americans, as shown most brutally in his repressive treatment of anti-Soviet elements in Poland. In 1940 the Soviet Secret Police massacred some 20,000 Polish officers and other civilians in and near the Katyn Forest (an atrocity denied by Soviet authorities until 1990) and in August and September 1944 Stalin halted the westward-advancing Red Army on the outskirts of Warsaw to allow the retreating Nazi regime time to annihilate members of the Polish resistance movement there.[39]

It is true that Churchill and Stalin had privately agreed to a division of territory whereby much of southeastern Europe would fall under Moscow's control. Roosevelt had also conceded that the United States could do nothing about Soviet action in the East, and he took steps to make sure that nations under Washington's political influence in western Europe and elsewhere maintained capitalist-oriented and subordinate governments. Roosevelt and to a greater extent Churchill understood the Kremlin leadership's obsessive fear of a German revival and its determination to do whatever was necessary to thwart that possibility, or at least delay it. They further acknowledged that the Soviet Union's huge land-mass, three times larger than that of the United States and covering twelve time zones, was not easy to defend, and they sympathized with Stalin's desire to dominate the states that separated Russia from Germany, as a way to create a security buffer against another invasion from the west. Indeed, by postponing the opening of a second front until 1944, the United States and Great Britain in essence wrote off eastern Europe in a geopolitical sense, their inaction effectively ensuring that this region would be dominated by the Red Army.

But Stalin's actions showed more than his unwillingness to go along, even superficially, with the idea of national self-determination. They also showed his resistance to the idea that international politics must change after the war. Roosevelt aimed to develop a collective security regime based on domination by the "Four Policemen"—the United States, Great Britain, the Soviet Union, and China. The primary mission of these four actors would be to cooperate among themselves in order to prevent the formation of military alliances and power blocs which, in Roosevelt's view, inevitably precipitated war. Stalin had other ideas. His actions seemed geared toward creating a bloc in eastern Europe by resorting to precisely the kind of power politics the four policemen were supposed to oppose. Roosevelt accepted this reality; he was not going to cut off relations with the USSR in response to its repression of the Poles, despite what he sometimes implied to domestic audiences.[40] What concerned the American president more was the blatant cynicism of Stalin's policies—the fact that the Soviet dictator gave no more than lip service to international ideals of any kind.[41] It hardly augured well for a new Rooseveltian world order.

FDR's growing doubts about cooperation with the USSR were intensified by Stalin's insistence that the new Security Council of the United Nations, which was being developed toward the end of 1944 in Washington, D.C., incorporate a veto provision. The two leaders went back and forth on this issue over the last several months of Roosevelt's life.[42] The delegates at Dumbarton Oaks had tried to paper over this problem, but Roosevelt's concern revealed that he understood its gravity. The veto would allow any permanent member of the Security Council to prevent any council action, including a decision to authorize the use of force against an aggressor. As a result, any permanent member could itself engage in aggression without fear of reprisal, making the council's power to prevent war among the world's five major powers illusory.

To be sure, Stalin had good reason to insist on a veto, for without one the other members of the council—the three other policemen plus France, all of them presumably allied with the United States as part of its new world order—could gang up on the USSR in the name of collective security. But this suspicion itself put the lie to the idea of great power cooperation, the premise that the allies could and would work together after the war, and it also signaled to smaller states that they could not rely upon the United Nations to protect them if they were attacked by one of the Security Council's permanent members. What kind of new world order was this? The great wars of the twentieth century had been initiated not by small powers but by large ones. If the major powers could not be curbed in the name of collective security, what actual force did the United Nations possess?[43]

Roosevelt could not be sure why Stalin refused to go along with his broader plan for postwar peace. Certainly he had good reason to suspect that the postponement of the second front played a central part; he had warned Churchill in 1942 and 1943 that the USSR would regard the delay as a cynical Anglo-American ploy to exhaust the Red Army by forcing it to bear the brunt of the war against the Nazis. He also was not so naive as to be shocked by Stalin's unwillingness to embrace global capitalism—FDR seemed to believe all along that postwar cooperation could be achieved even in a world of opposed economic and ideological blocs. The president could see why the Soviet Union preferred to rely on its own power rather than collective security in the event of German resurgence, a factor that FDR clearly acknowledged in Tehran. But Roosevelt regarded the colossal destruction of the two world wars as self-evident proof that the victorious nations now had to build a fundamentally different international order. Stalin was making it clear to the American that he disagreed.

Yalta

These problems weighed on the president's mind as he, Stalin, and Churchill met for a final time at the Crimean resort town of Yalta in early February 1945. By this time the European war was almost over, and the projection of both American and Soviet power into the European continent was a geopolitical fact. Roosevelt's health, meanwhile, was in rapid decline—he was a dying man, and he knew it. But he also knew that he faced a grim choice at Yalta. He could confront Stalin on economic integration, Poland, and the Security Council veto, with the aim of achieving a real post-armistice collective security order. Or he could avoid these hard questions and instead aim to maintain friendly relations with Stalin, in the hope that somehow things would work out. The president was able to get Stalin to sign the Declaration on Liberated Europe, a statement that the victorious powers would respect national sovereignties and human rights. The conspicuous absence of any enforcement mechanism behind this declaration, however, ensured that few, least of all Stalin, took the statement seriously. Fundamentally, Roosevelt chose the second course of action, and in so doing left for the future the task of securing a workable arrangement.

Why did FDR, at the moment of imminent victory over Nazi

Germany, relent on issues he believed central to the establishment of a genuine and enduring postwar peace? For the remainder of the century and beyond, the mantra among many on the right was that Yalta represented a sellout, an abandonment of principle by an American president who ended his presidency preferring a cordial and superficial summit conference to confrontation with a Soviet aggressor clearly bent on expansion and hostility.[44] Perhaps, some of the critics have allowed, his failing health entered into the equation: he may simply have been physically unable to face the prospect of turning the summit into a power struggle with Stalin.

But a simpler and better explanation for Roosevelt's behavior holds that the only way he could compel Stalin to accept integration into the American economic order, relinquish his grip over eastern Europe, and abandon the Security Council veto was to threaten him with war. In early 1945 FDR simply had no other plausible means of persuasion. The Soviet leader had already shown that he could not be bought off by an American loan. The war against Hitler was reaching its end, and though American and British forces were moving steadily through France and into Germany, the Red Army was also advancing swiftly from the other direction. By this point, therefore, all hopes of using the second front as a lever to coerce Stalin into compliance had disappeared.[45]

There was the atomic bomb, but the scientists at Los Alamos had not yet finished it, and even if they had, a threat to destroy Moscow unless Stalin changed his tune would have almost certainly failed to impress. In a top secret meeting in 1944, Roosevelt and Churchill had agreed to seek an Anglo-American monopoly over the bomb for the indefinite future, to keep the atomic project secret from other states (namely, the USSR), and to reject the program of international control which some of FDR's atomic advisers had been suggesting. By doing so, the president was communicating to the handful of people who knew about the bomb that he regarded the prospective new weapon as a tool of American power.

Among these people was Stalin, who had long since learned of the project via his spies in the West, and because Roosevelt and Churchill knew all about the espionage, they knew as well that they were quietly informing Stalin that his main wartime allies meant to keep the bomb to themselves.

Did the prospect of the bomb play some part in FDR's decision-making at Yalta? Possibly. Desperate for some means to somehow bring Stalin around, mortally ill and out of options, Roosevelt may have hoped that the mere prospect of a revolutionary new weapon would persuade his Soviet counterpart to soften his position.[46] We know now that Stalin would never have done so in a million years, but FDR could not be sure of that. In any event, Stalin did not budge, and that put an end to Roosevelt's hopes of a comprehensive new world order.

A few American and British military figures, including General George S. Patton, raised the possibility of attacking the USSR, perhaps even by joining forces with the Germans, but this was never in the cards. Neither the American nor the British public would have accepted such a campaign, which would certainly have meant many more years of fighting the largest army in the world, with untold thousands of casualties. Hitler's failed expedition recalled what Napoleon had learned a century and a half before—that invading Russia was a fool's game in the best of times. In 1945, with the victorious Red Army implanted throughout eastern Europe, it would be a taller order still. Furthermore, the very idea of turning on an ally after four years of fighting together was close to inconceivable to most American officials, including Roosevelt and Supreme Allied Commander Eisenhower, and to an American public eager to bring the boys home.[47] Added to all that, the war against Japan remained to be won. No, a war to force the USSR to accept an American peace was not an option. To achieve his postwar vision, Roosevelt in early 1945 had no recourse but to try to cajole Stalin into joining America in an idealistic new order. That was a losing cause, and the president, mindful of Wilson's experience and nearing his death, did not pursue it.

Mr. Truman from Missouri

The Yalta Conference ended on February 11, 1945, and eight weeks later, on April 12, Franklin D. Roosevelt died at his vacation home in Warm Springs, Georgia. Less than a month after that, on May 7, Germany surrendered. Roosevelt's successor, Harry S Truman, was ill-prepared for the role now thrust upon him. A plainspoken, largely self-educated man, Truman had served as a junior officer during the First World War and, after a series of professional failures, had joined the Democratic machine of Kansas City, where he found his calling as a competent and partisan Democrat. As a U.S. senator Truman had been primarily concerned with domestic politics; Roosevelt chose him as his running mate in 1944 mostly because he passed muster with southern Democrats and party elders wary of the liberalism of the current vice president, Henry Wallace. Truman had been vice president only a few months when FDR died. He possessed few considered ideas about foreign policy, apart from a midwestern populism that had led him to oppose American interventionism during the 1930s. He would be forced to learn quickly. For during the first year of his administration Truman would preside over the conclusion of the Second World War and the beginning of a new conflict: the Cold War.

Many historians have suggested that Truman shifted U.S. foreign policy to a more aggressive stance against the Soviet Union —that, influenced in part by anti-Soviet and conservative advisers, Truman accepted a postwar confrontation between the United States and the USSR that Roosevelt could, or would, have found a way to prevent.[48] That a shift occurred with the presidential transition is clear enough. Truman was a different sort of man. Roosevelt had managed during his tumultuous twelve-year reign to achieve his goals—preventing the Great Depression from destroying American democracy, and winning the Second World War—by avoiding rigid positions, keeping his true intentions to himself, maintaining a kind of moral flexibility, and focusing on what seemed to work on a given day. His self-confidence and native optimism allowed him to live with gaping inconsistencies, sure that his big-picture instincts were correct.

The new president lacked such sanguinity. Prone to seeing the world in black and white, Truman often glossed over nuances, ambiguities, and counterevidence; he preferred the simple answer stated in either/or terms. As Winston Churchill, who admired Truman's decisiveness, once observed, the president "takes no notice of delicate ground, he just plants his foot firmly on it." Shortly after taking office, Truman hosted a meeting at the White House with the Soviet commissar of foreign affairs, V. M. Molotov, and scolded his guest for Moscow's failure to fulfill the Yalta agreement on Poland. Molotov stormed out. Keen to impress his new advisers, Truman had used what he called his "tough method." He bragged after the encounter: "I gave it to him straight, one-two to the jaw."[49] It is hard to imagine a comparable scene under FDR.

Truman's tougher line was taken up also by those in lower echelons of the administration. The altered outlook was subtle, and it might have occurred regardless of who was in the White House. Especially at more senior levels, however, it reflected in part the new access of officials who had chafed under what they saw as FDR's misplaced faith in Soviet-American cooperation and who saw the possibility of shaping the views of an inexperienced new president. Several advisers—including the U.S. ambassador in Moscow, Averell Harriman, who was now more gloomy on the outlook for bilateral ties than he had been earlier in the war, and Secretary of the Navy James Forrestal—encouraged Truman to take a tough position with the USSR, to indicate to the Kremlin that the United States would seek accommodation from a position of strength and hard dealing, a stance that appealed to Truman's political combativeness.[50]

Yet too much can be made of this leadership change in Washington. Roosevelt's policies during the war paved the way for a showdown with the Soviet Union, even if he himself hoped to keep it from happening. By going along with Churchill's postponement of the second front in order to maintain a victorious alliance with Great Britain, he stoked Stalin's suspiciousness while delivering eastern Europe into his hands. For similar reasons, FDR agreed to keep the atomic project secret from Stalin. He failed to take the steps necessary to have any hope of securing genuine Soviet cooperation in enforcing postwar peace and national security—steps that in early 1945 would have amounted either to an outright attack on the Soviet state or, conceivably, a series of major concessions to Stalin. Neither of these scenarios was within the realm of political possibility in the winter and early spring of that year. The geopolitical storm clouds had been gathering for months when the great man died, and they were drawing ever closer when his successor took the oath of office.

By this time, Americans had less reason to be hopeful about a postwar Grand Alliance than before. The Kremlin leader seemed to have no interest in running any kind of serious risks for the sake of greater cooperation with the West. Once the war in Europe was as good as won, Stalin made little attempt to pretend that Moscow would tolerate free elections in Poland or to reconsider his insistence on the Security Council veto. He patiently tolerated American and British talk about human rights and self-determination, signing documents if that would make his allies happy, but he never indicated that he took these notions seriously. He left little doubt in his communications with Washington and London that his government planned to practice power politics as usual after the war. There was only one language Stalin understood, Truman said, not long after the war ended: "How many divisions have you?"

Truman's analysis here was correct but incomplete: it missed Stalin's cautiousness in world affairs during this period. However paranoid and murderous he was at home, Stalin as statesman was a thoroughgoing realist. For the foreseeable future, he had to be careful. The Soviet Union had suffered horrendous casualties and almost unfathomable physical destruction—the extent of the devastation in some parts of European Russia had to be seen to be believed. Reconstruction would take years. He knew he was in a very weak position with respect to the United States and had virtually no navy or strategic air force to speak of. Eventually, Stalin believed, Germany would rise to threaten the USSR again, probably by the 1960s, and so probably would Japan. As for the capitalist powers, only a fool would trust them, though Stalin aimed to make whatever deals were necessary to buy time to rebuild the Soviet Union's military and economic strength.[51]

From Potsdam to Tokyo Bay

Notwithstanding his scolding of Molotov, Truman too moved cautiously in his early weeks, seeing as his duty to ensure stability by maintaining Roosevelt's foreign and domestic policies. This meant, among other things, working to preserve the Grand Alliance after the war, which Truman took to be the main outcome of the Yalta Conference. Having no urgent reason to act otherwise, and conscious of the late president's tremendous political popularity, Truman tried to be cooperative with Moscow during his first few weeks. When Lend-Lease shipments to the Soviet Union were accidentally canceled in May 1945, Truman restored them immediately. When he learned from James Byrnes, a close adviser whom he would soon appoint secretary of state, that the Yalta agreements could clearly be interpreted as giving Stalin a free hand in eastern Europe, he took no steps to try to reverse or redefine that interpretation. Like Roosevelt, Truman understood that he simply had no leverage to do so.[52]

With his Soviet options limited, Truman felt free to focus his attention on the last great problem of the war: securing Japan's unconditional surrender.[53] This task dominated his thinking about foreign policy in the early summer, because it presented a political dilemma that he could not easily resolve or pass on to associates. Despite the continuous advance of U.S. forces across the Pacific, the destruction of Japanese air power, the bombardment of Japanese cities by the American air force, and the surrender of Germany on May 8, 1945, the imperial government in Tokyo continued to refuse to accept the Allied demand of unconditional surrender. Peace factions within the government issued vague statements to neutral governments like Switzerland and the USSR (which would not declare war on Japan until early August), but these fell far short of the criteria Roosevelt and Churchill had agreed upon in Casablanca in 1943.[54] Until the government issued an unambiguous surrender to the United States, Truman felt bound to proceed with the war, which meant, if Japan were to be militarily defeated, an invasion of the Japanese islands.

The experience of the island-hopping campaign in the Pacific over the previous two years suggested that an invasion of the Japanese homeland would be a horrible ordeal, leading to tens of thousands of American casualties and untold millions of Japanese deaths. That was an especially miserable prospect because Japan was so manifestly beaten. For Truman, it was also a political nightmare, as he considered the public reaction to an ongoing and bloody campaign that extended into 1946 or even beyond.

What to do? Several of his main advisers, including Secretary of War Henry Stimson and Joseph Grew, a leading Asianist in the State Department, urged Truman to consider quietly assuring Japan that it would be allowed to retain its emperor after surrender.[55] By doing so, Washington could perhaps give the peace factions in Tokyo the argument they needed—that defeat could be accepted with honor—even though such an assurance was in clear contravention of unconditional surrender. Stimson and Grew argued that the Japanese were certain to fight suicidally as long as they believed that the emperor would be deposed—perhaps even executed—by the invading American forces. By granting Japan this one promise, invasion could be averted and the war brought to a speedier conclusion. Since Japan had scientists familiar with atomic energy, Undersecretary of the Navy Ralph Bard urged that the United States should give Japan a two or three day warning that the bomb would be used, and at the same time inform them of the Soviet Union's imminent entry into the war.[56]

Truman rejected the advice. He wanted, for the time being at least, to wait for the final Big Three conference, scheduled for the middle of July in Potsdam, a suburb to the south of Berlin. His contempt for the Japanese made him reluctant to soften the surrender terms, as did his fear of a domestic political backlash should he deviate from unconditional surrender, an objective that so many American soldiers had died for in the island warfare of the past two years. At Potsdam, moreover, he could try to get Stalin to participate in the invasion of Japan, which would reduce American casualties. Also, and of greater importance to Truman, he knew that the scientists at Los Alamos had scheduled a test of the atomic bomb that would coincide with the beginning of the conference, which he had postponed for just that reason.[57]

It was the last of the Grand Alliance conferences, and the agenda was enormous. With the war in Europe won, the Big Three set to work negotiating the details of postwar occupation and treaty arrangements, finalizing in a sense the basic agreements that were made at Yalta and Tehran. The Soviet Union also secured a more formal acceptance by all other parties of its sphere of influence in eastern Europe, and details concerning the occupation of Germany—and within it, Berlin—were thrashed out. In a discussion with Truman on the evening of his arrival, Stalin reaffirmed his promise made at Yalta to join the war in Japan as soon as possible.

For the most part, Stalin, Truman, and Churchill engaged in general discussions about postwar cooperation, though their cordial relations were interrupted by Churchill's shocking electoral defeat and his replacement at the conference by the new Labour prime minister, Clement Attlee.

For Truman, Potsdam was dominated by big news from home: the atomic test in New Mexico, codenamed Trinity, had succeeded. Truman, who had been deliberately kept ignorant of the Manhattan Project during FDR's presidency, had not discussed the bomb at length with his advisers before arriving in Germany. Secretary of War Stimson had called the bomb a "master card," while other advisers, including his new secretary of state, James Byrnes, and Undersecretary of War John J. McCloy, had hinted at the possibility that its use could preclude Soviet participation in the Pacific War. In late May, a committee of high-level scientists and policymakers had formally recommended that the bomb be dropped on a Japanese city rather than, as a few had suggested, on an unpopulated area or a neutral test site with international observers. The fact that this was debated at all shows that the few people in Washington who knew about the atomic bomb were aware of its revolutionary possibilities—they did not think of it as just another weapon.[58]

Truman understood that too. But he had approved the plan, drawn up by General Leslie Groves, military head of the Manhattan Project, to order the U.S. Air Force to use the two atomic bombs at its disposal as soon as they were ready. The president did not officially accept the suggestions of Stimson and Byrnes that the bomb could be used to intimidate the USSR, but now that the bomb had been proven to work, Truman and his aides made two key moves in that direction. First, they authorized the release of a new communication to Japan, the Potsdam Declaration, which reiterated the demand for unconditional surrender and threatened a "rain of ruin" if the Japanese refused it. Stalin was not invited to participate in this declaration, even though Truman the previous week had made a point of securing the Soviet leader's affirmation that his armies would soon enter the war, even though the Soviet delegation had drafted its own declaration that was remarkably similar to the American one, and even though Britain and China (who would not be fighting in Japan) did sign it.[59] With the bomb now available, Truman moved to make the war on Japan an exclusively American operation.

Second, toward the end of the conference Truman walked over to Stalin and personally informed him that the United States now possessed a weapon of unusual destructive capabilities. It was the first time an American official had formally told a Soviet counterpart of the atomic bomb since the beginning of the Manhattan Project in 1941. The irony was that Stalin had learned of the project from his spies long before Truman himself had any inkling of its existence.[60]

Hiroshima and Nagasaki

On August 6, 1945, while Truman was sailing home from Europe, a single American bomber, the *Enola Gay,* dropped a uranium bomb on the Japanese harbor city of Hiroshima. The explosion killed about 40,000 residents instantly, mortally wounded perhaps 60,000, and injured tens of thousands more, many of whom suffered grotesque wounds and disfigurement. Over the ensuing weeks many survivors of the blast succumbed to new forms of illness caused by atomic radioactivity.[61] Two days after the destruction of Hiroshima—on August 8—Stalin declared war on Japan, and on August 9 the United States dropped a second atomic bomb, this time on the industrial city of Nagasaki, which eventually killed a total of about 70,000 residents.[62] The Japanese government asked for terms from the United States on August 10 and formally surrendered three weeks later. Despite its professed insistence on unconditional surrender, the United States accepted Japan's demand that the emperor be allowed to remain as a figurehead on the Japanese throne.

The brutality of the two atomic attacks, taken together with the timing of their occurrence—at the end of the Second World War, with the United States on the cusp of its confrontation with the Soviet Union—raises the question: did the decision to drop atomic bombs on Japan represent an attempt by the Truman administration to intimidate the USSR? Was the bombing of Hiroshima and Nagasaki, in other words, the first gambit of the Cold War rather than the last move of the Second World War? Scholars have debated this question for decades, and the matter has not yet been settled.[63] The basic facts related to the decision are not in dispute, but the intentions of Truman and his key advisers are, as is the question of the necessity of the bombing.

Truman never stated in official meetings during the months leading up to Hiroshima and Nagasaki why exactly he rejected the alternatives to the Groves plan to attack when ready. There was little official White House discussion of the subject. As with many issues related to the history of foreign policy, the intentions of the decisionmakers are hard to discern definitively from the internal record. This is especially true in the case of the atomic bomb, which was treated with absolute official secrecy until August 6, 1945. Even at the highest levels of the government, few knew anything about the weapon. Given the absence of hard evidence, the best that historians can do is to deduce the likely motivations behind the decision and offer the most logical explanation.

The official justification for the attacks, given afterward by Truman, Stimson, and many others, was simple: the bombs were dropped for the single purpose of ending the war as quickly as possible. There can be no doubt that Truman himself dreaded the prospect of a U.S. land invasion of Japan, as it would probably have led to tens of thousands of American casualties and extended the war into 1946 or beyond. The American air force had been bombing Japanese cities ruthlessly for more than a year, with the aim of forcing a surrender, but it hadn't happened, despite hundreds of thousands of Japanese civilians dead. Under the circumstances, why wouldn't the president have dropped atomic bombs for the sole purpose of securing the quickest possible Japanese surrender? If his plan was simply to save American lives by bringing the war to a close, it certainly worked.

But what if Truman's intentions were not so straightforward? Several threads of evidence suggest that the president had additional reasons for the bombing, beyond his desire to avoid the American land invasion scheduled for November 1945. First, Truman knew that peace factions in the Japanese government had been communicating their desire to surrender for months. To be sure, these communications were likely to be conditional, and the United States had previously insisted on unconditional surrender.

But in the end, the Truman administration accepted the retention of Japan's emperor as a condition of peace, which suggests that the terms of surrender were always negotiable. If simply ending the war without an American land invasion had been Truman's only priority, he could have more vigorously pursued this backdoor path to peace before resorting to the bomb.

Second, Truman knew well before August 6 that the imminent entry of the Red Army into the war against Japan would hasten the Japanese surrender and might make the American invasion unnecessary. If the prospect of additional American casualties had been his only concern, he could have postponed the bombing in order to play out the option of a Soviet invasion. But from a geopolitical perspective, the president understood that if the USSR intervened in Japan, the Soviets would send their military forces through Manchuria, where some of them would likely remain long-term. Moreover, they would participate in the occupation of Japan itself—a "fact on the ground" that would allow Stalin to extend his power considerably into East Asia.

Finally, the president and Stimson claimed after the war that the American ground invasion might have cost as many as 500,000 American lives, even though both men knew that the army had projected many fewer combat deaths, along the lines of 50,000.[64] Why would these two men lie about this number, if not to disguise their true agenda in dropping the bomb?

To tease apart the answer to this question, we must consider the possibility that the Truman administration's motives for bombing Hiroshima on August 6 were different from its motives for bombing Nagasaki on August 9. Scholars who see both bombings as being primarily motivated by a desire to intimidate Moscow and prevent it from expanding its presence in Asia face a tall task. In the case of the first attack in particular, they must demonstrate that Truman was more influenced by postwar geopolitical considerations than by the more straightforward objective of avoiding a bloody ground invasion in November. In other words, they must show that absent an interest in influencing Soviet conduct, the United States would not have dropped the bomb on Hiroshima.

This is simply an untenable claim. U.S. officials were indeed aware of the peace feelers sent out by elements of the Japanese leadership, through intercepted communications. But these were not formal requests, and they came from factions that were not clearly in control of the Tokyo government. And while Truman may have believed that the imminent participation of the USSR would likely lead to a Japanese surrender before an American invasion became necessary, he could not count on this outcome. Warfare is inherently unpredictable. The president knew, for example, that Germany had fought on for months after its defeat became inevitable, and the Japanese had demonstrated a fanatical capacity to keep fighting that surpassed even that of the Nazi regime. Truman was not morally repulsed by the prospect of bombing cities in order to bring an end to this suicidal behavior. He had been tolerating the terror bombing of civilians since the day he became president, and he knew that America's incendiary bombing of Japanese cities in 1944 and 1945 had already killed several hundred thousand Japanese.

Moreover, if the president had made a different choice about the atomic bomb, and if the American public had later discovered that he could have used it to end the war but chose instead to authorize an invasion that killed tens of thousands of American soldiers, his political life likely would have gone up in flames. So for all of these reasons, even if the Soviet Union had been completely out of the picture, Truman almost certainly would have proceeded to drop an atomic bomb on Hiroshima on August 6, the first day it was ready to use. And had Japan refused to surrender shortly thereafter, the president almost surely would have used the next atomic bomb in his arsenal for the same reasons.

The question, then, is not why Truman permitted a second bomb to be dropped, but why it was dropped so soon after the first. We know that Truman had reasons to avoid a second bombardment if possible. If the president was not morally repulsed by the bomb, he was nevertheless aware of the moral implications of atomic warfare. Truman knew that his own key advisers had discussed the possibility of dropping the bomb on an unpopulated area or a test site in the Pacific, and that Secretary of War Stimson had flatly rejected the air force's request to use the first bomb on the ancient cultural center of Kyoto.[65] After Hiroshima became the target, Truman was bothered by initial reports of the gruesome destruction the bomb had caused. In short, the president understood that dropping an atomic bomb on a city full of civilians was a momentous, world-changing thing to do. Yet he did nothing to prevent the second attack on Nagasaki, only seventy-two hours after Hiroshima. Why?

Truman must have known that the Japanese government would need several days to discover what had happened in Hiroshima and to work out a formal surrender. If he had preferred not to use the second bomb, and if his only aim had been to avoid the November invasion, he could have postponed the second attack for a week or even two. Because the air force, and not the president, had determined the initial dates and targets of attack, Truman would have had to intervene deliberately in the decisionmaking process —but if he had wanted to give Japan a reasonable window of time to capitulate, he could have done so. Yet he did not make a move to avert the destruction of Nagasaki.

Truman's disinclination to delay the second bombing brings the Soviet factor back into consideration. What the destruction of Nagasaki accomplished was Japan's immediate surrender, and for Truman this swift capitulation was crucial in order to preempt a Soviet military move into Asia. By dropping the second bomb quickly—just one day after the Soviet Union declared war on Japan—Truman ensured that the Japanese government, reeling from the devastation of two attacks and worried that its cities might be flattened one by one, would lose no time in coming to terms with the United States. This explanation of Truman's timing is supported by the administration's acceptance of Japan's one condition of surrender—that its emperor be retained. Once the second bomb had pushed the Tokyo government to discuss terms, it became critical to reach a deal quickly, before the Soviets could make their move, even if the principle of unconditional surrender had to be abandoned. An American government indifferent to Soviet actions probably would not have accepted these terms, at least not until the eve of the planned invasion three months hence.

In short, the first bomb was dropped as soon as it was ready, and for the reason the administration expressed: to hasten the end of the Pacific War. But in the case of the second bomb, timing was everything. In an important sense, the destruction of Nagasaki—not the bombing itself but Truman's refusal to delay it—was America's first act of the Cold War.[66]

Seeds of Conflict

President Franklin Roosevelt developed a new American foreign policy in the early years of the Second World War. The demise of free security and the specter of Axis domination of Eurasia led him to conclude that the United States was truly, for the first time since it had become a modern and unified nation after the Civil War, insecure. This did not mean that the American people faced an imminent threat of conquest or invasion but that the technological shrinking of the oceans and the prospect of a victorious German-Japanese alliance in command of all Europe and Asia meant that Americans could no longer remain indifferent to power politics in the larger world. Perhaps these new developments would not ever threaten American sovereignty, but serious observers of world politics at the time of Pearl Harbor had to believe the possibility existed. These fears were magnified, if murkily, by the possibility of the atomic bomb, and the entirely reasonable prospect that a Nazi Germany in control of all Europe would build one first.

Roosevelt also believed that it was time for the United States to assume leadership of the western world, to build a new global order out of the rubble of prewar international politics, an order based on American notions of self-determination and free-market capitalism. The president was not motivated by base economic considerations only, but he was not indifferent to them either. For him, economic interest went hand-in-hand with national identity, the idea of American civilization. He believed, like Niebuhr, that the United States now faced a choice between projecting its power and civilization globally or having another nation's power and civilization—most vividly, that of Nazi Germany—imposed upon it. American capitalism could not survive a Nazi-controlled world, and neither could American values. Alternatively, in a world defined along American lines, the United States could enjoy decades of prosperity and retain its liberal political tradition. Free security had allowed the United States to ignore this choice for generations—the United States had been able to pursue prosperity and cultivate its liberal polity without sustained engagement with international power politics. That utopia was no more.

By the summer of 1944 it was clear that Germany and Japan could not win and that the United States would be the undisputed leader of the capitalist world. Yet Roosevelt's plans were complicated by the fact that the Soviet Union had withstood the ferocious onslaught of the German *Wehrmacht* and now was poised to emerge as a dominant power in Europe. As the world's only communist state, and a survivor of four years of devastating war, the USSR was unlikely to accept America's world leadership and the globalization of free-trade capitalism. Stalin's diplomacy during the last two years of the war seemed to confirm this. By dismissing American criticism of his Polish policy, by insisting on the Security Council veto, and in general by appearing entirely uninterested in idealistic plans for the postwar period, Stalin communicated the message to American leaders that he would not participate in their new world order.

America's increasingly adverse attitude toward Soviet power by the end of the Second World War was thus caused largely by U.S. leaders' own desires and Stalin's rejection of them rather than by a fear of Soviet designs per se. The Kremlin's disavowal of the American plan for peace seemed inexorably to mean the establishment of competing economic blocs in Europe and possibly elsewhere and a United Nations that would be largely ineffective.

Leading officials in Washington during the period 1941–1945 rarely expressed a fear of Soviet aggression. Nor did they often or loudly stress the malign nature of the Stalinist regime when considering postwar foreign policy. We now know, more than American leaders did then, the colossal scale of Stalin's brutality toward his own people. Retrospectively, this inclines us to regard the Cold War as a moral contest, as a struggle against evil. But that is not how American leaders of the day perceived it. During the Second World War, Roosevelt, Truman, and the men who most influenced them on matters of foreign policy did not approach the USSR with moral revulsion. Rather, they began to regard the Soviet Union as an adversary because its army stood astride much of eastern Europe, and because it was refusing to go along with Washington's global plans.

2

CONFRONTATION

In a Navy Day speech delivered in New York City in late October 1945, President Harry Truman declared that the victorious nations of the Second World War must liberate the peoples of the earth from the enmities and conflicts of power politics. The world, he said, "cannot afford any letdown in the united determination of the allies in this war to accomplish a lasting peace."[1] Cooperation with the other great powers would be necessary to avoid yet another global war. The United States would commit itself to this noble objective.

Even as he spoke these words, however, Truman strongly doubted that any kind of "united determination" to create a lasting peace —a world without great-power hostility and military confrontations—existed. Like Franklin Roosevelt before him, the president believed that a new world order could be created by establishing more open international trade, as well as a regime of collective security under which no nation would be immune to sanctions and military intervention. But this would mean the triumph of global capitalism and the development of a veto-proof United Nations Security Council composed of the United States, its three capitalist allies, and the Soviet Union. The world's only communist state had just turned back the Nazi onslaught, fighting for years without major assistance from the Western powers, and had helped to crush the German war machine. The Kremlin was not about to accept America's claim to global leadership, an international economic order defined by free-trade capitalism, and a Security Council dominated by the United States if it could avoid it.

And Stalin could avoid it. The only way the United States could compel him to go along with its postwar vision was to wage war against the USSR. But Stalin's Red Army, the largest in the world, was now deployed throughout eastern Europe, and the Soviet Union had already proven how difficult the nation was to conquer by conventional invasion. The American public, eager for peace after four years of sacrifice, would never support a harrowing major war on the other side of the world just to overthrow its former ally for the idealistic purposes of establishing "a new world order." This was the overarching reality facing the U.S. government as the World War II came to an end. What remained undecided was how the Truman administration would respond to this international situation.

Many in Washington, including—at least rhetorically—the president himself, believed that the colossal horrors of the Second World War, along with the specter of the atomic bomb, made it imperative for the United States to seek some kind of collaboration with its Soviet rival, whatever the odds. Perhaps Truman could negotiate with Moscow to reach formal agreements on Europe, Asia, and the international control of atomic energy. If Soviet-American relations could remain on an even keel, maybe a global conflict could be avoided. This view had prominent supporters in Washington in the final months of 1945. Others believed that the Soviet Union could not be trusted, that it was committed to global revolution and the destruction of regimes like the United States, and that Americans would do better to acknowledge this reality now and confront the Kremlin rather than pursue futile, or perhaps even dangerous, agreements with them. These observers pointed to reports from eastern Europe indicating widespread oppressive actions by Soviet proconsuls backed by the Red Army, especially in Bulgaria and Romania. They ignored cases where the USSR had kept its agreements and had followed more conciliatory policies, as in Hungary and Czechoslovakia.

Truman and his key advisers were not committed formally to one path or another in the autumn of 1945. They possessed no grand, forward-looking strategy. Over the next few months, however—driven by turmoil in Europe and Central Asia, a closer assessment of Stalin's motives, the revelations of Soviet atomic espionage, and perceived domestic political imperatives—the administration moved decisively toward the second approach. By late 1947 the phrase "Cold War" had entered the political lexicon, and America's containment strategy had been implemented. Moments of acute East-West tension followed; and each time, the United States and the West emerged in a stronger position than before. By the spring of 1949, a serious observer could argue that the trendlines were clear: containment's core objectives had been achieved.

Toward Cold War

At the end of World War II the United States possessed far and away the world's largest economy. Its Gross Domestic Product (GDP) was five times that of Great Britain, four times that of the Soviet Union, and it accounted for more than half of the world's economic output. America had been spared the immense physical destruction inflicted on much of Europe and East Asia, and it had suffered far fewer battlefield deaths than most of the other major belligerents, and almost no civilian casualties. Moreover, the United States alone possessed the atomic bomb. By any reasonable definition, American enjoyed preponderant power in the immediate postwar period. How could it use this power to contend with the Soviet Union?

Truman, together with his secretary of state, the South Carolina power broker and former U.S. Supreme Court justice James F. Byrnes, seemed initially inclined to pursue the old FDR notion that the simple reality of overwhelming American force, together with tough give-and-take negotiation, could impel Stalin to compromise on the vexing issues dividing the two nations.[2] War was not an option, but maybe American pressure could push the Soviets to moderate their behavior in eastern Europe, agree to U.S. occupation policies in Germany, and follow Washington's lead on the looming problem of international atomic arms control. Indeed, Byrnes hoped to use the promise of weapons control as an inducement to obtain Soviet concessions on the other issues. If Stalin would relax his repressive policies in his European sphere, particularly Poland, and if he would work with the United States and other occupying powers to establish a functional government in Germany rather than savagely looting the Soviet sector there, then Washington might take steps to transfer its atomic monopoly to an international body.

To Byrnes, this seemed like an entirely plausible notion. But during the first Council of Foreign Ministers (CFM) conference, which took place in London from September 11 to October 2, the Soviet foreign minister Vyacheslav Molotov belittled the American monopoly, despite Byrnes's use of both threats and encouragements.[3] In December, at the second CFM conference in Moscow, Byrnes tried again to obtain firm deals on these issues, and again failed. Molotov rejected the United States' demands for a liberalization of eastern Europe, refused to cooperate on Germany, and dismissed Western complaints about the establishment of undemocratic regimes in Bulgaria and Romania.

Even if Molotov had been receptive, Byrnes learned in mid-December that he was to refrain from reaching any agreement with the USSR on the bomb until the White House had developed a policy on atomic weaponry. Truman ordered him not "to disclose any information regarding the bomb at this time." Arriving back home empty-handed, Byrnes found himself increasingly isolated in White House decisionmaking. In Truman's view, he had exceeded his mandate—he had sought to conclude a deal in Moscow without obtaining prior approval from Washington, a transgression for which the president upbraided him upon his return. Long resentful of Byrnes's lack of deference and his independent dealings as secretary of state, Truman used the Moscow conference as an excuse to marginalize his adviser and demonstrate his anti-Soviet toughness. It was time, Truman said privately, to stop "babying the Russians."[4]

Why did Truman reject negotiations with Moscow on the question of atomic control? He was not unaware of the stakes. In September the departing secretary of war, Henry Stimson, suddenly made an impassioned plea for international atomic control, spelling out to the president and the rest of the cabinet very clearly exactly what was required. "I consider the problem of our satisfactory relations with Russia as not merely connected but as virtually dominated by the problem of the atomic bomb," the veteran statesman said in a secret White House meeting.[5] His logic was simple. The United States and Great Britain had kept the building of the bomb a secret from their Soviet ally and had used it ruthlessly to end the war in Japan. This collusion and secrecy with respect to a manifestly powerful weapon was so threatening to the Kremlin that it would take all steps necessary to build a comparable weapon for itself. Once it did so, Stimson maintained, an arms race would ensue and the prospect of international cooperation would disappear. Hence the necessity of moving quickly to reach a deal with the Soviet Union that could lead to the establishment of a truly international agency in control of all atomic technologies. Without such an agency, the two new powers would sooner or later commence an atomic arms race. History taught that this would eventually result in another world war, this time fought with the kind of weaponry that laid waste to Hiroshima and Nagasaki.[6]

Stimson's pleas fell on deaf ears. Though Truman in early October 1945 did call for international atomic control and cooperation with the Soviet Union, soon afterward he indicated that he was unwilling to take even the minimum steps Stimson, along with many other advocates, deemed necessary to achieve these goals. Speaking to reporters "on the record," the president vowed that the United States would never transfer its atomic material and scientific facilities to an international agency, and added that if other nations wanted the bomb they should acquire it "on their own hook."[7] In a speech to Congress in December he called for a foreign policy built on military power. By these unequivocal and public statements the president indicated that the United States would not cooperate seriously with the Kremlin on the question of atomic control and would not use its bomb monopoly as a negotiating tool to secure Soviet concessions either. Stimson's logic had no place in the administration's emerging policy.

Ordinary political calculations played an important role in Truman's reasoning. He wanted to focus on the domestic economy, to avoid recession, and to maintain the Democratic party's majority in Congress after the 1946 midterm elections. Talking tough on foreign policy was a way to disarm Republican critics and appeal to eastern European voters in key states such as Michigan and Illinois.[8] Also, like Roosevelt, Truman believed that the Kremlin should be making the concessions, not the much stronger United States. Soviet obstinance at the two CFM meetings certainly did not encourage the president to conclude that cooperation with the USSR would likely get anywhere, particularly on an issue as revolutionary as establishing international control over a new form of weaponry.

But the most immediate factor pushing Truman away from cooperation with the Soviet Union on the question of atomic control was one that the public would not know about until February 1946: Soviet atomic espionage. In September, just as Stimson was pleading for cooperation and as Byrnes and Molotov were meeting in London, FBI director J. Edgar Hoover informed Truman that a massive spy ring operating out of Ottawa had infiltrated the Manhattan Project with Canadian and American spies working for Moscow. Washington officials had known of this network since 1942, but new revelations from the Canadian government indicated that the scale of the espionage was much greater than had been previously suspected.[9]

The espionage report from Hoover indicated two things to Truman. First, it gave him a clear, simple explanation for Soviet intransigence. Why was Stalin defying the United States by acting as he liked in eastern Europe? Why were the Soviets unyielding and obstinate at international meetings, despite the USSR's relative weakness? Why did Stalin appear indifferent to American offers of cooperation? Perhaps because the information he had received from his spies made him confident he could build a bomb soon and thereby contend with the United States as a military equal. Just how much the Kremlin had stolen Truman did not know, could not know, but Stalin's actions suggested the amount was substantial.

Second, and much more important, the revelations of atomic espionage were, for Truman, political fireballs. If word got out that the Soviet Union had spied on its ally during the war, that many of its spies were American citizens, and—as Hoover would later make abundantly clear to Truman—that many of these individuals had connections to leading Democratic Party figures in the State Department and elsewhere, the damage to his party and to his own political stature could be devastating. But if such revelations were made public at the same time that Truman was proposing to give away America's atomic bombs to an international agency, well, the ensuing political assault on the White House would have been incalculable. The espionage revelations made serious international control a political impossibility for the president, and further inclined him to regard the Soviet Union with suspicion and hostility.[10]

Five Fateful Weeks

None of this was yet public knowledge. As far as the American people were aware, the Soviet Union was still an ally, and the administration's plans for the postwar world were still wholly undetermined. President Truman thus faced an array of foreign policy criticism on this question in the first weeks of 1946. There was still a lingering suspicion of American internationalism throughout parts of both the Democratic and Republican parties, especially among politicians wary of Great Britain and those keen to reduce the power of the federal government now that the war had ended. Many liberals in the Democratic Party—led by Henry Wallace, vice president under Roosevelt during much of the war and now Truman's secretary of commerce—were unhappy with the increasingly frosty nature of the Soviet-American relationship and demanded that Truman honor Roosevelt's call for a perpetuation of the Grand Alliance to keep the postwar peace. Conversely, many influential Republicans, sensing a political opening, argued that the administration was dangerously slow to respond to the Soviet threat and pressed for a more resolute policy.[11]

Truman did not know exactly how to answer these criticisms. Philosophically, he sympathized with fiscal conservatives' aversion to big government, and since the end of the war he had moved to cut military spending substantially and demobilize millions of American soldiers. He had much less affinity for the old Rooseveltian left and its calls for closer ties with Moscow, but he could not respond to its criticisms as openly as he liked because Soviet espionage was still a closely guarded Washington secret. Also, he wanted to appear as a president who was simply carrying on the cooperative policies of FDR. Yet Truman, a canny political operator, well understood that a policy of continuity carried its own risks. He grasped that his conservative Republican critics could try to brand him as insufficiently tough by drawing on memories of the Munich appeasement in 1938, when British prime minister Neville Chamberlain granted the Sudetenland to Hitler in an attempt to secure the peace.[12]

Over the space of about five weeks in February and early March, the political climate in Washington shifted dramatically toward the view advocated by Truman's Republican critics, and several of his own advisers, that the United States must confront the Soviet Union decisively as a serious enemy. Truman had little control over the four events that precipitated this shift, but he responded in ways that worked to his political advantage and reflected his straightforward approach to international relations.

The first and perhaps most important (though least noted) of these events was a radio address given by the syndicated columnist Drew Pearson on February 3. Pearson told his listeners that he had received secret information from inside the government (probably from Hoover) about an extensive Soviet atomic espionage network operating out of Canada.[13] The network, he warned, was not simply localized in the atomic project itself but could well have spread throughout the United States. The ensuing scandal and outrage caused by Pearson's remarks and by the Canadian government's official acknowledgment of the spy network two weeks later triggered what the historian Gregg Herken has called a "near-hysteria" in many newspapers and throughout Washington during the second half of February.[14] Not only had America's wartime ally run a major—and apparently quite effective—espionage operation during the war; the operation evidently had been conducted largely by American citizens, secretly working for Moscow while they went about their treacherous business in Los Alamos or Washington.

CONFRONTATION

Republican critics demanded that the administration respond to the charges and identify the traitors within the government. Newspaper editorial pages around the nation warned of subversion. Did Pearson's charges mean that the Soviet Union would soon have its own atomic bomb, stolen right out from under the nose of Roosevelt and Truman?

The public effect of the Pearson revelations did not come to full fruition until the heyday of McCarthyism in 1950–1953, but the political impact on Truman's foreign policy was immediate. The president had already privately abandoned the idea of seeking genuine international cooperation on atomic matters with the USSR, but the Pearson address closed this possibility off for good. As Hoover (or whoever provided Pearson with his information) must have known, Truman now could not risk any kind of atomic deal with Moscow, no matter how minor, for such a move would spell political disaster. Indeed, the president was so shaken by the Pearson scandal that he canceled an atomic cooperation deal with Great Britain, reneging on a promise Roosevelt had made to Churchill in 1944.[15] The idea of pursuing any kind of collaboration on atomic control with the Soviets disappeared from White House discussions after early February.

As if on cue, Stalin provided even more fodder for those in Washington who were looking for a reason to regard him as an adversary. In a public speech on February 9, he announced that his government would maintain its wartime (and prewar) policies of state control over the economy and would continue to divert maximum resources toward heavy industry and military production. Stalin did not attribute the policies he was announcing to American behavior as such but rather to the need for the USSR to maintain its military strength in a world of continuing imperialism.[16] He endorsed Lenin's line that the nations of the West were impelled by the logic of late capitalism toward unending conflict and war.

The Soviet Union would not be caught up in this logic, but

it could find itself—as it did in 1941—in a capitalist war not of its own making. Until the global triumph of communism, Stalin maintained, the world would be dangerous and the threat to the Soviet Union imminent. The aspirations of the long-suffering Soviet citizenry for prosperity and domestic reform would have to wait. Indeed, he saw another world war as inevitable. "We shall recover for fifteen or twenty years," he told his biographer Milovan Djilas, "and then we'll have another go at it."[17]

The Stalin speech was not, as some Washington commentators described it, a "declaration of war."[18] He said nothing that could not have been uttered at any time in the Soviet past, issued no direct threats toward the United States, and emphasized above all else the security of the Soviet state and the communist experiment. Rather, Stalin showed, if his previous words and actions had been insufficient, that he regarded the postwar world as a continuing realm of competition in which the Soviet system would fight for its survival in the face of capitalist encroachment. Close ties with the West were not in the cards. The situation, as far as he was concerned, was the same as it had been before the Great Patriotic War: rivalry was inevitable, broad-ranging cooperation all but impossible.[19]

Enter George F. Kennan, counselor at the American embassy in Moscow. Asked to explain Stalin's position, Kennan responded with an 8,000-word answer in the form of a telegram he sent to the State Department two weeks later. A cerebral Russia expert with a tendency toward melancholia, Kennan had boundless affection for pre-revolutionary Russian literature and music but none at all for the Bolsheviks and their philosophy. Stalin's purges of the 1930s appalled him, and he thought any notion of postwar Soviet-American friendship and collaboration was naive and dangerous. With the Grand Alliance a rapidly fading memory, Kennan seized the chance to tell official Washington what it could and could not expect to see from Moscow's secretive leadership.

CONFRONTATION

The impression of fatalism given by Stalin's February 9 speech, Kennan wrote, was amply justified. The Soviet Union's relations with the West were merely the latest rendition of the long Russian tradition of diplomatic cynicism and duplicity. Russian statesmen regarded international cooperation as a ruse to lower the guard of the gullible. Only fools kept their word on the international stage. This had always been the attitude of Russian leaders, and such cynicism was only magnified and given ideological depth by the struggle between Soviet socialism and the imperialist West. Nothing the United States might do would earn Moscow's trust, so irreducibly hardened were these views.

Yet the Soviet Union was no Nazi Germany. It was not bent on global conquest, Kennan maintained, and even if it were it was too devastated by the war to act upon such dreams. But this did not mean that the Kremlin was simply content to exist within its present sphere of influence. Presented with opportunities to expand, Stalin would take them. Indeed, in the absence of countervailing force the Soviet Union would project its power, gradually and tentatively but inexorably. By doing so, Stalin could spread socialism, enhance Soviet power, and—to Kennan, perhaps most important—maintain a political culture of international action and danger that provided him with an excuse to exercise dictatorial control over the Soviet people and avoid the domestic reforms they required. The Soviet Union thrived on constant external crisis. Without it, the dysfunctional political system of Stalinism would have to turn inward, causing it eventually to implode.[20]

America's fundamental task was to establish firm barriers to Soviet expansion. By making clear to the Kremlin that a strong and unified West would act to prevent encroachment, especially in western Europe, Soviet leaders would be forced to abandon a foreign policy of opportunistic expansion and deal instead with their internal problems. In other words, by simply containing the Soviet Union, the United States could weaken and potentially even destroy its adversary without having to wage war. This was the basic strategy that Kennan developed over the next two years, as head of the State Department's Policy Planning Staff.

Because Kennan's telegram was a secret State Department missive rather than a public address, its impact on the Truman administration and Washington politics generally is hard to assess. But clearly many senior policymakers were taken with Kennan's analysis, for it provided both a straightforward explanation of Soviet behavior and a simple, achievable strategy to contend with it. Kennan was telling Washington what some highly placed observers already believed: that cooperation with the Soviet Union was pointless but that contending successfully with its power could be done short of war, and even short of massive expenditure and mobilization. As Kennan later acknowledged, he understood that this message would find a welcome audience in the Truman administration.[21]

The last, and certainly most conspicuous, of the four events that transformed the political culture of Washington in 1946 was a speech given in early March by Winston Churchill at Westminster College in Truman's home state of Missouri. Like Stalin's speech of four weeks earlier, it was prepared for public consumption. Truman had read a draft in advance and approved it, though he would later equivocate on this point.[22] He sat behind Churchill as the legendary leader, speaking in the great rolling cadences now so familiar to Americans, declared that an "iron curtain" had fallen on Europe, dividing the free people of the West from a tyrannical, totalitarian regime in the East. Sometimes called the opening shot of the Cold War, this passage is one of the most often-quoted in post-1945 world affairs:

> From Stettin in the Baltic to Trieste in the Adriatic, an iron curtain has descended across the Continent. Behind that line lie all the capitals of the ancient states of Central and Eastern Europe. Warsaw, Berlin, Prague, Vienna, Budapest, Belgrade,

Bucharest and Sofia, all these famous cities and the populations around them lie in what I must call the Soviet sphere,
and all are subject in one form or another, not only to Soviet
influence but to a very high and, in many cases, increasing
measure of control from Moscow.[23]

Other parts of the speech were less bellicose. "I repulse the idea
that a new war is inevitable; still more that it is imminent," Churchill said near the end. "I do not believe that Soviet Russia desires
war. What they desire is the fruits of war and the indefinite expansion of their power and doctrines . . . What is needed is a settlement, and the longer this is delayed the more difficult it will be and
the greater our dangers will be." The West, he declared, should
have "frequent and growing contact" with the leadership in Moscow.[24] Few commented on this part of the speech at the time, and
fewer still remembered it later. What people took away from that
day in Missouri was the image of the great wartime British leader,
already a living legend, appearing on a stage in the heart of America with Harry Truman seated behind him and announcing the division of Europe. They took away the notion that there must now
be an Anglo-American agreement to stand up to the Soviets, to
prevent them from pushing the iron curtain westward across Europe.

These four developments of February and early March went a
long way toward solidifying American attitudes with respect to the
Soviet Union. The Pearson revelations and the Stalin speech demonstrated to lawmakers of both parties that continued efforts at
cooperation with the USSR would be risky to sustain in the hardening atmosphere of American politics. General suspicion of the
Soviet Union moved to the mainstream—it was now the easier,
politically safer stance for a congressional representative or senator to take. To the White House, meanwhile, Kennan's long cable
provided both a vivid and coherent explanation of Soviet foreign
policy and a blueprint for action. And Churchill's arresting address

in early March (or at least part of it) provided the anti-Soviet position with both a gripping metaphor (the Iron Curtain) and the imprimatur of a widely respected statesman who had roused America to fight Hitler. It also gave Truman a bit of cover on his right flank. Add the four together and the picture was clear: Stalin's Soviet Union presented no immediate danger, but neither could it be trusted. Because the Soviets could not be trusted, the United States needed to act, rather than stand idly by as it had in the 1930s.

Containment on the Cheap

Having committed itself to countering Soviet expansionism, the Truman administration needed to decide just how expansive its own campaign ought to be. Anything too costly or too belligerent was out of the question: the American public would balk—or so the president and several senior officials, including Byrnes, believed. America had no tradition of high military budgets and elaborate security policies during peacetime. Many in Congress, and probably the president as well, continued to regard the United States as an exceptional nation that did not play the corrosive and expensive game of power politics "perfected" by the defunct and discredited Europeans. Truman was also personally committed to keeping the federal budget low and balanced and to avoiding inflation and the economic distress that many predicted would accompany the reconversion of the American economy to consumer production and the return home of millions of GIs.[25]

Because the danger of Soviet power remained fairly distant, the administration could afford to develop its confrontational policies gradually and, for the moment, cheaply. It therefore embarked upon several policies in 1946 that, while keeping the pressure on Moscow, did not portend massive expenditures or, even worse, the possibility of war. In Iran, where Stalin demanded an oil concession equal to that held by Britain, American and British diplomats worked with the Iranian leader Ahmad Qavam (and, surreptitiously, with the heir to the Persian throne, Reza Pahlevi) to demand the removal of Soviet troops sent by Stalin to the northern part of the country and to suppress the Iranian communist party, Tudeh. The Soviet leader agreed to withdraw his forces in exchange for an oil concession; but once the troops were out, the Iranians—backed by Washington—reneged on the oil agreement, and Iran settled back into the Western camp.[26] At about the same time, the administration pushed through Congress a low-interest $3.75 billion loan to Britain. A tough sell initially, it won approval in July, justified not only by new geopolitical imperatives but also by the claim that the United Kingdom would become a lucrative market for American goods and by Britain's willingness to make its pound sterling convertible to American dollars.[27]

In occupied Germany, meanwhile, American forces and diplomats worked to solidify political control over the sections of that nation occupied by the three Western powers. The extreme economic deprivation throughout the beaten Reich made radical ideologies, especially communism, attractive to many Germans, and U.S. officials, led by General Lucius Clay, sought to quash that appeal by backing anti-communist groups and taking rudimentary steps to restore the German economy. The United States could not move quickly on this front, however, because several European states, most notably France and the USSR, were unwilling to tolerate any policies that might revive German power, and this hampered America's efforts to contain Soviet power in Europe.[28] Quietly, the administration also developed modest aid packages for pro-Western forces in several other European countries, and it continued to support Chiang Kai-shek's nationalist government in China, despite its inability to suppress the growing communist movement there led by Mao Zedong. In Indochina, the administration tolerated and indeed covertly backed French efforts to beat down nationalist foes dominated by the communist-led Vietminh under Ho Chi Minh.[29]

Finally, in the area of atomic weapons control, Washington put forth an inexpensive and disingenuous scheme known as the Baruch Plan. It came about after the United States Atomic Energy Commission developed a classified plan to achieve international control, which came to be known as the Acheson-Lilienthal report, and submitted it to Secretary of State Byrnes in January 1946. The plan was immediately leaked to the press, and the administration was faced with a political dilemma. If it simply abandoned its long-standing commitment to international atomic control, it would have to take the blame for ruining a centerpiece of Roosevelt's postwar order. Though Truman had personally given up any remaining hopes of forging a lasting atomic settlement with the USSR, he had little interest in emphasizing this fact, and even less in taking personal blame for it.

To get around this dilemma, the administration cleverly altered its proposal. Bernard Baruch, a wealthy financier and Democratic Party figure whom Truman had appointed to be the U.S. representative to the UN Atomic Energy Commission, delivered a speech to the commission in June stating that the United States would agree to transfer its bomb to the United Nations, but only under certain conditions. First, the UN Security Council would have to begin a process of thorough worldwide inspections to ensure that no state was attempting to build a bomb surreptitiously. Any state caught doing so would be subject to immediate and harsh penalties, which meant, as far as the Security Council was concerned, military attack. Second, no nation on the Security Council would be allowed to use its veto on matters of international atomic control. Truman and Byrnes quickly approved these new stipulations. It was a brilliant move. The administration knew from the espionage revelations that Moscow was working on a bomb. If the Kremlin accepted the new provisions, it would open itself up to a military attack by the United Nations that it could not veto. This the USSR would never do. And if it rejected them, the Soviets—not the Americans—would be held responsible for crushing the dream of international atomic weapons control. Sure enough, late in 1946 the Soviet Union rejected the plan. For the first time, but not the last, the United States had developed a strategy that forced Moscow to shoulder the blame for initiating a conflict to which the United States had already committed itself.[30]

The Truman Doctrine, Abroad and at Home

So far, the United States had committed little fiscal or political capital to its confrontation with the Soviet Union. Truman wanted to keep the project small and unobjectionable. Tough words were cheap, and they allowed the president to deflect criticism unleashed by right-wing anti-Soviet elements in American politics, along with Republicans eager to use the espionage revelations to go after the Democratic Party. Aid to Britain, small-scale interventions in European and Central Asian politics, a nice strategem to make Stalin responsible for the failure of international atomic control—these were hardly the acts of a nation hell-bent on confrontation with the USSR.

The great question that loomed in late 1946 and early 1947 was whether the United States would assert its military and economic influence on the European continent, the locus of two calamitous world wars and the obvious theater for a direct Soviet-American confrontation. U.S. diplomatic tradition stipulated that the United States should avoid direct intervention in European affairs during peacetime, and it was not at all clear that Truman had decided once and for all by year's end to forsake this practice. Powerful voices in American society, including Senator Robert A. Taft of Ohio, son of the twenty-seventh president and known simply as "Mr. Republican," opposed high government spending and large-scale expansion of American power abroad, a stance taken also by recently elected Republicans John Bricker of Ohio and Joseph McCarthy of Wisconsin. Traditionally isolationist publications, including the *Chicago Tribune* and the *New York Daily News,* also criticized Truman's internationalism from the right.[31]

On the left, some still voiced hope for Soviet-American reconciliation. Secretary of Commerce Wallace, discerning the actual nature of the Baruch Plan, charged that Truman's get-tough policy was substituting atomic coercion for diplomacy. He told a Madison Square Garden audience in September 1946 that "'getting tough' never brought anything real and lasting—whether for schoolyard bullies or businessmen or world powers. The tougher we get, the tougher the Russians will get." Although Truman soon fired Wallace from the cabinet, blasting him privately as "a real Commie and a dangerous man," he was not yet prepared to order an ambitious and expensive projection of American power overseas.[32]

But the trend was in that direction. Within the White House, Truman faced increasing pressure to commit to full confrontation. Two weeks after Wallace's firing, White House aides Clark Clifford and George Elsey submitted an 82-page report on Soviet-American relations solicited by Truman. Based on information provided by senior military and civilian officials, the report warned ominously of the Kremlin's hostile designs and demanded that the United States must check this expansionism by all means available. Negotiations were futile; Stalin only understood tough talk and military power. Clifford and Elsey made no attempt to be nuanced or balanced—they were well aware, as Clifford candidly recalled, that Truman liked things spelled out in black-and-white terms. The report offered worst-case assessments of Soviet intentions and ignored instances in which the Kremlin had kept agreements. Should Washington and its allies fail to act resolutely, Clifford and Elsey declared, it would be a repeat of the 1938 Munich appeasement.[33]

Truman was becoming politically predisposed to accept the Clifford-Elsey line, but he was reluctant to move without an obvious justification. In early 1947 he got one. On February 21, the British government under Clement Attlee informed Washington that it would no longer subsidize pro-Western forces in Turkey and Greece, two nations in which Britain had wielded informal colonial power since the nineteenth century. The British departure was a clear sign, if one was still needed, that the old empire would not take responsibility for European security, not even in cases where strategically important nations faced the risk, or so it seemed, of political collapse.

Senior U.S. analysts debated what to do. Most of them believed that failure to support the pro-Western (or at least anti-communist) governments in these two nations would cause them to fall to the revolutionaries, who upon seizing control would likely join the Soviet bloc. Did that possibility justify American action? Truman and his aides, including his increasingly influential undersecretary of state, Dean Acheson, considered this question intensively over the end of February and the beginning of March. In a secret meeting with congressional leaders on February 27, Acheson referred to the potential collapse of Greece as "Armageddon." Like "apples in a barrel infected by a rotten one," he warned, its loss could "infect Iran and all of the East" and even Africa and western Europe. Many interventionist lawmakers, including the influential Republican senator from Michigan, Arthur Vandenberg, urged action. Truman concurred. With Poland now firmly under Soviet control and with communist satellite governments having gained power in Bulgaria and Romania, the United States had to act to prevent Turkey and Greece from falling as well.[34]

But how to do it? Could the American public be persuaded to support a substantial economic and political commitment to Greece and Turkey? Unlike, say, Poland, neither country had been a clear victim of ferocious wartime *Machtpolitik,* and while there were millions of American voters of Polish descent, the Greek and Turkish voting blocs in the United States were negligible. Some

U.S. leaders had a sentimental attachment to Greece as the cradle of Western civilization, but current pro-Western figures in both Greece and Turkey tended to be right-wing militarists, hardly the kind of democrats American policy was supposed to defend. Furthermore, the two Mediterranean nations were not threatened by imminent Soviet aggression; they were on the fringe of the European continent, not at its center. Truman and Acheson, together with the new secretary of state, George Marshall, saw but one option: in order to get Congress to allocate aid to the two nations, an abstract, universal case would have to be made emphasizing the importance of overseas American commitment generally, rather than the specific merits of supporting Greece and Turkey. As Vandenberg famously put it, Truman would have to "scare hell out of the American people" to get Congress on board.

And so on March 12, 1947, before a joint session of Congress, President Truman articulated, for the first time, a comprehensive American foreign policy for the postwar world. He did not mention the Soviet Union by name, or refer to the need to contain its power in Europe, though he did place American freedom against "totalitarian regimes." Appealing to American universalist ideals, he declared that U.S. foreign policy henceforth must side with any nation facing aggression, anywhere in the world:

> I believe that it must be the policy of the United States to support free peoples who are resisting attempted subjugation by armed minorities or by outside pressures. I believe that we must assist free peoples to work out their destinies in their own way . . . The free peoples of the world look to us for support in maintaining their freedoms. If we falter in our leadership, we may endanger the peace of the world—and we shall certainly endanger the welfare of our own nation.[35]

The implications of the Truman Doctrine, as it was quickly dubbed, were revolutionary. In a single speech, Truman announced that the United States, recently a country that eschewed power politics everywhere, would henceforth take an interest in the affairs of any nation that faced aggression from abroad or—even more remarkable—insurrections from within. It was, rhetorically, a staggering change of course, not only since 1940 but even since 1945. And in terms of its immediate political effects it worked: the president received the decisive support he coveted from internationalist Republicans such as Vandenberg and Massachusetts senator Henry Cabot Lodge. The bill to commit American funds to Greece and Turkey passed the Senate easily, by 67 votes to 23.

The political benefits of a Cold War hard line were becoming apparent. The popularity of the Truman Doctrine throughout America as well as in Washington led the president—one eye as always on his 1948 election campaign—to recognize that much could be gained by adopting an aggressive stance against the Soviet Union, even if it had little to do with what was happening in Greece and Turkey. Siding with either the old Rooseveltian left or with the small-government conservatives in Congress, on the other hand, would be to court unnecessary political danger. Why take chances? Harry Truman was coming to the realization that if he wanted to obtain political advantage by talking and acting tough on the Cold War, it would not do to wait for the Soviet Union to give him a reason.

In an extraordinary 43-page memo in November 1947, Clark Clifford and former FDR assistant James Rowe hammered the point home. The two strategists predicted that relations with the USSR would be the key foreign policy issue in the upcoming presidential campaign; that those relations would get worse during the course of 1948; and that this would strengthen Truman's domestic political position. "There is considerable political advantage in the administration in its battle with the Kremlin," the two men told the president. "The worse matters get . . . the more is there a sense of crisis. In times of crisis, the American citizen tends to back up his president."[36] The message was unmistakable. Cold War tensions would benefit Truman's political prospects, Clifford and Rowe were saying. But the White House could not orchestrate Soviet actions; it couldn't force Stalin to act rashly in Europe or to give another belligerent speech just in time for the presidential campaign. If Truman wanted to capitalize on the Cold War, the two men maintained, it would be necessary to rally the nation behind him irrespective of what the Soviet Union was actually doing. It would be necessary to generate Cold War tensions in Washington.

Already, signs of this internal belligerence were appearing throughout the nation's capital. In the 1946 midterm elections the Republicans had scored major gains, taking control of both houses for the first time since 1928. Many of those elected were more conservative and more anti-communist than the candidates they replaced; many resorted to Red-baiting in their campaigns. The exultant incoming speaker of the house, Joseph Martin of Massachusetts, declared open season on Reds: "They should be—they must be—removed." Democratic leaders vowed not to be caught flat-footed again: in the 1948 campaign they would highlight Truman's intense opposition to Stalin's takeover of eastern Europe.[37]

What was more, the president moved on the domestic front to go after Americans sympathetic to communism or the Soviet Union. Two weeks after announcing his doctrine, Truman established the Federal Employee Loyalty Program, which gave government security officials authorization to screen three million employees of the federal government for any hint of political deviance. The workers were required to show their patriotism without being permitted to confront their accusers or, in some cases, knowing the charges against them. Hundreds were fired, and thousands more resigned rather than submit to investigation. In most cases there was no evidence of disloyalty. The House Un-American Activities Committee (HUAC), meanwhile, initiated a series of hearings to determine the extent of communist influence in Hollywood.

Some screenwriters and directors were imprisoned for contempt of Congress after refusing to "name names" of suspected communists, and hundreds of others in the industry were blacklisted.

As author David Halberstam astutely put it, "Rather than combating the irrationality of the charges of softness on communism and subversion, the Truman Administration, sure that it was the lesser of two evils, moved to expropriate the issue, as in a more subtle way it was already doing in foreign affairs. So the issue was legitimized; rather than being the property of the far right, which the centrist Republicans tolerated for obvious political benefits, it had even been picked up by the incumbent Democratic party."[38]

But Truman himself was careful not to go too far. He continued to deflect critics on his right who demanded greater investigations of the American left or a major expansion of the Cold War. On the left, Henry Wallace was able to commence a serious run for the presidency in 1948 based largely on a policy of defusing tensions with the USSR. Truman perceived the political logic of the Clifford/Rowe memorandum, but it remained to be seen how far he, and other politicians, would take it.

Lippmann's Critique

This conscious melding of domestic and foreign communism—which began in a serious way in 1947–48, well before McCarthy had become a household name—would in time have hugely important ramifications for Cold War America.[39] But in the short term, some serious-minded internationalists had begun to question whether it was necessary to develop a foreign policy to contain the Soviet Union that shelved entirely the art of diplomacy. Walter Lippmann, for example, derided both Wallace's "naive" idealism and Taft's supposed isolationism. The prominent columnist needed no one to tell him that Stalin was a ruthless dictator, and he did not blame the United States and the West for the emerging

Soviet-American antagonism. He fully agreed with Kennan's contention, published by the diplomat in mid-1947 in *Foreign Affairs* under the pseudonym "X," that the Soviet Union would expand its influence unless confronted by American power.[40]

Yet the columnist worried greatly about the direction American foreign policy seemed to be heading. Moscow officials had genuine security fears, he reasoned, and were motivated primarily by a defensive concern to prevent the revival of German power—hence their determination to assert effective control over eastern Europe. It distressed Lippmann that the administration seemed blind to this reality, and to the possibility of negotiating with the Kremlin over issues of mutual concern. Even Kennan, whom Lippmann respected and had met on occasion, seemed to have ruled out diplomacy.[41]

Kennan's "X" article, coming in the wake of the Truman Doctrine, had made a great splash in Washington, where it was seen (correctly) as a systematic articulation of the administration's latest thinking about foreign policy. Lippmann understood that an effective way to attack the new approach was to go after the article itself, which he did in a remarkable series of columns in the *New York Herald Tribune* in September and October. These were then gathered in a slim book whose title, *The Cold War,* gave a name to the confrontation.[42] Lippmann predicted that a policy of containment, at least as outlined by Kennan, could draw the United States into defending any number of far-flung areas of the world. Military entanglements in such remote places might bankrupt the treasury and would in any event do little to enhance American security at home. American society would become militarized in order to fight a "Cold War." What's more, he maintained, the containment doctrine gave the strategic advantage to the Soviets, by permitting them to initiate confrontations in areas where they were stronger. To compensate for America's comparative weakness in these locations, Washington would be forced to recruit a "heterogeneous array of satellites, clients, dependents, and puppets," any number of whom could be expected to pull in the United States to defend them when trouble arose.

But if not containment, then what? Lippmann advocated a European settlement whereby American, Soviet, and British forces were withdrawn from Germany and eventually from continental Europe. If the Soviets' presence in eastern Europe was the result of the Kremlin's security concerns, after all, the way to get them to leave was to mollify those concerns. Under this plan, Germany could be reunified under strict guarantees of demilitarization, and reciprocal trade agreements could be vigorously pursued that promised to open up large holes in the Iron Curtain. No less important, the plan would be the "acid test" of the Kremlin's agenda, confirming whether it was intent on conquest or whether it would agree to a reasonable settlement in eastern Europe.

Diplomacy, the columnist emphasized, should not be seen as an act of surrender. It was a means of achieving mutually beneficial objectives, of gaining in this case at least a partial resolution of Soviet-American differences. A principal flaw with containment was its failure to envisage a role for good-faith negotiations; and in that sense, Lippmann continued, it went against how great powers typically acted. Traditionally, so long as war was not imminent, even bitter rivals engaged in diplomacy of the most basic sort, to avoid needless antagonism and misunderstanding. Thus, Churchill in his Iron Curtain speech had advocated seeking a settlement through "frequent and growing contact" with the Kremlin. In order to frustrate Soviet designs, the Briton seemed to be saying, the United States and Great Britain should confront the USSR with their power, while at the same time seeking to finalize some kind of deal, especially in Europe. Lippmann agreed. It made sense to negotiate with Stalin particularly over the question of Central Europe, and above all Germany, if the containment of Soviet power within eastern Europe was the goal. You stay on that side, we stay on this side. Stalin, arch-realist that he had often shown himself to be and with his country still recovering from a brutal war, might agree to a treaty based on that. Or he might refuse. There was no way to know without trying.

Ironically, Kennan agreed with much of this. Though he had himself downplayed the utility of diplomacy in his "X" article and his earlier long telegram, he, no less than Lippmann, bemoaned what he saw as the black-and-white dichotomies of Truman's speech. Earlier in the year, Kennan had told a meeting of the Russian Study Group of the Council on Foreign Relations in New York that Russian diplomacy had always been characterized by both cautiousness and flexibility, and that therefore Washington should be forthright in its dealings with Moscow and always be willing to negotiate while never appearing false or weak or arrogant. "Nothing is to be gained," the diplomat told his audience, by "fatuous concessions without receiving a *quid pro quo*. They balance their books every night and start over every morning . . . They expect you to proceed in a hard-boiled way and not to give them things without getting something from them."[43] The passage could have come straight from a Lippmann column.

In a sense, though, Lippmann had jumped the gun. He and Kennan worried that the White House was rejecting diplomacy and traditional political dealing in favor of the sort of universalistic campaign implied by the Truman Doctrine. But would the administration really operate that way in practice? Would Washington in fact support any nation anywhere, offering what amounted to a blank check to any regime that could claim it represented a "free people" threatened from without or within? Not yet. Although the Truman administration rejected the kind of diplomacy advocated by Lippmann, it stopped short of embarking on total Cold War. As Kennan had advocated in 1946 and reiterated in his "X" article, the strategy was to contain Soviet power on the Eurasian landmass by deterring Moscow from expanding into western

Europe. Between the middle of 1947 and the middle of 1949 the United States zeroed in on the objective of strengthening that region to the point where its peoples would not succumb to external pressures from the Soviet Union or internal subversion from leftist political movements.

Highlighting American foreign policy during these two years were three American demonstrations of serious commitment in that region: the European Recovery Program, better known as the Marshall Plan; the Berlin blockade and airlift; and the creation of the North Atlantic Treaty Organization. Only later would the full ramifications of the Truman Doctrine hit home.

The Marshall Plan

Two years after Hitler's defeat, western Europe still remained prostrate and impoverished.[44] Mother Nature played a role—the winter of 1946–47 was the worst in a hundred years. But the war and its after-effects were the real causes. The three main belligerents fighting in this part of the world—the United States, Britain, and Germany—resorted early and often to terror-bombing civilian populations, leaving many of Europe's metropolises, from London to Naples to Rotterdam, badly damaged, and many German cities, including the rubble that was once Berlin, in total ruin.[45] Cities and towns caught in the path of the allied invasion of Europe were also heavily hit. In France, Belgium, the Netherlands, Luxembourg, and western Germany, railways, bridges and roads were blown up, factories smashed, farms and fields ravaged by tank battles and firefights.[46]

The war had also forced the old European colonial powers, most notably Britain and France, to begin the painful and, they soon learned, financially costly process of withdrawing from some of their overseas possessions, either as a result of military retreat or simply because they could no longer afford their imperial commitments. The First World War had shattered European society in many respects, but industrial cities and empires had remained intact. And in the case of British and French overseas possessions, they had even grown, as remnants of the defeated German and Ottoman empires were added. Now, the major European powers found themselves in retreat abroad and physically ravaged at home. It was a long way from the Age of Empire half a century earlier.

Harder to measure, but perhaps even more important, was the bleak political mentality overcoming postwar Europeans. In the space of thirty years the most powerful nations in the history of the world had set upon themselves in two ruinous wars. The epic struggles had killed tens of millions of their citizens, injured tens of millions more, and had stripped from each of them, even Great Britain—unconquered in either war, victorious in both—the rank of first-class power. A belief in the superiority of European civilization, so obvious to Europeans (and others) at the beginning of the twentieth century that it barely required discussion, was now, in the eyes of many, a cruel joke. Superior civilizations do not elevate warmongers to absolute political power in order to destroy themselves in unremitting industrial warfare. They do not bombard defenseless civilians, send conscripted soldiers to certain death in battle after battle, massacre ethnic minorities, or attempt to exterminate Jews. The conclusion seemed inescapable: the European way of politics had wrought disaster.

Throughout western Europe, political movements emerged advocating radical change. Left-wing parties, many of them loyal to Moscow, seemed poised to seize political power in places like Greece, Italy, and France, where they enjoyed wide political credibility as a result of their dominant role in resistance campaigns against fascism. Now, the European left zeroed in on economic deprivation. In France, meat was unobtainable except on the black market, while bread rations had been further reduced. In Britain, which suffered far less than most of the continental nations, the economy had hit rock bottom. Throughout the once-mighty British realm, two years after a war they had won, people lived on bare rations and in unheated homes, often without electricity. The worst suffering by far, however, was taking place in western Germany, a fact that caused few Americans, remembering Nazi brutality, to shed tears but which raised dire questions about whether that region could become a bulwark of containment.[47]

American diplomats and military men stationed in Europe repeatedly conveyed the same message during the dark winter of 1946–47: the United States had done right to commit itself politically to defending western Europe from Soviet encroachment, but if it did not act immediately to restore some sense of economic well-being and political optimism in the region, that commitment could be rendered meaningless. Radical movements throughout the continent would capitalize on despair and anarchy, delivering western Europe into the hands of Stalin without his having to lift a finger. Those American officials who were most concerned with Europe—Marshall, Acheson, Kennan, and Assistant Secretary of State for Economic Affairs William L. Clayton—realized that the United States, if it were to contain Soviet power, had first of all to resuscitate the economy of western Europe and the political morale of its peoples.[48] In the spring of 1947, these officials crafted a European Recovery Program, which Secretary of State Marshall introduced to the world during his Harvard University commencement address in June. The proposal was simple and straightforward. The United States would offer to extend a massive grant to the ravaged states of Europe, with the only condition that these states devise a coordinated strategy to use the funds for economic revitalization.[49]

The simplicity of the plan belied the brilliance of its conception. The Marshall Plan, if it were accepted, would serve American goals on several fronts. To begin with, the aid would signal to Europeans that the United States was not indifferent to their suffering. The Soviet Union had spent much of late 1945 and 1946 systematically looting the territories it controlled in eastern Germany and elsewhere, generating massive resentment among local populations in the process. The United States would act differently. In addition, and as it was largely advertised, American aid would strengthen the economies of its recipients, giving Europeans a reason to feel hopeful about the future and to reject radical political solutions. Moderate regimes in Europe that dispensed the aid would gain legitimacy and domestic power. Moreover, by agreeing to a common plan to use the American money, the participating states would naturally integrate their economies, avoiding the autarky and economic nationalism that had been one of the main causes of the two world wars, at least in the eyes of American planners.

Marshall and Truman understood full well that it would be extremely difficult to sell the plan to a Congress that had expressed repeatedly its aversion to subsidizing the governments and peoples of Europe. The British loan of 1946 had barely passed, after all, and the Marshall Plan not only proposed sending far more money to the Europeans but also giving it to Germans and Italians who had recently been fighting Americans. The only way to push the plan through would be to portray it as a means of strengthening European resistance to external threats and internal subversion. The Marshall Plan had to be sold as a central weapon in the Cold War. On top of all this, the plan promised to enhance long-term American economic objectives. At the State Department, planners such as Lovett and Acheson were convinced that the United States would require markets for its goods after the war. Many Americans, including Truman, feared that with the war over the economy could slip into another depression. But a wealthier Europe that needed to rebuild its own industrial base after the war would serve as an ideal market for American goods. Moreover, as long as the plan to use American funds to revitalize the region's economy promoted free trade and rejected autarky, the United States would be guaranteed access to the European market indefinitely, even after factories were rebuilt and railroads repaired. U.S. policymakers had long wanted to promote open markets around the world— this had been one of Roosevelt's original objectives in pushing for American participation in the war. The Marshall Plan could not deliver a global system of free trade, but at least it would integrate the United States with Europe. It could create a more substantial foreign market for consumer goods and other products fabricated in the new American factories built during the war, and jobs for soldiers returning home to work in them.[50]

And there was one other gem in the American proposal—a clever element certain to pressure the Soviet leadership. The administration extended the Marshall Plan offer to *all* the states of Europe, including not only the eastern European nations under Soviet control but also the USSR itself. American officials were confident that Stalin would refuse the aid and force his client states behind the Iron Curtain to reject it as well. For by participating in the Marshall Plan, the Soviet Union would have to agree to integrate its economy with the other states of Europe under the rules of their common proposal for acceptance, a proposal that would of course be based on free-market capitalism.[51] When Stalin duly turned down the offer, the success of the gambit was immediately evident. His rejection was met with groans in eastern Europe, where leaders were desperate for economic assistance and, in several cases, actively interested in accepting the American offer. By rejecting the aid, Stalin effectively took responsibility for dividing Europe along economic lines. The nations that received Marshall Plan aid would develop integrated free market economies connected to U.S. capitalism; the nations that rejected aid would remain, by definition, outside the capitalist order. Thus the brilliance of the scheme: even though the Truman administration had by early 1947 become resigned to the division of Europe, the Marshall Plan forced Stalin to shoulder the blame for this division, just as the Baruch Plan had made him assume responsibility for the failure of atomic weapons control.

This outcome was confirmed in February 1948, when the Kremlin engineered a coup in Czechoslovakia and installed a puppet communist regime. In March the former Czech foreign minister Jan Masaryk jumped (or was pushed) to his death from a window in Prague. That same month, as a contentious election loomed in Italy, Congress approved the Marshall Plan. The Organization of European Economic Cooperation gratefully accepted the $4 billion that lawmakers initially authorized, an amount that they increased to about $11 billion by 1951. It is difficult to measure precisely the effect of economic aid upon political outcomes, and historians disagree about the impact of American aid on Europe's economic recovery.[52] But there can be little doubt that the infusion of American money bolstered pro-Western governments in Europe and revived the sagging morale of ordinary people in these countries. It certainly tied the western European economy deeply to that of the United States, establishing a transatlantic capitalist system notable for its relatively free markets and its use of the American dollar as a base currency.

Finally, the Marshall Plan once and for all finalized the political divide between eastern and western Europe, a fact confirmed by the Soviet Union's weak attempt to imitate it through the Molotov Plan (a Soviet aid package for its eastern European client states). It is reasonable to argue that the Marshall Plan met every one of its key objectives, above all the American desire to contain Soviet power in Europe. It stands as perhaps the most successful single foreign policy initiative ever undertaken by the United States.

CONFRONTATION

The Berlin Blockade and Airlift

By the middle of 1948, European international politics had become more stable and better defined. The division between West and East had grown into a geopolitical reality, with western European nations clearly aligned with the United States and eastern ones with the Soviet Union. Both superpowers were openly describing one another as adversaries in Europe, and the Truman administration had begun to develop diplomatic and military strategies to deal with the containment of Soviet power there and the possibility of war.

The great exception to this more settled state of affairs in Europe was the question of Germany. Unlike the Japanese case, its formal postwar political status remained unresolved because no comprehensive, formal peace treaty had been signed with a defeated government. Three years after the Nazi surrender, even as Germany remained a single nation in name, the country was politically divided into discrete sectors and occupied by foreign powers. This indeterminate circumstance was epitomized by the uneasy situation in the former German capital, Berlin, which was itself divided into four zones occupied by the United States, Great Britain, France, and the Soviet Union, even though the city lay some 110 miles inside the Soviet sector of northeastern Germany. At Potsdam in mid-1945 the Big Three had vowed that the occupation would be temporary. In due course Germany would reemerge as a single nation, they had said. But the issues were complex, especially those surrounding the core economic question of whether a unified Germany would be capitalist or socialist. During the summer of 1945, continuing notions of Grand Alliance cooperation had led the conferees to avoid this question and to imagine that great-power security collaboration might make the economic orientation of smaller nations secondary. By 1948 that pipedream had been abandoned. Europe was divided along economic as well as political lines. Western nations allied with the United States were capitalist; eastern nations allied with the Soviet Union were socialist. The Marshall Plan turned this fact on the ground into a durable reality, and Germany's economic destiny took on urgent Cold War implications.[53]

Vivid memories of recent Nazi aggression led nations on either side of Germany, especially France and the Soviet Union, to oppose the political and economic rehabilitation of a unified Germany. For their own protection, both of these nations hoped to keep Germany militarily and economically weak. Moscow in particular was determined to exact horrific reparations from its sector of the former Reich. For Stalin, no outcome could be worse than an independent, unified, capitalist Germany that was completely beyond his control.

U.S. policy with respect to Germany, meanwhile, remained unformed. Would all Germans, or only those in the western sectors, receive Marshall Plan aid? Would the United States seek reunification if Germany were neutral and nonaligned, or only if it were clearly wedded to the West? Would Washington seek to revive Germany's economic and military might in order to withdraw its own forces, even if this move caused acute anxiety in France and elsewhere on the continent, or would America commit to a long-standing military presence there? Above all, how would the United States defend western Germany, if it came to that, in the face of the USSR's massive conventional military superiority in central Europe? These intertwined questions moved the German problem to the center of American Cold War policy during the late 1940s.[54]

And difficult questions they were. The Truman administration knew that it wanted a capitalist Germany, and it had been engaging in activities to further this objective since the end of the war. But how far should the United States go to make this fundamental objective a reality? Senior policymakers were still considering this matter in mid-1948 when Stalin obligingly forced the issue by erecting a blockade around West Berlin. His action sealed the division of Germany between East and West and became the greatest symbol of the Cold War in Europe. The ensuing crisis—the first real confrontation of the Cold War—was, once again, laid at the feet of the Soviet Union, even though it had been quietly triggered by American actions.

In the previous March, after a conference in London, officials from the United States, Britain, and France had declared in a joint announcement that it was now their objective to establish a pro-Western economy in western Germany. This came despite formal opposition to such a scheme by the Soviet Union and despite the fact that it left the question of Germany's unification unresolved. Some Western military planners worried that the announcement would provoke a confrontation that might culminate in hostilities. Sure enough, in initial protest the Soviets began to harass western transportation around Berlin, though both sides were careful not to escalate this into a crisis. To push for a more substantial solution, however, the American occupying command, under the leadership of General Lucius Clay, secretly initiated Operation Bird Dog, which quietly dispersed a Western-linked currency throughout western Germany and, in June of 1948, in the western sectors of Berlin. As Clay and his adversaries knew perfectly well, this would have the effect of tying west Germans and west Berliners to the American side without having to engage in open political conflict. It was the Marshall Plan logic again, this time implemented covertly.[55]

Unwilling to accept what appeared to be a western outpost in its sector of Germany, the Kremlin upped the ante. On June 24 Soviet authorities began to erect a physical blockade around Berlin to prevent all traffic from the west from entering the city. Stalin hoped that West Berliners, starved of resources, their Western currency now meaningless, would be forced by economic necessity to reject their alliance with the Americans and throw their lot in with East Germany and the USSR. Stalin's strategy also put the Western powers in the position of either relenting or attempting to overcome the blockade—a step that could lead to a war in which they were seriously outmanned. Would Americans be willing to risk their blood to hold on to Berlin? This was the question Truman now had to confront. Some of his advisers, including the ambassador to Moscow, Walter Bedell Smith, urged him to back off, to accept the division of the nation along regional lines and leave Berlin for East Germany.

The president's response, issued on June 28, was blunt: "We are going to stay, period."[56] But what did that mean? Some in the uniformed military advocated military action to break the blockade, but Truman rejected that idea. Raising an army that could contend with the Soviets in East Germany was simply beyond American capabilities. And the initiation of a possible third world war in order to liberate the residents of Hitler's capital would not be a popular move in the United States, not to mention Britain or France. American and British planners found another way almost as dramatic: they commenced a round-the-clock airlift of supplies to West Berlin, in order to forestall an economic collapse that would have driven residents into the arms of the Soviets. This placed the responsibility for war in Stalin's hands: his only choices were to shoot down the supply planes, an act that would surely trigger retaliation, or let the airlift continue and hope it would be inadequate. He opted for the latter.

A remarkably mild winter and an extremely able airlift operation conducted by the American and British air forces delivered an average of 8,000 tons of food and fuel each day. On April 16, 1949, the single busiest day, some 1,400 planes brought in nearly 130,000 tons within twenty-four hours—an average of one plane touching down every 62 seconds. Stalin offered better rations to any West Berliner who registered with communist authorities, but only 20,000 took him up on it. His hopes frustrated, Stalin lifted the blockade and in May 1949 authorized talks with the Western powers about formalizing the status of Berlin.[57]

The West had scored another clear victory. The role played by the United States in this first Berlin crisis had far-reaching effects throughout Europe; arguably, it was as important for the long-term as the more carefully conceived Marshall Plan. It established, on the ground, the division of Germany into economic sectors and Berlin into a permanently occupied city. Before June 1948 the status of Germany remained up in the air; by late spring 1949 it had become as politically settled, at least apart from Berlin, as the rest of Europe. That fall, the (East) German Democratic Republic and the Federal Republic of (West) Germany were formally established.

The Berlin blockade and airlift were not the only causes of this resolution, but they played a decisive role. The blockade forced American officials and their allies in Europe to take action. The airlift demonstrated, in a way that only the possibility of violence can, that the United States was committed to the defense of Europe and willing to run the risk of war to protect a place of symbolic, if not strategic, importance. If the Americans were prepared to risk another war to provision a handful of West Berliners, Europeans told themselves, surely they would spare no effort to defend West Germans, Italians, Belgians, and French. In clamoring for action, Clay and other military officials on the scene and in Washington delivered this message over and over: Europeans were watching to see if America would come through.[58]

The Berlin crisis also forced the Truman administration to examine more carefully how it would respond to another such confrontation, whether over Berlin or elsewhere. For all the bravado of the airlift, the fact remained that the Western powers were in no position to wage a land war in central Europe. Indeed, as things stood in the spring of 1949 it was highly unlikely they could stop a full-scale Soviet invasion from taking all of Europe. Few in Washington, and even fewer in other Western capitals, believed that the USSR had anything like this in mind, but no one familiar with the recent history of European conflict could rule out the possibility that a war might start nevertheless. What if a maverick Soviet colonel had shot down an American plane flying into Berlin's Tegel airport? What if Stalin had refused to lower the barricade? Major wars had begun over similar incidents in the past.

The administration's response to this question came in the form of National Security Council document No. 30 (NSC-30), completed in September 1948 during the middle of the Berlin showdown. This report clarified what was evident already to military thinkers in Washington and around Europe: the United States, in the event of war, would rely heavily on its monopoly of atomic weapons to defeat the Soviet Union. Rather than deploy a massive and expensive land army on the European continent, America would drop atomic bombs on Soviet political and military targets, with the aim of forcing a Soviet surrender at home rather than defeating the Red Army on the field of battle.

NSC-30 reflected an underlying reality of the early Cold War. Before it was issued, the United States had gotten its way in its various struggles with the Soviet Union—over Iran, in Berlin, and in general in its successful anti-Soviet containment policies. These outcomes had come about not only because the USSR was exhausted and averse to war, though this was important, but also because Stalin knew that if the two Cold War antagonists commenced World War III, atomic bombs would fall on Moscow and Leningrad but not New York and Washington. The simple existence of America's monopoly in atomic weapons, rather than any explicit threat, convinced the Kremlin dictator to act cautiously, probably more cautiously than if atomic weapons did not exist— which was why he had ordered his scientists to spare no cost in building a bomb as quickly as possible. In NSC-30, American military planners developed a more official strategy to exploit this reality, to be implemented in the event of another confrontation in Berlin or somewhere else.[59]

America's First Peacetime Alliance

NSC-30 was fine as far as it went, but the British and the French wanted more. For two years London and Paris had been pressing the United States to sign a formal defense treaty with its western European allies. The Attlee government sought American protection so as to avoid spending its own scarce revenues on defense.

France had six different governments during the years 1947–1949, but to a greater or lesser degree all of them wanted the United States to commit to a strategy of defending the western European continent from Soviet invasion. The natural step for the Americans to take in defending western Europe from the USSR was to strengthen Germany, as it was a large and populous state that Soviet tanks would have to pass through on their way to the Atlantic. The French would have none of it. They wanted Washington to deploy GIs in Germany instead and to agree in writing that America would come to the defense of the West in the event of war.

The reality of American atomic power complicated these aims. As the reasoning of NSC-30 suggested, the United States could avoid having to deploy a large and expensive army in Europe by relying instead on atomic deterrence. If the Red Army moved westward, Washington could threaten to drop the bomb. But this strategy worried continental Europeans almost as much as the plan to rebuild Germany's military forces. What if deterrence failed? The Soviet Union might be able to overrun Europe long before the Western allies could cobble together some kind of conventional military response. And the destruction of Moscow or Leningrad with an atomic bomb would not do much for a besieged France or

Belgium apart from making the advancing Red Army even more vengeful. Were the Americans to use atomic bombs on the battle-field, the targets could be in Germany or even France rather than the Soviet Union, and the casualty figures would be colossal. No one in France had forgotten that the destruction of coastal cities like Cherbourg and Saint-Malo after D-Day was caused not by German airplanes but by the RAF and the U.S. Air Force.[60] West Germans were beginning to realize as well that World War III would turn their country into an atomic battle zone.[61]

The Europeans got their way. While the Berlin airlift continued in early 1949, U.S. officials led by the new secretary of state, Dean Acheson, concluded a deal with European delegates that committed the United States, for the first time in its history, to the formal defense of other large nations. In early April Truman signed the North Atlantic Treaty, which obligated the United States, along with Canada, to come to the defense of the member nations of the previously signed Brussels Pact (Belgium, Britain, France, Luxembourg, and the Netherlands), along with Italy, Portugal, Denmark, Iceland, and Norway.[62] It was a formal military treaty, in that an attack on any member nation was to be regarded as an attack on all of them. But in reality, of course, it was a one-way commitment: the United States did not sign the treaty so that it could be defended by Luxembourg.

The move that put teeth into the treaty was the forward deployment of American troops in West Germany. These troops would serve as a trip-wire: any Soviet westward campaign would quickly lead to American casualties and bring the United States into the war at the outset. Several critics of the treaty, including Kennan, whose influence was waning in Washington, thought NATO (as the alliance became known) to be unnecessary, as the American atomic monopoly and Soviet weakness made the prospect of a Red Army invasion remote. More and more, Kennan had come to regret his own alarmist portrayal of the Soviet Union in 1946 and

1947. Echoing Lippmann, he now proposed that, in lieu of NATO, a deal be struck with the Soviets to demilitarize Germany while America still remained the world's preponderant power. Administration supporters of the new treaty, notably Acheson, agreed that the threat of invasion was low but proceeded anyway, probably because they saw NATO principally as a means to strengthen relations between the United States and key European nations, particularly France. It committed the United States to defending that region while at the same time keeping Germany weak. The French could hardly have hoped for much more than that.[63]

Containment in Europe and the Atomic Monopoly

The American bid to protect western Europe from Soviet penetration is widely regarded as the most successful component of its Cold War foreign policy. It's hard to disagree. The United States managed to develop an effective defense system there without having to coerce its allies into accepting it (as the Soviet Union was forced to do in the east); without spending itself into insolvency; and without provoking the Kremlin to the point of war. It did not have to endure defections from its camp, as Stalin did when Yugoslavia's communist government under Josip Broz Tito successfully broke away in 1948. Washington also was able to portray the Soviet Union as the nation responsible for the division of Europe, Germany, and Berlin, even though in key respects all three situations were the result of American actions. By relying on economic coordination, symbolic demonstrations of commitment (as in Berlin), and a defense treaty agreed to by all parties rather than imposed by Washington, the Truman administration constructed an alliance that can be seen as a model of careful multilateralism and strategic foresight.

True, Truman established new institutions in Washington that, as many critics of the day pointed out, threatened to wield unaccountable power. These included the Central Intelligence Agency, designed to correlate and evaluate intelligence activities, and the Department of Defense, created to replace the three independently run military services. In signing the National Security Act of 1947 that created these agencies as well as the National Security Council and that institutionalized the wartime Joint Chiefs of Staff, Truman also transferred a great deal of potential authority away from Congress and toward the White House. But the far-reaching effects of this landmark legislation would fully manifest themselves only later.[64] At the outset, many legislators on both sides of the aisle professed to believe that they would be able to retain their say over the great questions of peace and war. And after four years of post-war confrontation with the Soviet Union, America's defense budget remained low, its army small, and its "security state" tiny when compared with the great military bureaucracies of the European powers just a few years before.

But if American foreign policy during the early years of the Cold War was effective, this happened in large part because it was developed under highly advantageous conditions. The Soviet Union was devastated by the Second World War, while the United States emerged from the fighting far stronger than it had been in 1941. No less important, the projection of American power into Europe between 1946 and 1949 came under the unique protection of its atomic monopoly. Truman, his advisers, and informed members of the public all understood that the risks of provoking the Soviet Union were quite low for the simple reason that if the provocation led to war, the USSR would be hit by atomic weapons and the United States would not.

The weakness of the Soviet Union and its inability to respond in kind to an American atomic assault meant that the United States during the late 1940s was effectively invulnerable to external threats, whatever alarmists in Washington occasionally said. It wasn't a reincarnation of free security, for it was no longer free, and the possibility of Soviet domination over the Eurasian land-mass, however distant, meant that the United States could no longer regard the balance of power in Europe with indifference. But the United States' atomic monopoly ameliorated this problem to a large extent. And now that western Europe was protected by treaty and on the way to recovery, Americans had good reason to feel safe.

3

TO THE ENDS OF THE EARTH

The halcyon days of mid-1949 did not last long. Two events in the late summer and early fall, both of them outside American control, led the Truman administration to expand its Cold War policy radically. In early September a specially-equipped U.S. weather plane detected radioactivity in Soviet air space above Siberia, a clear sign that the USSR had tested its own atomic device. America's monopoly in nuclear weapons, which had helped to encourage the United States to act assertively in Europe, was over. Then, a few weeks later, the nationalist government in China collapsed and fled to the offshore island of Formosa (Taiwan), leaving the Chinese mainland controlled by a communist regime led by the peasant revolutionary Mao Zedong. Suddenly, a vast nation, with the world's largest population, was on the communist side, in apparent alliance with the Soviet Union against the West.

While both events shocked many Americans, neither came as a great surprise to senior administration officials. Based on information they had obtained about the Soviet espionage program, President Harry Truman and many of his advisers felt certain that the Soviet Union was working to obtain its own bomb. No one in the United States could know exactly when Moscow would succeed, but most U.S. strategists believed it was only a matter of time. Still, Truman himself had predicted only a few months earlier that the monopoly would last several more years, and even after the evidence of a successful test arrived, the president seemed to disbelieve it for a time.[1] Others in the government were less taken aback.

The victory of the Chinese communists was even less unexpected. Since 1945 the administration had spent millions of dollars and dedicated substantial effort to building up the political power of Chiang Kai-shek's nationalist regime. But most American experts on China, along with George Marshall, who was sent by Truman on a special year-long mediation mission to the country in late 1945, agreed that Chiang's government was deeply dysfunctional (the "world's rottenest," according to Truman), at once corrupt, inefficient, and out of touch.[2] The Chinese communists had long appealed to discontented peasants with promises of land reform and to urban elites with plans for radical political change. The nationalists had few natural constituents, having failed to resist Japanese aggression during the war or to run the country effectively once it was over. Most American officials felt certain that Chiang's government would collapse unless the United States intervened militarily during the civil war, a step Truman never seriously considered. "We picked a bad horse," he merely said. Secretary of State Dean Acheson speculated that once the "dust settled," Washington could extend diplomatic recognition to the new government and probe the nature of its ties to Moscow.[3]

Others felt very differently. China's destiny had long been a central preoccupation of many American politicians, particularly those on the right. The Republican Party had been Pacific-oriented since the days of William McKinley and for decades had regarded China with special affection. (It was as if each party had its own ocean, the Democrats claiming the Atlantic.) The same was true of leading voices in the American press, including *Time* magazine publisher Henry Luce, who was born in China to missionary parents, and of prominent industrialists who saw enormous potential profits in the China market. "The China lobby" was the pejorative name for the group of journalists, business leaders, and right-wing lawmakers who had become arch defenders of Chiang Kai-shek. As expected, they expressed outrage that hundreds of millions of people and a huge chunk of Asia had "suddenly" gone communist, and they blamed Truman and the Democrats, rather than the nationalists' incompetence, for making it happen. The "dust" continued to swirl, and the administration did not offer diplomatic recognition to Mao's government.[4]

Neither of these developments endangered the basic U.S. Cold War strategy of containing Soviet power and preventing the USSR from some day dominating the Eurasian landmass. True, in the short term the Soviet bomb complicated America's military commitment to western Europe, as both American and European officials now had to contemplate the possibility that a war over Europe could lead to the atomic destruction of U.S. cities, or at least western European ones. This new factor made the unconditional promise by the United States to defend its NATO allies somewhat less credible. But if Washington's determination to prevent Soviet domination of Eurasia by containing its power in Europe was as central to its basic national security as American officials constantly said it was, then even this terrifying prospect did not invalidate the strategy of containment; it just made it more dangerous— or, to put it another way, as dangerous now to the United States as it had already been to the Soviet Union and other European states.

Similarly, Mao Zedong's victory in China did not necessarily undermine the balance of power across the Eurasian land mass that the containment policy had been designed to establish. This is more clear today than it was in 1949—materials released since the end of the Cold War show in stark relief the abiding mutual distrust and suspiciousness of Mao and Stalin and the degree to which the Soviet leader was anything but thrilled to have a new, more powerful Chinese state on his southern border.[5] But even at the time, some close observers could and did make the case that nothing fundamental had changed. When Kennan was director of the Policy Planning Staff, he had argued that the United States could prevail in the Cold War by making sure it retained political influence over the major industrial regions outside the Soviet sphere, namely, Britain, western Europe, and Japan. He did not consider the China outcome catastrophic.

Other senior analysts agreed. China was an impoverished pre-industrial state that could not threaten America. Even if it became a totally subservient client of the USSR, it could not enhance Soviet military power sufficiently to allow Stalin to take on the United States directly. To be sure, the defection of China into the communist camp posed serious problems with respect to the economic destiny of Japan and to the fate of noncommunist forces in Southeast Asia, but these problems were hardly immediate threats to the viability of containment. The geopolitical logic that underlay the American decision to contain Soviet power in Europe was not rendered invalid, though it was made more complicated, by the events of August and September 1949.

Nevertheless, the "twin shocks" of 1949 would have major long-term implications for America's Cold War. Instead of responding to the Soviet bomb and Mao's triumph by developing specific strategies to deal with these two predictable events, the Truman administration made the momentous decision to embark on a colossal expansion of its Cold War foreign policies. The relatively limited, sober, and inexpensive efforts of 1946–1949 would be replaced by a huge and costly military buildup, by a campaign of political repression the likes of which had never been seen before in the United States, and by a grinding, stalemated war in Korea.

From Fission to Fusion

America's first response to the twin shocks initiated a new stage in human history. In January 1950, some five months after the Soviets' successful atomic test, President Truman authorized a special committee to investigate the possibility of building a hydrogen bomb, or "superbomb." Since the days of the Manhattan Project, several nuclear scientists, including Ernest Lawrence and Edward Teller, had been arguing that it might be possible to develop a nuclear weapon that harnessed the power of nuclear fusion, or the merging of atomic nuclei. Fusion, these experts contended, would trigger an explosion of far greater magnitude than that created by fission (the "splitting" of atoms).

Not everyone welcomed this news. Several administration officials, including David Lilienthal, a member of the special committee, and George Kennan, who was about to leave office, believed that such a project was unnecessary and immoral. Lilienthal argued that atomic weapons were sufficient to deter the Soviet Union—a claim seconded by J. Robert Oppenheimer, the scientific head of the Manhattan Project.[6] Kennan, for his part, in what he later described as the "most important memorandum" he had ever written, said it would be wrong for the United States to be responsible for unleashing the destructive power of the superbomb, a power so vast that it could threaten all of civilization. A war fought with such weapons could not achieve any political objectives; it would only destroy everything that the war had been waged to defend.[7]

Truman rejected these arguments. Instead, he ordered the military to build thousands of new atomic weapons and authorized the U.S. Atomic Energy Commission to embark on a crash project to build the superbomb. The scientists and military officials assigned to this task worked quickly and effectively, so that already by 1952 the United States was able to conduct its first test of the new weapon at the Eniwetok atoll in the southwestern Pacific. The explosion vaporized an entire island, unleashing roughly 500 times the blast and fire caused by the Hiroshima and Nagasaki bombs.[8] No one witnessing the test could fail to realize what a war waged with such weaponry would do to the human species. The thermonuclear age had begun.

The decision to build the superbomb is often included within historical accounts of Truman's expansive Cold War policies during the last three years of his administration. But the reasoning behind it actually had much more to do with traditional security policy. As many supporters of the project argued and as Truman himself believed, the United States really had no choice: it could build the weapon, or wait for the Soviets to build it first. Under the latter scenario, Stalin's USSR would occupy a position similar to that enjoyed by the United States during the years of its atomic monopoly. In the event of a confrontation between the two superpowers, the Kremlin could threaten the United States with a thermonuclear attack, and Washington would be unable to respond in kind. U.S. cities could be destroyed in an instant; Russian ones could not. Had the Soviet Union been a small country with a few big metropolitan areas, populated by a citizenry unused to wartime suffering, perhaps its leaders could have been deterred from exploiting their nuclear advantage by the threat of atomic retaliation. The USSR, however, was no such state, and its dictator had demonstrated few qualms about subjecting his people to whatever hardships he deemed necessary to achieve his political objectives. The Lilienthal–Oppenheimer argument, that a Soviet Union equipped with superbombs could be deterred by atomic bombs alone, was not difficult to refute.

Indeed, the American response was no different from what it had been a decade earlier, when the United States was faced with the prospect of a Nazi atomic bomb. Then as now, the only sure way to avoid being on the losing end of a monopoly was to build the weapon, the sooner the better. Truman might well have agreed with Kennan that the world would be better off if no nation had thermonuclear bombs, but he was not about to assume that the leaders of the Kremlin would feel the same way. Truman's response to the conclusions of his special committee reveals his grasp of the "security dilemma," the tragic dynamic whereby nations escalate tensions between themselves even though they both may have only defensive motivations.[9] He asked: "Can the Russians build one?" Yes, came the answer, they obviously could. "Then we have no choice but to go ahead."[10]

At one time it might have been plausible to argue that the Soviet Union lacked the technical know-how to succeed, or that it could not do so for decades. But its 1949 atomic test demolished that proposition. Truman and many of those around him believed strongly that espionage was one reason why the Soviet Union had been able to build its atomic bomb so quickly. Their fears were magnified by Britain's arrest of the atomic spy Klaus Fuchs in February 1950 and by the FBI's apprehension of American spy Julius Rosenberg and his wife and alleged accomplice Ethel in New York in July and August. Who could be confident, now that the Soviets had tested their atomic weapon, that their espionage network had not also given them decisive information about thermonuclear technology?[11]

The Blueprint

At the same time that Truman authorized the superbomb program he also asked the National Security Council to review overall U.S. Cold War policy in light of the new developments. The result was NSC document No. 68, written largely by the new director of the Policy Planning Staff, Paul Nitze, though with input from other officials, including Secretary of State Dean Acheson.[12] As with all such policy papers, NSC-68 did not automatically determine action. Government file cabinets are full of papers that never see the light of day; one of them was NSC-20/4 from 1948, which reached some of the same conclusions as this new effort. But times had changed. NSC-68 was different because of the twin shocks that came before, and because of what was to come shortly: a major military conflict, with strong Cold War implications, on the Korean peninsula. Like Kennan's 1946 telegram, NSC-68 provided Harry Truman with a timely depiction of the new state of world affairs and, even more important, a blueprint for action that was politically attainable. The authors of the document surmised that the president would be receptive to vivid, stark scenarios that would not be politically costly to him or the Democratic Party—and might indeed pay political dividends. They framed their argument accordingly.

The Truman Doctrine of 1947 had stated that the United States would assist any nation facing internal subversion or external aggression. Everyone understood at the time what the president meant by this: that the United States would help regimes to suppress *communist* movements and to resist *Soviet* pressures, though Truman was careful in 1947 to avoid such political specificity. In any event, the administration chose not to back up its universalistic promises with action. It implemented the doctrine fairly faithfully in western Europe and Japan, but in other parts of the world, most obviously in China, the United States did not do whatever was necessary to stop the advance of communist or left-wing movements. For three years, the administration proved willing to tolerate setbacks in several peripheral locales, preferring instead to focus on its key objective of containing Soviet power in Eurasia.

True, during the late 1940s the United States provided military and financial aid to anti-communist forces in China, Indochina, the Middle East, Latin America, and elsewhere. It would be wrong to claim that Truman and his advisers cared only about the fate of Europe during this period. But the administration did not regard the rise of communist or left-wing movements in the Third World (as the preindustrial areas of the planet became known, with the First World consisting of the United States, western Europe, and Japan, and the Second World consisting of the Soviet Union and countries within its sphere) with anything like the same kind of urgency that it regarded challenges to the West in Europe. In China, Mao's communists won victory after victory without facing U.S. intervention, while Truman risked war in order to defend the tiny enclave of West Berlin. In Indochina, when the socialist Ho Chi Minh threatened to overthrow French colonial rule and establish a left-wing regime in Vietnam, Truman took no decisive action to stop him; yet the United States intervened heavily in Italian and Greek domestic politics to ensure the defeat of socialists. This willingness to tolerate defeats in less industrialized parts of the world allowed the United States to contend with a weak if opportunistic USSR cheaply and efficiently.[13]

NSC-68 argued that the Soviet bomb and the fall of nationalist China had made this strategy obsolete. The United States must rid itself of the illusion that the struggle with the Soviet Union was a traditional contest of power politics, with both sides content to dominate their own spheres of influence and assert their power only gradually and carefully. No, the Soviet Union was bent on world domination, on "the complete subversion or forcible destruction of the machinery of government and structure of society in the countries of the non-Soviet world and their replacement by an apparatus and structure subservient to and controlled from the Kremlin."[14]

Before gaining the bomb, Nitze and his colleagues asserted, Stalin had to move cautiously, for he knew that a war with the Americans could endanger this global mission. Now, he could move anywhere and everywhere, undermining pro-Western regimes with impunity, probing in Europe, establishing influence over the new regime in China—and all the while daring a soft United States, fearful of atomic war, to stop him. His tactic would not be the traditional one of establishing alliances or declaring formal wars but of fomenting the spread of left-wing movements that he would inevitably control in every corner of the globe. For Stalin, NSC-68 argued, the practice of communism abroad involved "total conformity to Soviet policy."[15] As China demonstrated, in the absence of American counteraction, country after country would fall to communism and be incorporated into the Soviet sphere. Soon the United States could be encircled by a ruthless foe governed by a tyrannical ideology and bent on total victory.

To those who might have objected that Stalin did not have the military means to achieve such a victory, that his nation was still deep in the recovery phase from a brutal war that had cost one-tenth of its population and half of its industry, NSC-68 had a reply: the Soviet Union could rely more on ideological subversion and revolution than major war to achieve its planetary domination. Consequently, any victory of left-wing movements anywhere constituted a basic threat to the security of the United States. The implications of such a worldview were huge: previously, and despite the Truman Doctrine, Washington had generally conceived of its Soviet adversary as a territorially bounded nation-state whose influence rested almost solely on the political and military power it could muster. Now, it must define its enemy as the ideology of communism. If the United States were to survive, American foreign policy had to become a policy of global anti-communism.

What would such a foreign policy entail? NSC-68 provided a vivid answer: the United States must wage the Cold War on every front. It must fight communism by every means, not only political and economic (had these not failed in China?) but also military. It must project its own armed forces to the far corners of the world, in order to meet the Kremlin's pressure with countervailing American power. To succeed in this new global policy, the United States would therefore have to vastly increase its military expenditures. It would have to train foreign armies and equip them with advanced weaponry. It would have to deploy American soldiers and materiel not only in Europe but anywhere on earth where communists threatened to prevail. This would of course mean raising a huge peacetime army and massively expanding the national security institutions involved in running such a project.

This tremendous expansion of American military might would signal to Moscow that it could not expect to get away with easy aggression outside Europe. To America's allies it would signal that Washington was committed to waging the Cold War even in an age of Soviet atomic power. But the buildup would also give the United States a means of contending with the USSR without instigating the "annihilation" of atomic war.[16] The authors of NSC-68, like most analysts before them, did not expect the Soviet Union to initiate direct war against the West. Nor did they believe that the United States should initiate preventive war against the USSR— that option, they declared, was "morally corrosive." The difference now was that the Kremlin could extend its influence more confidently in areas outside vital American interest, aware that Washington would be afraid to respond for fear of inadvertently triggering an atomic catastrophe. By deploying conventional forces in trouble spots away from the strongpoint frontiers, Washington could deter such attacks. And if deterrence was unsuccessful, the United States could wage a minor war with the USSR in the hopes that it would not escalate into World War III.

To put it another way, according to NSC-68 the United States would henceforth have to wage a far more onerous and dangerous Cold War against the Soviet Union while at the same time avoiding total (meaning nuclear) war. To wage such a protracted conflict successfully, the government must persuade the American people to commit for the long haul. They must be willing to regard the Cold War as a vital national struggle to be fought worldwide, but at the same time to accept that this struggle must never culminate in a decisive conflagration. They would have to become accustomed to long-term political conflicts in remote corners of the globe, where no final resolution, no dramatic surrenders on battleships, and no ticker-tape victory celebrations would ever be possible.

Nitze and his co-authors understood that this last demand would be difficult to sell.[17] One of the principal reasons Truman—not to mention many on Capitol Hill—had endorsed the policy of containment in Europe was because it made relatively few demands on an American public eager for prosperity and peace. Truman had long feared that a president who asked for a more substantial commitment would lose popular backing. He also knew that influential Republicans, among them Senate heavyweight Robert Taft and former president Herbert Hoover, still rejected the idea of the United States as a global policeman. Taft saw no contradiction between blaming the administration for Chiang Kai-shek's defeat and advocating a return to a hemispheric strategy (but in alliance with Great Britain and Japan) that bore more than a little resemblance to the original containment blueprint.[18]

Taft's and Hoover's concern was in part financial. The United States, they maintained, could not afford a globalist foreign policy. NSC-68 did not deny that the costs would be huge, and it suggested that the government might have to raise taxes and cut spending to pay for its larger military project. Several officials involved in the preparation of the study, however, including the future chairman of the president's Council of Economic Advisers, Leon Keyserling, had a better answer to this problem. In their view, the massive military buildup NSC-68 envisioned could be financed not by radically higher taxes or serious reductions in domestic government spending but rather by the deliberate acceptance of government deficits. Indeed, if the government used deficit spending to increase military spending, this could have the effect of energizing the economy—just as had happened in the late

1930s. As the British economist John Maynard Keynes had argued during the interwar era, an advanced industrial economy like the United States could not only tolerate large budget deficits but could actually prosper from them, as the money the government spent on military production and the salaries of soldiers and government employees was plowed back into the domestic economy. The American economy, Deputy Secretary of Defense Robert Lovett quietly noted, "might benefit from the kind of build-up we are suggesting."[19]

In sum, NSC-68 provided a comprehensive strategy for dealing with a Soviet Union now in possession of the atomic bomb, and at the same time encouraged the Truman White House to reach for Keynesian solutions to the massive expenditures this strategy would require. It offered a recipe, one scholar has said, for the "permanent militarization of U.S. policy."[20] Yet it was only a document—it did not compel Truman to act according to its recommendations. As late as June 1950 the president seemed resistant to a ramping up of the Cold War, and committed to keeping the defense budget in check. Late that month, however, an event occurred that seemed to be precisely in accord with the gloomy predictions made in NSC-68 and caused him to change his mind: the outbreak of military conflict in Korea.

The Korean War

In the predawn hours of June 25, 1950, North Korean forces attacked across the 38th parallel that divided the country into a pro-Western regime in the south and a pro-Soviet regime in the north. The division had occurred in mid-1945, as Washington and Moscow agreed to share the task of occupying Korea and disarming the Japanese there. They also agreed to work for the reunification of Korea at the earliest practicable time. But as Cold War tensions increased in the following years, the divisions of occupation hardened. A civil war broke out, pitting left-wing and right-wing Koreans against each other, and by spring 1950 this struggle had claimed 100,000 lives.

Early U.S. accounts of the June invasion told a simple story of North Korean aggression undertaken to serve the cause of Soviet-led communist expansion. The reality was different. Many figures associated with the southern regime of Syngman Rhee, subsequent research showed, sought to unify the peninsula under his right-wing rule and had been conducting forays into the north for years. Some Americans, both inside and outside the Truman administration, supported Rhee in those efforts. To complicate matters, in January 1950 Acheson gave a public speech in which he excluded South Korea from America's defense perimeter, though he added that states outside the perimeter might be defended by the United Nations. The historian Bruce Cumings has offered a circumstantial argument that the United States, together with South Koreans, effectively instigated the war in order to sell the expansionist strategy of NSC-68 to Truman, Congress, and the American public and to establish American economic hegemony throughout Asia.[21]

Cumings's account of the origins of the conflict remains controversial, but it puts to rest any claims that the outbreak of fighting in late June came as a total shock to all Americans—that South Koreans and Americans were simply minding their own business when the North Korean army attacked. It is also now clear, however, that the North Korean leader, Kim Il Sung, wanted a war of unification and that the invasion of South Korea was approved in advance, albeit with reluctance, by both Stalin and Mao Zedong. Historians have demonstrated that Stalin remained ambivalent about Kim's unification plans, signing off on them only after Kim had promised a quick victory and had secured support from Mao. All too aware of his strategic inferiority with respect to the United States, Stalin did not wish to be dragged into a costly war. "If you get kicked in the teeth," he cautioned Kim, "I shall not lift a finger."[22]

Our knowledge of the motivations and decisionmaking of these actors in the early summer of 1950 was not available to the Truman administration at the time. But what senior policymakers did know was that U.S. officials and agents were operating to undermine unsympathetic regimes in many places, including North Korea. They knew that many right-wing Americans, including especially those involved with the China Lobby and likeminded organizations, were clamoring for the United States to flex its muscles in Korea and elsewhere in Asia. These sorts of operations and campaigns had not, in the recent past, triggered a serious military invasion in response. This time, however, North Korean troops were pouring over the 38th parallel.

Moreover, and most important, the invasion took place in the wake of the Soviet atomic test and the collapse of Chiang Kaishek's China. Stalin had previously responded to American provocations in limited ways, but this was different—it was a major military operation, violating an agreed-upon border and attacking a regime allied to the United States. If the Soviet Union was behind this—not a far-fetched notion for most Americans in late June 1950—it represented a new kind of aggressiveness, one not seen before. That many Koreans on either side of the parallel regarded the attack as simply an escalation of an ongoing civil war across an artificial border imposed on their country by foreign occupiers does not mean that Truman or his top aides regarded it in this way. The Truman administration was not stunned by the invasion, and indeed the evidence shows that many in Washington believed that something like it was going to happen soon. Nor had it been stunned in 1948 by Stalin's blockade; but if the Kremlin leader had responded to Western intrigue in Berlin by invading western Germany, this would have meant something entirely different to Washington. The outbreak of the Korean War seemed to fulfill NSC-68's prediction that while Stalin had been cautious before 1950, his new bomb had given him the confidence to intensify his

efforts to spread communism. The bomb, after all, had had a gal-
vanizing effect on American foreign policy five years earlier—why
should it be any different with the USSR?

Hence the exquisite timing of the new document. The general
thrust of American Cold War policy before NSC-68 did not dictate
a major U.S reaction to an event like this. The logic of Kennan's
containment was fairly clear on this question: since Korea was not
a center of industrial might, Washington's response should be limited, because the fall of South Korea to a communist regime would
not threaten American security. Containment did not dictate pas-
sivity outside the industrialized world, but it did argue that Washington should not spend vast amounts of money and commit major military forces in these areas. NSC-68, on the other hand,
suggested that the nation must now regard any communist victory
anywhere as a threat to American survival, and must act to prevent
it. Crucially, it also argued that the nation could afford to do so.
Many administration officials, including some who had dissented
from a number of NSC-68's conclusions, added another critical argument: that America's key ally in Asia, Japan, could not withstand
the loss of all of Korea to the communist side.[23] Already deprived
of the China market, Japan needed a nearby trading partner. An
American military effort to save South Korea for capitalism would
persuade the Japanese that the United States would defend their
interests just as it would defend those of its European allies.

Truman, who was tending to family business in Missouri when
the invasion occurred, responded swiftly. Eager to score political
points at home by demonstrating his anti-communist credentials
and to show that the United States would not back away from conflict even after the setbacks of 1949, he returned quickly to Washington and almost immediately decided on a military response,
embracing enthusiastically the expansive logic of NSC-68. He authorized the commander of American forces in East Asia, General
Douglas MacArthur, to prepare a counterattack that would push

North Korean forces out of the south. At the same time the president organized a formal United Nations Security Council response that allowed him to characterize the largely American military operation as a UN "police action" and to avoid having to ask Congress for a formal declaration of war. Such a declaration, he and Acheson feared, could easily lead to an all-out effort resembling World War II. Truman received an unwitting assist from the Soviets, who were boycotting the Security Council to protest the exclusion of Communist China from the United Nations and were therefore not present to veto the plan. Sixteen nations contributed troops to the UN command, but 40 percent were South Korean and about 50 percent were American.

Early on, North Korean forces used tanks and superior firepower to make rapid progress, pushing UN forces down to the tiny Pusan perimeter at the tip of South Korea. But in September General MacArthur launched a successful amphibious invasion at Inchon, on the western coast of Korea more than a hundred miles behind North Korean lines. Over the next two months UN forces pushed North Korean troops back across the 38th parallel and then continued northward. This defied the stated goal of the war, to defend South Korea and re-establish the status quo ante. But it followed perfectly the more aggressive approach of NSC-68. "The only way to meet communism," Truman would tell the alarmed British prime minister, Clement Attlee, in explaining his decision to approve MacArthur's offensive, "is to eliminate it."[24]

In addition, midterm elections were fast approaching, and the president feared that what Melvin Small has called "the prudent but not-anticommunist-enough decision" to halt at the 38th parallel could hurt the Democrats at the polling booth in November.[25] MacArthur, "the sorcerer of Inchon," was hugely popular with voters, and the White House had no desire to take him on. Nor did it wish to tangle with California Republican William Knowland, the China Lobby's most powerful spokesman in the Senate, who hinted that limiting an offensive into the North would signify presidential timidity and weakness. Knowland and other lobby members were not alone in this view. The Republican National Committee was urging its candidates to depict the war as a "story of blind, blundering and almost treasonable foreign policy," and aired a radio spot warning Americans to take heed of the "Atom-bomb secrets lost to Russia . . . Appeasement of Communism . . . unpreparedness in Korea." On the campaign trail, GOP candidates accused Dean Acheson of being soft on communism and blasted Secretary of Defense Louis Johnson for leaving the U.S. military underequipped to fight through to full victory in Korea. A group of moderate Senate Republicans charged in a statement that as a result of the Truman administration's "ineptitude," the Kremlin had in effect been "given a green light to grab whatever it could in China, Korea, and Formosa."[26]

The expansive logic of NSC-68, together with Truman's desire to appear tough to the American electorate, impelled the president to accept an offensive strategy in Korea. Initially, the action in the North went well. But as American forces neared the Chinese border and U.S. aircraft bombed targets along the Yalu River separating Korea from China, Mao Zedong responded by launching a Chinese invasion across the frontier. Mao had publicly warned the United States that he would not accept the annihilation of North Korea, but MacArthur shrugged off the warnings. Over the winter of 1950–51 Chinese armies pushed UN forces back toward the 38th parallel. Truman saw no choice but to send more troops to stem the Chinese advance.

A stalemate took hold, leading some to call for a ceasefire and a return to the status quo ante. Yet earlier, by approving MacArthur's advances into the North, Truman had seemed to seek more than the status quo: he appeared to desire a conquest of the entire country. And especially now that China had entered the war, why should the United States not "eliminate" communism there as well by taking the war to the Chinese mainland? Chiang Kai-shek pressed for such action, as did some Cold Warriors in Congress and the press. More important, so did MacArthur. He openly hinted that Truman, in keeping the war confined to Korea, was guilty of "appeasement"—now a four-letter word in domestic American politics—and he famously told a congressman that there was "no substitute for victory." The United States should hit China with atomic strikes; it should use the Korean War as a platform to roll back communism and oust Mao's regime.[27]

Truman would not go that far. A war with China would likely be long and exhausting, but even worse, it could bring in the Soviet Union, now presumably armed with atomic bombs. Even if the Soviets stayed out, Stalin could sit back and watch as the Americans and Chinese bloodied each other in a long war of attrition. The president had been persuaded by the expansive demands of NSC-68 and had taken a range of extraordinary measures while the Korean War raged: he acted to quadruple U.S. military spending, deploy much larger conventional forces to Europe and elsewhere, build thousands of atomic and thermonuclear bombs, and step up political and economic anti-communist campaigns throughout the Third World. But he would not take the war to the Chinese mainland. In April 1951 he fired MacArthur and ordered his replacement, General Matthew Ridgway, not to advance ground forces into China. At the same time, the U.S. Air Force stepped up its campaign of bombarding civilian and industrial targets throughout the North, killing as many as one million people and turning much of the territory into a wasteland—a horrific strategy remembered for decades by North Korea's population and its leadership.[28] As it had during World War II, the United States would not shrink from bombing enemy civilians indiscriminately if this action could further the war effort. A brutal form of containment was substituted for victory in Korea.

All the while, negotiators sought to conclude terms for a ceasefire. Both sides adhered to a hardline posture, which in the case of the Americans can be understood only in light of the charged domestic atmosphere in which that posture was adopted. White House officials knew all too well that political critics stood ready to equate compromise with surrender or appeasement and to revive support for MacArthur's "no substitute for victory" dictum. The general's firing had galvanized the Republican right, whose spokesmen hit hard on the theme that Democrats were handcuffing military leaders and showing undue timidity about using force to thwart communist designs. When the presidential election campaign geared up in 1952, Republican leaders, including nominee Dwight D. Eisenhower, asserted that Truman had been foolish to agree to negotiations and that he was compounding the error by continuing diplomacy in the face of clear evidence that the communists were using the time to build up their forces. Even the apparent economic health of the nation was turned against the White House: the prosperity, GOP spokesmen charged, "had at its foundation the coffins of the Korean war dead," a slaughter that as yet appeared to have no end. Truman, who had wavered on the question of running for reelection in late 1951 and early 1952, decided to let another Democrat bear the brunt of this criticism and announced in March that he would not seek reelection.[29]

Even so, partisan pressure contributed to the hardening of the administration's bargaining posture in 1952. In the words of the historian Rosemary Foot, "Sensitivity to public charges, to congressional attacks, and to electoral charges that the Democratic administration had been led into a negotiating trap by its 'cunning' enemies, all reinforced the administration's preference for standing firm rather than compromising."[30] North Korea and China insisted on the repatriation of all POWs, but Truman rejected their demands. Apart from his political reasons for doing so, the president was genuinely averse to forced repatriation. Many U.S. military officials also believed that the merciless bombing campaign would compel North Korea to accept American terms, a conclusion that turned out to be incorrect. The war's increasing unpopularity at home drove Truman's ratings to unprecedentedly low levels as the 1952 election approached. When he left office in January 1953, "Mr. Truman's War" still raged.

Red Scare

Thomas Dewey's surprise come-from-ahead loss to Truman in the 1948 election had stung Republicans deeply. They had been out of the White House since the early days of the Depression—sixteen long years—and they knew it would be four more before they would get another chance. Increasingly in 1949 and 1950, and especially after the fall of China, Republicans used the anti-communism club to beat up on Democrats, and Democrats used the same club, though much less effectively, to defend themselves. More and more, the Cold War encouraged Americans to draw a sharp line between those who were patriotic and those charged with disloyalty. Truman's federal loyalty program, established in mid-1947, had failed to uncover any serious cases of espionage, but by the end of the decade investigators were closing in on several wartime spies, including Julius Rosenberg, Morton Sobell, Elizabeth Bentley, and David Greenglass (who claimed to have stolen uranium from Los Alamos by putting it in his pocket). This operation intensified when Britain announced the arrest of Klaus Fuchs.[31]

The search for American spies who had been working for the USSR was hardly a sign of political repression or government paranoia. The United States was engaged in a serious international confrontation with the Soviet Union; had it chosen to overlook the infiltration of its military and governmental institutions by agents in the pay of its principal adversary, it would have been the first nation in history to do so. The question was not whether the careful, long-term investigation of atomic spies was in the national interest—it clearly was.[32] The question was whether spying constituted a low-level operation undertaken by a small number of disaffected Americans, whose network was largely shut down after 1947, or whether it reflected a larger conspiracy.

As early as 1945 and into 1946, FBI director J. Edgar Hoover suggested that atomic espionage represented only the tip of a much larger iceberg. Via an aide, he quietly informed Truman that State Department officials, including Deputy Secretary of State Dean Acheson, were part of a much greater subversive conspiracy.[33] A few years later, political figures such as Richard Nixon, then a little-known California congressman, and Senator Pat McCarran, a rabidly anti-communist Democrat from Nevada, began to conduct hearings on the possibility of such a conspiracy. In 1948 Nixon accused former State Department official Alger Hiss of espionage, and in early 1950, after a high-publicity trial, Hiss was convicted of passing documents to the Russians—an act of treason motivated presumably by his sympathy for communism in the 1930s.[34]

Hiss's conviction coincided almost to the day with the appearance on the national stage of Senator Joseph McCarthy, a hitherto obscure Republican from Wisconsin. In a speech in Wheeling, West Virginia, in February 1950 McCarthy announced that the State Department was "thoroughly infested with Communists," and moreover that he had a list to prove it. The list, he declared, contained the names of 205 "card-carrying" communists. In subsequent days, he lowered the number to 57, then raised it to 81, then made it "a lot." It is now clear that he had no list, and that he likely had no proof that *anyone* in the State Department actually belonged to the Communist Party. There were, to be sure, plenty of Americans working for the government and elsewhere with general left-wing sympathies; some of them had joined socialist or communist organizations, as had many Americans during the depths of the Great Depression. But to claim that these Americans were *prima facie* disloyal to their country, and actively working against it as the atomic spies had done, was another thing entirely. They were guilty of holding dissenting political views, but that was not a crime in the United States.

In reality, McCarthy had little genuine interest in either communism or espionage. "Joe couldn't find a Communist in Red Square—he didn't know Karl Marx from Groucho Marx," George Reedy, a journalist and later an aide to Lyndon Johnson, memorably said. McCarthy merely needed an issue with which to revive his flagging popularity in Wisconsin, where he faced a difficult reelection run in 1952.[35] By making such grandiose claims, however, he conveyed the message that there must be some validity to the charge that the government was filled with traitors secretly working for the Soviet Union. His timing, he knew, was right: his speech came a few months after the Soviet test and Chiang Kaishek's defeat and mere days after the Hiss verdict. The speech gained McCarthy the headlines he craved—reporters knew both that he was an unreliable source and that sensational stories sell papers. When the Korean War commenced in June, the senator began a more comprehensive campaign to expose communist subversion throughout American society.[36]

The war gave McCarthy a moral advantage. With American soldiers being shot at by North Korean and Chinese communists, few people in or out of Washington had the courage to denounce his outrageous crusade. Almost no one spoke up when he attributed the war and the failure to win it to the "Commiecrats," "homos," and "pretty boys" in the State Department "with silver spoons in their mouths."[37] Many Republicans welcomed McCarthy's campaign, even if they privately thought it excessive, because he went after Democrats and liberals almost exclusively and because they discerned that his portrayal of these liberals as privileged and effete elites could enhance GOP appeal to ordinary, heartland Americans.[38]

As a consequence, the senator and his colleagues could say almost anything without much fear of contradiction. Anyone even vaguely associated with the left was fair game, and so, apparently, were others. Dean Acheson, a Cold War hawk of the first order, was accused of weakness in the face of communist aggression—a "pompous diplomat in striped pants," McCarthy called him. China experts in the State Department who criticized the corruption of the nationalist regime and predicted a communist victory—which is to say, those who saw reality—were forced out. HUAC and other government entities, meanwhile, probed the entertainment industry and began investigating educators. High school teachers and university professors who taught about socialism, Russia, or China, even from critical standpoints, lost their positions or were forced to change specializations. Countless others, afraid of HUAC's reach, downplayed controversial material in their courses. In the labor movement, the CIO expelled eleven unions, with 900,000 members, for alleged communist domination. At one point, the American Legion accused the Girl Scouts of preaching communistic "one world" ideas in their publications.[39]

By comparison with Stalin's gulag, this repression was mild. Still, the climate of fear fostered by the senator and his congressional allies, and by professional anti-communists such as McCarthy's lieutenant Roy Cohn, had a pernicious effect on American society. Film, literature, and journalism veered toward the uncritical and banal. Unscrupulous individuals in Hollywood and academia accused their rivals of having secret left-wing pasts, as did candidates for office at the federal, state, and local levels. It's not much of a stretch to say that at the height of his power in 1952–53 McCarthy reigned over Washington, his strength deriving partly from his skill as a demagogue ("No bolder seditionist ever moved among us," Richard Rovere wrote, no one "with a surer, swifter access to

the dark places of the American mind") and partly from the acqui-
escence of those around him. Few dared challenge him, least of all
publicly.[40]

With the election of a Republican administration and the establishment of a ceasefire in Korea in June 1953, however, the political
ground under McCarthy began to shift. Dwight D. Eisenhower,
though he had been unwilling to challenge McCarthy during the
campaign and in the first months of his term, worked quietly to
undermine the senator during the second half of 1953. The end of
the fighting on the Korean peninsula, meanwhile, deprived Mc-
Carthy of a major rallying cry. Desperate, he tried to raise the
stakes by accusing the United States Army of being a communist
organization and by naming George Marshall, widely regarded as
an American hero, as a possible Soviet agent. In televised Senate
hearings in 1954 McCarthy advanced his wild claims in a forum
that was becoming less intimidated by his "big lies." The attorney
for the army, Joseph Welch, effectively pushed McCarthy into a defensive corner, making him appear brutish and unstable in front of
millions of TV viewers. The army was cleared of all accusations,
and soon afterward McCarthy was formally censured by the Senate. He descended into acute alcoholism and died in 1957, a lonely
and marginalized figure.[41]

But McCarthyism would live on, if in mellower form—in the
campaign strategies of politicians at all levels of government, in
the actions of federal, state, and local agencies, and in the pronouncements of business organizations, veterans groups, and religious leaders. McCarthy's very extremism had the effect of solidifying the anti-communist consensus in Middle America by making
it appear moderate by comparison with his own recklessness.[42] At
the same time, his "outrageous exaggerations and inventions," as
the historian Christopher Andrew has noted, in a way transformed
him into an effective Soviet agent, because his zealotry made most
American liberals skeptical of *any* claims of Soviet espionage, no

matter how valid—a theme later introduced in the film *The Manchurian Candidate.*[43]

Explaining the Expansion of America's Cold War

America's Cold War changed shape after 1950. It became a global campaign, much more ideologically charged, far more expensive—the military budget shot up from $14 billion in 1949 to $53 billion in 1953—and a substantially greater factor in the lives of ordinary Americans. The Korean War, in which some 33,000 American soldiers, along with hundreds of thousands of Chinese and perhaps more than a million Koreans were killed, helped create this new Cold War, but the stirrings of change were evident even before Kim Il Sung's troops attacked. The earlier containment strategy promised a limited and inexpensive project that would keep America safe, and it appeared to have done so. What, in the end, led the Truman administration to depart from that strategy and embark on such a fateful course? Scholars have offered two general answers to this question.

Many historians contend that the main foreign policies associated with NSC-68—the decision to intervene in Korea, and to embark on a global campaign of military anti-communism—were rational, if sometimes excessive, strategic responses to the twin shocks of September–October 1949. It was not unreasonable, Melvyn Leffler has argued, for Truman and his key advisers to conclude that the communists would go on the offensive after the successful Soviet bomb test and Mao's victory in China, and that the balance of world power remained so delicate in 1950 that such an offensive could succeed unless the United States stepped up its efforts to thwart it. The decision to intervene in Korea exemplified this way of thinking. If the United States allowed the entire peninsula to fall to the North Koreans, not only might Japan abandon its alliance with the United States and defect to the other side, but other nations in Asia might follow suit. What is more, European allies could conclude that the United States had no stomach for sustained military confrontation and that therefore the Soviet Union, now armed with atomic bombs, could begin to push westward without fear of American response. By drawing a line at the 38th parallel, so this "strategic continuity" argument goes, the United States demonstrated to its putative allies that it was willing to commit blood and treasure to its Cold War campaign even after its atomic monopoly disappeared. Korea demonstrated the credibility of American commitments, a word that would be much used in the decades to come.[44]

Other historians argue, quite to the contrary, that the development of NSC-68 and America's global anti-communist project was not a defensive act at all but rather the commencement of a full-fledged neocolonialist campaign to establish American hegemony across Asia, which in turn stemmed from a U.S. desire to expand its capitalist world system into every corner of the globe. The most persuasive of these "revisionist" authors avoid crude economic determinism in their analyses, and they do not claim that U.S. officials had a grand plan to master the Asian continent. Their argument, rather, is that American planners felt certain that the survival of a functioning global trading system depended on preserving Western Europe and Japan in a U.S.-centered system, which in turn required keeping certain parts of the Third World—notably Southeast Asia—out of communist hands. The world was interconnected; defeats in some places could produce losses elsewhere, ultimately unraveling the global trading system on which American prosperity depended. Hence the determination of leading officials, including especially Secretary of State Dean Acheson, to put important economic resources and sectors under America's effective control. The Soviet bomb and the fall of China, according to this view, served as pretexts to enact a policy already conceived.[45]

There is power in each of these analyses, but neither can fully explain key decisions made by the Truman administration during the early stages of the Korean struggle. Choices made in war, after all, reflect the true intentions of governments better than declared policies. The strategic continuity thesis stumbles on the decision to attack across the 38th parallel in Korea late in 1950. Had the Truman administration been following the strategic logic of Kennan's containment, as these scholars suggest it was, the president and his aides would not have supported MacArthur's rapid incursions into North Korea and toward the Yalu River, actions that were sure to antagonize China and almost certainly prompt it to enter the war—as critics of this expansive strategy repeatedly warned.[46] How could a defensive strategy of containment, now threatened by the Soviet bomb and Mao's takeover, be enhanced by getting into a war with China that might lead to an atomic war with the USSR or a war of attrition in Asia? The reasoning behind MacArthur's offensive was too consistent with the new thinking of NSC-68, and the new anti-communist crusade at home, to affirm claims that Washington's Cold War strategy had not substantially changed.

The United States had a clear opportunity after the invasion of Inchon, and then again after the counterattack against the Chinese, to secure a ceasefire and restore the antebellum border, as the United Nations resolution decreed. Containment as originally conceived would have dictated negotiation and compromise on a second-level confrontation such as this one. NSC-68 advocated a more aggressive strategy against communism anywhere, and it was this mentality that now drove the Truman administration after the start of the war. The respective career trajectories of Acheson and Kennan are illustrative of this change. Acheson, a clear advocate of the offensive strategy in Korea during the second half of 1950, had by that time come to dominate foreign policymaking in the Truman administration. Kennan, a thoroughgoing critic of the escalation, was on his way out of Washington.[47]

The neocolonialist thesis, on the other hand, is complicated by the next major development in the struggle, namely, Truman's firing of MacArthur and his decision not to expand the war to include China. An administration driven by the imperative of achieving hegemony in Asia would likely have followed MacArthur's lead and used Korea as a platform to "liberate" China. For a world-system hegemon, after all, China was the great prize, with its 650 million consumers and massive supplies of raw materials and cheap labor, compared to which Korea was an economic pygmy. Yet Truman declined to start a general war with China and instead presided over a defensive, limited war that in time would cost him dearly in political terms.

Why did Truman shrink away from starting a war with Mao Zedong's China? A key part of the answer surely lies in the new reality of the Soviet bomb. Waging direct war against the Beijing government could lead to Soviet intervention and the outbreak of World War III. Such a struggle would become much more difficult to wage, and far more destructive, both in Asia and in Europe, now that the Soviets had joined the atomic club. The aggressive designs of MacArthur and other American militarists ran up against the fearsome prospect of atomic war, and Truman wanted no part of such an escalation. A "fearful difficulty lay in the fact that the course advocated by MacArthur might well mean all-out, general world war—atomic weapons and all," he recalled in his memoirs. "But because I was sure that MacArthur could not possibly have overlooked these considerations, I was left with just one simple conclusion: General MacArthur was ready to risk general war. I was not."[48] A self-justifying recollection made years after the fact? Certainly, but one that is consistent with what we know about Truman's state of mind at the time of decision.

But do Truman's actions necessarily contradict the hegemonic theory put forward by revisionist historians? One could argue, as Bruce Cumings has, that Truman's decision to avoid risking World War III was not based on any diminishing American interest in economic expansion; rather, the Soviet bomb forced an otherwise rapacious United States to back off at the last moment.[49] This acknowledgement, however, only begs the question. It is not difficult to understand why Truman wanted to avoid a general war in early 1951—as far as he knew, the Soviet air force might have been able to drop atomic bombs on American cities, not to mention European and Japanese ones, and the man who authorized the attacks on Hiroshima and Nagasaki needed no instruction on the colossal destruction such bombings would cause.[50] But it is hard to see how Truman's reasons for wanting to prevent such a catastrophe can be explained by the hegemonic, economic imperatives that revisionists believe were driving his policies in Korea. Far more likely, he was motivated by the simple desire to avoid the atomic destruction of dozens of his country's cities and those of close allies—a motivation, that is to say, based on fear rather than on economic interest. And this, of course, was precisely the concern of NSC-68. For all of the expansive and universalistic rhetoric of that document, the position of its authors on the new realities established by the Soviet bomb was clear: the primary purpose of the United States must now be to wage the Cold War without getting into an atomic war, and without having to concede to Soviet demands to avoid one. As we shall explore further below, it is implausible that such a tremendous global campaign, not to mention the original offensive toward the Yalu River, was needed to accomplish this goal; therefore, other factors must have contributed to Washington's new policies. But it is simply untenable to argue that NSC-68 was a blueprint for absolute global hegemony, because one of its central conclusions was that with the advent of the Soviet bomb a policy of unlimited U.S. expansion was not possible. The Kremlin could no longer be militarily defeated at acceptable cost, and major wars that risked bringing in the Soviets were now too dangerous. The question NSC-68 sought to answer was not how to overcome this new reality but how to respond to it. If Truman's determination to expand the war in Korea reflected the reasoning of NSC-68, so did his decision to fire MacArthur and avoid war in China.

If American action in Korea during the pivotal months of late 1950 and early 1951 contradicts both the argument that the United States was maintaining its original policy of containment and the counter-argument that it would pursue maximum economic expansion at all costs, how then does one explain Truman's decision to markedly intensify the Cold War during this period, both abroad and at home? To be sure, the setbacks in 1949 created genuine problems for the original containment policy: the Soviet bomb made the promise to defend western Europe and Japan more dangerous and less credible, and Mao's victory created a major new ally for Moscow and also put serious pressure on Japan. But why did Truman reply with such a heavy hand? To explain this, we must turn to the domestic politics of insecurity.

Had the Truman administration stayed wedded in 1950 to the concept of basic containment, it could have decided in general to approve greater military spending in the event of Soviet advances and to work to assure its key allies in Europe and Asia that it would defend them irrespective of the Soviet bomb. It could have conducted limited operations in Korea, keeping the South Korean regime afloat while at the same time doggedly pursuing negotiations to restore the status quo ante, an objective that probably could have been achieved in late 1950 or early 1951. Instead, it went much farther. Truman quadrupled the military budget. He gave MacArthur free rein in Korea for several months, triggering a Chinese counter-attack and a great intensification of the war and raising the possibility of an all-out global conflagration—a Third World War. The U.S. Air Force bombed North Korea, a nation that had not attacked the United States, killing hundreds of thousands of Koreans and leaving countless more homeless. Meanwhile, on the domestic front, American society suffered its worst case of political repression in the modern era.

Understanding this overreaction requires understanding the changing nature of domestic politics in Cold War America. It is crucial to recall that Americans had been introduced to power politics via the total, unconditional war against Germany and Japan; yet a strict adherence to Kennan's finite, geopolitical strategy of Eurasian containment asked them to accept the existence of Soviet power and take limited, long-term steps to deal with it. Strategists like Paul Nitze and many politicians, including the prominent internationalist Republican John Foster Dulles, recognized that Americans would be more receptive to the clear-cut morality of active anti-communism than the cool logic of defensive containment. Once the Truman White House began to move in this direction, the gates opened, and when the war began in Korea, Kennan's realist logic was trampled underfoot, the victim of a surging American globalism.

Partisan electoral politics played a key role. To an extent not seen elsewhere in the Western world, crusading anti-communism became intimately bound up with practical politics.[51] Candidates for office learned quickly that opposing radicals and the Soviet Union was the sine qua non of effective campaigning, that there were few votes to be gained and many to be lost by preaching conciliation in East-West relations. The range of acceptable political debate narrowed sharply. In 1948 Henry Wallace, the former vice president under Franklin Roosevelt, ran for president on the Progressive Party ticket advocating a left-of-center agenda and conciliation toward the USSR, thereby attracting the open support of socialist and other left-wing groups; such a national candidacy would have been unthinkable in 1952.

Even without McCarthy's immense influence on the campaign trail that year, Democrats would have felt especially vulnerable to the "soft on communism" charge, for they had "allowed" the Soviets to get the bomb and, even worse, had "lost China." Never mind that the Republicans offered no alternative policy on China, or that indeed there was no policy to offer, China not being America's to lose. Events were outside U.S. control—a reality that was lost in the supercharged atmosphere. Truman was put on the defensive and sought to validate his anti-communist credentials by vastly increasing military spending and by refusing to compromise in Korea. Almost certainly, a calmer and more bipartisan political climate during the 1950–1952 period would have allowed Truman to achieve an earlier ceasefire in Korea and to restrain military spending. Partisan politics, in other words, paved the way both for the perpetuation of McCarthyism and for Truman's gravitation toward a harder Cold War line.[52]

The premise of Eurasian containment indicated that the United States in 1950 had accomplished its major strategic goals. By this time western Europe was firmly in the American camp. Although Japan's economic future was endangered by the communist takeover in China and the possibility of communist victories in Korea and Indochina, it was much more under the control of American power than was western Europe. The Japanese would likely remain on the American side as long as the United States proved willing to defend them and incorporate their nation into an industrial trading system. Containment did not require that American allies become rich. As Kennan understood, this did not mean that international politics had come to an end and that the United States could let down its guard. It did mean, however, that no further grand initiatives along the lines of the Marshall Plan or NATO were needed in the foreseeable future. Vigilance in Europe, perhaps minor interventions in Korea or elsewhere in East Asia, assurances that the USSR would not achieve nuclear superiority—such measured steps could provide the United States with the continued confidence that the Soviet Union would not conquer Eurasia and that therefore America and its civilization would be secure.

The problem with regarding the original architecture of containment as adequate was that this view served few entrenched political and economic interests in American society. Many more powerful interests stood to benefit from a vigorous prosecution of the Cold War and from increased military spending—the armed forces themselves, civilian officials associated with defense issues, arms industrialists, labor unions associated with weapons industries, universities and businesses that benefited from military research. Few organizations—at least few powerful ones—had reason to fight such a rise. New, politically potent government entities such as the CIA, the National Security Resources Board, and the Atomic Energy Commission had a stake in the Cold War's perpetuation, as did the many communities in the West and the Northeast whose economic destiny was beginning to depend on large-scale military spending. So as well did the 1.3 million Americans who now worked for the Department of Defense.[53]

In the same way, influential entities favored a greater projection of American power in Asia—corporations with ambitions in the region, certainly, but also right-wing politicians and press barons who believed that America's destiny lay in the East. A much smaller number tried to resist, and still fewer had any incentive to champion the careful and inexpensive monitoring of a containment project effectively completed. Just as the New Deal created an array of institutions and interests that saw their prosperity and even their existence tied to the ever-growing expansion of the American state, the Cold War did the same thing after 1950 in the arena of foreign policy, though on a greater scale.

Politicians in the early 1950s were no different from what they are today: then as now they recognized that in a democratic system, the meaning of political concepts can be altered by political pressure as well as dramatic events. "National security" meant one thing to Kennan, Marshall, and other strategists of the early Cold War, and something else to those in Washington who stood to benefit from its expansion into something far more ideological and open-ended. The twin shocks of 1949, followed by the outbreak of war in Korea, encouraged these politicians to take that power, by exaggerating the dangers to the United States caused by these events and by working to redefine national security into a doctrine of Us versus Them.[54]

American politics changed in important ways after 1949. The ideology of anti-communism, already ascendant in the political culture, become more acute, leading to increased repression at home and calls for victory, not just containment, abroad. Politicians, Democratic as well as Republican, recognized the electoral benefits of Cold War belligerence and called for an unyielding line. The Korean War intensified these impulses, as only a fighting war can do. It was in this political climate that a new president would take the oath of office, as a new age—the thermonuclear age—was dawning.

4

LEANER AND MEANER

On January 20, 1953, Dwight D. Eisenhower took the oath of office as the thirty-fourth president of the United States. Like Truman, he came from the rural Midwest, born in Texas but reared in modest circumstances in Kansas. From there he made it into West Point, afterward settling into what seemed a dead-end officer's career in the army. The Second World War changed all that, as it would for so many once-anonymous Americans. Having demonstrated peerless managerial and political abilities during the early years of the war, Eisenhower was given command of the Allied Expeditionary Force in Europe in 1943. Over the next two years he worked tirelessly to oversee the buildup to the D-Day invasion and then the war to defeat Hitler, redirecting both subordinate military commanders and political figures from the United States, Britain, and France away from their own objectives and toward his single-minded goal: the unconditional surrender of Nazi Germany.

Unlike Truman, Eisenhower had kept his distance from party politics, turning away overtures from the Democratic Party to replace Truman as its candidate in 1948 and voicing on numerous later occasions his unwillingness to seek political office.[1] But this reticence was a calculated stance by an ambitious politician-to-be, and when Eisenhower—then NATO commander—finally accepted the Republican Party's nomination in the summer of 1952, he quickly shifted into high gear. On the campaign trail that fall he told voters that he would "go to Korea," implying that he would find a way to end the war where Truman had not, and on terms favorable to the United States. The promise appealed to an American public tired of two years of military stalemate and anxious to see Eisenhower ("Ike" to his supporters) as the one man who might carry it off. He denounced the Democrats and their standard-bearer, Adlai E. Stevenson, for being soft on communism, and he selected for his running mate the Red-baiting senator from California who "got" Alger Hiss: Richard Nixon. Eisenhower also trod carefully around Joseph McCarthy, appearing with him on a stage in Milwaukee even though the Wisconsin senator had denounced George Marshall, Eisenhower's mentor and friend, as a possible communist agent.[2]

The president's choice for secretary of state, John Foster Dulles, had already articulated the broad outlines of a Republican Cold War policy. The grandson of one secretary of state and the nephew of another, Dulles seemingly had been groomed for this appointment his whole life—as Eisenhower quipped, "Foster has been studying to be Secretary of State since he was five years old." A high-powered Wall Street lawyer and a leader in the Presbyterian Church, Dulles was not quite the inflexible ideologue that legend would have it. Behind closed doors he could show a nuanced grasp of the complexities of world affairs. But he believed that the Cold War was fundamentally a struggle between good and evil, in which there could be no middle way, and that it was necessary to frame American foreign policy accordingly.

In several writings, most notably a 1952 article in *Life* magazine called "A Policy of Boldness," Dulles attacked the Truman administration for reacting to Soviet aggression rather than going on the offensive.[3] Containment, he maintained, was an immoral strategy, for it ceded the initiative to the Soviet Union and implied that the

United States was willing to tolerate indefinitely co-existing with a godless, totalitarian regime. This was particularly unacceptable in the European theater, which Dulles regarded both as the central battlefield of the Cold War and also the home of Western civilization. Thus the effort must be made not merely to contain communism but to roll it back. It would have been difficult for Dulles to come up with a better foreign policy to appeal to an electorate driven into an anti-communist frenzy by McCarthyism. Rollback, Eisenhower's adviser Emmett Hughes once said, was "all domestic politics."[4]

Eisenhower and Dulles knew that rolling back communism was a rather tall order now that the Cold War was moving toward its second decade. They recognized that political calls for Cold War victory would have to be scaled back once they took office. But they agreed that, after winning the election, a new policy would be needed to replace Truman's containment, which was synonymous in their minds, and in the minds of voters, with the stalemated war in Korea. They called their strategy the New Look.[5] Eisenhower wanted to manage the Cold War more efficiently, avoiding large land wars, reducing military spending, while bringing the Cold War to the doorsteps of the Kremlin in innovative ways. Dulles, for his part, wanted to take the moral offensive, rejecting what he saw as the reactiveness of Truman's policies in Korea in favor of an assertive strategy that might, someday, vanquish the Soviet Union.

Despite their somewhat different objectives and their outwardly differing styles—Eisenhower pragmatic and outgoing; Dulles bombastic, severe, and socially awkward—the two men worked together during Eisenhower's first term to wage an aggressive Cold War, playing hardball in the Third World, maneuvering to control the playing field in Europe and other arenas of direct Cold War confrontation, brandishing America's atomic and nuclear superiority. The question that would ultimately divide them was how far these policies should be pushed as the thermonuclear age dawned.

A Missed Chance for Peace?

The new administration had been in office for only a few weeks when shocking news arrived from the east: Joseph Stalin, the personification of godless, totalitarian Soviet communism, had died. His passing opened the possibility of seeking a less confrontational relationship with the new leadership, whatever its makeup—a view advanced forcefully by Winston Churchill, who had returned to power in Britain. Since 1948, even before the Soviets had tested their atomic bomb, Churchill had advocated a grand settlement with the Soviet Union, believing that greater engagement between the two sides would play to the West's advantage. In November 1951, shortly after returning to 10 Downing Street, Churchill called for "an abatement of the Cold War by negotiation at the highest level." Now, with Stalin gone and his lieutenants making reassuring noises about their geopolitical intentions, the prime minister renewed his effort.[6]

Churchill's aims were, of course, not wholly idealistic—an "abatement" of the Cold War between the two superpowers could mean a resurgence of British influence and a more prominent place for him personally on the world stage.[7] Still, he had reason to believe that the new American president might be interested. Eisenhower had long demonstrated a greater faith in the notion of cooperation with the Soviet Union than many others in Washington. At the end of the European war in 1945, he had resisted demands from both London and Washington, as well as from many on the scene, to race to Berlin ahead of the USSR. Although military considerations played a role in his decision, almost certainly he also believed that letting the Red Army have the honor of seizing the Nazi capital would facilitate better Soviet-American relations in the postwar period.[8] On numerous occasions in the war's aftermath, not only in private but also in print, he expressed an interest in cooperating with the Soviets and perpetuating the Grand

Alliance. In a fascinating conclusion to his 1948 memoirs of the European campaign, Eisenhower wrote that during his meetings with the Soviet Marshal Grigori Zhukov at the end of the war he had hoped that the United States and the Soviet Union could achieve a cooperative postwar order. If "mutual confidence and trust could be developed between America and the Soviets," the president wrote, "the peace and unity of the world could be assured."[9]

Furthermore, Eisenhower retained an affinity for the so-called Old Guard Republicans, the Taft wing of the party that hoped to reduce military spending and limit American involvement overseas. He rejected their opposition to NATO, as well as the more radical notion that the United States could retreat to the Western hemisphere, and he wanted nothing to do with the nativism of Old Guard figures such as Senator John Bricker. He excoriated Taft on these matters during their primary presidential campaign. But the new president had been sympathetic with the Old Guard's general demand that the United States avoid an expensive global Cold War that would bankrupt the nation and entangle it in innumerable foreign squabbles. Seen in that light, a deal with the USSR would make a lot of sense. The United States could negotiate mutual withdrawals from Europe and Asia (while assuring key allies that it would send troops back whenever necessary) and concentrate on national defense. The wild spending and universal commitments of NSC-68 would become a thing of the past. Eisenhower's first major speech on foreign policy, in which the new president issued a general plea for nuclear disarmament and said the United States should always "display a spirit of firmness without truculence, conciliation without appeasement, confidence without arrogance," suggested that perhaps Churchill's wishes might be fulfilled.[10]

The speech belied Eisenhower's true intentions. By 1952 he had abandoned his earlier notions of cooperation and instead was determined to ramp up the Cold War. If any doubts remained, the president dispelled them in a December 1953 meeting with Churchill in Bermuda. In talks that also included the French, Churchill suggested there might be a "New Look" Soviet policy as well; perhaps now was the time to move aggressively to reduce East-West tensions and to organize a stable European order. Using crude language to swat away that notion, Eisenhower said Russia was a "woman of the streets," and whether the dress was new or just the old one patched up, she was "certainly the same whore underneath."[11]

Whatever Moscow's intentions might have been in 1953, there was little chance for a grand settlement for the simple reason that the new administration in Washington was not interested.[12] For Dulles, cooperation was a nonstarter: the secretary of state was never inclined to think in terms of substantial Cold War compromise.[13] The new president, for his part, had abandoned his earlier hopefulness. Two factors appear to have altered his attitude toward the Soviet Union. The first was simple political expediency: he understood that pursuing international conciliation in the run-up to the 1952 election would have endangered his candidacy for the presidency at a time of rabid anti-communism in the United States and especially within the Republican party. He had no desire to invite attacks from Joe McCarthy, then at the height of his power, by talking about making overtures to the communists. After his victory, the president knew that his prospects for reelection in 1956 would not be enhanced by a campaign, waged in defiance of major elements within his own political party and possibly his secretary of state, to conciliate the USSR during his first term.

Eisenhower also seemed to have become genuinely more hostile toward Moscow as a result of Stalin's purge of his friend Zhukov from Soviet politics shortly after the war and his own experience as NATO commander between 1950 and 1952.[14] Nor did he hold out much hope that the post-Stalin leadership in the Kremlin would initiate lasting changes in policy. In short, Eisenhower and Dulles had little personal inclination and even less political incentive to seek a grand Cold War compromise with the Soviets. Instead, they turned up the heat on several fronts.

Massive Retaliation

The foundation of the new administration's foreign policy during Eisenhower's first term was simple: the threat of nuclear war. NSC-68 postulated that the Soviet acquisition of the atomic bomb meant that the United States could no longer regard major war with the USSR as an acceptable option. Neither Dulles nor Eisenhower was indifferent to this state of affairs, and Eisenhower had expressed on several occasions his concerns about atomic warfare. Indeed, the new president had confided to many colleagues since the war that he had opposed dropping the bomb on Hiroshima and Nagasaki. And after leaving office he publicly criticized the decision, saying it had not been necessary "to hit them with that awful thing."[15] But the fact remained that as the new administration took office, the United States still possessed a substantial superiority over the Soviet Union in atomic armaments, not only in the number of actual bombs it deployed but also, and more important, in the means of delivering these bombs to Soviet targets.[16]

Dulles proposed to use this advantage strategically. In his "Boldness" article in *Life,* and then in a famous 1954 essay in *Foreign Affairs,* he argued that the United States ought to answer communist aggression, such as had occurred in Korea, not by responding in kind and deploying large armies to the scene but rather by attacking the source of the aggression.[17] After all, he asserted, communist incursions around the world were directed by Moscow. Why not threaten the Kremlin with a direct atomic attack in the event of such incursions? Such a policy would be much cheaper, would avoid unpopular, draining wars such as Korea, and would play to

America's strategic advantages. What is more, Dulles added, the threat could deter communist leaders from authorizing aggressive actions in the first place, thus clearing the way for the United States to take the initiative around the world. Here, in short, was an aggressive, active strategy, one that could tilt the balance against the communist threat, rather than a reactive containment policy that accepted things as they were. Or so he presented it.

Following an early exercise called Operation Solarium, in which Eisenhower commissioned three alternative strategies for waging the Cold War, the National Security Council produced the foundational document of America's new basic security policy, NSC-162/2. In this paper the administration articulated its new vision of contending with Kremlin aggression. The United States would deploy limited tactical atomic forces, enact a modest Civil Defense program, and authorize the Strategic Air Command, a branch of the air force, to develop a massive bomber capability that could strike Soviet targets from European and other bases. In the event of substantial communist aggression, the United States would unleash this bomber force against Soviet targets rather than attacking directly with ground troops.[18] "Massive retaliation" became the centerpiece of Eisenhower's basic security policy during the years 1953–1956, despite the fact that the USSR tested a thermonuclear device in 1953. A core component of NSC-68 was discarded in favor of a new strategy that seemed to invite rather than reject nuclear war.

Massive retaliation was a general threat to deter the "Sino-Soviet bloc" from sponsoring further Koreas, but it had another purpose as well. If the United States could establish a general nuclear deterrent at the level of direct Soviet-American confrontation—if it could make Moscow believe that intervening in a Cold War hotspot might well trigger a nuclear attack—then it could wage a more militant campaign against communist or other anti-American forces around the planet. During Eisenhower's first term, the

United States radically stepped up its efforts in the Third World by threatening atomic war in Asia, overthrowing popular regimes in the Middle East and Latin America, and contending with so-called nonaligned governments in many parts of the world.

Atomic Diplomacy

Eisenhower and Dulles believed that a tacit threat of atomic war might serve American goals in Asia, where the Cold War had already divided several nations. Truman had eschewed the use of open atomic threats in Korea, but Eisenhower and Dulles were not bound by this tradition. Why not hint at atomic attack there, or elsewhere in Asia? After all, a new Soviet government would surely be very reluctant to support its Asian allies in the face of American atomic superiority. And Mao Zedong's government in Beijing, a crucial backer of Kim Il Sung's North Korean regime, would be certain to take notice as well. Shortly after assuming the presidency, Eisenhower set out to the test the idea as a means to bring the Korean War to a successful end.[19]

His campaign vow to go to Korea had worked wonders with the American public, who took it to mean that he would use his unparalleled military experience to end the desultory conflict on American terms. But that would be no easy task, Eisenhower knew. Both sides were dug in, unwilling to agree to a ceasefire. Both preferred to continue waging limited warfare rather than give in on outstanding issues, including the precise demarcation of North and South Korea into separate states and the exchange of prisoners of war. The United States had abandoned the idea of "liberating" North Korea and expanding the war to China, and—despite continuing support for such a move within American right-wing circles and the nationalist government in Taiwan, and regardless of the New Look's aggressive rhetoric—Eisenhower had no interest in moves that risked precipitating a third world war. He merely wanted to end the fighting. To that end, he instructed Dulles to communicate to the government of India that if China and the North Koreans continued to reject a ceasefire and refused to repatriate American POWs, the United States would consider using atomic bombs to destroy Chinese and North Korean forces.[20]

North Korea and China, who had earlier relaxed their opposition to American demands and agreed to ceasefire talks, softened their position further. In June 1953, only five months into Eisenhower's term, the opposing sides concluded a ceasefire, establishing a boundary at the 38th parallel, where it had been when hostilities began three years earlier and where it would remain in the decades to come. The war had been fought to a draw. Was Eisenhower's atomic diplomacy responsible for this change in the enemy's posture? Recent scholarship indicates that it was not the crucial element driving the Chinese and North Koreans to agree to a deal. Almost certainly they were motivated more by the death of Stalin and hence the uncertainty of continued Soviet support, as well as their own desire to end a bloody and exhausting war, than by the tacit American threat.[21] But of course Eisenhower and Dulles could not be certain about what broke the logjam. From the American perspective, the atomic threat seemed to work—if not alone, then in conjunction with these other factors.

Little wonder that at the Bermuda meeting in December 1953 the president told his startled British and French counterparts that he would consider using atomic weapons against Chinese targets if the communists violated the Korean truce. The bomb, he told them, was just another weapon in the U.S. arsenal, which meant London and Paris should not expect to be consulted prior to its use. A horrified Churchill said such action would likely bring Soviet nuclear retaliation. And because the Kremlin was believed to lack the means to drop a bomb on American soil, its likely target would be U.S. air bases in East Anglia. This atomic exchange would be the start of World War III. With London's defenses inadequate, the prime minister continued, his emotion rising, he "could not bear to think of the destruction of all we hold dear, ourselves, our families and our treasures; and even if some of us temporarily survive in some deep cellar under mounds of flaming and contaminated rubble there will be nothing left to do but to take a pill to end it all." Eisenhower coolly replied that he did not think Moscow would attack in the West if atomic weapons were used against bases and troop concentrations in China.[22]

In the spring of 1954 a second opportunity for atomic diplomacy arose. In Indochina, France had been waging a protracted and losing war against the Vietminh in order to retain colonial power. The fighting had begun in late 1946 but for the first three years it remained in essence a localized colonial war. But when Mao's communists won victory in China three years later, the Truman administration made two crucial decisions, both in early 1950 before the Korean War began. It extended recognition to the French puppet government of Bao Dai, an intelligent but indolent former emperor who had collaborated with the French and Japanese, and it pledged to furnish France with military and economic assistance for the war effort.[23] With the Soviets and especially the Chinese simultaneously throwing their weight behind the Vietminh led by Ho Chi Minh, the Franco-Vietminh War now took on a new cast as simultaneously a colonial conflict and a Cold War confrontation—a Soviet-American war-by-proxy with the potential to escalate into direct military confrontation.

As the fighting raged on, the United States kept raising the level of its material aid, and by spring 1954 American taxpayers were carrying almost three quarters of the financial cost of the French effort. Yet despite some tactical French successes in 1951–52, the overall strategic situation favored the Vietminh. In March 1954 Vietminh commanders, aided by Chinese logistical and material support, attacked a large French garrison at Dien Bien Phu in remote northwest Vietnam. Paris alerted Washington that if Dien

Bien Phu fell France would abandon Vietnam, and asked for military support. Some of Eisenhower's advisers recommended a massive American air strike against Vietminh positions, perhaps even using tactical atomic weapons, but the president moved more cautiously than his Bermuda bravado might have suggested. He questioned whether air power alone would do the job, and said he did not want to act unilaterally. Moreover, influential members of Congress, including Senator Lyndon Baines Johnson of Texas, told Eisenhower they wanted "no more Koreas" and warned him against any U.S. military commitment, especially in the absence of cooperation from America's allies. Some felt very uneasy about supporting colonialism. The issue became moot on May 7, when the weary French defenders at Dien Bien Phu surrendered.

The Vietminh stood ready to take all of Vietnam. Yet at the Geneva Conference two months later the Vietminh delegation and its Chinese and Soviet allies agreed to an American-backed temporary partition of the country at the 17th parallel, with elections for reunification to follow within two years. Why did the Vietminh, in command on the ground, relent? Their motives for agreeing to the Geneva Accords were complex, including pressure from their Soviet and Chinese patrons to compromise and their own felt need for a respite from almost eight years of warfare. The evidence is clear, however, that an additional factor was their deep desire to avert a direct U.S. military intervention, one they knew would involve massive air power and potentially atomic weapons.

Mao, however, was not inclined to rest easy. He decided to turn up the heat on another hot spot in Asia: Taiwan. In the fall of 1954, soon after the French collapse in Vietnam, China began to harass the Quemoy-Matsu island chain—tiny atolls held by Chiang Kai-shek's nationalists which he hoped to use as a point of embarkation for the great counter-revolution on the Chinese mainland. Over the next few months, Beijing ramped up the pressure, attacking the even smaller Tachen chain to the north, launching regular artillery attacks against Quemoy and Matsu, and amassing a large invasion force on the mainland coast directly opposite the islands. In the face of incredulous resistance from several allies, including Great Britain, Eisenhower and Dulles opted to define the defense of Quemoy-Matsu as central to American security. Letting the Chinese take Quemoy and Matsu, Eisenhower argued, would mean that the United States would have to force Chiang to remove his forces from the islands—a humiliation that would surely undermine his regime and lead to the fall of Taiwan. With Taiwan in the hands of the communists, South Korea and then Japan would in all likelihood soon succumb. Just like that, America's allies in East Asia would be gone.

The president's private views were different. He didn't actually believe that the loss of Quemoy-Matsu would inexorably lead to the collapse of all East Asia—he once joked that he wished "the damned little offshore islands" would sink. Rather, he saw the political benefits of hard-nosed atomic diplomacy. At home, a tough stance on the offshore crisis would please the China lobby and other voices pressing for a stronger U.S. stand in Asia. Senator Knowland compared the islands to Berlin and warned ominously that failure in the crisis could represent a "second Munich," while Henry Luce's *Time* asked mockingly "at what special, awkward point the U.S." would begin "to care deeply." *Life,* another Luce publication, was even more blunt: "Stand by Free China!"[24] Abroad, a resolute posture in the straits would demonstrate America's resolve to U.S. allies, including Europeans wondering about America's commitment to their defense now that the Soviets had the bomb. And, he reckoned, the chances that his bet would be called were low. China was a long way from obtaining its own atomic arsenal, and he knew that the USSR was far behind the United States in nuclear weaponry and did not yet have a deployable thermonuclear bomb. Soviet leaders would not risk a confrontation over the issue.

As a result, Eisenhower and Dulles engaged in their most overt atomic diplomacy yet over the defense of Quemoy-Matsu. In March 1955, not long before a superpower summit in Geneva, Dulles spoke publicly of new American nuclear weaponry that could "utterly destroy military targets without endangering unrelated civilian centers," a clear reference to the Chinese military bases being built across from the islands. A week later, Eisenhower bolstered Dulles's tacit threat: in a combat situation, the president said, the United States would use tactical nuclear weapons "just exactly as you would use a bullet or anything else." The intimidation worked. Beijing soon put a halt to its aggressive activity against Quemoy-Matsu, and the nationalist garrisons remained on the islands.[25]

On three separate occasions during Eisenhower's first term, then, his administration engaged in coercive diplomacy by brandishing atomic weaponry. The president's goal was to win victories in Asia without getting bogged down in "another Korea"—to prevent left-wing and communist expansion in that part of the world, but to do so on the cheap. Eisenhower seemed to target his adversaries indiscriminately—the Kremlin leadership, the Chinese armed forces, and the indigenous nationalists in Vietnam. It is now clear from the documentary evidence that in each of these three episodes the American threats—tacit or, in the case of Quemoy-Matsu, overt—probably had little effect on the outcome. It is also evident that in each case the United States did not win a lasting victory. In Korea, Vietnam, and the Taiwan Straits, atomic diplomacy turned out only to "hold the line" in Asia, no more.[26] But Eisenhower did not have the advantage of hindsight nor access to the thinking of leaders in Moscow, Beijing, Hanoi, and Pyongyang. He wanted to prevent communist expansion at that moment, without spending money or committing troops. And from his point of view, atomic diplomacy worked.

Which, in turn, raises an intriguing question. Was Eisenhower really prepared to use the bomb? Was he willing to perpetrate more Hiroshimas in order to force a ceasefire in Korea, or defeat a popular anticolonial rebellion in Vietnam, or defend the tiny outpost of Quemoy-Matsu? He later claimed that the strategy was a bluff—he had pushed in a big stack of chips but would have folded if the other side called. When many of his aides, including perhaps Dulles, seemed open to the idea of actually using the bomb at Dien Bien Phu, Eisenhower reportedly replied: "You boys must be crazy. We can't use those awful things against Asians for the second time in less than ten years. My God." The quote may be apocryphal, though it has the ring of truth, especially in light of his later actions. But then, that's the beauty of a winning bluff: no one gets to see your cards.[27]

Subversion, American Style

In addition to using America's atomic superiority more aggressively, Eisenhower and Dulles wanted to employ more unorthodox methods to contend with America's adversaries. Truman, to be sure, had not eschewed the dark arts of foreign policy. The CIA had opened for business in 1947, and NSC-68 had stressed the importance of using that agency and other secret means to take on the Soviet Union in the arenas of espionage, subversion, and covert action—fields in which Moscow was seen to have had a serious head start. Eisenhower and Dulles, eager to wage the Cold War more efficiently and effectively, wanted to take these arts to another level. One of their major goals was political subversion. On two occasions, the administration worked covertly to topple unfriendly governments, inspiring anti-American feelings that would linger for decades.

In 1951 Iranians elected the nationalist but avowedly anticommunist Mohammed Mossadeqh as prime minister. Mossadeqh had no interest in allying his nation with the Soviet Union or

pursuing radical policies, though some of his supporters entertained such objectives. He did, however, seek to nationalize Iran's
oil holdings and eject the British and American companies that
had controlled Iranian production since the nineteenth century—
a form of modern-day colonialism that allowed Iran to claim only
about 20 percent of the profits from its own wells. Western Europe
relied heavily on access to cheap and reliable petroleum from the
Middle East, and many U.S. and British companies stood to lose
vast profits should Mossadeqh's nationalization policy succeed. A
boycott of Iranian oil failed to cause his overthrow, and many industry figures worried about a sustained absence of Iranian production from the world market.

Pushed into a corner and finding his power slipping, Mossadeqh called for a referendum on his policies, and then fixed the results to give himself more than 95 percent of the vote. He also
threatened to turn to the Soviet Union for support. Soon after taking office, Eisenhower—prodded by the British to make an example of Mossadeqh and concerned as well that permitting one Middle Eastern nation to control its own oil might encourage nearby
states to follow suit—approved a plan to use covert operations to
undermine the new Iranian government and replace it with one
led by the heir to the ancient Persian throne, Reza Pahlevi.

Agents employed by the CIA and the British secret service, MI6,
moved into the capital, Tehran, in July 1953. The head of the
American operation, Kermit Roosevelt (grandson of Theodore),
employed right-wing figures on the scene to orchestrate a coup,
elevating to power Fazlollah Zehedi, who would eventually cede
actual power to Pahlevi, the new shah of Iran. Several hundred Iranians, mostly those allied with Mossadeqh, died in the street violence, many of them pummeled to death by CIA-financed local
toughs and other opponents of the regime. One of the rabble-
rousers was a 51-year-old cleric named Ayatollah Ruhollah Musavi
Khomeini. Mossadeqh was arrested and sent to prison. The United

States recognized the new government immediately, sending $45 million of aid to the shah and providing him with advisers trained in repressing domestic unrest.[28]

The following year the administration acted again, this time in Guatemala. Its leader, Jacobo Arbenz Guzman, had come to power in 1951 after perhaps the fairest election in the country's history, succeeding the reformist president Juan Jose Arevalo. Arbenz, like Mossadeqh, was a non-communist nationalist whose new government included a handful of political leftists. Also like Mossadeqh, he hoped to nationalize Guatemalan resources owned by foreign companies—in this case, several hundred thousand acres of land, much of it unused, owned by the United Fruit Company of Boston, a corporation with close ties to the White House. He expropriated United Fruit's uncultivated land and offered compensation. The company rejected the offer and trumpeted the claim around Washington that Arbenz posed a communist threat. The CIA began outlining a plot to overthrow him, and American suspicions were reinforced when intelligence reports revealed that Arbenz had received arms from Czechoslovakia.[29]

Dulles, playing up the arms deal, tried to organize Latin American nations against the Arbenz regime. He urged an inter-American conference in Caracas in March 1954 to come together around a policy of opposing the spread of communism in the Americas. Though a generic resolution along these lines passed, it became clear to Dulles that most of the delegates to the conference, excepting only right-wing dictators such as President Perez Jimenez of Venezuela and Anastosio Somoza of Nicaragua, were reluctant to move beyond vague support for U.S. policy and condone direct action against Guatemala. There the matter might have ended, at least for the moment, had the Czech arms deal not been disclosed in the American press. The prospect of a communist state in Central America, armed by the Soviet bloc, seemed to violate the Monroe Doctrine's prohibition of hostile-power encroachment in the Western Hemisphere. Politicians from both parties outdid one another in exaggerating the threat posed by the tiny impoverished country. Speaker of the House John McCormack, a Democrat from Boston, beat them all by describing the Guatemalan arms deal as "an atom bomb planted in the rear of our backyard." It was as if a Soviet ship had smuggled a nuclear weapon into New York Harbor, "confident that at any time it could blow up the City of New York."[30]

The White House took up the challenge. In June 1954 CIA-led exiles moved from bases in nearby Honduras and Nicaragua, while a U.S.-backed Guatemalan military officer, Castillo Armas, worked to instigate a coup in Guatemala City. The coup stalled. Desperate, Allen Dulles—director of the CIA and brother of John Foster Dulles—persuaded Eisenhower to approve a comprehensive CIA air attack on the capital, financed privately by an American businessman in order to keep it away from Congress and the public.[31] Arbenz saw the writing on the wall and abdicated, leaving the door open to Armas, who quickly established a military dictatorship and put hundreds of Arbenz's followers before the firing squad. The weapons went back to Czechoslovakia, and United Fruit kept its land. John Foster Dulles crowed that Guatemala had been saved from "Communist imperialism" and that Armas's takeover added "a new and glorious chapter to the already great tradition of the American States."[32]

No Room for Neutrality

By brandishing atomic weapons and overthrowing two governments outright, the Eisenhower administration indicated during its first term that it would play tough in the struggle to defeat any forces in the Third World that were communist-leaning or just insufficiently pro-American. But what about those players in underdeveloped countries who staked out an openly neutral position in the Cold War? How would the administration respond to them? Less harshly, as it turned out, but often with the same fundamental objective in mind: to undermine national leadership.[33]

The neutralist challenge was hardly unexpected. Great-power rivalries create opportunities for small states, and the Cold War was no exception. After 1950 it became obvious to the leaders of several impoverished nations, most of them only having recently thrown off the yoke of European colonialism, that economic and military aid could be obtained by amplifying the communist (or capitalist) threat in their nations. Even better, ambitious states could play one superpower off against the other, attracting aid and political support from both the United States and the Soviet Union in a kind of Cold War beauty contest. Finally, such regimes could stress the eternal ideals of independence and nationalism—causes that naturally appealed to populations remembering decades, even centuries, of subservience to European imperialists. To accomplish this nice trick, nationalist leaders had to avoid declaring for one side or the other and instead remain neutral. Several statesmen spearheaded this movement: among them were India's Jawaharlal Nehru, Egypt's Gamel Abdel Nasser, Yugoslavia's Josip Broz Tito (who had wrested his country from Stalin's grip in 1948), Ghana's Kwame Nkrumah, and Indonesia's Achmed Sukarno, who in 1955 hosted a conference of "nonaligned" nations in Bandung.[34]

Neutralism in the Third World might well have fit in quite nicely with Kennan's old containment blueprint, with its limited conception of America's national interests and its emphasis on preserving America's political preponderance primarily over the major industrialized states of western Europe and Japan. But that logic had long since disappeared from Washington. Eisenhower and Dulles determined that the United States should oppose neutralism and nationalism all over the preindustrialized Third World, not by engaging in the heavy-handed tactics seen in Quemoy-Matsu or Guatemala but by seeking to politically undermine or at least weaken prominent nonaligned regimes and impel them to side with Washington. In India, Washington secretly funded anti-Nehru factions, and it did the same to opponents of Sukarno in Indonesia.[35] The administration declined to provide material aid or diplomatic support for the fledgling Tito regime, despite its success in fending off Soviet domination. In 1954–55 Eisenhower, working with old colonial allies in London and Paris, moved to establish formal alliances in the Middle East and Asia in the form of the Baghdad Pact and the Southeast Asian Treaty Organization (SEATO), under which Third World nations that openly sided with the West would receive economic and military aid.[36]

These moderate steps failed to halt the nonaligned movement. Nasser, Sukarno, and other leaders simply had too much to gain by playing off the United States and the USSR against one another and by appealing to their suffering constituencies' sense of emergent nationalism.

Psychological Warfare

A final way that the administration intensified the Cold War during Eisenhower's first term was to contend directly with international communism in manipulating public opinion around the world. The president believed that the USSR had jumped to a commanding lead in this arena, especially in shaping European opinion. That was not surprising: while the Soviet state had long perfected the art of propaganda, it was a rather new enterprise for the United States. But that was no reason for Washington to admit defeat. Eisenhower was convinced that in the nuclear age the Cold War was in large measure a psychological struggle, a battle—to use the Vietnam-era phrase—for hearts and minds.

Moscow certainly saw these kinds of techniques as central to its campaign to wage Cold War by other means. In particular, the Soviets sought to portray themselves as the champions of peace and the common man in the global struggle against colonialism and capitalist exploitation.

To surmount this communist "peace offensive," America must innovate, rather than merely respond to Soviet actions. The result, as the historian Kenneth Osgood has shown, was a campaign of psychological warfare that comprised several objectives. To counter anticolonial Soviet propaganda in Latin America and Africa, the administration worked to demonstrate America's support for freedom of religion, thereby appealing to the large Christian populations in these regions. In Europe, a major theme was freedom of speech, a message thought to resonate with societies in southern and eastern Europe that had experienced fascist and communist repression.[37]

In the People-to-People campaign, a state-private venture initiated by the United States Information Agency (USIA) in 1956, U.S. propaganda experts sought to use ordinary Americans to promote confidence abroad in the basic goodness of the people of the United States and, by extension, their government. Simultaneously, officials hoped, the program could serve a domestic mobilization function, reminding Americans of what the Cold War was about while avoiding the use of overtly anti-communist sloganeering. Americans were told, for example, that thirty dollars could send a ninety-nine-volume portable library of American books to schools and libraries overseas. People-to-People committees organized sister-city affiliations and pen pals, hosted exchange students, and organized traveling People-to-People delegations representing various communities. To extol everyday life in the United States, Camp Fire Girls in more than 3,000 communities took photographs on the theme "This is our home. This is how we live. These are my People." The photographs, assembled in albums, were sent to girls in Latin America, Africa, Asia, and the Middle East. Corporations earmarked portions of their overseas advertising to facilitate a "better understanding" of the United States.[38]

The Kremlin's peace offensive presented a peskier problem. To begin with, it was not easy to argue against "peace" in a propaganda campaign. Moreover, America's superiority in atomic weaponry and its commanding overall geopolitical position made Eisenhower loathe to endorse Soviet campaigns for nuclear disarmament and neutralism. Instead, the administration tried to emphasize the peaceful uses of atomic energy, an effort highlighted by Eisenhower's famous "Atoms for Peace" speech to the U.N. General Assembly in New York in December 1953 and by further campaigns for atmospheric test bans. All the while, U.S. officials pounded away on the theme that the communists sought to expand not by overt territorial conquest but by subversion, and that freedom-loving peoples everywhere must work to thwart them.

Their task was not made easier by the glaring gap between American practices and ideals, especially on the subject of race. Dulles realized early on that segregation practices in the United States were a "major international hazard," spoiling American efforts to win friends in Third World countries and giving the Soviets a propaganda advantage. Accordingly, when the U.S. attorney general appealed to the Supreme Court to strike down segregation in public schools, he underlined that the humiliation of dark-skinned diplomats—who were often refused service in whites-only sections of restaurants while visiting the States—"furnished grist for the Communist propaganda mills." This image problem was not helped after a U.S. nuclear test in the South Pacific in the spring of 1954 spewed lethal radiation on several hundred Marshall Islanders and the crew of a Japanese fishing boat, the *Lucky Dragon*, reviving terrible images in Asia of American nuclear brutality. So when the court banned public school segregation in *Brown v. Board of Education of Topeka*, the administration quickly broadcast news of the decision around the world in thirty-five languages on its Voice of America overseas radio network. It was not much, but the administration was eager to claim what little success it could.[39]

By radically expanding the American propaganda and public relations machine, the Eisenhower administration contributed to the trend in American Cold War policy of becoming more like the adversary. If NSC-68 responded to the Soviet Union's propensity for ideological power politics by coming up with an even more ambitious American version, the new campaign to win the hearts and minds of people everywhere resembled, if in a less cynical form, the Soviet tradition of political intrigue and agitprop. In this key respect, Eisenhower's new strategy of psychological warfare represented better than any other policy his administration's determination to wage total Cold War against the Soviet enemy.

By 1956, in sum, as their first term neared an end, Eisenhower and Dulles could claim success in their mission to expand and intensify the Cold War in more innovative, less expensive ways. The administration had used America's atomic superiority in a fashion Truman had rejected to intimidate both Mao Zedong's China and the new Soviet government, as well as to hold the line in Korea, Indochina, and the Taiwan Straits—or so Eisenhower and Dulles believed. It had used the old-fashioned techniques of political subversion and covert action to overthrow unfriendly governments, even ones that were hardly client states of the Soviet Union. It had identified the nonaligned movement not as a force to be welcomed in a world of containment and nationalism but as one to be strenuously opposed. And it had dedicated billions of dollars and the efforts of new government agencies to spread American propaganda around the world. In short, while avoiding direct military action, Eisenhower had expanded America's Cold War in order to contend more vociferously with the USSR, international communism more generally, and the left-wing and anticolonial nationalists that the Soviet Union had been cultivating since 1945.

Was he prepared to go farther? Would he now raise the stakes and use America's nuclear and economic superiority to confront the Soviet Union directly? Dulles had repeatedly suggested, in public and private, that this objective naturally followed. If coexistence with the Soviet Union was an immoral foreign policy—as both the president and his secretary of state had declared—and if the United States had successfully replaced containment in the Third World with an aggressive and dynamic offensive strategy, then why should the United States not use these techniques to take the Cold War right to the Soviet Union's doorstep, rather than simply containing communism's further spread?

Indeed, the administration's first-term policies pointed toward two ultimate objectives. On one hand, the United States should intensify its attempts to destroy neutralism and undermine hostile regimes in the Third World—in other words, to become more like an empire, demanding overt subservience from weaker states rather than letting them go their own way. On the other, Washington should take the Cold War more directly to the Soviet Union in the central theater of Europe, using its improved techniques of political warfare, together with its nuclear superiority, to begin the process of rolling back communism in eastern Europe and forcing a showdown with Moscow. There was no shortage of administration officials and politicians in Congress keen to make this happen.

Eisenhower began to shrink from this ambitious, dangerous strategy. In long debates with Dulles, he was coming around to the position that a bid for Cold War victory was too dangerous in a thermonuclear world. Then suddenly, in October 1956, right before the general election, the president faced two crises that put his position to the test.

From Suez to Budapest

Earlier in that year, Britain and France had hatched a plan with Israel to take the Suez Canal away from Egypt. In late October they set the operation into action. Simultaneously, Nikita Khrushchev, an earthy Russian, reared in the Ukraine, who the previous year had cemented his control over the post-Stalin Kremlin leadership, sent Red Army units to crack down ruthlessly on anti-Soviet rebels in Hungary. The aggressive Cold War stance that Eisenhower and Dulles had so far adopted clearly suggested that American should support its allies in their struggle against Egypt, whose leader, Nasser, had just received military aid from the USSR and had recognized Communist China. Even more did this approach dictate coming to the rescue of the fearless Hungarian rebels, who were quite literally taking on Soviet tanks with sticks and stones. On both occasions, Eisenhower chose the opposite course of action.

The Suez crisis was a complicated affair, originating in a burgeoning Egyptian nationalism, the rise of Israel as a regional power in the Middle East, and the gradual diminution of British and French power in world affairs.[40] Nasser, a towering figure in the pan-Arabic movement fighting against Western interests in the Middle East, vowed to expel Britain from the Suez Canal and Israel from Palestine. Eisenhower sought to tread a fine line, alienating neither the Arabs, who controlled valuable oil supplies, nor Israel, which had enjoyed the support of many American citizens since Truman's recognition of the Jewish state in 1948. But when Nasser declared neutrality in the Cold War during the summer of 1956 and made overtures to the Soviet Union and China, the president lost patience. He withdrew U.S. financial support for the Aswan Dam, a project to secure cheap electricity for the Nile River Valley.

The Egyptian leader hit back hard: he nationalized the Suez Canal, which had long been controlled by British and to a lesser extent French interests. Officials in London and Paris regarded Nasser's move as a direct challenge to long-standing colonial influence in that region and an economic catastrophe for influential British and French concerns. They drew up a plan with the Israeli government whereby Israel would invade the Suez region through the Sinai on the pretext of seizing territory used for attacks on the new Jewish state, whereupon France and Britain would move in under the transparent excuse of keeping the canal open for vital international commerce. A few months of diplomatic efforts failed to persuade Nasser to relent, and on October 29, just a few days before the American election, the Israelis struck. Two days later Britain commenced a bombing campaign against Egyptian forces near the canal zone, while the Israelis moved into Gaza and the port city of Sharm el Sheikh.[41]

Furious at what he regarded as a blatant act of neocolonialism, Khrushchev informed the British that continued attacks on the Soviet Union's new friend Egypt would force him to attack British and French cities with rockets, an act that might trigger a third world war. Eisenhower too was angry—but not at Moscow. Instead of siding with his three allies against the mercurial Nasser and the USSR, the president exerted severe economic and diplomatic pressure on the allies to abandon their campaign and leave the canal in Egyptian hands. While election day came and went, Eisenhower threatened British prime minister Anthony Eden with a run on the pound sterling, made plans for an embargo of Middle Eastern petroleum to Europe, and organized a freeze on private American funding for Israel. In other words, during the Suez crisis the United States acted effectively to achieve the same outcome that the Soviet Union had demanded: an end to hostilities directed against Egypt and the relinquishment of the canal.

The allies relented. For Britain and France, it was a geopolitical disaster of the first order, leading to the quick demise of the Eden government and the marked diminution of European influence in the Middle East. Not a few analysts have called the loss of the Suez the symbolic end of the British empire. As for Israel, this overt political defeat at the hands of a U.S. administration led the young nation's leaders, along with many of their conservative supporters in the United States, to take a more focused interest in American foreign policy.[42]

The unexpected American decision to confront its allies over the Suez Canal can be explained by several factors. Among the most important, certainly, was a determination to replace the Europeans as the major Western power in the Middle East, to stand up against Old World colonialism, and to secure its oil supply. When Eisenhower obtained a congressional resolution soon after his reelection suggesting that the United States regarded the Middle East as an area of vital national interest—a policy that soon became known as the Eisenhower Doctrine—he was only affirming the reality that the West, especially Europe, had by 1956 become dependent on cheap Middle Eastern oil. In this respect at least, America's Middle East policy resembled that of a traditional great power interested in acquiring cheap material resources from stable client regimes, more or less irrespective of ideology. Quite possibly, the United States would have developed a similar policy toward the Middle East even if the Soviet Union had not existed.[43]

What distinguished American actions in the region from those of a traditional great power was Eisenhower's simultaneous desire to avoid conflict with the Soviet Union. In earlier eras, an American president might have sided with Britain, France, and Israel not only to seize control of Suez but also to parlay that victory into a larger imposition of Western power over the oil-producing countries, as had been done by imperial powers in the nineteenth and early twentieth centuries. That kind of approach seemed to grow naturally from the aggressive Third World policies the administration had been pursuing over the past few years. But Eisenhower's careful diplomacy during the Suez crisis indicated that he regarded old-fashioned gunboat imperialism in the Middle East as excessively dangerous. It would alienate nonaligned and other Arab regimes America was trying to attract, of that there could be no doubt. But more important to the president, it ran too great a risk of major war. The United States would continue to safeguard its supply of inexpensive oil in the Middle East, but not in ways that would antagonize the Soviet Union. If that practice meant defying its traditional allies in order to establish credibility among Arab states and avoid military escalation, so be it.

If Suez indicated that Eisenhower was becoming more cautious in a thermonuclear age, American inaction during the Hungarian uprising confirmed it. At precisely the time that the Suez crisis was slipping into outright warfare, Khrushchev opted to crack down brutally on political rebellion in Budapest. Earlier in the year he had taken the unprecedented step of denouncing Stalin's repressive rule and cult of personality and had announced a "de-Stalinization" campaign. Thousands of opponents of the corrupt client regime in the Hungarian capital took his words to heart and rose up in an attempt to overthrow the government and reject Soviet domination of their nation. Many counted on receiving American support, just as Radio Free Europe, broadcast throughout eastern Europe, implied. But when the Soviet tanks moved into Budapest, crushing the uprising and installing a new and completely subservient government, the United States did nothing.

In the three-day conflict 22,000 Hungarians and 2,300 Soviet soldiers died or were wounded. Senior U.S. officials, including Eisenhower and Dulles, denounced the Soviet behavior, but the president ruled out the military response that conservative critics and representatives of eastern European interest groups demanded. Even Democrats chided the administration for talking about "liberation" yet refusing to act. Hungary, the president retorted, was "as inaccessible to us as Tibet." The use of nuclear weapons was out of the question: "To annihilate Hungary . . . is no way to help her."[44]

What neither Eisenhower nor his aides fully understood at the time is that Khrushchev's action was borne out of deep concern over the fragility of the communist bloc. He and his Kremlin colleagues worried that the Hungarian revolution would spread into other states in eastern Europe—Czechoslovakia and Romania were particularly vulnerable—and possibly into the USSR itself, causing the entire edifice to come tumbling down. Anti-Soviet protests had broken out in the Soviet republic of Georgia in recent months, and demonstrations in favor of the Hungarians had been staged at Moscow State University. While the Republican right and its journalistic allies at William F. Buckley's *National Review* could wax indignant about the Hungarian invasion being proof of the USSR's global designs, on the contrary it demonstrated nothing so much as the weakness of the Soviet system. It showed the extent of popular opposition both to the communist regime in Budapest and the Kremlin's role in eastern Europe.[45]

The Divergence

Eisenhower's policies with respect to Suez and Hungary had broad support within his administration, including from John Foster Dulles. In the case of the Suez crisis, the secretary of state was incensed by the duplicitous actions of Britain and France, and he actively endorsed Eisenhower's decision to force the two nations to end their colonial adventure. On Hungary he felt differently. He certainly did not advocate responding to the Soviet crackdown by initiating major war, but America's failure to answer such brazen repression in the heart of Europe tormented him. There must be some way, Dulles thought, for the United States to contend with the Soviet Union even in the thermonuclear age.[46]

And this age had definitely dawned. In 1955 the White House received top-secret reports from the CIA and other departments stating that the Soviet Union now possessed a substantial arsenal of multi-megaton nuclear bombs and that it would probably attain intercontinental missiles to deliver these weapons by about 1958. This meant, quite simply, that in the event of superpower war the United States, along with its allies in western Europe and Asia, could be hit by thermonuclear attacks that would kill tens of millions of people.[47] A highly classified study commissioned by Eisenhower in late 1956 made this point clear. It showed that, once the Soviet Union obtained a large missile arsenal, an all-out nuclear war would kill or seriously injure fifty million Americans (about a third of the population at the time) and destroy the country's social and political institutions. The United States as it had existed would be no more. It would be, Eisenhower said, a "business of digging ourselves out of ashes, starting again."[48]

The implications were hard to miss. In the near future, a general war with the Soviet Union—like World War II—would be an absurdity. Any attempt to defend the United States through total war would destroy it. If the administration's first responsibility was to safeguard America, it had to find a way to prevent this calamity from occurring. The strategist Bernard Brodie predicted this turn of events soon after Hiroshima and Nagasaki: "Thus far," he wrote in 1946, "the chief purpose of our military establishment has been to win wars. From now on its chief purpose must be to avert them. It can have almost no other useful purpose."[49] This truth was coming home to the Eisenhower administration. But what was to be done?

The first order of business—and here Eisenhower and Dulles were in full accord—was to build an airtight deterrent. Accordingly, in early 1955 Eisenhower authorized the Pentagon to build new strategic nuclear weaponry to be deployed by land, sea, and air and to construct new advance-warning detection systems, to be run by the Strategic Air Command. His reason for commissioning this new system was simple: he sought to deter the Soviet Union from ever launching a first strike against American soil. As long as the United States possessed a nuclear strikeforce sufficiently large that it could not be reliably destroyed by a Soviet first strike, only a Kremlin bent on self-destruction would ever initiate a new world war. Thus was born the perverse logic of Mutual Assured Destruction (MAD).[50]

Eisenhower authorized the building of the nuclear triad to deter the Soviets from launching a sudden first strike, a "bolt from the blue." It would prevent another world war from beginning in that fashion, as long as the men in the Kremlin did not go insane. By the end of the 1950s, therefore, the United States deployed an arsenal that included thousands of nuclear weapons. This policy of overkill reflected Eisenhower's determination to foreclose any possibility that the Soviets might ever consider a first strike, while revealing as well his inclination to appease hardline critics demanding ever more American military power.[51] But no matter how many nuclear bombs the United States built, the possibility of nuclear war remained. The enduring problem, one that Eisenhower and Dulles had long discerned, was how the United States should respond to a smaller crisis. What if the Soviet Union invaded West Berlin, for example, or if China attacked Taiwan? What should the United States do now that a regional conflict could escalate into a thermonuclear war?

It was on precisely this point that the president and the secretary of state began to diverge. Dulles's view of this emerging dilemma reflected his belief that the United States must maintain firm pressure on an illegitimate Soviet state. The secretary of state argued that total war, once the two sides had sufficient bombs and missiles, was no longer a rational option. What was the purpose of waging a struggle that would destroy both sides beyond recognition? Not only would such a war constitute an immorality of the greatest conceivable order; it would also become an increasingly implausible response to aggression. The communists in the Kremlin would naturally conclude that the United States would never risk such a war to defend its allies in Europe and Asia. Armed with thermonuclear missiles, the Soviets could therefore commence a gradual expansion into these regions, Dulles feared, aware that Washington would be too terrified to respond. The thermonuclear dilemma threatened to undo containment and eventually lead to a Soviet victory.

To prevent such a disastrous outcome, Dulles insisted that the United States must develop military strategies that could allow it to defend its allies in Europe and Asia without triggering total nuclear war. By enhancing America's conventional military presence on the Eurasian landmass and devising strategies for a limited nuclear engagement, Washington could wage a war with the Soviet Union without destroying Western civilization. Such a strategy would affirm American credibility with key allies by assuring them that the United States would come to their defense. They could be confident that NATO had not become a suicide pact. But time was of the essence: American military policy had to be upgraded now so as to avoid being frozen by fear of total nuclear war. In 1954 and 1955, during tense White House debates, many military advisers to the president sided with Dulles. Without a substantial upgrade of America's conventional military power, Air Force chief of staff Arthur Radford proclaimed, "at some time or other the Soviet Union will elect to force the issue."[52]

Eisenhower saw the logic in the Dulles argument, but his experiences during World War II and his philosophical grasp of the nature of major war led him to reject it. Would it be better to wage a limited war with the Soviet Union than to blow up the planet? Obviously. Would it be better to put forward a military policy that could assure U.S. allies in Europe and Asia? That went without saying. Would a dynamic military policy play to America's advantages, as it had before? Yes again. But the problem with all of these reasonable objectives was that they presumed a war with the USSR could be contained. Eisenhower thought otherwise. During his time as supreme commander in World War II, he had presided over an allied military strategy that progressed, inexorably, toward total war with the Nazi adversary. If the United States and the Soviet Union commenced hostilities, the same escalation would happen again, of that the president felt certain.

Thus the problem with the claims by Dulles, Radford, and other officials, including Army Chief of Staff Maxwell Taylor, that a Soviet-American war could be kept limited: it could not. Should the Soviets decide to go to war, Eisenhower lectured an incredulous Taylor at the White House on May 24, 1956,

> the pressure on them to use atomic weapons in a sudden blow would be extremely great. He [Eisenhower] did not see any basis for thinking other than that they would use these weapons at once, and in full force. . . . To him the question was simply one of a war between the United States and the USSR, and in this he felt the thinking should be based upon the use of atomic weapons—that in his opinion it was fatuous to think that the U.S. and the USSR would be locked into a life and death struggle without using such weapons.[53]

In the president's mind, the reality was stark. The United States and the Soviet Union had both recently experienced absolute, life-or-death wars and had witnessed these conflicts escalate, unstoppably, toward total war. Both nations knew that this is what happens when titans lock forces in battle. So what was the point of developing strategies of limited nuclear or conventional wars when the Russians, if pressed to the wall, would fire back with everything they had? It was "fatuous," Eisenhower told the head of the U.S. Army, to think otherwise. Hence developing strategies of limited war was pointless. More than that, it was dangerous. If the United States deployed weapons to wage such wars and developed doctrines to fight them, then when a crisis arose with the USSR, American leaders could regard recourse to limited war as a thinkable option. In other words, if limited wars were destined to escalate to total war, having a strategy of limited war in place would actually make total war more likely. The only solution, therefore, was to develop a new military policy of all-or-nothing nuclear war, not so much to deter the Soviet Union as to give military and civilian leaders in the United States no reason to believe that a limited war was possible.[54]

In 1957, following his second convincing election victory over Adlai Stevenson, Eisenhower pushed through the National Security Council precisely such a policy. He demanded that the NSC eliminate sections of its basic policy that envisioned limited nuclear war or conventional war with the Soviet Union and replace them with sections stipulating that any war with the USSR would be total nuclear war. He rejected military requests for limited nuclear war weaponry, and he cut the budget for spending on conventional forces. He personally informed civilian and military advisers that in the event of armed hostilities with the USSR, he would commence a general nuclear attack. From now on, it was all-or-nothing: in a serious Cold War crisis, both sides would compromise, or everyone would die.[55]

Sputnik America

In short, by 1957 the world's two superpowers were threatening to blow up the planet. They were deploying thermonuclear megaton weaponry (equal to millions of tons of TNT, as compared with the kilotons of atomic fission bombs) against one another, and anyone who had paid attention during the first half of the twentieth century could have little confidence that the bombs would not eventually go off.

And if they did go off? More and more in the late 1950s, nuclear strategists contemplated that question, envisioning what a nuclear war might really be like. One of these "wizards of Armageddon," Herman Kahn of the RAND Corporation, in an astonishing book called *On Thermonuclear War,* speculated giddily on the effects of thermonuclear attack on American society and the ways a new order might emerge afterward. One of the strategies he discussed, an immediate retaliation to Soviet attack with every American weapon available, he called a "wargasm."[56] Somewhat more soberly, Henry Kissinger of Harvard University argued, *contra* Eisenhower, that it was just as possible to wage limited war in the nuclear age as it had been before, and moreover that Washington would have to develop a strategy of waging and winning such a war if it expected to prevail in the Cold War. An intensely ambitious academic who hungered for access to political power, Kissinger calculated that a dense body of work making a detailed, scholarly case for limited nuclear war might attract the attention of leading Democrats in Washington.

And indeed, Kissinger's 1957 book *Nuclear Weapons and Foreign Policy*, despite being riddled with elementary errors and inconsistencies, won plaudits from leading Democrats anxious for prestigious scholarly ammunition with which to attack the president's foreign policy.[57] They had been on the defensive for close to a decade, since Truman allegedly "lost China"; here was a chance to turn the tables. A key figure among them, Senator John F. Kennedy of Massachusetts, was photographed carrying a copy of the book. He and other Senate Democratic hawks such as Stuart Symington of Missouri and Henry Jackson of Washington, when informed about Eisenhower's new policy by sympathetic figures in the military, began to criticize the president's position. Industrialists and military leaders, especially in the traditional services, could likewise be heard making grumbling noises. Some of them began to channel funds and offer support to the Democratic Party.[58]

This trickle of criticism turned into a downpour following the Soviet Union's test of its unmanned *Sputnik* satellite in October 1957. *Sputnik* (short for *Sputnik Zemlya,* Companion of Earth) suggested to an alarmed American public that the Soviet Union might be well ahead in the race to build nuclear missiles. It raised the specter of a scientifically advanced USSR moving past a decadent and lazy America. Jackson, whose state was home to the nation's largest military contractor, Boeing, called for a "national week of shame and danger." Pressured by events, Eisenhower appointed an independent committee (later known as the Gaither Committee) to investigate America's strategic vulnerability and the possibility of Soviet superiority. The committee's report, drafted primarily by Paul Nitze, recommended an immediate and radical military buildup lest the Soviet Union attain an overwhelming advantage. Eisenhower also signaled his approval of the National Defense Education Act, which began pumping $2 billion a year into the "battle of brainpower." The act funded new elementary and high school programs in mathematics, foreign languages, and the sciences, and subsidized construction costs and student loans on college campuses. By 1960 the federal budget provided 20 percent of university operating expenses nationwide.[59]

But the Democrats had their issue, and they played it for all it was worth. As 1958 dawned, they proclaimed the existence of a "missile gap" between a declining America and a confident, aggressive Soviet Union.[60] Senator Kennedy compared the situation to Europe in 1940 when "the Germans achieved victory not because of the overall scale of her military force relative to France's and Britain's but because of her development of a new *blitzkrieg* technique built around mobile tanks and dive-bombers."[61] Eisenhower knew that the alarmism was misplaced and that the claims of a missile gap were totally bogus. According to U.S. intelligence, it was the United States that possessed, and would continue to hold, a substantial advantage over the Soviet Union in all categories of nuclear weaponry. But he could not announce this fact publicly, for fear of drawing Moscow's attention to American intelligence sources. Furthermore, the president was determined to maintain his new all-or-nothing nuclear strategy in the face of intense private and public criticism. If that meant accepting new military programs and commissioning independent committees, he considered it an acceptable price to pay. In short order, he called for an increase in defense spending.

The irony was thick. Eisenhower and Dulles had risen to office by brazenly attacking what they saw as Truman's weak and passive Cold War foreign policy; now the Democrats had found a way to turn the tables against them. Eisenhower's political agonies only worsened in December, when America's answer to *Sputnik,* the *Vanguard* satellite, exploded on the launch pad. Many Republicans began to distance themselves from the president as the 1958 midterm elections beckoned. That included his vice president, Richard Nixon, who had eyes on the Oval Office himself.[62] Eisenhower, however, was becoming less and less interested in partisan politics. For one thing, he was prohibited by law from seeking a third term. For another, he had found a cause—avoiding nuclear war—that transcended electoral grandstanding and drew directly on his strengths as a politically adroit statesman. Others could play politics; he would make sure America did not spend its way into oblivion and that the world did not blow up.

In adopting this posture, he had a quiet ally in George Kennan, who himself had long lamented the influence of domestic politics on American foreign policy and who had left government service to commence a distinguished academic career as a diplomatic historian at the Institute for Advanced Study in Princeton. On his own accord, Kennan was beginning to reach the same conclusions as Eisenhower. The idea that nuclear war could be limited or useful was insane, he now wrote, a dehumanized abstraction in which "everything else, including all normal political purposes and calculations, pales into insignificance." On the contrary, a war between the two sides could be "the final episode of our civilization."[63]

Neither Eisenhower nor Kennan knew it, but the Cold War was about to enter a new phase, a five-year crisis period in which the United States and the Soviet Union would come so very close to starring in that final episode.

5

THE NUCLEAR RUBICON

The year 1958 began inauspiciously for the Eisenhower administration. The Democrats were on the offensive on foreign policy, keen to reverse their fortunes after successive defeats in the elections of 1952 and 1956. The Soviet Union, they charged, was moving decisively ahead of the United States in missile technology, with disastrous implications for American security.[1] Some academic strategists, meanwhile, accused the administration of gross negligence, while economists claimed it was inviting a recession by refusing to spend more on the military. Astute political observers, among them senator and likely presidential contender John F. Kennedy, recognized that a winning coalition could be built upon these grievances, and upon the obvious remedy: a new military buildup that would not only overcome the Soviets' supposed superiority but also recharge the American economy. In this atmosphere Eisenhower's repeated, if quiet, insistence that the United States actually held the lead disappeared unheeded into the political winds.

The president also felt pressure from inside the administration. His senior foreign policy and military advisers, led by the ailing secretary of state, John Foster Dulles, found his new all-or-nothing nuclear policy dangerous in the extreme and certain to alienate close allies in Europe and Asia. Several top military figures, including especially Army Chief of Staff Maxwell Taylor, regarded the president's new policy as virtual surrender. A bookish soldier-intellectual, Taylor would soon leave office, write a book denouncing the administration's policies, and join forces with the Democrats.[2] Even Eisenhower's vice president, Richard Nixon, himself a presidential aspirant, publicly hinted at some doubts about the new policy. On the matter of basic Cold War foreign policy, Eisenhower by this point stood almost alone.

He held his ground. He had begun his presidency with the intention of waging the Cold War with more determination and innovation than the Truman administration had, while at the same time avoiding expensive, Korea-type wars. That policy appealed to a Republican base eager to fight communism worldwide but averse to large military commitments and high government spending. Eisenhower would persist with one aspect of this policy until the end of his presidency: dirty covert actions to undermine unfriendly or nonaligned governments in the Third World, including, most notably, Achmed Sukarno's regime in Indonesia. But toward the end of his first term he began to reassess his larger Cold War strategy of using American nuclear superiority to take the offensive against the USSR, as he considered what a major war with the Soviet Union would mean in an age of nuclear missiles. By 1957, avoiding nuclear war had become his main strategic preoccupation; in the event of an acute superpower crisis, diplomacy and compromise would have to prevail over hostility and violence. Secure in the knowledge that the United States remained militarily superior to the Soviet Union (by 1960 the U.S. nuclear stockpile would reach almost 20,000 warheads, compared with 1,600 for the USSR, and the new nuclear-equipped Polaris submarines would be ready) and confident that Soviet leader Nikita Khrushchev also grasped the meaning of war in the thermonuclear age, Eisenhower hoped in his final three years in office to preside over a period of superpower stability.

It didn't quite turn out like that. In the summer of 1958 China reignited a second confrontation over the disputed Quemoy-Matsu island chain. This incident inaugurated a four-and-a-half year period during which the Cold War came close to exploding into thermonuclear war—making this the most dangerous era in all of human history. Five crises of these years stand out, together with a sixth event inextricably linked to them, the election of 1960. The United States pursued other foreign policies from the summer of 1958 to late 1962, some of which rose to the forefront in later periods, but over these four years the specter of a third world war dominated White House considerations of its Cold War strategy. Many informed observers were sure that a nuclear conflagration was coming and that the human race was doomed. In October 1962, during the Cuban Missile Crisis, that moment seemed to have come, and the world held its breath. Yet the two sides managed to avoid war. Their leaders kept their wits about them when it counted most.

The Second Quemoy-Matsu Crisis

The first of the four crises occurred in 1958, when those now-familiar minuscule islands in the Taiwan Straits—Matsu and the chain known as Quemoy—returned to international attention. Little by little during the first months of the year, Mao Zedong's People's Republic of China began to denounce the continued possession of Quemoy-Matsu by the "American lackeys" in Taiwan. Four years had passed since the first crisis in the straits, and Beijing leaders were frustrated by the continued intransigence of Chiang Kai-shek's government—and by his efforts, following the earlier crisis, to bolster his military presence on the islands. With the United States having signed a mutual defense treaty with Chiang's government, Mao also sought to determine Washington's real intentions toward the island, and in addition he hoped to use a renewed confrontation to drum up revolutionary zeal among Chinese as part of his emerging Great Leap Forward domestic campaign. Accordingly, Beijing again demanded that the small islands, much closer to the mainland than to Taiwan, be returned to Chinese control.

The possession of the island chain by Taiwan did not make much strategic sense, but Chiang had made a point of seizing them as a means of defying the communist regime, and both Truman and Eisenhower, wary of antagonizing the Taipei regime's fervent supporters on Capitol Hill, had long pledged to support him.[3] Mao's ultimate intentions were unclear to Washington, but if he attempted to take the islands by force, the National Security Council had a contingency plan to stop him. According to NSC planning document No. 5723, it would be impossible to defend Quemoy-Matsu against a large Chinese invasion with conventional forces. The U.S. Seventh Fleet would move to guard the island chain, but as Gerard Smith, director of the Policy Planning Staff, reported in a follow-up memo, current war plans envisioned responding to a major Chinese attack with "nuclear strikes deep into Communist China," resulting in "millions of non-combatant casualties." This in turn would likely bring a major Soviet retaliation in defense of its ally, in the form of nuclear strikes against Taiwan and the U.S. Seventh Fleet. "Under our present strategic concept," Smith wrote, "this would be the signal for general nuclear war between the U.S. and the U.S.S.R."[4]

Just like that, Eisenhower's new nuclear policies were being put to the test. If the Chinese invaded the tiny islands—barely more than rocks jutting out of the South China Sea—America's official policy was to respond with a nuclear attack that, according to U.S. estimates, would initiate global thermonuclear war. Behind the scenes, Eisenhower had devised his policies so that, in the event of a serious Cold War showdown, he would have to push matters toward compromise and away from military conflict. Quemoy-Matsu, which the United States defended largely for domestic political purposes, was an unexpected venue for the first implementation of his strategy, but he now had no choice but to follow through. On August 23 China began shelling the sparsely populated islands with artillery. No one could know whether these attacks foreshadowed a general invasion, but Chiang Kai-shek begged the White House to back his armies in a campaign to retake the mainland. Senior American military officials, both on the scene and in Washington, likewise demanded a military response, preferably with nuclear weapons.[5] Eisenhower refused, stating publicly that the United States would come to the defense of *Taiwan*— not the islands alone—and denying requests for military action.

Dulles had spent months strenuously objecting to Eisenhower's nuclear policies, going so far as to dissent from his president in the pages of *Foreign Affairs*.[6] He believed that the United States should prepare to fight limited nuclear war, not because he sought such a war but because he was convinced that Ike's all-or-nothing policy would demoralize American allies and give the initiative to a ravenous and ruthless USSR. In this case, however, he agreed with Eisenhower's decision. Getting into a war over Quemoy-Matsu made no sense to him. Even if the fighting did not escalate into general thermonuclear war, the use of atomic weapons would terrify American allies in the Cold War theater that mattered much more in his eyes: Europe. There was no alternative but to cut a deal with the Chinese. On September 4, following secret conversations with Eisenhower, the secretary of state communicated to the British ambassador that the United States might be amenable to a plan to demilitarize the islands as long as Beijing recognized them as Nationalist possessions. Unlike America, Great Britain had normal diplomatic relations with Beijing and could make sure the message got through.

The Chinese were responsive. On September 6 premier and foreign minister Zhou Enlai announced his government's willingness to commence talks with the United States. Two weeks of haggling ensued, whereupon delegates from the United States, China, and Taiwan met in Warsaw to work out an arrangement. Over the rest of September, while the diplomats negotiated, China maintained its daily bombing campaign. On October 6 the communist government and Taipei announced a ceasefire, even though Quemoy-Matsu had not been demilitarized—as new documentation shows, this was probably due to Soviet pressure on Beijing not to escalate the conflict as long as Taiwan and the United States held their fire.[7]

In one of the many geopolitical curiosities of the Cold War, China indicated that it would respect the demands of its Soviet ally, but only halfway: in late October the communist regime recommenced its artillery bombardment *on every other day.* By that time, however, the United States had extricated itself from the conflict. The Chinese governments on either side of the Taiwan Straits would have to learn to live with the bizarre, unresolved situation. Beijing's alternate-day bombings of the islands continued into the 1970s, and Quemoy artisans made a profitable business by forging iron implements from the spent Chinese shells.

The Eisenhower administration's behavior during the second Quemoy-Matsu crisis alarmed the British, who wondered whether the White House had actually been willing to risk global war over the tiny islands in the South China Sea. Foreign Minister Selwyn Lloyd traveled to Washington in the middle of September and listened in horror as Dulles calmly told him that the United States had indeed been ready to use nuclear weapons in the crisis.[8] Lloyd then discussed the matter with Eisenhower himself. The British, Lloyd stated, were terrified at the thought that the Americans might start a war over such small stakes. The president reassured him. If the United States were to use nuclear weapons, he said, it would be "in an all-out effort rather than a local effort." And he had no plans, Eisenhower continued, "to use nuclear weapons in any local situation at the present time." The foreign minister left the Oval Office in a better mood.[9]

Berlin Ultimatum

The actions of the United States also received close scrutiny in Moscow. Khrushchev could see that the Americans were behaving differently. In 1955 Eisenhower and Dulles brandished atomic threats over Quemoy-Matsu, but three years later they hurriedly cut a deal with the hated Chinese. That raised the possibility of further adventures. For thirteen years, the West had rubbed the Russian nose in the dirt by keeping its forces in Berlin, deep inside East Germany, despite the cemented division of the nation. But this particular locale had far larger geopolitical importance. Khrushchev decided to force the issue.

In November 1958 the Soviet leader declared it was time to resolve once and for all the abnormal situation in the city. The occupying powers, he demanded during a Polish-Soviet "friendship rally," must turn control of the city over to East Germany. No one doubted his motivation: the island of West Berlin served as a continuing source of aggravation to the Kremlin and as a practical nightmare for its client state in East Germany. For one thing, it symbolized America's earlier Cold War superiority in Europe, when the Soviet Union could do nothing about the West's determination to remain in Berlin. In addition, it was a destination for thousands of East Germans and other East Europeans, most of them educated and highly skilled, who had had enough of the workers' paradise and found it easy to defect to the West simply by walking into West Berlin. For Khrushchev, Berlin was "a bone in my throat."[10]

Moreover, the Kremlin leader believed he had cards to play. He had committed himself over the past two years to transforming his nation into a genuine superpower. In 1956 he had denounced Stalinism, demanded that the USSR modernize and rationalize its economy, and abandoned the idea of immediate global revolution. "Peaceful coexistence" was now the Soviet policy, and Khrushchev aimed to defeat the United States by outperforming it economically and scientifically. It was a long shot, given America's vast superiority in these fields, but Khrushchev believed that in the nuclear age he had no choice. A continuation of Stalinism at home and radicalism abroad would bankrupt the nation and quite possibly lead to a nuclear war that would destroy socialism forever.[11]

And Khrushchev made progress. By 1958 the Soviet premier had reason to believe that his nation was no longer an inferior power. *Sputnik* had demonstrated that, as had Eisenhower's trepidation over Quemoy and Matsu. Khrushchev's demand for an end to the occupation of Berlin therefore was not an empty request but an ultimatum: the Western powers had to leave by May 1959, or else. The Quemoy-Matsu crisis, as dangerous as it was, was not started by the Soviet Union. The Kremlin's prestige had not been directly on the line. Berlin was different. Get out of the city within six months, the Soviet premier demanded, or face the prospect of war.

For Eisenhower, the Berlin ultimatum raised the stakes of his all-or-nothing gamble. Conciliation was possible over the offshore islands, but how could he compromise on Berlin? Since the days of Truman's airlift, the United States had made West Berlin a focal point in the center of Europe—the city was the very symbol of America's commitment to European defense. On some level it made no sense to continue to occupy a defeated capital some thirteen years after the war had ended—Eisenhower privately admitted it was an "abnormal situation." But there it was, a product not of domestic lobbying so much as geopolitical symbolism. Current American policy was clear: if the USSR tried to force the West out of the Berlin, the United States would respond with general war. Dulles declared immediately after Khrushchev's speech that the

Western alliance depended on this commitment, for if the United States folded over Berlin, western Europeans would no longer be able to count on Washington to defend them. American credibility would be fatally undermined.

Because no one in the White House was willing to question the importance of Berlin, and because Khrushchev had put forward a simple six-month ultimatum, Eisenhower had little room to maneuver. He could not get around the commitment to prevent the loss of West Berlin, and his new military policy implied that his only answer to a Soviet move to seize the city was to commence general nuclear war. With both military and civilian aides now urging him to commit to a concrete plan for the day the Red Army advanced on Berlin, Eisenhower groped to find another way.

In March the British government threw the president a lifeline. Prime Minister Harold Macmillan traveled to the United States to express horror at the idea that the administration might begin a new world war over West Berlin. In the event of war, "eight bombs" could put an end to Great Britain, he said repeatedly. Echoing Churchill's earlier concerns, Macmillan wondered how the United States could even think of initiating a conflagration over an issue like this, when it could lead to the disappearance of Britain. Surely Berlin didn't matter that much, considering how many years had passed since the war ended and considering it was the former capital of a nation that had tried twice to conquer Europe. If the United States insisted on fighting such a war, Macmillan said, his government would "need time to remove all their young children to Canada so as to keep their stock alive as against the total devastation of nuclear war." In one emotional meeting with Eisenhower on the evening of March 20, Macmillan wept.[12]

But the prime minister had an ace up his sleeve. NATO policy stipulated that no nation could initiate the use of nuclear weapons without the concurrence of all members. Macmillan, insisting that the United Kingdom could not endorse the resort to nuclear war without some attempt at a diplomatic solution, urged Eisenhower to invite Khrushchev to a summit meeting before the May deadline expired. This could defuse the crisis and pave the way to a general European agreement. Here was a perfect way for Eisenhower to escape his dilemma, except for one small problem: American policy dictated clearly that the United States would not negotiate under ultimatum. Eisenhower got around this by telling Macmillan that he would accept the Soviet invitation to convene a foreign ministers meeting, and that he would propose a summit if "there was even slight progress" at the talks.

In late March, the United States signaled its willingness to hold four-power talks on Berlin, and the May deadline passed without incident. In that month as well, Dulles succumbed to the stomach cancer he had been fighting for two years. Christian Herter replaced him, but in the short term Eisenhower was on his own. Despite the absence of "even slight progress" in the four-power discussions, he invited Khrushchev to visit the United States. He came in the fall, touring American farms and cities, sometimes noticeably stunned by the scale of American affluence.

At the end of the trip the two leaders met for a few days at the presidential retreat at Camp David, where Khrushchev promised not to issue another ultimatum on Berlin and informed the president of his determination to cut military spending. The tensions of the previous months were, for the moment, put aside, with a relieved Eisenhower having found a way secretly to conciliate the Kremlin and a contented Khrushchev delighted to reciprocate. The two heads of state agreed to convene a grand summit in Paris, to be held in the spring or summer of 1960. Perhaps the two superpowers could now engage in real negotiations that might lighten the thermonuclear shadow, and maybe even lead to a broad political settlement.

U-2 and the Collapse of the Paris Summit

It was not to be. An altercation intervened—at 70,000 feet. American CIA pilots had been penetrating Soviet airspace for years, in Lockheed U-2 aircraft designed to fly at extremely high altitude, too high for all but the latest Soviet anti-aircraft missiles. Once again, the United States was using its tremendous advantage in technology to gain an edge in the Cold War. Satellites and U-2 planes photographed large swaths of the Soviet interior, looking particularly for missile facilities and installations. Armed with such information, Washington could learn key information about the nature and extent of Soviet missile production and, more urgently, determine if the Kremlin was preparing for a first strike.

The photos revealed no such plan. They showed, rather, that the USSR's missile project, far from bounding dangerously ahead as the doomsayers charged, was well behind that of the United States. In early 1960, for example, a National Intelligence Estimate asserted that the United States possessed a clear lead, with the Soviet Union possessing only 100 or so operational nuclear missiles, as contrasted with several hundred on the American side. A second study, completed in August of that year and provided to Kennedy and other Democratic critics, indicated that the CIA and other intelligence agencies could not find *even one* operational Soviet ICBM facility. We now know that these top-secret studies actually exaggerated Soviet capabilities. The United States enjoyed a vast superiority over the USSR in every category of nuclear weaponry, even as critics of the White House were thundering on about imminent Soviet dominance.[13]

In late April, Eisenhower gave the go-ahead for another U-2 flight. With the summit scheduled to begin on May 15, some Washington analysts questioned whether it made sense to conduct a mission so close to Eisenhower's departure for Europe. Other officials saw it differently, including Richard Bissell, the CIA's head of clandestine operations, who pleaded with the reluctant president to authorize one last flight. The Kremlin was aware of the U-2 flights, after all, but not protesting against them for fear of admitting weakness. (What superpower cannot control its own skies?) No doubt the flights enraged Khrushchev, and no doubt little useful information would come from this last U-2 mission, but the risks were small. The planes normally flew too high for Soviet defenses, and were they to get lucky and shoot one down, almost certainly the plane and the lone pilot—in this case, CIA airman Francis Gary Powers—would not survive. Pilots carried with them a needle that offered instant suicide in the remote event they were captured alive. Eisenhower approved the mission, delayed by weather until May 1, the international workers' day and a major Soviet holiday.

Against all odds, the worst scenario occurred: the U-2 flight was shot down on the eve of the international summit, and the pilot survived. The Soviet missile aimed at the plane exploded just behind it, allowing Powers to eject safely and some of his plane to survive as wreckage. He chose not to use the needle. He was captured by villagers not far from the city of Sverdlovsk in the Urals and whisked quickly to Moscow. When Powers failed to return to base, the CIA knew that something had gone dreadfully wrong.[14]

The president, not yet knowing that Powers had survived, went along publicly with a CIA cover story that an American "weather plane" had accidentally strayed into Soviet territory. On May 7 Khrushchev announced via the Soviet press that an American airman had been captured, putting the lie to the weather plane tale. He demanded that the American president apologize for the treachery. Eisenhower now faced a dilemma. He could claim—and Khrushchev certainly wanted him to claim—that the flight had gone ahead without his knowledge. By doing so, the president could meet with his Soviet counterpart in Paris and then proceed with a planned visit to the Soviet Union, without the embarrassing scandal completely souring their negotiations.

But having already been caught in one lie, Eisenhower refused to utter a second one. Perhaps he was reluctant to give credence to the Soviet suspicion that "imperialist" circles in the United States wanted to derail the summit. He also might have wanted to deflect accusations that he was out of touch, no longer in control of things at the White House. More likely, remembering from his days as a military officer the credo that a real leader does not place the blame on subordinates, he was unwilling to make the CIA a scapegoat for a decision he had authorized. In any event, Eisenhower refused to apologize for the U-2 flight or claim it had occurred without his approval. Khrushchev saw this as a personal slight. The Paris summit began as scheduled on May 15 but the truculent Soviet leader, following a few hours of unpleasant formalities, headed into the French countryside, helped himself to large quantities of local red wine, and announced that the Soviet delegation was returning home. The Paris summit, and with it hopes for a broader relaxation of the Cold War, collapsed.[15]

Kennedy vs. Nixon

The failed Paris summit took place only eight months before Eisenhower's departure from office. In that period he would make no further attempt to deal with Khrushchev or to alter American Cold War strategy. More and more as the year progressed, foreign policy moved largely from the realm of Eisenhower's secret maneuverings to the open and messy spectacle of domestic politics.

The Democratic candidate for the presidency, John F. Kennedy, had long believed that a sustained attack on Eisenhower's Cold War was the surest route to the White House, particularly given that his opponent in the race was Vice President Richard Nixon.

Kennedy's main pollster, Louis Harris, repeatedly stressed this point as the campaign hurtled toward election day. The vice president should be put on the defensive, in order to force him to admit that the United States was slipping behind in the superpower struggle for mastery. If Nixon refused to concede the point, Harris emphasized, he could then be hit with the charge that he was dangerously naive. If, on the other hand, he accepted the claim that Moscow had surged ahead, he would be acknowledging that the Republicans, including himself as vice president, had failed. It was a foolproof line of attack. Kennedy resorted to it over and over again during the fall of 1960.[16]

Scion of a prominent Boston family, graduate of Choate and Harvard, the aristocratic Kennedy had been groomed for high office since his youth, if not initially as high as his older brother Joseph Jr., who was killed in World War II. Following distinguished service in the Pacific in the war, the handsome young man— backed heavily by his wealthy father, Joseph Kennedy, a liquor importer during Prohibition in the 1920s and U.S. ambassador to Britain in the 1930s—won a seat in the House of Representatives and then the U.S. Senate. Now he stood on the cusp of attaining the highest office in the land. Sensing Republican weakness and keen to demonstrate his own toughness, Kennedy attacked on every front. He accused the administration of neglecting relations with Third World nations, especially those in the Western Hemisphere. He suggested that Eisenhower was bound by a conservative, lethargic attitude toward the Soviet Union and international communism, ironically echoing many of the charges Eisenhower and Dulles themselves had leveled against Democrats in their 1952 campaign. Influenced by the many strategists hoping to attach themselves to his presidency, the senator advocated a more flexible Cold War military policy, enhanced by much higher spending on conventional forces and weapons useful for waging limited nuclear war. Eisenhower's all-or-nothing nuclear policy, Kennedy charged, forced the United States to choose, in the event of crisis, between "holocaust and humiliation."

As if that were not enough, the Kennedy campaign also accused the Eisenhower-Nixon team of allowing the Soviet Union to establish a lead in nuclear missile production—creating a "missile gap" which, if left unchallenged, could allow the USSR to achieve clear military superiority over the United States in the near future. Not only did JFK have no credible evidence for this charge; he had been given top-secret intelligence demonstrating that the missile gap actually vastly favored the United States.[17] Kennedy chose to disbelieve the intelligence, or disregard it, in order to press home the alarmist message that the United States, under Eisenhower's leadership, was on the verge of falling under Soviet military domination. In other words, Kennedy ran on the claim that the United States was falling dangerously behind the Soviet Union in the one category that still truly mattered—nuclear deterrence— even though he possessed clear evidence that the United States held the lead.[18]

Of course, short of traveling to Russia and counting the missiles himself, Kennedy could not know for certain that the missile gap did not exist, but the evidence Eisenhower provided was as definitive as he could obtain. Accepting the president's assurances of American superiority, however, would mean losing a lethal campaign weapon. This the senator would not do. Though the private Kennedy was not a reflexive Cold Warrior—he was a cautious, quite cynical pragmatist—that was the image he now sought to project. He and his aides were aware that Nixon had made his name in national politics as a demagogic anti-communist, and they knew all too well how effectively Republicans had used the "soft on Communism" charge against Democrats in recent elections. In 1960 the Democrats proved themselves quite willing to take these tactics to a new level.

And it worked. As the historian Christopher Preble has shown, by stressing that he would redress the supposed missile gap and in general beef up the American military after years of neglect, Kennedy gained the support of many voters, and donors, who might otherwise have supported Nixon. He campaigned heavily in districts that had lost jobs in defense industries and solicited contributions from aerospace contractors. Voters in industrial regions of the northeast and Pacific coast that relied heavily on military spending turned out for him. On Election Day Kennedy won in an extremely close race, defeating Nixon by very narrow margins in several key states. All other things being equal, had he not exaggerated American military weakness and peddled false charges about a missile gap, he probably would have lost. "The missile gap issue," as Preble concludes, "worked for Democrats."[19]

A Farewell Address

All eyes were now on the youthful president-elect, but Eisenhower still had one more turn on center stage. Three days before Kennedy's inauguration he delivered one of the most striking farewell addresses in American history, as notable perhaps as Washington's in 1796.

The president had grown alarmed by the relentless pressure on him to expand the military budget and threaten nuclear war, especially during the last years of his administration. He had spent billions on America's nuclear arsenal, to ensure beyond any doubt that the Soviet Union would never attack unless it wished to commit national suicide. He had held the line in Southeast Asia, Central America, and elsewhere, working to prevent communist advancement through every manner of covert action and subversion, but always avoiding war. Moreover, he had achieved these objectives without sacrificing the life of a single American soldier.[20] Yet critics from academia, labor unions, the Democratic Party, arms industries, and—what incensed him the most—the uniformed military continued to demand more spending, more weapons, more confrontation. In an earlier day this was bad enough, but now, in the nuclear age, such belligerence threatened all of civilization. Eisenhower determined that he must speak out.

With the help of Malcolm Moos, a former political scientist at Johns Hopkins University recently appointed as a White House speechwriter, Eisenhower produced a speech that had one central aim: to alert the American people to the dangers of the "military-industrial complex," the alliance of interest groups who benefited from endless growth in military spending and endless confrontation overseas. Ralph Williams, another speechwriter called in to assist with the drafting, noted in an internal memo: "For the first time in its history, the United States has a permanent war-based industry. Not only that, but flag and general officers retiring at an early age take positions in a war-based industrial complex, shaping its decisions and guiding the directions of its tremendous thrust." The phenomenon must be confronted, all three men agreed. An early draft discussed a "military-industrial-congressional" complex; Eisenhower, believing it inappropriate to lecture Congress, ordered the legislative reference dropped.[21]

The Cold War was a noble and necessary struggle, Eisenhower told the American people on the evening of January 17, 1961. The Soviet Union was a ruthless, hostile adversary, whose power and expansionist capability had to be checked. But in the process of pursuing this laudable and essential objective, the United States had created, for the first time in its history, permanent military institutions and a vast industrial sector to supply them. Hundreds of thousands of Americans depended on this new economy for their livelihood, many of them earning fantastic wealth. Unless contained, this complex of military and industrial groups would naturally grow larger and larger, manufacturing greater and more outlandish threats in order to justify ever-higher defense spending. The very soul of America was at stake:

In the councils of government, we must guard against the acquisition of unwarranted influence, whether sought or unsought, by the military-industrial complex. The potential for the disastrous rise of misplaced power exists and will persist. We must never let the weight of this combination endanger our liberties or democratic processes. We should take nothing for granted. Only an alert and knowledgeable citizenry can compel the proper meshing of the huge industrial and military machinery of defense with our peaceful methods and goals, so that security and liberty may prosper together.[22]

The greatest tragedy of all, Eisenhower continued, was that the United States might sacrifice what it was trying to preserve—not just the physical existence of the nation, but its institutions of free enterprise and individual liberty—in the name of total Cold War. "As one who knows that another war could utterly destroy this civilization," the president demanded of his fellow citizens that they stand guard against the military-industrial complex, that they question and resist its demands for ever more spending and ever more conflict.

Never before had such sentiments been expressed by a U.S. president, or indeed any senior official—at least not in a public forum. Little wonder that the speech would resonate deeply in the years to come. Of course, as several observers pointed out, Eisenhower himself was hardly blameless for the rise of the military-industrial complex. It was he who intensified the Cold War during the early years of his administration, wreaking havoc in several Third World countries; it was he as much as anyone who had created a nuclear weapons system that could "destroy civilization."

But by the late 1950s the Soviet Union could no longer seriously threaten the United States by spreading its ideology via subversion and propaganda—it was steadily losing popular backing even within the Eastern Bloc. Nor could the Kremlin plausibly consider launching an attack against the United States or its key allies. In a real sense, therefore, American security was now largely assured. Yet Eisenhower had come to the deeply troubling realization that this very fact—security—threatened the power and livelihood of a growing force in U.S. society, a powerful conglomeration of strategists, industrialists, lawmakers, and Pentagon leaders. It was in the interest of this complex to deny, always and forever, that America had done all it could do to make itself safe. He determined he must confront it.

Presidents can change while in office. As we shall see, another Republican would manage that feat in the 1980s. Eisenhower came into power in 1953 eager to wage Cold War more aggressively, if also more cheaply. He was hardly unaware of the domestic political gains that could be had by adopting a hard line, and he chose to associate closely with industrial and military leaders. By the end of his first term, however, he was beginning to understand that the nuclear weapons at the foundation of his new strategy threatened to destroy everything that the United States was trying to protect. This new fact necessitated an overhaul of America's strategy, for the simple reason that actual hostilities with the Soviet Union were now too dangerous to allow.

Eisenhower waged protracted political warfare to force this view on his advisers and military subordinates. He was determined that American leaders must never allow themselves to believe that a nuclear war could somehow be won. The stakes were too high. Do not risk war for political gain—this was the president's message to his successor.

Kennedy and Berlin

John F. Kennedy had campaigned on the premise that his administration would expand America's military capabilities so that, in the event of another major Cold War crisis, the United States would have an alternative to "holocaust or humiliation." Upon taking office, the president assigned his new secretary of defense, Robert S. McNamara, the task of overhauling America's military posture accordingly. A brilliant young executive (age forty-four) who had been an assistant professor at Harvard Business School at twenty-four and later the president of Ford Motor Company, McNamara eagerly embraced the assignment.

Together with many ambitious social scientists working under him at the Pentagon—the so-called Whiz Kids who flocked to the government from the Ivy League as well as institutions such as Stanford and MIT—McNamara began to develop a new military strategy of "Flexible Response."[23] In the event of another showdown with the Soviets such as had just occurred over Berlin, McNamara wanted to provide the president with a number of military options, rather than just the one—all-out war—that Eisenhower had available to him. The idea was to use the creativity of the Whiz Kids, along with Kennedy's desire to spend much more on the military, to come up with original and effective ways of contending with the Soviet Union. There had to be a better way than Eisenhower's blunt threat of general nuclear war.

Kennedy, McNamara, and others in the White House, including National Security Adviser McGeorge Bundy, another *wunderkind* (age forty-one) who had been appointed dean at Harvard at age thirty-four with only a bachelor's degree, moved with dispatch to implement Flexible Response. Just before taking office, the new president called for a "crash program" to catch up with Soviet superiority. His new military adviser, General Maxwell Taylor, wrote at the same time that the "military trend is running against us and decisive measures are needed to reverse it" and called for a "flexible military strategy designed to deter war, large or small."[24] By emphasizing the importance of waging a more dynamic Cold War, JFK and his advisers knew that they could benefit politically. They could demonstrate their anti-communist credentials, maintain a crisis atmosphere in Washington, and signal to key campaign supporters that military contracts and jobs were in the offing. But their goals were quickly sidelined by events. Kennedy had barely settled into the Oval Office when Nikita Khrushchev activated a new crisis over Berlin. And when the new administration confronted the very real possibility of war, many of its members began to have second thoughts about Flexible Response.

The trouble started for Kennedy not in Germany but in America's backyard. He decided to give the go-ahead to a plan, conceived during Eisenhower's last months, to land a force of CIA-trained Cuban émigrés and other paramilitary operatives on Cuba's Bahia de Cochinos—the Bay of Pigs—in order to oust Fidel Castro's government. In early 1959 Castro and his rebels, or *barbudos* ("bearded ones"), driven by a deep sense of nationalism, had ousted long-time U.S. ally Fulgencio Batista from power. Batista had welcomed American investors, U.S. military advisers, and tourists to the Caribbean island, and his government was corrupt and inefficient. The Central Intelligence Agency, after flirting with backing Castro, worked to thwart his rise to power, but to no avail. After assuming control, he moved fast to break the American grip on Cuban trade and, after some hesitation, concluded a trade treaty with Moscow. Eisenhower ordered the CIA to come up with plans to overthrow the Castro government, and the agency also began to plot an assassination of the Cuban leader. Castro in turn solidified his ties to the Soviet Union.[25]

The CIA, still headed by Allen Dulles, believed that Castro's government commanded little popular support. A small amphibious invasion would likely trigger a widespread revolt that would overthrow Castro and restore a pro-American government. Despite widespread doubts at the CIA that the plan was anywhere close to sufficient, the invasion took place on April 17, 1961. Roughly 1,500 irregular soldiers landed at the swampy bay early in the morning, but their appearance failed to trigger widespread rebellion, despite the efforts of CIA operatives in Havana and other Cuban towns.

As the invading force ran up against Castro's army, Kennedy, still seeking vainly to keep the United States' participation in the scheme hidden, refused to provide air cover for the attackers, who were swiftly surrounded and captured. Henceforth in American political parlance, the word "fiasco" would be attached to the end of "the Bay of Pigs."[26]

For Nikita Khrushchev, though, the more apt word was "opportunity." Still eager to secure a deal on Berlin after the disaster in Paris, and now witnessing the new American president's Caribbean misadventures, the Soviet leader agreed to a U.S. proposal for the two heads of state to meet in Vienna. Kennedy had sought such a meeting because he wanted to secure an agreement from the Soviet leader on Berlin and to discuss other possible hotspots, including Indochina. But when the two leaders met in June, a confident Khrushchev took the initiative. He rebuffed Kennedy's declarations that the United States would support non-communist regimes in Indochina and said he would reactivate the Berlin ultimatum he had let pass in 1959. Kennedy replied that it was not in Moscow's interest for the United States to suffer the humiliation of abandoning Berlin, but the Soviet leader stood his ground. Despondent, JFK warned Khrushchev as the two men prepared to part that the new ultimatum would make for a "cold winter." On that dismal note the encounter ended, and Kennedy returned to Washington, having failed to outfox his adversary and carrying a Soviet ultimatum on Berlin in his pocket. Khrushchev just "beat hell out of me," a dejected Kennedy confided to *New York Times* columnist James Reston soon after he arrived home.[27]

The Berlin ultimatum was back, and Kennedy, like Eisenhower thirty months earlier, had to fashion a response. The older man's task had not been easy, but it was straightforward: because he would not countenance any talk about limited war in Central Europe, the only sane option was to find some means of compromise. The new administration had officially rejected this way of thinking, but its problem was that now, in the summer of 1961, Flexible Response was still only an idea. There were no new weapons systems to speak of, no new strategies; and American and other NATO military commanders in Europe were still adhering to the premise that a Soviet military move against West Berlin in all likelihood meant World War III.

Fundamentally, the new administration had painted itself into the same corner Eisenhower had once occupied. The United States needed to find a surreptitious way to compromise. Kennedy, together with Bundy, McNamara, and special adviser Arthur M. Schlesinger Jr. convened a special Berlin steering group to seek alternatives short of war. The president also consulted Eisenhower, who counseled restraint and diplomacy. Rejecting the militaristic advice of ex-secretary of state Dean Acheson, whose input the president had also sought, the steering group discovered a possible out. During the third week of July, the administration began to communicate to London and Paris that the United States would accept a change in the legal status of Berlin, whereby the entire city would no longer be legally under the supervision of the four occupying powers, on the pretext of the eventual unification of the city. Rather, the Western powers would only insist upon having access to West Berlin and the security of its soldiers and diplomats there. This signified a formal change in the position of the United States and its NATO allies, who had long supposed that the de facto division of the city had no permanent or official status and hence demanded access to all areas of the city. Now, Kennedy was referring only to West Berlin, and on July 25 he announced this in a public speech that Khrushchev could hear.[28]

The Soviet leader now had to find an answer. His problem was threefold: the irritating presence of the Western powers in Berlin, sixteen years after the end of the war; their freedom to roam around the entire city, infiltrating themselves throughout the capital of Moscow's key client state, East Germany (Berlin, Khrushchev once complained, was a "nest of spies"); and, most urgent, the continuing hemorrhaging of East Germany's educated classes, who were now fleeing to the West in record numbers following his June ultimatum. Under severe pressure from East German President Walter Ulbricht, Khrushchev arrived at a grim solution.

On the night of August 12–13, East German soldiers, under Soviet authority, began to close down traffic between West Berlin and the East German territory surrounding it, taking care to keep the main arteries linking West Berlin and West Germany open. Over the next several weeks the soldiers erected a wall around West Berlin to physically isolate it from East Berlin and the rest of East Germany. By doing so, Khrushchev and Ulbricht solved the second and third of their problems, while avoiding war. The Berlin Wall reflected miserably on the appeal of the socialist bloc, and it also imprisoned West Berliners on a kind of Cold War island. Families were separated from one another, and countless Berliners found themselves suddenly without work. But war was averted, and the abnormal situation in Berlin was stabilized. It was an expedient local solution to a volatile geopolitical problem.[29]

Kennedy and his advisers denounced the action, but privately they were relieved. They had campaigned for a new foreign policy based on vigor and aggressiveness, for taking the offensive against America's Cold War adversary, but they were more than content to accept the Berlin Wall as a means of avoiding a major confrontation, leading perhaps to the ultimate catastrophe. When belligerent Americans on the scene, led by General Lucius Clay, commander of American forces in Berlin, tried in October to force a confrontation at Checkpoint Charlie—the main crossing point between the sectors of West and East Berlin, not far from the Brandenberg Gate—Kennedy shut them down. "A wall," he memorably said, "is a hell of a lot better than a war."[30]

To the Brink over Cuba

Yet the outcome of the crisis left a bitter aftertaste in the mouths of Kennedy and his top aides. They had been forced to compromise over Berlin, and had precious little to show for their campaign promise to strengthen America's military capacity. Led by Secretary of Defense McNamara, the administration sought in 1962 to overhaul U.S. security policy. McNamara, influenced heavily by civilian strategists such as Thomas Schelling, introduced the "no-cities" nuclear doctrine in the summer of that year. No longer would the United States regard war with the Soviet Union as an occasion for total nuclear destruction. It would target Soviet military installations and missile sites, not Warsaw Pact cities, in the event of war. It would strengthen its conventional forces in Europe and elsewhere and prepare strategies of limited nuclear war. Should World War III begin, America would try to win it in a specific and carefully calibrated fashion, rather than by simply blowing up the planet. The ideas resonated in elite opinion. Many congressional hawks, nuclear strategists, and arms manufacturers applauded the new direction.

But how determined was the administration to follow through with this new policy? Kennedy would soon have his opportunity to test it. On Tuesday, October 16, 1962, the CIA reported that their U-2 surveillance aircraft had photographed Soviet missile installations in Cuba. Reports had already indicated that the Soviets might be up to something on the island, but now National Security Adviser Bundy told the president that there could be little doubt that Khrushchev was deploying medium range nuclear missiles on the Caribbean island. Thus began the final, and most dangerous, of the five major Cold War nuclear crises between 1958 and 1962.[31]

Historians have long debated Khrushchev's reasons for taking this risky step. The evidence suggests he had several motives. He knew, first off, that Kennedy remained determined to overthrow Castro's government, now one of the USSR's most important allies. He may not have known just how determined: in the wake of the Bay of Pigs operation, Kennedy gave the go-ahead to a CIA project, Operation Mongoose, to disrupt the island's trade, support raids on Cuba from south Florida, and plot to kill Castro. Among the assassination schemes: providing Castro with poisoned cigars and harpooning him while he was snorkeling at a Caribbean resort. In recent months the United States had tightened its economic blockade of the island and had undertaken provocative military maneuvers in the Caribbean. An American invasion seemed highly likely, to both Khrushchev and Castro. By deploying nuclear weapons on Cuban soil, the Soviet Union would drastically raise the stakes of such an attack.

Moreover, by siding with the Cuban government in such a dramatic fashion, Khrushchev could show that the Soviet Union was still committed to the cause of world socialism, that it had not become the conservative, risk-averse superpower many critics, especially in Communist China, had portrayed it to be. Sino-Soviet tensions had deteriorated sharply in recent years, and the two powers had now essentially split. Khrushchev did not want to give Castro any reason to drift toward Chinese patronage.[32] He had also felt a powerful personal bond with Castro ever since the two men met briefly in Harlem in September 1960, during a UN General Assembly meeting. When the six-foot-four Cuban bent down to embrace the five-foot-three Russian in an exuberant bear hug, "He made a deep impression on me," Khrushchev later said. In due course, he would come to love Castro "like a son."[33] Another motivation was the more conventional one: Khrushchev hoped by the deployment to rectify the balance of power. As Aleksandr Fursenko and Timothy Naftali have demonstrated, the Soviet leader was determined to redress—when and where he could—the minor victories the United States had won during its period of nuclear superiority. The USSR had not yet reached parity with the Americans in terms of long-range rockets and planes (so-called strategic weapons), he knew, but it had plenty of medium-range ballistic missiles (MRBMs) targeted on western Europe. By moving some of these to territory ninety miles from Florida, he could give the

Americans a taste of their own medicine. The United States, after all, had allies encircling the Soviet Union. Its nuclear missiles were deployed in Turkey, West Germany, and other European states not far from Russian borders, and the Western powers retained a foothold in Berlin. A Soviet missile base in Cuba seemed only fair. Indeed, for Khrushchev, obsessed with obtaining recognition of the USSR as a legitimate superpower, this idea of redressing a manifestly "unfair" situation may have been the most important factor behind his fateful decision.[34]

Some American officials agreed, at least to a point. Robert McNamara, for one, initially asked colleagues what difference it made to the larger strategic picture if the Soviets had missiles in Cuba. Would it change the balance of nuclear terror? McNamara thought not, though the Joint Chiefs of Staff (JCS) disagreed.[35] Kennedy's focus, though, was elsewhere. He had suffered a humiliating setback at the Bay of Pigs and had got the worst of the Vienna encounter with Khrushchev. In Berlin he had accepted the Wall, rightly in his own mind but to the distress of right-wing figures in Congress and the press, who saw it as an obvious *casus belli*. For Kennedy, geopolitical fairness was not an issue. His, and his country's, reputation was on the line. If he did nothing about this Soviet provocation, Khrushchev would have every reason to conclude that he could peck away at American positions, confident that the administration would always back down. And Kennedy would face withering attacks from Republicans and conservative Democrats, with midterm elections only a couple weeks away.[36]

Already in September conservatives had accused the White House of underplaying growing evidence of a Soviet arms buildup in Cuba, causing Senate Majority Leader Mike Mansfield of Montana to express fear to JFK that "if public pressures on Democratic members now begin to lead them to engage in an attempt to outdo Republicans in militancy on Cuba, I am concerned as to where it might end." Democrats up for reelection might "have to leave you on this matter," Mansfield warned. On October 7, nine days before the U-2 discovery, Mansfield's GOP counterpart, Minority Leader Everett Dirksen of Illinois, announced that Kennedy had a "sorry record" on Cuba. "There is a mess in Cuba," Dirksen charged, "a mess of [America's] own making." And on October 16, mere hours before the discovery, the chairman of the Republican National Committee issued a statement condemning JFK's foreign policy and calling Cuba in particular "a symbol of the tragic irresolution of the administration."[37]

The political pressure on Kennedy was enormous. He convened an executive committee of the National Security Council (later called ExComm) to advise him on the proper response. Initially, Kennedy, along with his brother, Attorney General Robert Kennedy, considered authorizing a surgical air strike to take out the missile installations unilaterally (in part to give hawks the feeling that their views received due consideration). But General Maxwell Taylor, now chairman of the Joint Chiefs of Staff, could not promise that such a strike would disable every missile the U-2s had spotted, and there was no guarantee that the Soviets had not deployed other missiles the spy planes had missed (which, as it turned out, they had). On Wednesday, October 18, Taylor stressed that even a major air attack on Cuba would probably not destroy every missile, and even if it did the Soviets might respond to such an attack by beginning a general nuclear war. Still, at the end of that day an air strike remained one of two main options under ExComm consideration, the other being a naval blockade.

By the evening of Saturday, October 20, Kennedy, supported by his brother and McNamara, had made a tentative decision in favor of the blockade. More than many of those around him, JFK had a sense of the vagaries of history, of the tendency for things to happen differently from what you intended. Earlier in the year he had read Barbara Tuchman's *The Guns of August,* which detailed how European leaders stumbled into World War I; he came away so impressed that he often quoted from the book and urged aides as well as "every officer in the Army" to read it. Considering the stakes, and the possibility of nuclear war, the blockade seemed to him the safer option, and it would not put the United States in the morally dubious position of launching a surprise preventive attack, which is exactly what the Japanese had done at Pearl Harbor. A blockade could prevent the Soviet Union from increasing its deployment of missiles on the island and could create a more stable situation for negotiations to occur, without giving the appearance to the Soviets of being a military escalation. It could also deprive the Kremlin of an excuse to retaliate by moving militarily on Berlin. The president polled the group, and the supporters of the blockade prevailed. For the time being, there would be no U.S. attack.

By October 22 the general plan was set. The United States Navy would establish a blockade around Cuba (using the less aggressive word "quarantine"), while the president would demand publicly that the Soviet Union dismantle their missiles and take them home. At the same time, the idea of a trade with the Kremlin would be secretly floated—the United States would remove Jupiter missiles from Turkey if the Soviets removed its missiles in Cuba. That evening, the president went before a national and world television audience and announced the naval quarantine, demanded the removal of the missiles from Cuba, and warned that if any of the weapons were launched against any target in the Western Hemisphere he would order a full U.S. response—against the USSR itself. It would be Massive Retaliation, not Flexible Response. The European allies declared their support for the blockade, as did the Organization of American States. The Strategic Air Command went to its highest airborne alert: one in every eight strategic bombers was to be airborne at all times, to guarantee that some survived in the event of a Soviet first strike.

Around the world, and especially in North America and Europe, people began to think the unthinkable: a nuclear war might erupt at any moment. Would anyone be alive come morning? Would it be better to die instantly? Or try to survive, somehow? Nuclear war had been a persistent possibility during the previous crises, but never before had the two superpowers found themselves in a showdown like this. As far as anyone on the outside could see, one side would have to back down, and soon, or there would be war. Throughout the United States, men and women planned for the worst. Some moved their families into private bomb shelters, stocking them with rations, fresh water, and weaponry (in order to keep neighbors out). Others hastily made arrangements to emigrate to Australia or New Zealand. In Memphis, Tennessee, police discovered a man standing over a manhole in the middle of the night, trying to determine if his family could escape through it. Other Americans used mordant wit to keep a level head. Mocking his university's pointless system of warning signals, a student at the University of California concluded: "The air raid siren is preceded by a bright flash."[38]

People had reason to fear that their world was about to come to an end—more so than they could have known at the time. Khrushchev's initial reply to the Kennedy speech, a note that arrived in Washington early on the morning of the 23rd, took a firm line: the blockade was in violation of international law; the missiles were there for "defensive purposes"; the USSR would not back down. The moment had arrived for confrontation and war. Instead, over the final six days of the crisis the Kennedy administration determined that it would pursue peace and developed a brilliant strategy to achieve it. Robert Kennedy met with Soviet ambassador Anatoly Dobrynin to finalize the deal on the missiles in Turkey, and U.S. officials prepared to take the case to the United Nations and to ask Secretary General U Thant to intervene in the crisis. Meanwhile, the administration kept the blockade in place, along with its demand that the missiles be dismantled and removed. Then it waited.

On October 26 Khrushchev took one step backwards. Secretly, he sent a letter to Kennedy declaring that any further ships traveling to Cuba would not carry missiles. If the United States were to promise that it would never invade Cuba, or "support any sort of forces" that might do so, then the "necessity for the presence of our military specialists in Cuba would disappear." Was Khrushchev promising to withdraw the missiles? This letter implied as much, but it was vague. The next morning, Khrushchev sent another, less conciliatory letter, stating simply that the Soviets would remove its rockets from Cuba if the Americans took the Jupiters out of Turkey. This was a blow to Kennedy, because he wanted to avoid a public deal that might demoralize allies in Europe and bring accusations of appeasement at home, and also because Khrushchev seemed to be reneging on the offer he had just made the day before. Was the Soviet leader, once again, trying to manipulate Kennedy? That afternoon, news arrived that a U-2 had been shot down over Cuba. Had Kennedy been even somewhat inclined to return to the military option, to reject diplomacy, this was the time for that to happen. He would have had strong public backing, and with midterm elections only a few days away.

Instead, he ramped up his diplomatic efforts. He would not lose this opportunity to strike a reasonable deal with Moscow and avoid nuclear war, even as several of his advisers, including McNamara, were reviving talk of military action. Kennedy sent his brother to confirm to Dobrynin that the United States would in fact dismantle the missiles in Turkey within four to five months, as long as this could be done covertly, not part of a public deal. The promise never to invade Cuba, however, would be made public. In exchange, the USSR would agree to dismantle its nuclear missiles under supervision, take them home, and not deploy them on Cuban soil again. At the same time, the White House formally replied to Khrushchev's October 26 letter, promising simply not to invade Cuba, aware that Khrushchev already knew about the secret arrangement on the missiles in Turkey.

Khrushchev, desperate to seal the deal before the Americans changed their minds or some accident reignited the crisis, did not take the time to notify allies or draft a formal response. Instead, at 9:00 a.m. Washington time on Sunday, October 28, Radio Moscow announced that it would terminate its deployment of missiles on Cuban soil. This was how Fidel Castro, and the rest of the world, learned of the decision. Kennedy ordered the CIA to halt Operation Mongoose, the ongoing attempt to undermine the Castro regime. Soviet officials began to dismantle the medium range missiles in Cuba and put them on ships bound for Russia. The Cuban Missile Crisis was effectively over.

The Lessons of the Crisis

Kennedy and Khrushchev had done it: they had stepped back from the precipice. At the hour of maximum danger they showed themselves to be, in Michael Dobbs's words, "rational, intelligent, decent men, separated by an ocean of misunderstanding."[39] They were flexible at the key moments and demonstrated the ability to look a few steps ahead and resist the pressure from hawks in their midst. The president had a taping system installed in the Oval Office earlier in 1962, and most of the ExComm meetings during the crisis were recorded. These White House tapes reveal a deeply engaged, calmly authoritative commander-in-chief, capable of seeing the situation from his adversary's perspective.[40] When it came time to seal the deal with Khrushchev over the weekend of October 27–28, Kennedy moved decisively and creatively. A few critics on the right attacked the White House for not acting more aggressively, for failing to use tough military options in order to oust Castro's government once and for all; it was an idea that also held considerable appeal on the ExComm, particularly during the first week. We know now, though, that the Soviets had far more troops on the island than the administration was aware of at the time (42,000, not the estimated 8,000–10,000), that they had already deployed tactical nuclear missiles designed to defeat an invading force, and that the Soviet Union would almost certainly have responded to a serious attack on Cuba with actions that might have generated uncontrollable momentum toward general war. How many today lament Kennedy's caution?

Critics on the left, meanwhile, have faulted Kennedy on other grounds over the years. Some have blamed him for helping to cause the crisis in the first place with his anti-Cuban projects, and for failing to consider that quiet diplomacy could have achieved the same outcome without the extraordinary tension. Other skeptics assert that Kennedy rejected seeking an early diplomatic solution because he feared the Republicans would ride the missiles to victory in the upcoming midterm elections. There's a good deal of evidence to support these claims, but it was not Kennedy's decision to install missiles in Cuba just before the elections.[41]

American actions during the crisis provide two larger historical lessons about what effective leaders do when the moment of nuclear truth arrives.[42] The first reminds us of the difference between declared policy and actual intention. When assessing the history of an international crisis, one must examine what nations do, not what they say. The United States had begun to develop a policy of limited war with the Soviet Union, and Kennedy, McNamara, and other officials said on any number of occasions that they wanted to be able to respond to Cold War crises with more flexibility and creativity. The White House was particularly receptive to imaginative strategies, such as those put forward by Schelling, that urged an aggressive, risk-taking posture during a nuclear crisis, in order to put the USSR on the defensive. But when the actual possibility of war loomed—over Berlin and then, more acutely, Cuba—the American government responded by seeking compromise and making the avoidance of nuclear war its top priority. Eisenhower had perceived this truth and executed his policies accordingly. Kennedy tried to create something different but found himself gravitating toward Eisenhower's position when faced with Soviet missiles just off the Florida coast. His decisions in late October say far more about the actual nuclear policy of the Kennedy administration than do his administration's declared strategies and weapons acquisitions.

A second lesson speaks to the more general effect of nuclear fear. If nations are going to be as terrified by nuclear war as the United States and the Soviet Union were in 1962, then it becomes reasonable to conclude, as have many scholars over the past three decades, that war between nuclear states has become effectively impossible—that nuclear deterrence has become basically a perfect means of avoiding major war in our age. The political scientist Kenneth Waltz has advocated this view, and has therefore suggested that the acquisition of defensive nuclear arsenals by states is likely to promote peace.[43] Does the example of the Missile Crisis, and the proclivity of the United States (and the Soviet Union, as we can now see) to seek compromise during the entire crisis period give us reason to agree with Waltz, to conclude that nuclear deterrence has largely solved the problem of major war?

In a word, no. Waltz's conclusion is logical, but the Cuban Missile Crisis demonstrates the dangers of drawing too much from it. The United States gave very close consideration to attacking Cuba during the early days of the crisis. Had JFK known that such an option would probably trigger a Soviet nuclear retaliation, he likely would have been more cautious, but the salient point is that he did not, and could not, know this. More important, on several occasions during the crisis, accidents or unauthorized events occurred that could easily have caused a panic into war. If the Soviets had shot down the American U-2 flight on October 19 rather than October 27, Kennedy likely would have responded with military action. During a key moment of the crisis, the Strategic Air Command went ahead with a prescheduled test of an ICBM over the Pacific Ocean; before cooler heads prevailed, Soviet commanders viewed this as the initiation of major war. Perhaps most alarming and instructive, on October 28, at the pinnacle of the crisis, American defense officials were informed that a missile had been launched from Cuba and was about to hit Tampa, Florida. Only after frantic inquiries did they discover that someone was playing a simulation tape.[44]

On several occasions, clearly, the crisis could have easily spiraled into war. This is so even if one accepts the argument, as we do, that Kennedy became determined to avoid such an outcome. Accidents happen. Signals are missed. Officials panic. Nuclear deterrence is logical, but nations are not robots, and neither are the people who lead them. The Kennedy administration's behavior during the Cuban Missile Crisis—and that of the Soviet government too—gives us reason to endorse the optimistic belief that governments are likely to try to avoid nuclear war when it becomes a real possibility, whatever their official policies. This does not mean they will always succeed.[45]

A New Relationship

Like teenagers who have survived a terrifying game of chicken, the United States and the Soviet Union reached the common conclusion that they must make sure nothing like the Cuban Missile Crisis ever happened again. In 1963 they installed a coded wire-telegraph Hot Line staffed around the clock by translators and technicians, so as to prevent the kind of miscommunication that occurred on October 26 and 27. Both nations would also develop effective satellite systems that allowed them to monitor the other side's activities, and (even more important) neither nation tried very hard to prevent this. Washington and Moscow both recognized the value of transparency in the nuclear age—the importance of ensuring that one side was not uncertain about the other's military intentions. This represented a real revolution in the history of superpower diplomacy.[46]

Finally, and most important of all, both sides were beginning to understand that the Cold War must now be fought in a manner that would not bring about direct Soviet-American confrontation. Indeed, much of the hostility seemed to drain out of the bilateral relationship. In June 1963 Kennedy spoke at American University in conciliatory terms, urging cautious Soviet-American steps toward disarmament. More than that, he called on Americans to redefine some of their attitudes toward the USSR and toward communism, to try "not to see conflict as inevitable, accommodation as impossible, and communication as nothing more than an exchange of threats."

> So let us not be blind to our differences, but let us also direct attention to our common interests and the means by which those differences can be resolved. And if we cannot end now our differences, at least we can help make the world safe for diversity. For in the final analysis, our most basic common link is that we all inhabit this small planet. We all breathe the same air. We all cherish our children's futures. And we are all mortal.

Then, in August, defying the opposition in their respective bureaucracies, the two adversaries signed the Limited Test Ban Treaty prohibiting nuclear tests in the atmosphere, the oceans, and outer space. Individually, these steps were small, but together they reversed the trend of the previous years and began to build much-needed mutual trust. After the Cuban Missile Crisis, in sum, both superpowers started to reconceive the Cold War, to think carefully about how they might wage it now that the option of general war was off the table.[47]

Could one go further and argue that the Cold War had ended by mid-1963? One could. Such an argument would assert that those things that had made the superpower rivalry more than a rivalry no longer applied. American foreign policy, most evidently in NSC-68, had earlier characterized the Cold War as a titanic, life-or-death struggle, an ideological *guerre à outrance,* while Soviet foreign policy under Stalin had regarded its contest with the United States as a historically determined confrontation that could only end in war. Now, these views no longer prevailed in Washington and Moscow. Like the great powers of earlier eras, both sides now recognized, de facto, the legitimacy of the other; both moved beyond irreconcilable ideological hostility to a general affirmation of the need for peaceful coexistence.

This was the essence of the American University address and of other speeches JFK made, notably during a speaking tour of the western states in the autumn of 1963. Both Washington and Moscow implicitly acknowledged the existing geopolitical divisions and balance of power in the form of spheres of influence or control. Nuclear weapons, both sides agreed, would never be used except as a last resort. A spirit of competition remained, to be sure, and considerable mutual suspicion. But the contest could no longer be called a Cold War—not after the apparent settlement regarding Berlin and Germany, the irrefutable evidence of a Sino-Soviet split, the harrowing ordeal of the Cuban Missile Crisis, and the limited but symbolically crucial cooperation that followed with the Hot Line and the test ban treaty.[48]

It's a powerful argument, but so is the skeptical reply: that consequential though these developments were, they were not sufficient either individually or together to allow us to declare the Cold War over in 1963. For the fact remains that when assessing the history of American foreign policy, rather than retrospectively identifying the structural changes occurring over Washington and Moscow, the vast majority of politicians and statesmen who mattered in 1963 never imagined that the Cold War was over. The intermestic logic that drove American policymakers was as strong as ever. What Eisenhower said of the United States in his Farewell Address in 1961 (and which could have been said also of the Soviet Union) was no less true three years later: a great many people had a vested interest in the indefinite perpetuation of the Cold War, in the continuation of the arms race. This included key segments of American industry, the armed services, and powerful lawmakers in both parties. American political discourse had begun to change in subtle ways, but the underlying dynamic had not changed: vociferous anti-communism was still the lingua franca on Capitol Hill and among those who aspired to get there. If in doubt, spout the eternal verities: the Soviet menace is as great as ever, the Kremlin as untrustworthy.

But with containment complete, nuclear deterrence assured, and the Cuban Missile Crisis making direct confrontation with the USSR simply too dangerous to advocate, how—and where—could the United States continue the Cold War? A natural venue was the Third World. The Cold War may have begun in the mid-1940s as a struggle over Europe and the immediately contiguous areas of the Near East, but it had long since expanded to cover other parts of the globe. The United States in 1963 had security agreements with almost a hundred countries, on every continent but Antarctica. More than a million U.S. servicemen and women were deployed overseas, on close to two hundred bases. The Soviets' reach was almost as great. Thus, while it is true that, as one important study put it, 1962–63 witnessed the "making of a European settlement," this did not necessarily lessen the contest for the "periphery," especially with Mao Zedong's China loudly claiming to have supplanted the USSR as the true champion of liberation movements everywhere.[49] If anything, the locus of competition now shifted to these developing areas of Asia, Africa, and Latin America that together made up the Third World.

For the Kennedy administration, one Third World trouble spot loomed especially large during the summer of 1963: Vietnam.

6

GULLIVER'S TRAVAILS

With the stakes at their very highest, President Kennedy had avoided war over Cuba. Under pressure from various quarters to use military force against the Soviet missile sites on the island, he had instead deftly secured a compromise with Moscow, thereby avoiding a possible slide to a thermonuclear World War III. In 1963, in the months leading up to his assassination in Dallas, Kennedy appeared to question whether there was anything left to do in America's project to contain the Soviet Union, whether the time had not come to work toward a grand settlement with the Kremlin. In the months after the Missile Crisis, he and Soviet leader Nikita Khrushchev had already taken partial but important steps toward a Soviet-American rapprochement.

But there was a long way to go. Competition in the Third World continued that year, not merely with the USSR but with an aggressive-seeming People's Republic of China. More important, Kennedy proved unwilling to work to trim the power of the military-industrial complex at home. He had promised during the 1960 campaign to boost spending and revive struggling defense-industry sectors; and in so doing, he had created a political constituency he was loath to alienate.[1] Increased military spending promised, moreover, to prime the economy, a not unimportant consideration to the president and his aides as they began to look toward the 1964 reelection campaign.

Above all, there was that special burden borne by all Democrats during the Cold War: to demonstrate at all times the proper anti-communist *bona fides,* to show unyielding toughness and determination, to avoid giving Republicans any chance to use the cudgel they had wielded with such effectiveness against Truman for supposedly losing China. Kennedy chafed at this imperative on occasion, but he dared not try to contravene it—not fully—before the 1964 election. He allowed military spending to rise during this tenure, so that by fiscal year 1963 it was about ten percent higher than Eisenhower's last budget. When Kennedy left on that fateful trip to Texas in November 1963, the Pentagon was in robust financial health, numerous new weapons systems were in development, and defense contractors particularly in Sunbelt states of the West and Southwest were thriving.[2]

The new president, Lyndon Baines Johnson, showed little inclination to change this dynamic. Focused from the start on winning the presidency in his own right in 1964, the voluble Texan had been majority leader of the U.S. Senate before becoming Kennedy's vice president; few understood better than he the political and economic benefits of maintaining a high defense budget. For one thing, it would placate lawmakers whose states and districts benefited from the spending and whose support Johnson would need to pass his ambitious domestic legislative program, to be termed the Great Society. What is more, Johnson came to the White House with a deep and unquestioning commitment to a posture of staunch anti-communism in foreign affairs. His reading of history taught him that Truman and the Democrats had lost their effectiveness after China went communist in 1949. Johnson kept America on a Cold War footing and allowed the momentum built up by JFK toward improved relations with Moscow to flag. To be sure, that momentum might have ebbed also under Kennedy, had he survived, given the continued turmoil in the Third World and particularly the growing crisis in Vietnam. Johnson inherited a sticky situation in that former French colony, and from his first days in office he had a strong sense of what he must do: he would not be the president who lost Vietnam to communism, he vowed. Yet even as LBJ took the nation into full-scale war in 1964–65, he harbored deep personal doubts—shared by many in his administration—that long-term success in Vietnam could be achieved or that the outcome there really mattered to U.S. security. His eyes were on the home front and on the prospect that a failure to "stand firm" in Southeast Asia could harm him politically and undermine his historical legacy. Much more than any Cold War imperatives, these domestic political and reputational concerns drove Johnson's decision to escalate the conflict.[3]

Vietnam would be America's largest and longest military intervention during the Cold War, and by far the bloodiest. By the autumn of 1968, the United States was embroiled in a brutal war that had no end in sight and that many of Johnson's own aides, as well as a substantial section of the American public, believed was both unwinnable and immoral. By then, U.S. planes had dropped more than three million tons of bombs on Vietnam—twice the tonnage used on Germany and Japan in World War II. More than 500,000 American troops were in the field and were dying at a rate of a thousand per month. Hundreds of thousands of Vietnamese, most of them peasants who had taken no action against the United States or its soldiers, had been killed or maimed. At home, the largest antiwar movement in the nation's history had ruptured the Democratic Party and roiled American society. Abroad, longstanding Cold War allies found themselves alienated by U.S. policy and facing anti-American movements of their own. And Lyndon Johnson, who had long feared that Vietnam would be his undoing, announced he would not to run for reelection. In January 1969 he left Washington for his native Texas, a man broken by the war.

Kennedy's Early Decisions

Eight years earlier, when John F. Kennedy entered the White House, Vietnam had been but a cloud on the horizon, albeit an ominous one. Tensions within Vietnam were then on the rise, as a guerrilla insurgency in the South challenged the rule of noncommunist leader Ngo Dinh Diem. The Geneva Conference of 1954 had divided the country at the seventeenth parallel, with elections for reunification slated to take place two years hence. Diem, however, acting with Washington's support, had bypassed the election (U.S. analysts feared he would lose to the North's Ho Chi Minh) and instead set about solidifying his control in the South. For a time, his strategy worked. As American aid dollars and products flowed in, accompanied by technical know-how, some officials spoke hopefully about a "Diem miracle" and about South Vietnam being a "showcase" for Washington's foreign aid program.

Appearances deceived. Diem was a dedicated nationalist and anti-communist, but he had little mass support. He jailed dissidents and shut down newspapers critical of his government. He ignored entreaties from U.S. officials to implement meaningful land reform. Moreover, the America aid program fostered a dependency rather than laying the foundation for a genuinely independent nation. Gradually, an insurgency took root in South Vietnam. Ho's government in Hanoi initially focused on solidifying its control in the North, but in the late 1950s it began to send aid to the insurgents, who embarked on a program of terror, assassinating hundreds of Diem's village officials. In late 1960 southern communists, acting at the direction of Hanoi, organized the National Liberation Front (NLF).[4]

All the while, the Eisenhower administration, though aware of Diem's shortcomings and his disinclination to follow American advice, continued to affirm its Cold War commitment to the preservation of an independent, noncommunist South Vietnam. In 1954 Eisenhower had famously painted the metaphoric picture of what defeat in Indochina could mean: "You have a row of dominoes set up, you knock over the first one, and what will happen to the last one is the certainty that it will go over very quickly."[5] Though the metaphor was rarely trotted out again, the "domino theory" took hold in the popular imagination and continued to guide policy. The loss of Vietnam would represent a major gain for Soviet-led world communism and trigger a chain reaction among neighboring states; hence, such a result had to prevented. Never mind that in no previous case (including China in 1949) had the fall of a country to communism triggered the rapid fall of a whole string of other countries.[6] Never mind that Soviet leaders showed scant interest in Southeast Asia, either before Stalin's death or after; they considered the region a strategic backwater. For U.S. officials it was enough that Ho Chi Minh was a dedicated Marxist whose government enjoyed the backing of Moscow and Beijing.

Kennedy assumed the presidency just as the NLF came into being, and Indochina was from the start a significant policy issue for his administration. Initially, however, it was not Vietnam but neighboring Laos that loomed largest. Laos had been declared neutral by the Geneva conferees in 1954, and Washington had thereafter sent aid and advisory personnel to try to secure stable, pro-Western rule in this small, landlocked country. The North Vietnamese under Ho Chi Minh countered by building up the Pathet Lao in the east. By the time of Kennedy's inauguration, the U.S.-sponsored government of Phoumi Nosavan faced imminent defeat at the hands of Pathet Lao guerrillas, heavily backed by North Vietnam. Outgoing president Eisenhower and several senior officials urged JFK to intervene militarily, but he demurred, in part because of opposition from the British and French governments. Instead, Kennedy opted to back a Soviet-sponsored initiative to convene a new Geneva Conference on Laos for the purpose of negotiating a settlement among the competing factions. In July 1962 a deal was signed. It did not bring lasting peace, but it did remove Laos from the list of Cold War crisis points.

Diplomacy seemed to JFK the only plausible solution in Laos. But he feared that by choosing this course he had opened himself up to charges of being "soft on communism" from his domestic opponents, many of whom were also attacking him for the failed effort to overthrow Castro in 1961. Kennedy and other party leaders might privately mock the rigidity and bombast of John Foster Dulles and label as ludicrous the GOP charge that Democrats had lost China in 1949, but publicly they were careful. Behind closed doors they could say that America's China policy was quaintly irrational, that nonrecognition of Mao's government made no strategic sense, but they would not run the political risk of changing that policy or of reducing the commitment to Vietnam. Winning reelection in 1964 would depend in good measure on insulating JFK from charges that he was weak and had not stood up to the communists. His margin of victory over Richard Nixon in 1960 had been paper thin, barely 100,000 votes, and he had taken a beating over the Bay of Pigs disaster and gotten the worst of the encounter with Khrushchev in Vienna. Vietnam was the one place where the West was fighting communists with real bullets; that struggle could not be given up, at least in the short term.

The point bears emphasizing: to comprehend the dramatic escalation of U.S. involvement in Southeast Asia in the first half of the 1960s one must understand how heavily the shadow of Joseph McCarthy hung over the internal deliberations of Democratic leaders of the period—despite the fact that the senator had long since gone to his reward. Asia policy, it seemed, had been effectively frozen. It was one thing to stake out a rigidly anti-communist posture in the early 1950s when U.S. forces were battling in Korea and the French sought to hold the line in Indochina and when the United States at home was locked in Red Scare hysteria. It was quite another to embrace such policies in 1961. Yet that is more or less what Kennedy and his team did. McCarthy was no more, and the atmosphere in which the original policies had been set had changed, but the policies remained much the same. It's entirely possible, as David Halberstam would later suggest, that Middle Americans in 1961, if made aware of the key elements in the situation, would not have been that frightened of the communists taking over a small country 10,000 miles away. But no one wanted to test the proposition—not the Democratic leaders who had just agreed to negotiate in strategically less important Laos and against whom the soft-on-communism label might be applied, and not the Republicans who might do the applying.[7]

The issue transcended partisan warfare. Kennedy had run as a Cold Warrior in 1960 and had relished spouting the standard anticommunist shibboleths. He had taken a hard line on Fidel Castro, if anything harder than Nixon's. He had built up a "missile-gap constituency" that now expected him to follow through on his vows to fight the Cold War on all fronts—and, as part of that effort, to bolster America's military capabilities. Powerful committee chairmen in Congress, whose districts were counting on immense defense contracts to fuel their local economies, were watching to see what he would do. So were leaders in the uniformed military, who saw the Cold War as their mission, who had to be prepared to fight and die for that mission, and who viewed Southeast Asia as a likely theater of confrontation.

Which is not to say it was all about domestic politics and electoral strategizing. If JFK feared that his party's standing and his own political strength depended on taking a tough line on Vietnam, he and his aides also worried about the possible effects on *America's* standing and strength of an early withdrawal. This represented a shift in U.S. thinking about the Cold War strategic stakes in Vietnam. In the post-1960 documentary record, one sees less concern that the fall of Vietnam would lead immediately to the fall of the rest of the region; the CIA, the Intelligence and Research bureau (INR) at the State Department, and even numerous senior administration officials now conceded that, as Assistant Secretary of State for Far Eastern Affairs William Bundy put it in 1964, the original domino theory "is much too pat." Or, as his brother McGeorge Bundy, national security adviser under both Kennedy and Johnson, asserted in a later interview: "What happens in one country affects what happens in another, yes, but that you could push one down and knock the rest over, its extreme form . . . I never believed that."[8] Instead, the worry now was less tangible, more amorphous, as U.S. officials began to expound what Jonathan Schell has aptly called the "psychological domino theory."[9]

True, the domino theory had always, from its earliest incarnation, had a psychological dimension; now, however, that dimension became paramount. Vietnam was a test of America's *credibility*, policymakers grimly declared. Failure to stand firm in the struggle would cause observers near and far to question the strength of Washington's commitments, not merely in Southeast Asia but around the globe. Friends in the region and elsewhere might conclude that they could not count on the United States for their defense, and might succumb to enemy pressure even without military intervention by foreign communist troops—what political scientists refer to as a "bandwagon" effect. Foes, meanwhile, would be galvanized to challenge American interests worldwide.

Building Nations in the Third World

It mattered, in this regard, that more and more of the world seemed up for grabs. In Africa, for example, where in 1945 only Egypt, Ethiopia, Liberia, and South Africa could lay claim to independence, new nations were emerging seemingly by the month. In 1960 alone, sixteen new African states joined the United Nations. The departing colonialists had done little to prepare these nations for independence, and U.S. analysts feared that this would make them vulnerable to Soviet penetration.[10]

This seemed especially the case with the Congo, which received independence from Belgium in 1960 and quickly became a battleground for several tribal and political groups. The fledgling regime of Patrice Lumumba, leader of the most popular nationalist faction, waged a civil war against Belgian-supported secessionists in the mineral-rich southern province of Katanga, led by Moise Tshombe. In early 1961 Lumumba, who had received technical assistance and military equipment from Moscow, was assassinated by Katanga authorities at least encouraged, if not abetted, by the CIA. The United Nations sent a peacekeeping force to separate the warring sides, and eventually a pro-Western government under Joseph Kasavubu took power. Stability proved elusive, however, and in short order Joseph Mobutu, leader of the armed forces and Washington's favored figure, seized control. Mobutu enriched himself and a small group of supporters while impoverishing his resource-rich nation and aligning himself with the West. Washington had succeeded in thwarting Soviet aims in central Africa but at the cost, the historian Robert J. McMahon has concluded, "of imposing Cold War geopolitics on an impoverished, strife-torn former colony."[11]

Most U.S. officials would not have argued that they were doing otherwise, but they would have defended both their rationale and their tactics. After Khrushchev in 1961 endorsed "wars of national liberation" like the one in Vietnam, Kennedy called for a "peaceful revolution" in the Third World based on the concept of nation-building. Using the theories of modernization developed by Walt W. Rostow (Bundy's deputy at the NSC), Max Millikan, and other social scientists, the administration set out to push developing states through the early stages of nationhood with aid programs aimed at improving agriculture, transportation, and communications. The United States, these theorists argued, had experienced history's first "modern" revolution, and should now assist others to follow suit. One result was the multibillion-dollar Alliance for Progress, created in 1961 to spur economic development in Latin America. In the same year Kennedy created the

Peace Corps, which sent thousands of American teachers, agricultural specialists, and health workers, many of them right out of college, to assist authorities in the developing world and to improve the image of the United States there.

That the Alliance for Progress and the Peace Corps were Cold War weapons by which Kennedy sought to counter anti-Americanism and defeat communism in the developing world cannot be doubted. But they were also born of genuine humanitarianism. The Peace Corps, in particular, manifested Americans' historic faith in their capacity to exert moral leadership in the world and the idealistic can-do spirit of the 1960s. In later decades, cynics, among them many Americans, would explain away the United States' official pretensions to helping others as disingenuous farce. But, as the historian Elizabeth Cobbs Hoffman has noted, these observers would have difficulty explaining the Peace Corps, for the program went "to the heart of the nation's oldest and deepest conflict: how to reconcile its republican idealism with its powerful ambitions."[12]

This was the dilemma, and Kennedy and his aides did not know how to resolve it. Social revolution in the developing world was a good and necessary thing, they insisted, but they could not get their minds to accept the idea that communists could have a legitimate role in any such uprising. Nor could they tolerate Third World governments that might wish to be neutral in the superpower conflict. Alongside largely benevolent programs such as the Peace Corps, therefore, the administration also utilized the more pernicious concept of counterinsurgency to vanquish Third World revolutionaries who challenged friendly regimes. U.S. military and technical advisers trained native troops and police forces to put down disturbances.

Neither nation-building nor counterinsurgency achieved the results that their advocates promised. Under the Alliance for Progress, infant mortality rates in Latin America improved, but economic growth rates continued to lag and class divisions widened, furthering political turmoil. For the region as a whole, the growth rate did not come close to the targeted 2.5 percent.[13] The logic of nation-building, most vividly expressed in Rostow's best-selling book *The Stages of Economic Growth: A Non-Communist Manifesto,* assumed that the U.S. model of capitalism and representative government could be imposed successfully on foreign cultures.[14] But the reality was more complex. Many in the developing world resented meddling by outsiders and refused to be passive recipients of modernizing policies, even as they gladly accepted America's economic aid and craved its material culture. The self-interested elites through whom the assistance was usually funneled often failed to get it to the indigent population that was its target. To those who preferred the relatively quick results of a managed economy, moreover, American-style capitalism with its commitment to private enterprise seemed the wrong approach.

Kennedy's Escalation

These complications were slow to manifest themselves. Initially, the Kennedy administration pursued nation-building and counterinsurgency with gusto, and nowhere more energetically than in South Vietnam. As the fighting intensified in 1961 and 1962, the United States stepped up aid dollars, increased the airdropping of raiding teams into the North, and launched crop destruction by herbicides to starve the Vietcong (as the NLF insurgents in the South became known) and expose their hiding places. Kennedy also strengthened the U.S. military presence in South Vietnam to the point that by 1963 more than 16,000 military advisers were in the country, some authorized to take part in combat alongside the U.S.-equipped Army of the Republic of Vietnam (ARVN).

Meanwhile, opposition to Diem's repressive government increased, and not just on the part of communists. Peasants objected to programs that removed them from their ancestral villages for their own safety, and Buddhist monks, protesting the Roman Catholic Diem's religious persecution, poured gasoline over their robes and ignited themselves in the streets of Saigon. Diem countenanced corruption in his government, concentrated power in the hands of family and friends, and jailed critics to silence them. Eventually U.S. officials, with Kennedy's approval, encouraged ambitious South Vietnamese generals to remove him. On November 1, 1963, the generals struck, overthrowing Diem and on the following day murdering him.[15]

Just three weeks later, on November 22, while riding with his wife Jackie in a motorcade in Dallas, Kennedy himself was shot and killed. The almost-certain assassin, a troubled former marine named Lee Harvey Oswald, had his own connection to the Cold War, having once attempted to gain Soviet citizenship and later a Cuban entry visa. Partly for that reason, and partly because Oswald himself was murdered two days later (in full view of millions of TV viewers) by Jack Ruby—a local nightclub owner with connections to organized crime who died of cancer in prison two years later—speculation quickly turned to talk of conspiracy. The debate continues to this day. One recent account, by the historian David Kaiser, argues that Oswald pulled the trigger, but as a result of machinations within "a complex network of relationships among mobsters, hit men, intelligence agents, Cuban exiles, and America's Cold War foreign policy."[16]

What if Kennedy had returned from Dallas alive? What would he have done in Southeast Asia? The answer can never be known, of course, but that has not stopped scholars from speculating.[17] Consensus is almost always unattainable in such counterfactual exercises, and even more so in this case, given the timing and suddenness of Kennedy's death and given the complex nature of his Vietnam policy. He expanded U.S. involvement and approved a coup against Diem. On occasion he offered strong public endorse-ments of the domino theory, and he ruled out seeking a negotiated settlement. On the other hand, despite the periodic urgings of top advisers, he refused to commit U.S. ground forces to the struggle. Notwithstanding the sweeping pledge of his inaugural address to "pay any price, bear any burden," he generally chose the course of restraint in foreign policy, as in Berlin, Laos, and the Cuban Missile Crisis. Over time he became increasingly skeptical about South Vietnam's prospects and hinted that he would seek an end to the U.S. commitment. Had he lived into 1964–65 he might well have ordered a negotiated disengagement.

A few authors have gone further and argued that JFK had quietly commenced an American withdrawal from Vietnam even at the time of his death. The evidence for this claim is thin, however, and a good reason to doubt it is the fact that neither his vice president nor his top national security advisers were aware of any such decision. It is more likely that Kennedy arrived in Dallas still groping for a solution to his Vietnam problem, postponing the truly agonizing choices until later.[18]

Johnson Takes Charge

"Later" in this case meant after the 1964 presidential election. If at all possible, Kennedy wanted to avoid dramatic moves in any direction—whether toward withdrawal or large-scale escalation—until after voting day. In crass political terms, he and his aides knew that the safest choice was "stay the present course." His successor knew it too. A legendary political operator who had been Senate majority leader before becoming vice president, LBJ had little interest in diplomacy or in the world beyond America's shores. His passion was domestic politics, and his supreme desire was to surpass the legislative achievements of his hero, Franklin Roosevelt. To have any hope of enacting sweeping social legislation, however, and of emerging from the slain Kennedy's shadow, LBJ knew he had to win election in his own right on November 3,

1964—and win convincingly. All options with respect to Vietnam, in what would prove to be a critically important eleven months of the war, were viewed through the prism of the upcoming election.

The circumstances of his ascension to the presidency was another factor that inclined Johnson to maintain the status quo in Vietnam during the early months of his administration. The country needed to heal, and he needed to show the American people that he was a worthy successor to the martyred leader. Now was no time to initiate major changes in Kennedy's foreign policies, nor to question the Vietnam commitment. From the start LBJ had been a supporter of Eisenhower's decision to sustain a noncommunist bastion in South Vietnam, and he came to the White House with a deep and abiding belief that the United States must stand firm against communism throughout the world. After President Kennedy's assassination, Johnson resorted on occasion—privately as well as publicly—to the domino effect in describing the choices that lay ahead. "We could pull out of there," he declared in a phone conversation in February 1964, not long after another coup in Saigon underscored the continuing instability in South Vietnam. "The dominoes would fall and that part of the world would go to the Communists. We could send our marines in there, and we could get tied down in a Third World War or another Korea action. The other alternative is to advise them and hope that they stand and fight."[19] The status quo, in other words, was best.

But the status quo proved unsustainable. In early 1964 political instability in South Vietnam deepened, and the Vietcong continued to register gains. The possibility loomed that the Saigon regime might collapse without a major increase in U.S. involvement. In a May phone conversation with McGeorge Bundy, LBJ revealed the depth his doubts and misgivings:

> I just stayed awake last night thinking of this thing, and the more that I think of it I don't know what in the hell, it looks like to me that we're getting into another Korea. It just wor-

ries the hell out of me. I don't see what we can ever hope to get out of there with once we're committed. I believe the Chinese Communists are coming into it. I don't think that we can fight them 10,000 miles away from home and ever get anywhere in that area. I don't think it's worth fighting for and I don't think we can get out. And it's just the biggest damn mess that I ever saw.

The president alluded to a military aide who had "kids" being deployed to Southeast Asia and wondered, "What in the hell am I ordering them out there for? What in the hell is Vietnam worth to me? What is Laos worth to me? What is it worth to this country?" And later in the conversation: "It's damn easy to get into a war, but . . . it's going to be awful hard to ever extricate yourself if you get in."[20] Yet getting out was not an option in Johnson's mind. That spring and summer, the administration, still seeking to keep the war on the back burner through the election, secretly planned an expansion of the war into North Vietnam and sent more U.S. military advisers to the South. The Soviet Union and China, meanwhile, increased their aid to North Vietnam (though that assistance never came close to matching U.S. totals for Saigon), and Hanoi stepped up the flow of materiel and men into the South.[21]

In early August 1964 an incident in the Gulf of Tonkin, off the coast of North Vietnam, drew Johnson's involvement. Twice in three days, U.S. destroyers reported coming under attack from North Vietnamese patrol boats. Despite a lack of evidence that the second attack had occurred, Johnson ordered retaliatory air strikes against selected North Vietnamese patrol boat bases and an oil depot. He also directed aides to rework a long-existing congressional resolution on the use of force. By a vote of 416 to 0 in the House and 88 to 2 in the Senate, Congress quickly passed the Gulf of Tonkin Resolution, which gave the president the authority to "take all necessary measures to repel any armed attack against the forces of the United States and to prevent further aggression." In so doing, Congress essentially surrendered its war-making powers to the executive branch. The resolution, Secretary of Defense McNamara later noted, served "to open the floodgates."[22]

To Johnson's delight, his public approval ratings went up dramatically, and his show of force effectively removed Vietnam as a campaign issue for GOP presidential candidate Barry Goldwater. The Republican had spent the summer advocating a tougher American posture in Vietnam. Indeed, his foreign policy platform was far to the right of any previous major party presidential nominee, and he preached the gospel of victory in Vietnam. In his book *Why Not Victory?* published in 1962, Goldwater argued that the fight against communism was "the central reality of our time" and that America must "go on the offensive. We can't win merely by trying to hold our own." Negotiations with Moscow should be flatly ruled out, and self-determination ought to be rejected in the Third World if an election would produce a communist regime.[23] The book was a bestseller, but the message did not translate into mass appeal in a national campaign. Johnson had deftly pushed Goldwater into a corner by demonstrating Cold War toughness on Vietnam with his initial bombing campaigns and belligerent rhetoric, while at the same time repeatedly vowing that American boys would not be sent to fight in Asia's wars. On election day he won by the largest plurality in U.S. history, and the Democrats added to their majorities in both houses of Congress. Goldwater mustered barely 38 percent of the vote.

Decision for War

Would Johnson keep his promise not to send U.S. soldiers to fight in Asia? He had good reason to. He had just won a resounding election victory and possessed commanding power in Washington. He was no longer the tragic successor to the slain JFK but a president in his own right—more than that, he had beaten Goldwater by a much greater margin than Kennedy had defeated Nixon in 1960. His Democratic Party was dominant on Capitol Hill. Now he had the opportunity to push his Great Society domestic legislation through Congress without having to worry about a looming election or a united and powerful Republican opposition. The economy was strong, and he enjoyed broad popular support in all parts of the country. Goldwater's hawkishness on Vietnam, meanwhile, had been as thoroughly repudiated by voters as it could have been.

Furthermore, Johnson had few illusions that a ground war in Vietnam could be won quickly and easily. If anything, his skepticism was deepening, as the military situation worsened in the final weeks of the year and the Saigon government became still more ineffectual. Seasoned observers inside and outside the administration—among them Undersecretary of State George Ball and the Senate Democratic leadership on foreign policy, Majority Leader Mike Mansfield, Armed Services Committee chairman and LBJ mentor Richard Russell, and Foreign Relations Committee chairman J. William Fulbright—privately warned the president that Vietnam could become a quagmire and advised him to seek a way out. In the press, the *New York Times,* the *Wall Street Journal,* and other major newspapers expressed deep misgivings about any escalation of U.S. involvement, as did prominent columnists such as Walter Lippmann. More hawkish voices, among them Secretary of Defense Robert McNamara and National Security Adviser McGeorge Bundy, peppered their stay-the-course recommendations with gloomily realistic assessments of the prospects in the struggle. Nor did the uniformed military promise an easy victory: five years and 500,000 troops—that was the general estimate the Joint Chiefs of Staff offered the White House. The war would be difficult and bloody, in other words, and would still be far from over when the campaigning began for the 1968 presidential election.[24]

Overseas, Johnson faced scant pressure to raise the stakes. A few Asian governments did express trepidation about what a communist victory in Vietnam would mean for their national security. Most Western leaders, however, while not unsympathetic to what the United States sought to achieve in South Vietnam—to preserve an independent, noncommunist government in Saigon—emphasized the importance of nationalism and doubted that communism in one country inevitably meant communism in neighboring states. Among the most outspoken on this point was French president Charles de Gaulle, who urged Americans to learn from his own country's tragic experience in Vietnam. Some key allies, including Great Britain, did offer tepid rhetorical support for an Americanization of the war, but they were hardly urging Johnson on. And Washington proved almost totally unsuccessful in gaining meaningful material support from friendly governments for the war effort. Deeply skeptical that a lasting military victory against the Vietcong could be achieved—especially in view of the perceived politico-military weakness of the South Vietnamese government, and the apathy and war weariness of the southern populace—many allied officials also harbored doubts that the outcome in Vietnam really mattered to the West.

It all gave Lyndon Johnson maneuverability on Southeast Asia, as did a more basic fact: the United States was not yet committed to large-scale war. American ground units had not yet been deployed; U.S. casualty figures remained low. The general public knew little about Vietnam, and probably cared less. There were no dramatic battles or campaigns for them to follow, and few citizens had any idea who the senior American commanders there were. Hardly anyone had ever heard of places like Hue or Danang. What Americans did know was that there had been no invasion over a clear border, such as had occurred in Korea in 1950, and that South Vietnam was not being overrun by Soviet tanks or Chinese troops. Indeed, although allied with Hanoi, both China and the

USSR were playing it quiet in early 1965, the former undergoing intense political turmoil at home in the form of Mao's Great Leap Forward, the latter experiencing a succession struggle following the peaceful ouster of Nikita Khrushchev in late 1964.

No less a figure than Vice President Hubert H. Humphrey drove these points home to Johnson in early 1965. Writing to the president in mid-February—a particularly crucial period in U.S. decisionmaking—Humphrey argued that an expanded war was both inadvisable and avoidable. "It is always hard to cut losses. But the Johnson administration is in a stronger position to do so now than any administration in this century. 1965 is the year of minimum political risk for the Johnson administration. Indeed, it is the first year when we can face the Vietnam problem without being preoccupied with the political repercussions from the Republican right." The American people did not have confidence in the South Vietnamese government, Humphrey warned, and had not been persuaded that a major war on its behalf was justified. In such a situation, popular backing for a large war would evaporate before long, just as it had during the Korean conflict—when, Humphrey added, the stakes had been clearer than they were now. "If we find ourselves leading from frustration to escalation and end up short of a war with China but embroiled deeper in fighting in Vietnam over the next few months," he wrote, "political opposition will steadily mount," especially among Democrats and independents.[25]

Humphrey's credentials in making this case were sterling. He was not merely a giant in the Democratic party but also a veteran Cold Warrior, having helped lead the attack on communist-led unions after World War II. He understood Democratic precinct politics across the country as well as anyone, Johnson included. No one needed to remind Hubert Horatio Humphrey of the troubles that could befall politicians—and especially Democrats—who were perceived as insufficiently tough in foreign policy, as too willing to conciliate communists. And Humphrey did not deny that backing away from a fight in Vietnam would bring attacks from the right, from the alarmists, from the military-industrial complex. But he insisted that the onslaught would be manageable, so strong was Johnson's political position in early 1965. This was the time to incur the risks of getting out, he urged the president, for the risks of escalation were far greater.

Johnson was unmoved. "We don't need all these memos," he reportedly told Humphrey.[26] That same month, following Vietcong attacks on American installations in South Vietnam that killed thirty-two Americans, LBJ ordered Operation Rolling Thunder, a bombing program planned the previous fall that continued, more or less uninterrupted, from February 1965 until October 1968. Then, on March 8, the first U.S. combat battalions came ashore near Danang. The North Vietnamese met the challenge. They hid in shelters and rebuilt roads and bridges with a tenaciousness that frustrated and awed American officials. They also increased infiltration into the South.

In July 1965, LBJ convened a series of top-level discussions about U.S. war policy. Though these deliberations were not as consequential as many historians have suggested—Johnson had by then made his choice, and the escalation of the conflict was already well under way—they did confirm that the American commitment would be more or less open-ended. On July 28 the president publicly announced a significant troop increase and disclosed that others would follow. Lawmakers on Capitol Hill, keen as always to rally around the flag and around the president when U.S. troops were in harm's way, expressed their support. By the end of 1965, more than 180,000 U.S. ground troops were in South Vietnam. In 1966 the figure climbed to 385,000, and by 1968 it would reach more than half a million. The Soviet Union and China responded by increasing their material assistance to North Vietnam, though their combined contributions never came close to matching American totals.

Explaining Escalation

Why Vietnam? This used to be a fairly easy question for historians and other analysts to answer. Early on, some authors subscribed to the so-called quagmire thesis, which held that the president didn't know what he was getting into in mid-1965 and made no decision for war per se. Rather, he escalated U.S. involvement incrementally, much as his predecessors had done, confident that each step was the last that would be necessary.[27] The subsequent release of massive amounts of archival documentation, however, renders this interpretation untenable. Johnson and his top aides, it is now clear, understood very well that their actions in early and mid-1965 represented more than an incremental step; it was a move to major war, and one that would be difficult to win.

Other authors have acknowledged that Johnson knew what he was doing but have maintained in effect that he had no choice. It would have been unthinkable for him—or any American president of that era—to have rejected the escalation and chosen what by early 1965 was the only real alternative in Vietnam: negotiated withdrawal. His decision was inevitable—overdetermined—by two principal groups of factors, both shaped by the Cold War: the domestic political context, and the demands of credibility in the world arena.[28]

The notion that Johnson had no real choice is beguiling at first glance, and also comforting (why puzzle over a decision if it was bound to be made?). But it does not square with the reality of the political environment in early 1965, as articulated by the Senate Democratic leadership, by the vice president, and by influential voices in the media. If the proponents of inevitability insist that even in these circumstances LBJ had little or no choice but to escalate, then the domestic political and international Cold War contexts become effectively meaningless: no matter what was happening in Washington, or in Moscow or Beijing or London or Saigon, once the United States became involved in Indochina, Johnson had to go to war. Vietnam becomes a predetermined event in history, as unavoidable as the tides. It turns the president and his advisers into powerless cogs of historical destiny. This won't do.

Johnson and his advisers knew they could choose war or seek some kind of withdrawal. (The alternative of merely continuing the present course was no longer an option by early 1965, so grim had the outlook for the Saigon regime become.) To understand why they opted for the former we must look at two factors. On one hand, LBJ believed—with what degree of conviction can be debated—that the United States could be a force for good in Vietnam, that it could help the Vietnamese achieve a better way of life. He spoke of creating a Tennessee Valley Authority–type project on the Mekong River, one that would bring benefits to North as well as South Vietnam. Some intellectuals in the foreign policy bureaucracy believed likewise; the United States, they insisted, could use the tools of foreign aid, development planning, and technical assistance to modernize the country and make it more like the United States. As LBJ put it, "I want to leave the footprints of America in Vietnam."[29] Was this a convenient rationalization? In part, perhaps. But Lyndon Johnson had shown himself vulnerable to the temptations of idealistic nation-building, whether at home, with his desire to build a Great Society that would abolish poverty and injustice forever, or abroad. This instinct allowed him to sleep better at night, to explain his decision to escalate as a progressive political act, not just another Cold War operation.

More important, to turn back in Vietnam would be to acknowledge failure, never an enticing proposition for politicians—or indeed for human beings generally. As Humphrey put it in his February memo, "It's always hard to cut losses." The president and his top Vietnam aides had put themselves in a box with their repeated affirmations of South Vietnam's importance to U.S. security. In the case of top advisors McNamara, Bundy, and Rusk (all of them holdovers from JFK), the affirmations went all the way back to 1961, and it is easy to see why they might stay the course in the hope that new measures would work. The alternative—to accept the limits of America's power to effect change and admit that going all out for victory might not be necessary after all—was too loathsome to contemplate. In the short term, quiet escalation, if done gradually without putting the nation on full war footing, offered Johnson the path of least resistance.[30]

The issue was credibility and the concern that it might be irreparably harmed by a failure to stand firm in Vietnam. At home, this meant the administration's domestic political credibility and, especially, the personal credibility of the president and his leading aides. LBJ worried that failure in Southeast Asia could harm his ambitious domestic agenda to secure civil rights for black Americans and to wage a war on poverty. Even more, he feared the personal humiliation he imagined would inevitably accompany a defeat (and for him, a negotiated withdrawal constituted defeat). To use Eisenhower's metaphor, he worried that he would be the last domino in the line to fall. Top advisers, meanwhile, feared for their reputations and careers should they abandon their previous support for a staunch commitment to South Vietnam's survival.

Internationally, the tepid support for the war among major allied governments did not prevent U.S. policymakers from worrying that America's credibility was on the line. In 1965 Johnson warned that "around the globe, from Berlin to Thailand, are people whose well-being rests, in part, on the belief that they can count on us if they are attacked. To leave Vietnam to its fate would shake the confidence of all these people in the value of America's commitment, the value of America's word."[31]

A memo by Assistant Secretary of Defense for International Security Affairs John McNaughton early the following year put it this way: "The present U.S. objective in Vietnam is to avoid humiliation. The reasons why we went into Vietnam to the present depth are varied; but they are now largely academic. Why we have not withdrawn is, by all odds, one reason: to preserve our reputation as a guarantor, and thus to preserve our effectiveness in the rest of the world. We have not hung on (2) to save a friend, or (3) to deny the Communists the added acres and heads (because the dominoes don't fall for that reason in this case), or even (4) to prove that 'wars of national liberation' won't work (except as our reputation is involved)."[32] In short, according to McNaughton, maintaining America's international credibility was now the sole reason for the U.S. presence in Vietnam.

But this condition of credibility was created in the White House. America's NATO partners were not questioning Washington's commitment to the Western alliance in the key months of decision on Vietnam. Beijing and Moscow were not indicating a readiness to embark upon a Cold War offensive should the United States opt against large-scale war. And notwithstanding the nervousness regarding the communist threat among some Asian governments in early 1965, none argued credibly that it would switch sides in the Cold War unless Washington stood firm. As for the Saigon government, racked by in-fighting and corruption, and by a general unwillingness to engage the Vietcong on the field of battle, it commanded little emotional attachment in Washington. The "intermestic" interpretation of U.S. foreign policy stipulates that international problems and crises are often transformed by Washington officials into matters of domestic politics, and there may be no purer example of this process at work than LBJ's decision to escalate in early 1965. Because for him, the pursuit of credibility over Vietnam ultimately had little to do with appeasing the military-industrial complex, or seizing votes or donations, or pandering to high-powered interest groups. For him, credibility meant his own personal reputation and his historical legacy. Already in late 1963, shortly after taking office, he had vowed that he would not be the president who lost Vietnam; he still adhered to that conviction a year and a half later.

Wither the Consensus?

American forces fought well and succeeded in their most pressing aim: to prevent a collapse of the South Vietnamese government. But if the stepped-up fighting in 1965 showed Hanoi leaders that the war would not be swiftly won, it also demonstrated the same thing to their counterparts in Washington. As the North Vietnamese matched each American escalation with one of their own, the conflict reached a stalemate. Discontent among Democrats in Congress, which had been widespread in the lead-up to Americanization but was kept mostly quiet, now burst into the open.

William Fulbright, the powerful chairman of the Senate Foreign Relations Committee and a long-time LBJ ally, was especially troubled, not merely about Vietnam but about the rationale for another military intervention ordered by Johnson, this one closer to home, in the Dominican Republic. Here, military officers in 1963 had ousted the leftwing noncommunist Juan Bosch, the nation's first elected leader since 1924. In April 1965 another group of military leaders tried to restore Bosch to power but were thwarted by the ruling junta. Announcing that "people trained outside the Dominican Republic" were seeking to gain control and that he would not allow "another Cuba," Johnson sent nearly 23,000 troops to the country.

Unfortunately for him, the CIA determined that no communists were involved. Undeterred, Johnson ordered the FBI to "find me some Communists in the Dominican Republic," and the American embassy duly produced a weakly-sourced list of fifty-eight (or fifty-three) "Communist and Castroite leaders" among the rebels.[33]

The intervention put an end to the rebellion, but it outraged many Latin Americans. Fulbright, disturbed by what he saw as an evolving pattern of interventionism backed up by dubious justifications, and perhaps feeling guilty for failing to make his Vietnam misgivings public in a timely fashion, in the fall of 1965 charged the White House with following a policy of deception. Other critics concurred that Johnson was playing less than straight with the American people, and the term "credibility gap" entered the political lexicon.

In early 1966 Fulbright held televised public hearings on whether the national interest was being served by pursuing the Vietnam War. He denounced the "arrogance of power" that had characterized American diplomacy since World War II, and he asked what exactly was the threat in Vietnam. Ridiculing the credibility imperative in both its domestic and foreign-policy dimensions, the senator noted that "certain pledges must be repeated every day lest the whole world go to rack and ruin—e.g., we will never go back on a commitment no matter how unwise." Secretary of State Dean Rusk testified that global communism was on the march and had to be stopped in Southeast Asia; the war, he lectured the committee, "is as much an act of outside aggression as though the Hanoi regime had sent an army across the seventeenth parallel rather than infiltrated armed forces by stealth."[34]

Fulbright was unmoved, and he found support among several members of the foreign relations establishment who testified before the committee. George F. Kennan said the containment doctrine he had helped author was meant to apply to Europe and Japan, not the volatile environment of Southeast Asia, an area in which Moscow was in any event little involved. America's "preoccupation" with Vietnam, Kennan stated, was undermining its global obligations, a point seconded by the realist theorist Hans J. Morgenthau and former army general James Gavin. Johnson responded by denouncing "nervous nellies . . . who become frustrated and bothered and break ranks under the strain and turn on their leaders, their own country and their fighting men."[35]

The hearings were one sign among several that the so-called Cold War consensus was breaking down—or, perhaps more accurately, that its nature had changed. Containment remained the watchword, but for Fulbright and other Democratic liberals it was a different kind of containment, closer to Kennan's original formulation—one that allowed more prioritizing regarding which areas of the world were truly vital to American interests. What mortal danger, exactly, did a communist victory in Vietnam pose to America? The critics could find none. How did fighting in Southeast Asia further the nation's Cold War aims? No good answer seemed forthcoming. The skepticism on these points was reflected in behind-the-scenes opposition to Americanization in the spring of 1965, and burst out for all to see in the Fulbright hearings.

Even now, however, there were clear limits to how far most lawmakers and other establishment figures were willing to go. Johnson could still count on broad support in Congress and in the press, in part because of the rally-around-the-president phenomenon that always manifests itself when U.S. forces are in harm's way. Even Richard Russell switched from being a dove to a hawk in spring 1965, on the grounds that supporting the troops meant supporting the administration's policy. Moreover, the politics of insecurity remained powerful in American political discourse. Legislators, Democrats no less than Republicans, saw few votes to be gained, and many potentially to be lost, if they appeared insufficiently steadfast in their anti-communism. "Why take the chance?" had been the operative question among election candidates at the dawn of the Cold War; if somewhat weakened, it retained its grip in American politics two decades later. As the fighting ground on through 1966 and into 1967, most in Congress were content in public to affirm the vital importance of the mission in Vietnam and to trust the vows of military leaders (in a perfect echo of the French in Indochina in 1952–53) that things were getting better and the war would ultimately be won.[36]

Inside the administration, though, several top officials were despondent, none more so than Robert McNamara. Despite private misgivings that dated back to late 1963, the secretary of defense had been a key champion of Americanization in 1965. Soon, however, he became increasingly angst-ridden by the killing and maiming of civilians by American bombing. In November 1965 he expressed doubt that long-term victory could ever be achieved, and by the following fall he concluded that the enemy's morale had not been broken and that South Vietnamese political stability remained as elusive as ever. The air war was failing and had cost the administration mightily in terms of domestic and world opinion. Meanwhile, U.S. casualty figures continued to rise, with more than 4,600 troops dying in 1966 alone.

America's credibility, far from being protected by the unwavering commitment to fighting, was suffering grievous damage, McNamara feared. "The picture of the world's greatest superpower killing or seriously injuring 1,000 non-combatants a week, while trying to pound a tiny, backward nation into submission on an issue whose merits are hotly disputed, is not a pretty one," he wrote Johnson in May 1967.[37] That year, despondent and anxious over the war, McNamara ordered a huge study of all the documents on Vietnam, going back to the 1940s, a study that came to be called *The Pentagon Papers*. Upon reading part of the finished product, he told a friend, "You know, they could hang people for what's in there."[38] (In 1971 ex-Pentagon employee Daniel Ellsberg, a former hawk who had turned against the war, would cause a national sensation by leaking the papers to the press.)

Johnson himself was hardly immune to doubts. From early on he had grasped the weakness of his South Vietnamese ally, had sensed the limits of American power in that part of the world, had known that the odds against success were long, had wondered if the outcome in Vietnam really mattered to U.S. security. Yet he had never seriously considered backing away from the fight. After mid-1965 he pressed aides constantly for new negotiating ideas, but, as Undersecretary of State George Ball later put it, "he really meant merely new channels and procedures." The administration, Ball recalled telling colleagues, was "following the traditional pattern for negotiating with a mule; just keep hitting him on the head with a two-by-four until he does what you want him to do. But that was useless with Hanoi; the mule's head was harder than the two-by-four."[39] Though on occasion Johnson halted the bombing to disarm critics and to encourage Ho Chi Minh to negotiate on America's terms, such pauses often were accompanied by increases in American troop strength. Hanoi likewise drove a hard bargain, demanding a complete suspension of bombing raids before sitting down at the conference table.

The fighting continued. In the months before the onset of major war in 1965, numerous observers predicted that once the real shooting started and the body counts skyrocketed, both sides would dig in, and compromise would become more difficult. This proved to be all too correct. And as in World War II and Korea, the White House's first instinct when encountering a stubborn adversary would be to step up the bombing. From Roosevelt onward, leaders would almost always prefer military strategies that exploited America's technological superiority and promised to minimize U.S. casualties, even if that meant the mass killing of hundreds of thousands of civilians on the other side. Johnson was no exception: between 1965 and his departure from office in early 1969, the United States bombarded much of Vietnam, killing and maiming many hundreds of thousands of Vietnamese (including South Vietnamese that U.S policy purported to protect) and turning much of the countryside into a barren moonscape.

All the while, allied governments continued to complain that

Washington's fixation with Vietnam was diverting attention from other pressing issues. There is truth in this claim, but it can be overstated. Johnson worked quite hard to keep the Western alliance on an even keel and to maintain the improved Soviet-American relationship started by Kennedy and Khrushchev in the wake of the Missile Crisis.[40] On both counts he was broadly successful, though de Gaulle caused consternation in Washington with his decision to withdraw France from the military commitments of the NATO alliance (although not from NATO itself) and though the Vietnam escalation arguably retarded progress toward superpower détente. The nuclear arms race between the two giants continued. The Soviets, desperate to reach parity, had almost 900 intercontinental ballistic missiles (ICBMs) in their arsenal by 1967, while the United States had 1,054. Johnson and McNamara bemoaned the proliferation of weapons but did little to bring about a meaningful change. The military-industrial complex had lost none of its insatiable appetite for more warheads, additional troops, bigger bombers. And besides, Vietnam demanded so much attention, so much of the time. The administration also seemed slow off the mark when war erupted between Israel and three of its Arab neighbors, Egypt, Jordan, and Syria. After the Suez crisis of 1956, the USSR had supplied the Egyptian army while the United States had helped make Israel the strongest military power in the region. The Kennedy administration tried for a time to steer a middle course, maintaining the advantage of Israel's military power while also wooing Egypt's Gamal Abdel Nasser away from the Soviets. Over time, though, U.S. policy tilted more and more in a pro-Israel direction, especially after the sale of Hawk surface-to-air missiles in 1962 and Johnson's ascension to the presidency the following year. The flow of weapons expanded, and in 1965–66 Israel received the first shipments of U.S. tanks and Skyhawk bombers.[41]

The influence of right-wing pro-Israel groups at home help account for this shift. In large part stymied during the Eisenhower years, the Israel lobby under Kennedy and Johnson made its presence felt. Years later, reflecting on the Hawk sale, the U.S. ambassador to Cairo, John Badeau, acknowledged that the Pentagon thought Israel genuinely needed the missiles. "But I don't think this is why it was done." According to Badeau, the sale went through because contributors to various congressional campaigns withheld their funds in the summer of 1962 and said, "'You don't get this until we know what you're going to do for Israel.' And finally, the president said, 'Well, I've got military justifications, I'm going to sell Hawk missiles to Israel' and then he got the funds." Author Warren Bass, a careful student of this period, has been skeptical of Badeau's explanation, and it would certainly be too much to say that this domestic pressure was solely responsible either for the Hawk decision or the arms deals that followed. But the principal reason for Bass's doubtfulness—that the documentary record, he has maintained, does not support Badeau's claim—is itself open to question: such maneuverings and manipulations are hardly the type to be recorded on paper.[42] The partnership between Israel and the United States blossomed in the Kennedy-Johnson years, and it can hardly be doubted that Washington made policy partly with domestic political imperatives in mind.

Tensions in the Middle East grew. In 1967 Egypt threatened the Gulf of Aqaba, the entranceway to Israel's key southern port of Elat. Johnson begged Israeli foreign minister Abba Eban for more time to secure a peaceful settlement. The Israelis waited two weeks, then struck suddenly on June 5. In the resulting Six-Day War they scored a resounding victory by seizing the Sinai Peninsula and the Gaza Strip from Egypt, the West Bank and East Jerusalem from Jordan, and the Golan Heights from Syria. Instantly, Israel gained 28,000 square miles and could henceforth defend itself more easily against invading military forces.

But the victory came at a price. Gaza and the West Bank were the ancestral home of hundreds of thousands of Palestinians and the more recent home of additional hundreds of thousands of Palestinian refugees from the 1948 Arab-Israeli conflict. Suddenly Israel found itself ruling over large numbers of bitter Palestinians who naturally regarded the state as the enemy. When the Israelis began to establish Jewish settlements in their newly won areas, Arab resentment grew even stronger, and it began to turn on a United States that seemed unwilling to pressure Israel to cease its settlement activity, despite a UN resolution demanding just that. With U.S.-Israel ties growing ever closer, Johnson refused to criticize the Jewish state even after the Israelis bombed an American ship deployed in the Mediterranean, the *USS Liberty*, killing 34 sailors and injuring 171. He stayed mum even after senior aides questioned the official Israeli explanation that the attack was a case of mistaken identity.[43]

In the wake of the Six-Day War, Soviet Prime Minister Alexei Kosygin came to New York to attend a special session of the United Nations. While in America, he met Johnson for their only encounter, at a hastily planned summit conference in Glassboro, New Jersey. It was a small but meaningful step toward stronger bilateral relations. Johnson wanted Moscow, the largest supplier of military aid to North Vietnam, to pressure Ho Chi Minh to make peace. Kosygin was noncommittal, but he assured the American that his government would take no action that might lead to a direct Soviet-American confrontation in Vietnam. Soviet economic growth had slowed drastically, and Kosygin sought a way to limit the arms race between the superpowers. An impassioned warning by U.S. Secretary of Defense McNamara that the arms race was suicidal and must be eased helped Kosygin's cause, and the two sides announced a Nuclear Non-Proliferation Treaty (NPT).[44] The far right denounced the deal (William F. Buckley's *National Review* called it a "nuclear Yalta") even though, as American negotiators intended, it promised to lock in an inequality between nuclear and nonnuclear states.[45] But the Soviet invasion of Czechoslovakia in

August to crush an incipient reform movement known as "Prague Spring" prevented Johnson from sending the NPT to the Senate for approval. The invasion also killed a planned visit by Johnson to Moscow to discuss further measures aimed at improving bilateral relations. Cold War temperatures dropped markedly.[46]

Though Buckley and others on the right would have scoffed at the notion, the Soviet crackdown in Czechoslovakia was further evidence of Moscow's dissipating authority within the Eastern Bloc. The reform-minded Czech leader Alexander Dubcek had sought to meet popular clamor for greater political freedoms and economic reforms while reiterating fealty to the USSR, but it proved an impossible task. Kremlin leaders could not risk the spread of the "anti-Soviet bacillus" into other Warsaw Pact nations and so made the reluctant decision to use military power. Henceforth, few could doubt that Soviet control over eastern Europe rested solely on naked force and the readiness to use it. Western supporters of the Soviet Union, dwindling in numbers since the intervention in Hungary a decade earlier, were now almost nowhere to be found.[47]

"The Establishment Bastards Have Bailed Out"

Inside the Johnson White House, Vietnam still overshadowed everything. On January 31, 1968, the first day of the Vietnamese New Year (Tet), Vietcong and North Vietnamese forces struck all across South Vietnam, capturing provincial capitals. During the carefully planned offensive, the Saigon airport, the presidential palace, and the ARVN headquarters came under attack. Even the American embassy compound was penetrated by Vietcong soldiers, who occupied its courtyard for six hours. U.S. and South Vietnamese units eventually regained much of the ground they had lost, inflicting heavy casualties and devastating numerous villages.

Although the Tet Offensive was far from the resounding battlefield victory Hanoi strategists hoped for, the heavy fighting called into question American military leaders' confident predictions in earlier months that the war would soon be won. Had not the Vietcong and North Vietnamese demonstrated that they could strike when and where they wished? If America's airpower, dollars, and half a million troops could not now defeat the Vietcong, could they ever do so? Had the American public been deceived? In February, the highly respected CBS television anchorman Walter Cronkite went to Vietnam to find out. "We are mired in a stalemate," he announced on the evening news upon his return. "To say that we are closer to victory today is to believe, in the face of evidence, the optimists who have been wrong in the past."[48]

Top presidential advisers sounded notes of despair. Clark Clifford, the new secretary of defense, told Johnson that the war ("a sinkhole") could not be won, even with the 206,000 additional soldiers requested by General William Westmoreland, commander of U.S. forces. Aware that the nation was suffering a financial crisis prompted by rampant deficit spending to sustain the war, along with other global commitments, they knew that taking the initiative in Vietnam would cost billions more, further derail the budget, panic foreign owners of dollars, and wreck the economy. Clifford heard from his associates in the business community: "These men now feel we are in a hopeless bog," he told the president. To "maintain public support for the war without the support of these men" was impossible.[49]

Key architects of America's Cold War policies also chimed in. Former secretary of state Dean Acheson, NSC-68 author Paul Nitze, and veteran diplomat W. Averell Harriman—all top Truman advisers and all committed Cold Warriors—banded together with Clifford and other administration insiders to persuade Johnson to alter course. "Our leader ought to be concerned with areas that count," Acheson, previously a hawk on Vietnam, acidly observed. He and other so-called Wise Men attended a White House meeting on March 26–27 during which a dominant theme was put forth:

in Vietnam the United States could "no longer do the job we have set out to do in the time we have left and we must begin to take steps to disengage." A downcast LBJ is said to have mumbled after the meeting: "The establishment bastards have bailed out."[50]

Controversy over the war split the Democratic Party, just as a presidential election loomed in November. Senator Eugene McCarthy of Minnesota and Robert F. Kennedy (now a senator from New York), both strong opponents of Johnson's war policies, forcefully challenged the president in early primaries. Strained by exhausting sessions with skeptical advisers, troubled by the economic implications of escalation, and sensing that more resources would not bring victory, Johnson changed direction. Over a period of days in March, he made a decision that to many had been unthinkable: he chose not to run for reelection. The weight of the war was too much, the divisions in the country too deep.

LBJ announced his decision in a televised speech on March 31, during which he also called for peace in Vietnam. The United States would unconditionally halt the bombing of North Vietnam, with the exception of a small area just north of the DMZ, Johnson declared. Even that very limited bombing would end if Hanoi showed similar restraint. "Our purpose in this action," he said, "is to bring about a reduction in the level of violence that now exists. It is to save the lives of brave men—and to save the lives of innocent women and children. It is to permit the contending forces to move closer to a political settlement . . . I call upon President Ho Chi Minh to respond positively, and favorably, to this new step toward peace." The negotiations began in Paris in May.[51]

Progress on the diplomatic front came well too late for a burgeoning antiwar movement, one tied in many ways to other radical political movements of the late 1960s. Indeed, in the spring and summer of 1968 America appeared to be coming apart at the seams. Several cities erupted in violence after Martin Luther King Jr., the legendary civil rights figure, was assassinated on April 4.

Two months after that, Robert Kennedy was felled by an assassin's bullet in Los Angeles. At the Democratic National Convention in Chicago in August, Vice President Hubert Humphrey—who after prophetically warning LBJ against escalation in February 1965 had been banished from Vietnam deliberations, until he turned himself into an outspoken hawk—became the nominee in the midst of massive antiwar demonstrations. Hundreds of Chicago police joined 6,000 troops in clubbing the protesters, a frenzy of repression that would later be officially termed a "police riot." Johnson, fearful of the response that would greet him, stayed away from the convention.

The main beneficiary of these troubles was the Republican nominee, Richard Nixon, who was thought to be politically dead following his defeat by John Kennedy in 1960 and his failed bid for governor of California in 1962. Now, he was on the verge of an extraordinary comeback. Nixon campaigned tirelessly in the fall, vowing to "end the war and win the peace." How he would do so he didn't say, but he acknowledged the high price exacted by Vietnam on U.S. society and on America's standing in the world. The United States faced numerous challenges in world affairs, Nixon told aides, and would be unable to confront them so long as the fighting continued. What's more, his own political success depended on early resolution of the struggle. "I'm not going to end up like LBJ," he vowed after eking out a narrow victory over Humphrey in November. "I'm going to stop that war. Fast."[52]

7

NIXON'S WORLD

It was Richard Nixon's destiny to be president of the United States during a period of extraordinary tumult in world affairs. On his watch the cultural phenomenon we call The Sixties reached its zenith, and the East-West rapprochement over Europe begun in 1962–63 gained a firmer hold, by way of "détente." In the Middle East the fragile post-1967 truce between Israel and the Arab states broke down into renewed fighting, and an oil embargo directed against the United States created America's first energy crisis. In South Asia, warfare erupted between India and Pakistan, and a new state—Bangladesh—came into being. Skirmishing on the Sino-Soviet border in 1969 cast in stark relief the tensions between the two communist giants and helped facilitate a remarkable series of communications and meetings between U.S. and Chinese leaders that would culminate in the full restoration of diplomatic relations in 1979. Meanwhile, in Southeast Asia the 1973 Paris Peace Accords ended America's combat involvement in Vietnam, and two years later Saigon fell to North Vietnamese forces. In 1975, not long after Nixon resigned from office in disgrace over the Watergate revelations, the Helsinki conference on security and cooperation in Europe was convened, signifying further movement away from the bipolar Cold War verities of the past.[1]

To some degree, Nixon understood that he was entering office at a pivotal moment in postwar history. His inaugural address on January 20, 1969, implicitly acknowledged the erosion of American power vis-à-vis both rivals and allies, as he announced a new "era of negotiations" to replace the old one of "confrontation."[2] Eugene Rostow, undersecretary of state in the outgoing Johnson administration, had referred to a "diffusion of power" in the world system, and neither Nixon nor his principal lieutenant on foreign policy, National Security Adviser Henry Kissinger, questioned that characterization. They understood that the United States had over-reached in Vietnam with a military commitment that had caused massive bloodshed, deep domestic divisions, and economic dislocation. The difficulties of the war, coupled with the economic recovery of western Europe and Japan, signified to both men that American power was limited and, relative to its prior status, in decline.

Nixon and Kissinger moved quickly to reorient America's Cold War policy to take account of this new reality. In particular, they maintained that the United States had to adapt to a new, more multipolar international system; no longer could that system be defined simply by the Soviet-American rivalry. Western Europe was becoming a major player in its own right, as was Japan, while political unrest in the Middle East loomed large. Above all, the United States had to come to grips with the reality of China by re-thinking its policy of hostile isolation. Even without the "purgatory" of Vietnam, Kissinger later observed, "a major reassessment of American foreign policy would have been in order, for the age of America's nearly total dominance of the world stage was drawing to a close."[3]

To be sure, Nixon and Kissinger were hardly alone in grasping these realities. Their "Grand Design" in foreign policy was not quite as grand, or as novel, as they and their acolytes liked to claim.[4] Important groundwork for an opening to Beijing had been laid by the Johnson administration, and the first moves toward détente with Moscow had been made even earlier, in President Kennedy's final year. On Vietnam, LBJ's senior aides—though arguably not the president himself—had long since concluded that a drawdown of the American commitment was imperative. No less than Nixon and Kissinger, these officials understood that western Europe and Japan were now bigger players on the international stage and that the Middle East was a cauldron of tension.

The fact remains, however, that the full reassessment to which Kissinger referred took place only in 1969, after the new administration was in place. Circumstances at home and abroad were now more favorable than before. And the reassessment yielded a number of diplomatic triumphs, notably in the *annus mirabilis* of 1972, when extraordinary summit meetings in Beijing and Moscow were followed by a preliminary peace agreement in Vietnam. Nixon the arch anti-communist proved to be a nimble and flexible negotiator with communists, and more willing than many in Washington to acknowledge the existence of a new configuration of world power. He showed himself able to move beyond the simplistic, Manichean Cold War rhetoric that he himself had done so much to institutionalize two decades before. No longer was he the Red-baiter who in the 1952 campaign had relished taking the low road, who had saddled Adlai Stevenson, a confirmed Cold Warrior, with the designation "Adlai the Appeaser," and with having "a PhD from Acheson's College of Cowardly Communist Containment."[5]

Yet the Nixon era also witnessed major failures in U.S. foreign policy. By the time Nixon resigned in 1974, the Grand Design lay in tatters, the victim of his and Kissinger's penchant for secrecy and deceit, of a lack of cooperation at key moments by other governments, both friendly and not, and of the two men's unwillingness to do the laborious work of maintaining lasting domestic support for their initiatives.

This last failure is richly ironic, in view of the administration's obsessive interest in viewing all foreign policy options through the lens of domestic politics. Of course, Nixon and Kissinger always denied that crass partisan concerns ever influenced foreign policy. For example, in 1974, as the Watergate affair closed in on the White House and speculation was rife about the scandal's impact on diplomacy, Kissinger proclaimed that American foreign policy had always been, and continued to be, made on a bipartisan basis in the national interest. The internal record proves otherwise. Confident of the fundamental security of the American homeland, the two men allowed party politics to enter the policy equation from January 1969 to the end. To listen to even a few of the Nixon tapes (to his everlasting regret, Nixon began taping conversations in the Oval Office in early 1971) is to be struck by the degree to which foreign policy options were evaluated in terms of their likely effect on the administration's standing at home, especially among key interest groups, and how they would help or hurt Nixon's chances for reelection in 1972 and for keeping his job two years hence in the face of scandal.

Seizing Control of Foreign Policy

They were an odd pair—the reclusive, ambitious Californian, son of a grocer, and the sociable, dynamic refugee from Nazi Germany. Nixon, ten years older, was more or less a career politician, whereas Kissinger had made his name as a Harvard professor and well-connected foreign policy consultant. Nixon was a staunch Republican, while Kissinger would have been quite prepared to join Hubert Humphrey's administration had the Democrat prevailed in the election. (Covering his bases, Kissinger privately told Democrats during the campaign that Nixon was a "disaster" who was "unfit to be president.")[6] His deep German accent and slow delivery seemed to add *gravitas* to Kissinger's pronouncements, and he had a sense of humor that Nixon conspicuously lacked—even being willing to poke fun at his own vanity: "I have been called indispensable and a miracle worker. I know because I remember every word I say."[7] What the two men had in common was a love of power and zest for intrigue, a tendency toward paranoia with respect to their rivals, and a capacity to think in large conceptual terms about America's place in the world.

They also shared a conviction that foreign policy should be made in the White House—and only in the White House. "It is no accident," Kissinger wrote as early as 1961, "that most great statesmen were opposed by the experts in their foreign affairs, for the very greatness of the statesman's conception tends to make it inaccessible to those whose primary concern is with safety and minimum risk." Nixon, for his part, told a group of American diplomats in 1969: "If the Department of State has had a new idea in the last twenty-five years, it is not known to me."[8] Nixon accordingly tapped William Rogers, a New York lawyer and ally from the Eisenhower years, to be secretary of state. Discreet and loyal, Rogers knew little about foreign policy and could be counted on to keep the department quiet while the White House took charge.

On inauguration day the president issued a memorandum, drafted by Kissinger, that made clear who was boss on matters of high foreign policy. All policy papers, the directive demanded, must henceforth go through the National Security Council and receive clearance from Kissinger and his staff. A few weeks later, Nixon urged Anatoly Dobrynin, the Soviet ambassador, to bypass the State Department on vital issues and deal directly with Kissinger. Soviet-American relations would be conducted mostly through this backchannel during the Nixon years, with Dobrynin often meeting Kissinger in the White House's ground-floor Map Room, his car arriving through the service entrance to avoid detection by reporters.

Nixon distrusted the entire foreign policy bureaucracy, at the CIA as well as State, believing it to be peopled by "Ivy League liberals" who had always been out to destroy him politically. The Democratic Congress, too, should be circumvented as much as possible, and for the same reason. Centralizing foreign policy in the White House as much as possible was the only way to ensure its proper implementation and prevent political enemies from undermining the administration and thwarting the president's reelection four years hence.

De-Americanizing Vietnam

Vietnam of course posed a major potential threat to Nixon's reelection, and to everything that Nixon and Kissinger sought to accomplish in foreign policy. From the start the war was issue number one, a "bone in the throat" (as one adviser, recalling Khrushchev's earthy metaphor, put it) that had to be removed before real progress could be made on other pressing matters. Nixon and Kissinger liked to say that they were inheriting a Vietnam mess not of their own making, which ignored the fact that both had been hawks on Vietnam since well before the war's Americanization in 1965.[9] Indeed, Nixon's attitude toward the region could be traced back to his early days as vice president in 1953–54.[10] But they understood that the fighting was generating deep divisions at home and hurting the nation's image abroad and that some means must be found to wind down America's involvement. At the same time, like officials in the Johnson administration, they feared that a precipitous withdrawal would harm U.S. credibility on the world stage. And like LBJ, Nixon—who had led Republican attacks on Truman for "losing" China—feared for his political survival should he allow South Vietnam to fall to communism on his watch.

Did Nixon in these early months believe he could achieve victory in Vietnam? It's hard to be sure. Already the previous spring, in late March 1968, he had told a group of speechwriters that he believed there was no way the war could be won.[11] But there's also evidence that Nixon and Kissinger initially believed they could succeed where Johnson had failed and end the war "honorably," through an agreement that preserved, for the indefinite future, an independent, noncommunist South Vietnam. To accomplish this aim, they tried in the early months to convince Moscow to pressure Hanoi into ending the war on U.S. terms, in exchange for increased Soviet-American trade and diplomatic engagement. This effort bore little fruit, whereupon the administration embarked on a policy that at once contracted and expanded the war.[12]

A centerpiece of the policy was Vietnamization—the building up of South Vietnamese forces to replace U.S. forces. This idea to "de-Americanize" the war had taken root late in the Johnson period, and its chief proponent under Nixon was Secretary of Defense Melvin Laird, a former congressman who was acutely conscious of the national mood (and whose role has been underplayed in the literature). Nixon too came to see the logic, hoping such action would quiet domestic opposition and also advance the peace talks under way in Paris since May 1968. Accordingly, Nixon authorized the first of fourteen unilateral American troop withdrawals, which reduced the troop count from 543,000 in the spring of 1969 to 156,800 by the end of 1971, and to 60,000 by the fall of 1972. Vietnamization did help to limit domestic dissent—as did the implementation of a lottery system in the draft, by which only those eligible nineteen-year-olds with low lottery numbers would be subject to conscription—but it did nothing to end the stalemate in the Paris negotiations.[13]

Even as he embarked on this troop withdrawal, therefore, Nixon intensified the bombing of North Vietnam and enemy supply depots in neighboring Cambodia, hoping to pound Hanoi into making concessions. The bombing of neutral Cambodia commenced in March 1969. Over the next fourteen months, B-52 pilots flew 3,600 missions and dropped over 100,000 tons of bombs on that country. At first the administration went to great lengths to keep the bombing campaign secret. When the North Vietnamese refused to buckle, Nixon turned up the heat: in April 1970 South Vietnamese and U.S. forces invaded Cambodia in search of arms depots and North Vietnamese army sanctuaries. The president announced publicly that he would not allow "the world's most powerful nation" to act "like a pitiful, helpless giant."[14]

Instantly, the antiwar movement rose up as students on about 450 college campuses went out on strike and hundreds of thousands of demonstrators gathered in various cities to protest the administration's policies. The crisis atmosphere intensified further on May 4, 1970, when National Guardsmen in Ohio fired into a crowd of fleeing students at Kent State University, killing four young people and wounding eleven. In Congress, where opposition to the war had been building over the previous months, Nixon's widening of the war sparked outrage, and in June the Senate terminated the Tonkin Gulf Resolution of 1964. After two months, U.S. troops withdrew from Cambodia, having accomplished little. Even before the Cambodian setback, Nixon and Kissinger had begun to lower their expectations and redefine victory downward. Vietnamization was not having the desired results, and Hanoi stuck to a firm line in the Paris negotiations. The Saigon government, meanwhile, was weak and ineffectual. More and more, Nixon and Kissinger began to adduce a different measure of "success": no longer would it be achieving a victory over the Vietcong, or even establishing a solid South Vietnamese regime, but merely ensuring a sufficient length of time between the American exit and the almost-certain collapse of the government. A "decent interval" between the U.S departure and the fall of Saigon, Nixon and Kissinger hoped, could allow the administration to saddle Nguyen Van Thieu's government and the American antiwar critics with responsibility for the defeat. A second failed incursion, this one into Laos in early 1971 without American ground forces, was further proof of the South Vietnamese army's dependence on U.S. support. That summer, public disillusionment grew. A colossal 71 percent of citizens polled now agreed that the United States had erred in sending troops to Vietnam, and 58 percent saw the war as "immoral."[15]

Of course, there was no way to know in advance how "decent" the "interval" would be. Therefore, Nixon and Kissinger determined that the U.S. withdrawal would have to be gradual and that South Vietnam would have to be kept alive through the autumn of 1972, lest Nixon be tagged by voters as the president who lost Vietnam, the man who squandered 20,000 additional American lives for no good purpose at all. A March 1971 conversation recorded on the Oval Office taping system between Kissinger and Nixon captured the new thinking clearly:

> K: Well, we've got to get enough time to get out. It's got to be because—
>
> N: Oh, I understand.
>
> K:—we have to make sure that they don't knock the whole place over.
>
> N: I don't mean [*unclear*]. What?
>
> K: Our problem is that if we get out after all the suffering we've gone through—
>
> N: And then have it knocked over, oh [*unclear*]—
>
> K: We can't have it knocked over—brutally, to put it brutally—before the election.
>
> N: That's right.[16]

Détente

Even as they sought to achieve an "honorable" exit from Vietnam, Nixon and Kissinger pressed forward with the broader task of adapting U.S. foreign policy to a more even distribution of global power. This meant, in the first instance, increased burden-sharing with America's allies, through what became known as the Nixon

Doctrine: "We cannot supply all the conceptions and all the resources."[17] It also necessitated, in their judgment, a new relationship of détente with the Soviet Union—increased cooperation with Moscow through negotiations within a general environment of competition.

As this definition implies, détente did not mean the abandonment of containment or the end of the superpower rivalry. Checking Soviet expansion and limiting the Kremlin's arms buildup remained the primary purpose of U.S. foreign policy; the difference was that now this goal would be accomplished through diplomacy and mutual concessions. Kissinger, in particular, hoped to diminish the ideological intensity of Soviet-American relations, to make the Cold War more of a traditional great power rivalry like that of Europe during the nineteenth century.[18]

Specifically, the administration hoped to use "linkage"—tying American concessions in one area of the superpower relationship to positive results on issues of special importance to the United States. As Nixon put it not long after the inauguration: "Soviet leaders should be brought to understand that they cannot expect to reap the benefits of cooperation in one area while seeking to take advantage of tension or confrontation elsewhere."[19] Stern words, but ones that acknowledged a more level playing field than before. Since the Cuban Missile Crisis early in the decade, the Soviets had systematically built up their nuclear arsenal, to the point that by 1969 they had more land-based ICBMs than the United States. They still trailed in the number of submarine-launched ballistic missiles and nuclear-capable bombers, but overall the gap between the nuclear arsenals of the two superpowers was shrinking fast—from four-to-one in favor of the United States in 1964 to merely two-to-one now.[20]

Even that advantage might have been deemed adequate in Washington's eyes were it not for two other worrisome developments. One was the prospect of a viable system of antiballistic missile (ABM) defense, which had been contemplated since the mid-1950s but had always foundered on technical obstacles. In the intervening years, the obstacles had not disappeared, but the Soviets had begun building a local system around Moscow. If it was deemed to be workable, the delicate balance of terror on which nuclear deterrence had always been based would be upset. Second, in 1968 the United States began testing multiple independently targeted reentry vehicles (MIRVs)—missiles with several nuclear warheads, each capable of hitting a different target. As with the ABM system, MIRVs could tempt one side into risking a first strike on the other. The Nixon administration thought it imperative to engage the Kremlin leadership in discussions about the implications of these new technologies.

Nixon and Kissinger also felt pressure from NATO allies for improved East-West relations. Many of these countries were experiencing social turmoil within their own societies, and their leaders saw political benefits in promoting order in the global arena.[21] West Germany's Willy Brandt, through his policy of Ostpolitik, sought to build bridges across the Cold War divide by improving relations with East Germany and the USSR. The aim, said his foreign policy adviser Egon Bahr, was "change through rapprochement," in which "small steps are better than none." Several small steps were indeed taken, in summits between Brandt and the leaders of East Germany, Poland, and the Soviet Union. These efforts might have been seen by Nixon and Kissinger as complementary to their own attempts at achieving rapprochement, but instead the two men were annoyed. They did not wish to be upstaged, and they worried that Moscow might, in Kissinger's words, "use the climate of détente to argue that NATO is unnecessary."[22]

Soviet leaders had their own reasons for wanting détente. For a decade they had sought to regularize relations with the United States and to gain acceptance by the West of the USSR's status as the other global superpower; détente was one more step in that process. Détente might, moreover, generate serious progress on European issues, including the status of Germany and Berlin, and in the process raise the Soviet Union's standing on the world stage, which had been damaged by its brutal invasion of Czechoslovakia in 1968. Of greater importance, détente could ameliorate the USSR's worsening economic problems. Far more so than in the United States, the Cold War had been a drain on Soviet resources, and by the late 1960s defense spending and consumer demands were increasingly at odds. Agricultural productivity was consistently too low to meet the nation's needs, and industrial growth had lagged. The West's widening superiority in advanced technology led party secretary Leonid Brezhnev (who by this time had gained ascendancy in the Soviet collective leadership) and Prime Minister Alexei Kosygin to privately preach a new line wholly at odds with former premier Nikita Khrushchev's nationalist bluster: the need to secure technology transfers from the West.[23]

Détente with Washington would also allow the USSR to focus its energies on the threat from China. Sino-Soviet relations had deteriorated sharply during the 1960s, and Mao Zedong's Great Proletarian Cultural Revolution, launched in 1966 and aimed at purging party hacks and rejuvenating his revolution, had generated an intense xenophobic nationalism by the time it abated in 1969.[24] In March of that year Sino-Soviet tensions exploded into an armed clash along the Ussuri River, at the extreme northeastern tip of Chinese territory, between Vladivostok and Khabarovsk. The Chinese were the instigators, and several hundred casualties resulted. Although tensions eased eventually, Kremlin leaders remained acutely anxious about the bilateral relationship, particularly in view of China's fast-growing population.[25]

In October 1969 the two superpowers agreed to begin arms control talks in Helsinki and Vienna. Much of the real agenda, however, was shaped in secret by the Kissinger-Dobrynin backchannel in Washington. Often the two men met daily: in 1972 alone they spoke 130 times. These backchannel discussions undermined the morale of U.S. diplomats involved in the regular negotiations. Chief American arms control negotiator Gerard Smith was especially frustrated, denouncing what he termed Kissinger's "duplicitous diplomacy."[26] In the spring of 1971, after more than a year of wrangling over dizzyingly complex points, the two sides at last announced a preliminary agreement: they would negotiate an ABM treaty and simultaneously set general limits on offensive weapons. The accords would be formally signed at a summit meeting a year hence.

"The Week That Changed the World"

All the while, Richard Nixon moved with determination to secure what he hoped would be his crowning foreign policy achievement: the opening of diplomatic relations with the People's Republic of China. Though Kissinger would later refer to "our China initiative," it was in fact Nixon's brainchild.[27] For several years he had expressed interest in mending fences with the Chinese, and he was further encouraged by the deepening Sino-Soviet schism, which showed conclusively that the communist world could no longer be considered monolithic. Nixon also knew that his own anti-communist stridency, though it had mellowed as the 1960s progressed, provided him with important cover on the domestic front, immunizing him against charges of "appeasement" and being "soft on the Reds." In a well-known article in *Foreign Affairs* in 1967, he argued for ending China's separation from "the family of nations," lest it "nurture its fantasies . . . and threaten its neighbors."[28] Well aware that much of the foreign policy establishment and key segments of corporate America likewise favored an opening to China, and that a dramatic move in this direction could gain him domestic political advantage, Nixon pushed the issue quietly but firmly in the early months after his inauguration.

Kissinger was a more reluctant convert. Never much interested in Asian matters, he kept his focus resolutely on Europe and on American relations with the USSR. In February 1969 when Nixon made his hope for a China initiative clear, Kissinger reportedly told an aide, "Our Leader has taken leave of his reality. He has just ordered me to make this flight of fantasy come true."[29] In the months thereafter, the national security adviser remained staunchly skeptical; yet, lacking an independent power base of his own, he had no real option but to go along with Nixon's wishes. In time, Kissinger came to accept the president's arguments that rapprochement with Beijing could give the administration leverage in its dealings with the Soviet Union, and also bring Chinese help with Vietnam. China might be induced to put pressure on Hanoi to settle the war on terms reasonably favorable to the United States.

The Chinese, too, looked forward to turning the page in Sino-American relations. Both Mao Zedong and Prime Minister Zhou Enlai viewed with concern their country's isolation on the world stage. The Cultural Revolution had been disastrous for industrial production and had caused disarray in the educational system. Of the millions of well-educated Chinese who were sent to "reeducation camps" in the countryside, hundreds of thousands had perished at the hands of bloodthirsty political apparatchiks eager to demonstrate their fidelity to Mao's new political campaign. Chinese diplomacy was virtually nonexistent, as diplomats were recalled from their posts and persecuted for insufficient revolutionary ardor. Despite this zeal, Chinese leaders desperately sought to confirm the nation's status as a world power, and formal recognition by the United States would help in that regard. It would also give China greater access to Western technology and open up new opportunities for trade. Most of all, easing relations with Washington would serve Chinese aims in the escalating tensions with Moscow. When border clashes erupted, the United States could serve as a counterweight. If Nixon and Kissinger thought in terms of triangulation—playing their two principal adversaries off against each other—Mao and Zhou did precisely the same.[30]

The question now was how to proceed. After twenty years of hostility and name-calling, leaders on both sides felt compelled to move cautiously. Hardliners in their respective countries were opposed to a thawing of relations and had to be managed carefully. On the American side this group included California's Governor Ronald Reagan and Arizona's Senator Barry Goldwater, who made clear their enmity toward "Red China" and their unwavering support of Taiwan. Even backers of rapprochement retained some suspicion and worried about the potential for miscommunication. Little by little, however, contact was made, initially through intermediaries in Romania and Pakistan. In April 1971 Beijing officials invited the U.S. table tennis team to visit China. (Worried that his vastly superior players would make the Americans look bad, Zhou Enlai ordered the Chinese team to lose a few games.) Three months later, Kissinger, feigning stomach pains while on a visit to Pakistan, darted off to Beijing for a secret meeting with Zhou Enlai.

The talks were more substantive than Kissinger let on in his memoirs, and his concessions to his counterpart were greater. He did not object when Zhou referred to Taiwan as an "inalienable part of Chinese territory," akin to Hawaii or Long Island for the United States, and he pledged that Washington would not support independence for Taiwan. In addition, Kissinger shared U.S. intelligence on Soviet troop movements along the Chinese frontier and promised to keep Beijing abreast of useful information concerning China that might come out of the ongoing Soviet-American negotiations. Zhou Enlai, for his part, artfully deflected the American's request for assistance in the Vietnam talks and made only one substantive offer: Richard Nixon, he said, would be most welcome to visit China the following year—and, he assured Kissinger, no Democrat would be allowed to come before then.[31]

News of the Zhou-Kissinger encounter shook the world. In Taiwan, Chiang Kai-shek sputtered with rage, while in Tokyo senior Japanese officials were dismayed to be caught uninformed and unaware. Pakistan's Ayub Khan expressed satisfaction that his government's role as conduit had paid off, and in December 1971 when Pakistan's eastern province broke away and declared itself the independent nation of Bangladesh, Khan expected U.S. help in return. Sure enough, when war broke out between Khan's forces and those of India the United States—virtually alone among Western powers—tilted toward Pakistan, though not merely as payback: Nixon also disliked Indian prime minister Indira Gandhi, who he felt had snubbed him.[32]

In the United States, the announcement of Nixon's trip caused a sensation. Seeking to burnish his credentials as a statesman in an election year, the president left nothing to chance in planning the visit. He handpicked the reporters to accompany him and pored over even minute logistical details. A presidential memo instructed Kissinger to tell reporters that "Nixon is uniquely prepared for this meeting," that among his characteristics were "strong convictions; came up through adversity; at his best in a crisis. Cool. Unflappable." To the Chinese, meanwhile, Kissinger cautioned that a public relations avalanche was coming. "I warned Zhou Enlai," he wrote, that while "China had survived barbarian invasions before, "it had never faced that more fearsome prospect, the presidential advance party."[33]

And so, counterintuitive though it seemed to many who had followed his career, Richard Nixon landed in China on February 1, 1972. He shook hands with Zhou Enlai, reversing the old snub when John Foster Dulles had refused Zhou's hand at the Geneva Conference of 1954. He met with Mao, attended banquets, and took in the sights. (Upon seeing the Great Wall, he said, "This is a great wall.") The two sides agreed to disagree on a number of issues, but they concurred that the Soviet Union should not be permitted to make gains in Asia. They also signed a friendship treaty and vowed to open up bilateral trade and to work toward full diplomatic relations. Within months the Chinese entered the United Nations, and Chiang Kai-shek's Taiwan delegation was expelled.

"This was the week that changed the world," Nixon grandiloquently declared on his last evening in China.[34] The assertion brought derision from some, but he was right. Though the China opening came to be seen as a historical inevitability soon after it occurred, it bears remembering that decades of isolation preceded it, and that at the time of Nixon's visit Beijing was actively aiding America's enemies in Vietnam, and millions of Americans—among them deep-pocketed lobbyists in Washington—still believed that the real China was Chiang Kai-shek's Taiwan government, not Mao's People's Republic. The conditions may have been favorable for an easing of tensions, but it took Nixon and Mao to make it happen. By playing the "China card," Nixon acknowledged a new multipolar international system and helped bring China back into the community of nations. The world was indeed a different place when he boarded his plane for home, six days after he arrived.

The Politics of Foreign Policy

Of course, the China trip was not all about high-minded diplomatic engagement. Personal political advantage, never far from Nixon's concerns, figured heavily as well, as his obsessive interest in the public relations dimension of the visit illustrates.[35] The same calculation went into his other high-profile trip in 1972, this one to Moscow for a summit meeting with Brezhnev. The White House choice of the date for the visit, May 1972, was carefully considered: "close enough to the 1972 election campaign to be effective," Nixon's speechwriter William Safire explained, "far enough away not to be blatantly political."[36] The Beijing-Moscow twin bill would solidify Nixon's standing among voters as a world statesman and diminish whomever the Democrats selected to oppose him in the fall.

In the lead-up to the summit the negotiators worked feverishly to shape an agreement. Nixon, bored by the details of arms negotiations, left the field to Kissinger, who as usual conducted the real negotiations through his backchannel to Dobrynin. The final Strategic Arms Limitation Treaty (SALT), which Nixon and Brezhnev signed with fanfare in Moscow, did little to change the status quo. It limited to two the number of ABM systems the two countries could have (no big loss, Kissinger felt, for Congress would be unlikely to fund an expansion in any case, given the costs and the scientific skepticism that a workable system could ever be devised), and it froze the number of nuclear missiles at 1,600 for the Soviets and 1,054 for the United States. This discrepancy was not as one-sided as it seemed, however, for the treaty did not limit MIRVs, in which the Americans had a big lead. One U.S. submarine armed with MIRVs could inflict 160 blasts equivalent to Hiroshima, and the United States owned more than thirty such subs. SALT thus did little to halt the arms race, and the Soviets moved with dispatch to deploy their own MIRVs, which they did within a few years.[37]

But the summit was nevertheless a triumph for both Brezhnev and Nixon. The Soviet leader had tangible results to show his Kremlin colleagues—in addition to SALT, there were agreements in science and technology, as well as a joint space mission. Nixon, meanwhile, scored another public relations success through this first-ever visit by a U.S. president to the Soviet Union. His public approval rating rose to 61 percent a mere five months before the election. SALT would have an "enormous impact" among the swing voters who might be crucial in the campaign, one White House aide crowed.[38] Nixon had to work harder to sell SALT to Congress, but he succeeded in gaining the Senate's approval of the treaty. The price of overselling it was that he undermined political support for further agreements.

More and more as 1972 progressed, domestic political concerns shaped foreign policy. It showed in the strategizing around the China opening and the Soviet summit, and in the third big policy issue that year: Vietnam. The administration had hoped that the announcements of the Beijing and Moscow summits would induce an isolated Hanoi to come to terms, but it didn't happen, and as 1972 began the Paris negotiations had yielded little progress. But the North Vietnamese were unnerved by the prospect of their communist big brothers making nice with the Americans. Hoping to cripple Nixon's domestic position as they had Johnson's four years earlier and to send a message to their allies, on March 30 they launched a major offensive. Some 120,000 North Vietnamese troops, spearheaded by Soviet-made tanks, attacked on three fronts in the South: across the demilitarized zone, in the Central Highlands, and across the Cambodian frontier northwest of Saigon.[39]

Nixon was determined to "go for broke," as he put it. Polls indicated that voters wanted him to retaliate, and they would get what they wanted. He ended the restrictions on U.S. bombing that had been in place since the autumn of 1968 and launched a massive aerial onslaught against North Vietnam, including the bombing of Hanoi and Haiphong. In June alone, American planes dropped 112,000 tons of bombs, including new "smart bombs" guided to their targets by laser or television signals transmitted by computers. The president also ordered the mining of Haiphong and other harbors, a move the United States had previously avoided because it risked confrontation with Soviet ships, and because it would likely have little bearing on the outcome of the war, according to analysts. "The bastards have never been bombed like they're going to be bombed this time," Nixon vowed.[40]

His gamble paid off. The aerial attacks blunted the invasion, as North Vietnamese troops suffered huge losses. Nixon rightly anticipated that China and the Soviet Union would put rapprochement with Washington over ideological solidarity with Hanoi. Both continued their material support for North Vietnam and issued rhetorical denunciations of the new U.S. actions but went no further. To Hanoi's chagrin, Brezhnev refused to cancel the Moscow summit, and he sent a senior diplomat to urge the North Vietnamese to make peace. The Chinese likewise pressed Hanoi to be flexible in the negotiations, even as they assisted with minesweeping Haiphong's harbor. At home, meanwhile, Nixon also won broad backing. Most Americans considered his aggressive response justified under the circumstances, and Congress offered little resistance. The antiwar movement, weakened by Vietnamization and the phasing out of the draft, offered only token protest against the colossally destructive air attacks. The president's approval ratings rose further.

But if the military escalation that spring showed Hanoi that it could not win a rapid military victory, it also showed how utterly dependent South Vietnam remained on U.S. support. Absent Operation Linebacker (as the U.S. bombing campaign was called), the South's defenses likely would have collapsed altogether. With the military stalemate deepening, each side saw compelling reasons to settle. Already the previous year Kissinger had made the major concession that North Vietnamese troops could remain in the South after a ceasefire. Now, in mid-1972, Hanoi's leaders softened their position on several points, abandoning, most notably, their insistence that Nguyen Van Thieu's government in Saigon be removed before a deal. Still content to seek a "decent interval" between U.S. disengagement and South Vietnam's defeat, the administration stepped away from its full commitment to Thieu's government, agreeing to the post-ceasefire formation of a tripartite coalition commission that would be charged with facilitating a political settlement.

For Nixon, however, a large question loomed: should the deal come before or after the U.S. election that November? Kissinger thought before, but the president worried that a pre-election settlement might be interpreted as a naked ploy to win votes—and also that it would rob him of an issue on which blue-collar Democrats were prepared to vote for him. On August 14, Nixon told aides that Kissinger should be discouraged from expressing too much hopefulness regarding the negotiations, as that could raise expectations and be "harmful politically." On August 30 Nixon's chief of staff, H. R. Haldeman, recorded in his diary that the president did not want the settlement to come too soon. According to Haldeman, Nixon "wants to be sure [army vice-chief of staff Alexander] Haig doesn't let Henry [Kissinger]'s desire for a settlement prevail; that's the one way we can lose the election. We have to stand firm on Vietnam and not get soft."[41]

Nevertheless, the negotiations bore fruit, and by early October Kissinger and North Vietnam's chief negotiator Le Duc Tho had agreed on the basics of a deal. The American flew from Paris to Saigon with draft in hand in order to secure Thieu's approval. He didn't get it. Thieu was outraged at not being consulted about key issues, and he demanded wholesale changes. Nixon, feeling confident of reelection and resentful of his security adviser's "shuttle-diplomacy" fame and laudatory press coverage, backed Thieu. The agreement collapsed. In mid-December, fresh from his crushing defeat of Democratic candidate George McGovern, Nixon launched another massive air strike on the North. It was called Linebacker II by the air force, but to everyone else it was the Christmas Bombing. In a span of twelve days, breaking only for December 25, U.S. aircraft dropped some 30,000 tons of bombs on North Vietnam, more than during the whole of 1969–1971. Parts of the country were carpet-bombed. The attacks generated revulsion worldwide, with Pope Paul VI calling them "the object of daily grief" and Swedish prime minister Olof Palme likening them to the atrocities of the Nazis. Nixon was undaunted, but he also signaled his desire to secure a deal, if possible before Congress returned from recess and forced his hand.

On January 27, 1973, Kissinger and Le Duc Tho signed a cease-fire agreement in Paris, and Nixon compelled a reluctant Thieu to accept it by threatening to cut off U.S. aid while at the same time promising to defend the South if the North violated the agreement. In the accord, the United States promised to withdraw all of its troops within sixty days. North Vietnamese troops would be allowed to stay in South Vietnam, and a coalition government that included the Vietcong eventually would be formed in the South.[42]

Within a few weeks, the last American troops left Vietnam. Only some military advisers remained behind. To no one's surprise, both the North and the South soon violated the cease-fire, and fighting resumed. Hanoi leaders expected a long and bloody struggle ahead, but the fragile Saigon government could not hold out, even though its military at the start of 1975 possessed a huge numerical advantage in artillery, tanks, and combat-ready troops. The end came swiftly. On April 29, 1975, South Vietnamese leaders surrendered, and Vietnam was reunified under a communist government in Hanoi.

Vietnam and the Cold War

America's longest war—until the recent conflicts in Afghanistan and Iraq—was over. The overall costs were immense. More than 58,000 Americans and between 1.5 and 3 million Vietnamese—a majority of them civilians—had died. Civilian deaths in Cambodia and Laos numbered in the hundreds of thousands. The three Indochinese countries suffered colossal physical destruction, as the United States dropped some eight million tons of bombs (with half the total falling on South Vietnam). The price tag for the United States government was at least $170 billion, with billions more in veterans' benefits. The vast sums spent on the war weakened investments in domestic programs, and heavy borrowing by both Johnson and Nixon, to avoid raising taxes, triggered inflation and led the nation in 1971 to give up the gold standard as the basis of its monetary system. The war also solidified power in the White House, unbalancing the three branches of government on matters of foreign policy in ways that the authors of the Constitution had sought to prevent.

From the late 1940s on, U.S. policymakers had seen Vietnam partly through the prism of the Cold War. From the prevalent notion of neighboring "dominoes" falling one by one, it was but a short step to the more sophisticated "credibility" imperative: the idea that defeating Ho Chi Minh was essential lest both allies and adversaries *everywhere* lose faith in America's reliability and resolve. This new formulation was still a domino theory, only now it was psychological rather than geographical, global rather than regional.[43]

At various points since the war ended, writers have come forth to endorse the argument that the war decision was not merely understandable in the context of its own time but justified in retrospect.[44] For these revisionists, American credibility really *was* at stake in Vietnam, for it was a theater in a much larger struggle, the Cold War. Policymakers in Washington knew what they were doing, and the war was necessary for precisely the reasons they said it was. Though the Soviet Union had no hope of mounting a successful challenge to the United States in Europe or elsewhere in the industrialized world, in Asia and Africa the Kremlin could work stealthily to thwart U.S. aims and further its own. Ho Chi Minh's nationalist strengths, as demonstrated in the Franco-Vietminh War, and his willingness to accept Soviet and especially Chinese aid and counsel, made Vietnam an especially enticing opportunity. Given these realities, so goes the argument, American planners could hardly have remained aloof from the struggle. Failure to stand firm in Vietnam would have emboldened Moscow and Beijing to attempt subversion of Western interests in other parts of the Third World.

The revisionist line of reasoning falls apart on closer examination. It fails to square with what senior and midlevel officials knew in 1964–65 at the time of "Americanization": that the USSR and China were experiencing a deep split, that for Moscow a major war in Indochina would be the wrong war in the wrong place at the wrong time, that—far from wanting a confrontation with Washington—Kremlin leaders wanted to continue efforts toward achieving détente, and that China, too, sought to avert a major U.S. military intervention in Vietnam. It also fails to appreciate Ho Chi Minh's one great advantage in the struggle: his matchless nationalist credentials. As every Vietnamese schoolchild knew, he and his Vietminh comrades had not only led the fight against the French colonialists but had struggled against Japanese domination during the Second World War. No U.S.-backed leaders in the South could ever lay claim to the same degree of loyalty among the Vietnamese people. Nor could American officials ever surmount the widespread conviction among Vietnamese that the United States was merely a successor to France, another big foreign power imposing its will on the country through violent means.

What is more, the revisionists underestimate the degree to which American decisionmakers themselves privately doubted Vietnam's strategic importance. John F. Kennedy, a skeptic to the core, always held firm against committing U.S. ground troops to the conflict, and behind closed doors Lyndon Johnson and his aides frequently expressed uncertainty regarding the conflict's geopolitical importance—though they took the plunge. The same was true of Nixon and Kissinger. For all these men, Vietnam's importance derived in large measure from its capacity to do damage to their domestic political position and careers. It was about credibility, certainly, but personal and partisan credibility among voters as much as national credibility on the world stage.[45]

There's a deeper problem here. Even if one accepts, for the sake of argument, the existence in the mid-1960s of near-unanimous support for the proposition that America had vital interests in Vietnam, it is far from clear that had Washington opted against war, its worldwide credibility would have been seriously undermined. Harry Truman had not vowed to keep China from going communist in 1949, and Mao Zedong's victory did not lead to any meaningful pro-Moscow realignment in the international system. The same was true of Eisenhower's failure to trumpet his determination to keep Cuba from being lost a decade later. By the same token, no one concluded that because Nikita Khrushchev backed away from a hopeless position in Cuba in 1962, the United States was free to run rampant in eastern Europe. French prestige did not suffer when Charles de Gaulle withdrew from an untenable position in Algeria; if anything, it rose. As Undersecretary of State George Ball put it in arguing (too late, as it turned out) against Americanization in Vietnam in June 1965: "No great captain has ever been blamed for a successful tactical withdrawal."[46]

True, managing such a withdrawal became harder with time, as the fighting intensified and the body counts rose. Henry Kissinger was not altogether wrong to say—as he did, time and again—that the Nixon administration could not simply abandon South Vietnam after four presidents of two political parties had declared that the Saigon regime's survival was crucial to American security. But that is precisely the point: if U.S. credibility was on the line in Vietnam, it was only because successive administrations had put it there, with their constant public affirmations of the struggle's importance. They, not their adversaries, made Vietnam a "test case" of American resolve.

And even then, the stakes were not nearly as high as Kissinger suggested. Although the war undoubtedly undermined international confidence in the United States, the Western alliance emerged from it largely unscathed. The fall of Saigon was of modest international consequence, with marginal impact on the strategic balance between the United States and its communist rivals. Well before the fighting stopped, Washington had moved significantly in the direction of accommodation with Moscow and Beijing, the very nations Americans were purporting to contain by embarking on a bloody war in Vietnam. Outside of Indochina, the dominoes in Southeast Asia did not fall. True, in 1975 the Pathet Lao triumphed in Laos and the Khmer Rouge seized power in Cambodia, but no other nation in the region followed suit. They remained independent, noncommunist, and by and large friendly to the United States.[47] Some revisionists have suggested that, if the United States had prevailed in Vietnam, there would have been far less Soviet-sponsored meddling in Angola, Mozambique, South Yemen, and Afghanistan, and likely no toppling of the shah of Iran—as if such meddling and revolutionary activity were determined not by local politics and opportunities but by developments halfway around the world.

Thus, the core problem with the domino theory, whether in its original territorial or later psychological sense, was its failure to understand that political leaders from Vietnam to Guatemala to Iran were usually much more driven by their own local objectives and ambitions than by their participation in the Soviet-American rivalry. Yet even after American officials began to grasp this flaw in the prevailing paradigm, they continued to make dubious claims regarding the chain reaction that a premature U.S. withdrawal from Vietnam would trigger. Critics at the time rightly saw these claims as fanciful scenarios based on illusory, worst-case projections, but policymakers continued to articulate them year after year, administration after administration.

Why? In large part because depicting worst-case scenarios generally works well in American political discourse, at least in the short term. In the medium and long term, however, those who resort to it can find themselves backed into a corner. If you say often enough that failure to stand firm in such and such a place will have catastrophic consequences, you may find it hard—and politically very costly—to move away from that position. Commit troops to the cause and see them shipped home in body bags, and you will find it harder still to say that the whole idea was just a big mistake.

Crises Far and Near

Though Nixon and Kissinger had few illusions, the ultimate outcome in Vietnam was not known in January 1973, when the Paris Peace Accords were concluded and the president was glorying in his second inauguration. Free of the Vietnam quagmire, still basking in the afterglow of his China and Russia visits and the trouncing of McGovern, Nixon hoped in his second term to build on the successes of 1972. But barely had he resettled himself in office than problems began to surface. In the Middle East, the eruption of a new war entangled the United States and renewed Soviet-American tensions. In Chile, a democratically elected leader whom the administration had helped to overthrow was subsequently murdered. At home, détente encountered growing opposition.

But none of these problems held a candle to Watergate, a "third-rate burglary" and cover-up that, as historian David Greenberg has written, was the "consummate expression of Nixon's character and view of the world, rooted in his belief that he was entitled to violate established constraints—political, legal, ethical, moral—to promote his own advancement."[48] The break-in at the Democratic National Committee's headquarters in the Watergate hotel and apartment complex in Washington occurred in June 1972, but the scandal was slow to develop. It was the avalanche of stunning facts dislodged by the trial of the burglars and the Senate hearings in 1973 that buried the administration in scandal and ultimately forced the president from office.

In the Middle East the situation had grown more volatile in the aftermath of the Arab-Israeli Six-Day War in 1967. Terrorists associated with the Palestinian Liberation Organization (PLO) made hit-and-run raids on Jewish settlements, hijacked jetliners, and murdered Israeli athletes at the 1972 Olympic Games in Munich, West Germany. The Israelis retaliated by assassinating PLO leaders. Initially Nixon and Kissinger took a hands-off approach, delegating issues pertaining to this region to Secretary of State Rogers. They had bigger fish to fry, and besides, it gave him something to do. The president also worried that his "Jew boy"—Kissinger— might handicap the United States in dealing with the region.[49] But as tensions increased and as Rogers began receiving praise for his efforts to defuse them, the White House increasingly involved itself in policy. By late summer 1973 Rogers was pushed out altogether, replaced as secretary of state by Kissinger, who also retained his position as national security adviser.

Here as always, domestic politics played a role. In advance of the 1972 election, Nixon knew that the Jewish vote would go largely against him but that he couldn't simply write it off. He also was mindful of the deep reservoir of support for Israel in Washington and of the price he might pay if he backed an agreement perceived as insufficiently supportive of Tel Aviv. As the historian Robert Dallek has written, Nixon "had no intention of letting political opponents win any advantage in the contest to be seen as a firm supporter of Israel."[50]

In addition, notwithstanding their efforts to achieve détente with Moscow, Nixon and Kissinger saw the situation in the Middle East in much the same way as had their predecessors: through the lens of East-West relations. They worried about Soviet expansion in the region, especially after Egypt and Syria attacked Israel on October 6, 1973—the Jewish High Holy Day of Yom Kippur. The motives of these Arab nations were complex: they included a desire to avenge the 1967 war and a conviction on the part of Egyptian leader Anwar Sadat that his country could best come to terms with Israel by first standing up to it in another war. Caught by surprise, the Israelis reeled before launching an effective counteroffensive against Soviet-armed Egyptian forces in the Sinai. They were assisted by massive infusion of American military hardware in the second week; deliveries at times totaled 100 tons per hour. The Nixon administration, aware that Israel had recently joined the nuclear club (despite refusing to acknowledge the fact), had no desire to see Golda Meir's government use nuclear weapons to beat back Egypt and Syria. For this reason, the Americans worked hard to ensure an Israeli victory by conventional means.[51]

To punish Washington for its pro-Israel stance, the Organization of Petroleum Exporting Countries (OPEC), a group of mostly Arab nations that had joined together to raise the price of oil, embargoed shipments of oil to the United States and other supporters of Israel. An energy crisis and dramatically higher oil prices rocked the nation, confirming the extent to which Americans no longer fully controlled their own economic destiny.

Facing imminent defeat, Arab leaders appealed for Soviet assistance. The Kremlin demurred, but when the Israelis violated a ceasefire, Brezhnev implied that the Soviet Union might intervene to enforce it. Almost certainly he had no intention of doing so, but the National Security Council, with Kissinger presiding, ordered a worldwide U.S. nuclear and military alert. Nixon, in bed during the NSC session and reportedly drunk, later instructed Kissinger to inform journalists that Nixon had played a key role in the decision to order the nuclear alert, adding, "Who saved Israel? Would anybody else have saved them? You tell them that."[52] The crisis eased, but OPEC did not lift the oil embargo until March 1974— and even then, oil prices stayed high. Although the next year Kissinger persuaded Egypt and Israel to accept a UN peacekeeping force in the Sinai, peace did not come to the region. Palestinians and other Arabs still vowed to destroy Israel, while Israelis continued to build more Jewish settlements in the West Bank and Gaza.

In Latin America, the administration followed the broad policy aims of its predecessors: to preserve stability and to thwart radical leftist challenges to authoritarian rule. Neither Nixon nor Kissinger thought that the southern half of the Western Hemisphere mattered in the great game of world politics. Latin America, like the rest of the developing world, was "not important," Kissinger told the Chilean foreign minister, of all people, in 1969. "Nothing of importance can come from the South. History has never been produced in the South. The axis of history starts in Moscow, goes to Bonn, crosses over to Washington, and then goes to Tokyo." In such places history was made, Kissinger believed; and in such places he wanted to make his mark. "London, Paris, Rome, and Bonn seemed close," he wrote in his memoirs. "Mexico City seemed far away, Rio de Janeiro or Buenos Aires beyond reach." Chile, he quipped dismissively on another occasion, was a "dagger pointed to the heart of Antarctica."[53]

Yet Kissinger would have reason to revise such sentiments, at least for a time, demonstrating again how perceived Cold War imperatives could shape U.S. policy in all four corners of the world. In 1970, Chilean voters elected a devoted nationalist and sometime Marxist, Salvador Allende, as president. Like Mossadegh in Iran and Arbenz in Guatemala a decade and a half earlier, Allende moved swiftly to break Chile free of its domination by large landholders and American multinational corporations. He nationalized nearly $1 billion of U.S. investment.

Nixon and Kissinger reacted aggressively. They viewed Allende's government as a potential agent for Soviet expansion in the hemisphere. This worried them in terms of geopolitics, but also on the domestic front. Chile, Kissinger warned an aide, "could end up being the worst failure of our administration, 'our Cuba' by 1972." Accordingly, the White House turned the CIA loose to conduct secret operations to disrupt the Chilean economy and encouraged military officers to stage a coup. It was a long time coming, but in 1973 a military junta ousted Allende and installed an authoritarian regime under General Augusto Pinochet. (Allende soon died, probably by his own hand, using a rifle he received from Fidel Castro.) Washington publicly denied any role in the affair that implanted iron-fisted tyranny in Chile for two decades.[54]

In Africa the two men were content to maintain the status quo and let the State Department manage policy. "Henry, let's leave the niggers to Bill [Rogers]," the president (who could toss off racist remarks with ease) told Kissinger. On another occasion Nixon noted that "there has never in history been an adequate black nation, and they are the only race of which this is true."[55] He backed the white-minority regime in Rhodesia (now Zimbabwe) and used the CIA in a failed effort to defeat a Soviet- and Cuban-backed faction in Portuguese Angola's civil war. In South Africa, Nixon tolerated the white rulers who imposed the segregationist policy of apartheid on blacks and mixed-race "coloreds" (85 percent of the population), keeping them poor, disfranchised, and ghettoized in prisonlike townships. After a leftist government came to power in Angola, however, Washington took a keener interest in the rest of Africa, building economic ties and sending arms to friendly black nations such as Kenya and the Congo. The administration also began to distance the United States from the white governments of Rhodesia and South Africa. America, Kissinger emphasized, had to "prevent the radicalization of Africa."

The Ford Interregnum

On August 9, 1974, facing certain impeachment and conviction for his role in the Watergate cover-up, Richard Nixon became the first president of the United States to resign his office. Alongside major foreign policy achievements—the opening to China, détente with the Soviet Union, the broader recognition of the necessity and potential utility of negotiations, even with adversaries—stood glaring failures, foremost among them the perpetuation of the Vietnam War for four more years, at enormous cost and minimal gain. His conduct of the war deepened the domestic credibility gap opened up by Lyndon Johnson and generated unprecedented mistrust of the government by a large portion of the electorate. This mistrust in turned deepened Nixon's insecurities, his paranoia, and his vindictiveness toward perceived domestic enemies, and ultimately caused his undoing.

Enter Gerald Ford. A long-time congressman from Michigan before replacing Spiro Agnew as Nixon's vice president (Agnew left office under a cloud of criminal charges), the genial and unpretentious Ford had been a star football player in college and had turned down a chance for a pro career to attend Yale Law School. He came to the White House with a strong grasp of the workings of the federal government but with little background in world affairs. Once when he committed a faux pas in discussing Middle East affairs, a scribe remarked: "What the hell, it was just Jerry talking about things he doesn't understand."[56]

No one was surprised that Ford emphasized continuity in foreign policy—it is proper to speak of the entire eight-year span from January 1969 to January 1977 as the "Nixon era" in American diplomacy—or that he retained Kissinger as national security adviser and secretary of state. Both affirmed a commitment to promoting and furthering détente.[57] Yet the two men found it difficult to maintain established policies, in large part because of a change at the other end of Pennsylvania Avenue: the determination of Congress to reinsert itself into the foreign policy process. This legislative assertiveness was not new in 1974; it manifested itself early in Nixon's second term with various efforts to end the war in Vietnam or at least limit its expansion into Cambodia and Laos. But it gained more force at mid-decade: time and again the White House found itself stymied by lawmakers' refusal to rubber-stamp administration initiatives and by their eagerness to push measures of their own that undermined existing policies, most notably détente. Kissinger, disdainful of this Capitol Hill rebellion, later commented on the "irony that the Congress [Ford] genuinely loved and respected had harassed his foreign policy unmercifully from the beginning and encumbered it with unprecedented restrictions."[58]

The new president faced other challenges too, not least in the economic realm. A period of sustained economic expansion came to a pronounced halt in the early 1970s, as competition in global markets from Japan and western Europe hampered growth, notably in the steel and automobile sectors. The heavy costs of the Vietnam War were by this time making themselves fully felt in ballooning inflation figures: in July 1974 alone, prices increased 3.7 percent, the second largest monthly rise since 1946.[59] Gasoline and fuel oil prices remained high following the 1973 Arab oil embargo, and unemployment numbers crept upward. Add in the congressional resurgence and the popular cynicism and self-doubt generated by the Johnson/Nixon credibility gap and it becomes easy in hindsight to see that the new president faced a difficult path ahead. Ford and Kissinger traveled to Vladivostok in November 1974 and reached agreement with Brezhnev on the basics of a SALT II agreement that set new limits on nuclear arms. Hawks in Congress, led by Senator Henry Jackson of Washington, expressed opposition to the deal and delayed a vote on the agreement. A liberal Democrat on domestic issues and a hardline anti-communist, Jackson joined with Charles Vanik, a Republican congressman from Ohio, to approve the trade deal with the Soviets only on the condition that Jews would be free to emigrate from the USSR. Their amendment undermined U.S. leverage with Moscow and left Kissinger apoplectic. "The same sons of bitches who drove us out of Vietnam," he roared privately, were now trying "to destroy détente and assert that it is our moral obligation to change internal Soviet policies."[60] Ford suffered a further setback at the Helsinki summit in mid-1975. One of the largest such meetings ever, the conference brought together delegates from thirty-five countries, who accepted East European boundaries as permanent in exchange for a Soviet pledge to follow a more liberal human rights policy. The Helsinki Accords would in time contribute to the end of the Cold War by serving as a kind of manifesto for the dissident movement within the Eastern Bloc; but in the short term it merely weakened Ford at home. Eastern European ethnic groups condemned what they saw as his Yalta-like "betrayal" of their native lands. In Congress, conservatives in both parties were equally harsh.[61]

In Angola, which won independence from Portugal in early 1975 and immediately descended into civil war, Ford and Kissinger approved a new covert operation to defeat the Soviet-backed Popular Movement for the Liberation of Angola (MPLA). The Central Intelligence Agency secretly sent $32 million in cash and $16 million in weapons to the opposing National Front for the Liberation of Angola (FNLA), using as a go-between the CIA's great ally in the region, Zaire's ruthless dictator Joseph Mobutu. But the MPLA, aided by thousands of Cuban troops flown in by the Soviets, gained the upper hand. Decrying what he referred to as a dangerous escalation of the Cold War, Kissinger asked Congress for a massive infusion of additional aid. The lawmakers refused and indeed barred aid to Angola. Few of them saw national security interests at stake in the south-central African nation. When the MPLA took control of the capital, their victory gave ammunition to hawks in Washington who wanted a tougher line with Moscow. Ford, these critics charged, had opted to "toady up" to the Kremlin, and Angola was the result.[62]

By the start of the 1976 presidential campaign, the Nixon-Kissinger Grand Design barely registered a pulse. The Vietnam War had ended ingloriously the previous year, as North Vietnamese forces conquered Saigon. Détente had become an albatross around the administration's neck, so much so that pollsters advised Ford to drop the term from his speeches and Kissinger acknowledged that it "is a word I would like to forget."[63] By the early spring, Ford had shelved further arms control talks with the Soviet

Union, for reasons that had little to do with foreign policy and a great deal to do with electoral politics, he candidly admitted. "I never backed away from détente as a means for achieving a more stable relationship with our Communist adversaries," the president said, "but the situation that developed in connection with the presidential primaries and the fight at the convention made it necessary to deemphasize détente." By "situation" he meant in part the primary challenge of former California governor Ronald Reagan, who tapped into the frustrations among conservatives and blasted the Ford-Kissinger team for allowing the United States "to become number two in military power in a world where it is dangerous—if not fatal—to be second best."[64]

Indeed, Ford would encounter a familiar line of attack during his last year in office. Many on the right were horrified that a Republican administration had sought a negotiated compromise with the USSR. A range of conservative voices—William F. Buckley's *National Review,* think tanks such as the Heritage Foundation and American Enterprise Institute, and various activists and campaign professionals—banded together with congressional hawks to condemn "appeasement" of Moscow and America's newfound timidity in using force overseas. The Soviets could never be trusted, they charged, and moreover would take advantage of any diminution of American vigilance to expand their reach internationally.

Inside the administration, too, several hard-liners began to formulate a thoroughgoing attack on the central assumption of detente: that the United States and the Soviet Union possessed strategic parity. Pointing to an article in *Foreign Policy* by Albert Wohlstetter, in which the University of Chicago political scientist accused the CIA of systematically underestimating the USSR's missile deployment, the hawks successfully pushed for a review of official estimates about Soviet military capabilities, particularly those produced by the CIA.[65] Team "B" in this review process, led by the passionately anti-Soviet Harvard historian Richard Pipes, arrived at the conclusion that the USSR was rushing dangerously ahead. Dismissing the contrary evidence provided to them, Team B analysts working on Soviet strategic objectives argued that because it was impossible to ascertain definitive data on Soviet military power, the safest conclusion would be to assume that the CIA estimates were grievously wrong and that détente, therefore, courted national catastrophe. It was the logic of Kennedy's missile gap once more: because estimates could conceivably be wrong, they are wrong; and since they are wrong, those who believe in them are endangering the nation. It was a specious line of argument then, and it looks more so in hindsight—the CIA's estimates, we now know, radically *overestimated* Soviet capabilities. But a careful and measured assessment of the adversary's capacities was of no interest to Team B.[66]

Presidential adviser David Gergen reflected this shifting mood when he warned that in the nomination battle Ford needed to "posture himself as sufficiently hardline that no major candidate can run to the right of him on defense and foreign policy."[67] Ford got the message and turned Cold War hawk. He beat back the Reagan primary challenge, barely, but he began the general election campaign against a relatively unknown Democratic nominee, Jimmy Carter, deep in the hole. In the final weeks, Ford managed to make up most of a thirty-point deficit in the polls, but then a late gaffe stopped his momentum cold. During a televised debate, he responded to a question about Helsinki by saying that "there is no Soviet domination of Eastern Europe" and that the United States did not "concede that those countries are under the domination of the Soviet Union." He meant to say, of course, that the United States did not recognize the domination as legitimate. But Carter pounced on the misstatement, charging that it demonstrated the amorality of détente. Ford stubbornly refused to issue a correction.[68]

On election day Jimmy Carter, promising honesty in government and a new era in American foreign policy, claimed victory, with 297 electoral votes to Ford's 240.

8

A NEW COLD WAR

Jimmy Carter took office determined to conduct American foreign policy in a new fashion. Détente with the Soviet Union and the disastrous war in Vietnam convinced him that the United States had both the opportunity and motive to improve its reputation worldwide by embarking on a foreign policy based upon American ideals. An essential early part of this endeavor would be to shift the policy away from its singular focus on anti-communism. "An inordinate fear of communism," Carter declared in a commencement address at Notre Dame University in May 1977, "has led us to embrace any dictator who joined in our fear."[1] This must change. The time had come to move beyond the endless tit-for-tat of the bipolar contest, to deploy a more confident, more multifaceted American foreign policy. With reformist zeal, Carter vowed to reduce the U.S. military presence abroad, to cut back arms sales (which had reached the unprecedented height of $10 billion per year under Nixon), and to slow the nuclear arms race. He promised to avoid new Vietnams through an activist preventive diplomacy in the Third World and to give more attention to environmental issues as well as relations between rich and poor nations. He was especially determined to improve human rights abroad—the freedom to vote, worship, travel, speak out, and get a fair trial.[2]

It was a winning message. Americans were ready for a new direction. Most needed no convincing that American power had diminished over the past ten or fifteen years. They saw it in the high prices they were paying at the pump each week, in the steep increase in the cost of living during the first half of the 1970s, in the growing unemployment in "rust belt" states as foreign competition gained more and more of the global marketplace. Career politicians in Washington seemed hardly worthy of anyone's trust. Johnson and his credibility gap had been followed by the first man to resign from the presidency, and he in turn was pardoned by his successor, Gerald Ford, who was now running for reelection. Maybe this Carter fellow really would do what he promised: clean up the mess in Washington and bring about a new politics.

Few knew anything about him when the campaign began, and fewer still gave him much of a chance. When he told his mother that he had decided to run for president, she replied, "President of what?"[3] Raised in the rural south Georgia town of Plains, where his family owned a peanut farm, Carter attended the Naval Academy, graduating fifty-ninth out his class of 820, then served as an engineer in the navy's nuclear submarine program before entering politics. A deeply religious Christian, Carter had been elected governor of Georgia in 1970 on a platform of moderate civil rights and economic modernization. Six years later he won the highest office in the land despite his relative obscurity—or perhaps because of it.[4]

And he would achieve some successes, including foreign policy successes, though two of the more notable ones—reaching agreements with Panama over the canal and brokering a formal peace between Israel and Egypt—came by traditional diplomatic practice rather than Carter's new methods. Before long, however, problems appeared. For one thing, his promises proved hard to keep. It's not easy for a nation to appreciably reduce the size of its military footprint overseas when it has 400,000 military personnel stationed abroad and military agreements with ninety-two nations, as the United States did at the start of 1977.

Inexperienced in foreign policy matters, he had to put up with intense squabbling among his advisers, including National Security Adviser Zbigniew Brzezinski, a stern-faced Polish-born political scientist who blamed foreign crises on Soviet expansionism, and Secretary of State Cyrus Vance, a blueblood from the northeast who favored quiet diplomacy.[5] Carter also faced mounting outside criticism, especially from the right. Vocal neoconservative intellectuals such as Norman Podhoretz, editor of *Commentary* magazine, and the Committee on the Present Danger, founded in 1976 by Cold War hawks such as Paul Nitze, the man behind NSC-68 and the Gaither Committee, criticized Carter for any relaxation of the Cold War, characterized minor Soviet aggressions as imminent threats to American survival, and demanded that he jettison détente.

The hawks got their wish. Under Carter, détente deteriorated and the Cold War deepened, especially after the Soviet invasion of Afghanistan in December 1979. The president eventually succumbed, just as many of his predecessors had, to the reality that militarism was a necessary component of a successful reelection strategy. As long as the Cold War continued, the political culture in Washington would reward toughness and alarmism, and penalize equanimity and self-confidence, pretty much irrespective of what the Soviet Union was actually doing.

Unfortunately for Carter, he faced a formidable opponent in the 1980 election in Ronald Reagan, a former Hollywood actor and California governor whose genial personality belied keen political instincts and a capacity for bare-knuckle campaigning. Reagan promised to rejuvenate the Cold War against the Soviet Union and restore confidence to an America chastened by Vietnam and the setbacks of the Carter years. The message hit home with voters, and Reagan sent the Georgian packing.[6] Yet during his first term, Reagan simply intensified Carter's new Cold War; and by 1984, U.S.-Soviet relations had reached their lowest point in a generation.

The Campaign for Human Rights

Despite their diverse backgrounds, Carter, Brzezinski, and Vance had come together initially as leading members of the Trilateral Commission, a private organization founded by David Rockefeller to foster greater coordination and better relations among the three centers of world capitalism—the United States, western Europe, and Japan. The underlying strategy of the commission, and of the three men who took command of American foreign policy in 1977, was to de-emphasize the bipolar, geopolitical conflict between the United States and the Soviet Union, to regard that struggle in less urgent terms. By cultivating better relations with the Japanese and Europeans, by raising America's moral profile around the world, and by viewing the USSR as a declining, backward power that must still be contained but no longer deeply feared, the United States could lead the industrialized world into a post–Cold War era in which management and order, rather than confrontation and rivalry, were the main business of international politics.[7]

Within this larger vision, Carter initially hoped to achieve several specific aims, including a lasting peace in the troubled Middle East and the establishment of full diplomatic relations with the People's Republic of China. But the principal early effort was undoubtedly the administration's advocacy of human rights. Though political orators like to trace this concept back to age-old Judeo-Christian traditions, it is in fact a relatively modern proposition that emerged in a serious way only in the twentieth century. Out of two bloody world wars the conviction grew that crimes against humanity were humanity's concern. Woodrow Wilson's pronouncements endorsed this proposition, and Franklin Roosevelt, though never doubting that foreign policy must be based on calculations of national interest, believed that its ideals were an indispensable part of America's power. The UN Charter of 1945 pledged member nations to work to promote "human rights," and three years later the UN General Assembly adopted the Universal Declaration of Human Rights.

By then, the superpowers and their clients had already commenced bickering over the issue: the Western nations condemned the Soviet bloc for its abuse of civil and political rights; the Kremlin and its allies assailed the West for its neglect of social and economic rights. More and more, the concept became a theme in U.S. foreign policy, at least until Vietnam—a state engaged in massive aerial bombardment of an underdeveloped society could not readily claim a commitment to human rights. Its dormancy continued under Nixon and Kissinger, as the two men embraced Realpolitik and sought to downplay ideology as a driving factor in American foreign relations.[8]

Jimmy Carter was himself a late convert to the human rights cause, or so the evidence suggests. His 1975 memoir *Why Not the Best?* makes no mention of it, and in the early months of 1976 he condemned both the Helsinki Accords (with their strong human rights theme) and the whole business of interfering in the domestic affairs of other nations. But as the campaign heated up, he shifted course. Genuine conviction no doubt played a role, but so did political expediency. Human rights, he and his aides came to realize, was the perfect counterpoint to the seeming cynicism and amoral outlook of the Nixon years. The principle tapped the finest of American traditions, that of having a mission to the world, and also spoke to pressing contemporary concerns. It promised to restore America's tarnished international image, sullied by Vietnam, Watergate, support for right-wing dictators, and CIA assassination plots. It responded to the agitation in Congress to make human rights a centerpiece of American diplomacy. Best of all, the issue could win the support of Cold Warriors, who were eager to indict the communist world for its treatment of subject peoples, and also liberal idealists troubled by America's ties to dictatorships.

In the midst of a race for the White House, human rights seemed to the Carter camp like a grand unifying theory of foreign policy. The United States would act in accord with its own ideals, rather than hypocritically lauding its political liberties while bankrolling regimes that brutally suppressed them.[9] In 1977 White House Chief of Staff Hamilton Jordan put the matter bluntly: "Of our numerous foreign policy initiatives," he wrote to Carter, human rights "is the only one that has a broad base of appeal among the American people and is not considered 'liberal.'"[10]

Skeptics, straining to be heard over the din, pointed out that previous efforts to impose American idealism on the world had not always worked out as hoped. Wilson's grandiose plan to make the world "safe for democracy" after the First World War had foundered on the resistance of allies abroad and lawmakers at home. The skeptics cautioned that a human rights policy—if indeed it qualified as a policy—would be tricky to implement. And they warned that the concept could be seen by some around the world as ethnocentric and culture-bound, promoting a universal understanding of rights that in fact did not exist. Sure enough, in short order difficulties arose. Diplomats griped when the human rights effort interfered with delicate arms control negotiations, while the Pentagon brass complained when it imperiled military arrangements and alliances. Treasury officials noted the implications for the nation's balance book: trade restrictions, they said in late 1978, were costing up to $10 billion per year and increased the trade deficit. Captains of industry objected that the campaign hurt exports.[11]

In particular bilateral relationships, Carter likewise found himself pulled in different directions. Though he was able to preside over the transfer of the Panama Canal to the government of Panama, thereby removing long-running Latin American grievances against old-fashioned Yankee imperialism, the move exacted a serious domestic political cost. Right-wing lobbyists banded together to send out a "Truth Squad" to major media markets, charging that the withdrawal gave Moscow a stronger foothold in the region, an accusation repeated by congressional hawks.[12] Moreover, Carter ran into trouble on Nicaragua and Iran. In 1977 the administration announced that it would consider rescinding its support for these two long-time allies, both led by deeply repressive governments that had flourished as a direct result of American sponsorship. Anastosio Somoza ran Nicaragua with an iron hand, brutally terrorizing his political opponents and keeping the population mired in poverty. In Iran, the shah continued to reign a quarter-century after being put into power by Eisenhower's coup, and to deliver on his promise to keep the oil flowing. Determined to maintain secular values in the face of growing Islamist unrest, his secret police organization, SAVAK, imprisoned and tortured Islamic clerics and other dissidents by the thousands, using methods and equipment provided by the CIA.[13]

Carter needed no convincing that America's association with such regimes was damaging its reputation, turning many in Latin America and the Middle East who were uninterested in communism against the United States. But he also came to see a danger in undermining them. And so the presumed number-one human rights crusader could offer staunch support for the shah and send an effusive letter of commendation to Somoza, even as his administration moved to cut off U.S. support for both of these regimes.

Charges of hypocrisy flew, particularly when it became clear that the White House was holding strategically or economically "unimportant" countries—Paraguay, Uganda, and Cambodia, for example—to a higher standard than more important ones. (China, the cynics duly noted, received no administration pressure at all.)

Furthermore, by threatening to cut off support for Somoza and the shah, Carter gave political activists in those countries further reason to seek their overthrow. When the administration discontinued military assistance and opposed loans to Somoza's regime in 1977, left-wing activists, many of them with connections to Cuba and the Soviet Union, prepared for rebellion. In Iran, fundamentalist clerics, supported by radical students, rallied behind the Ayatollah Khomeini, who condemned Western materialism and promised to expel the corrupt shah and establish an Islamist republic. Carter thus confronted the dilemma that faces any leader promoting a moralistic foreign policy. Would the benefits of disassociating America from the repressive regimes in Managua and Tehran outweigh the risks of anti-American movements rising to political power?

The Soviet Union presented its own set of problems for the human rights campaign. Carter and Vance felt certain that U.S. foreign policy should reflect the new, more multipolar international system, but they also understood that it was still a two-superpower world. Issues remained that required negotiation and cooperation with the Soviet Union. For Vance, one such issue loomed larger than any other: arms control. The race between the United States and the USSR to acquire ever more nuclear weaponry had reached the point of absurdity, he was convinced—the two sides now had some 50,000 warheads between them. It was in the interest of both nations to agree to verifiable cuts, not only to avoid building expensive weapons that could only "make the rubble bounce," as Winston Churchill once put it, but also to get rid of weapons systems that could destabilize Mutual Assured Destruction. Certain kinds of nuclear weapons were clearly useful only for retaliation, but others could be used for offensive purposes. Washington and Moscow had a joint interest in preventing the proliferation of the latter.

Accordingly, during their first two years Vance and Carter sought to conclude a comprehensive deal with the Soviet Union that had originated during the Ford administration: the Strategic Arms Limitation Treaty (SALT) II.[14] They found a willing partner in Leonid Brezhnev, who was desperate to reduce military spending and who understood that arms control remained one of the few arenas in which the USSR could act as an equal. Carter, however, stung by the charges of hypocrisy, refused to abandon his criticism of Soviet human rights abuses for the sake of the treaty. He accepted a letter from the Soviet physicist and dissident Andrei Sakharov and publicly criticized the treatment suffered by Sakharov and other dissidents at the hands of Kremlin authorities. The White House also used moralistic language to denounce relatively minor Soviet involvement in the Horn of Africa—adventures that signified no nefarious geopolitical agenda but rather last-ditch attempts to expand its strategic reach and diplomatic influence, as great powers do.[15] The aging and ailing Brezhnev found this unacceptable. He threatened to cease arms control negotiations and abandon détente if the Americans continued to interfere in internal Soviet affairs. What had happened, he wondered, to the businesslike *Realpolitik* of the Nixon and Ford administrations?[16]

Carter was taking real risks with his get-tough moralism. Without receiving anything substantial in return, by the end of 1978 the administration had succeeded in contributing to the destabilization of Nicaragua and Iran and in antagonizing Moscow. The president gambled that the time was right to run such risks and that the United States, and his administration, could withstand any short-term repercussions.

Camp David Accords

Intrinsically connected to his larger campaign for a human rights–based foreign policy was Carter's deep interest in the longstanding conflict between Israel and the surrounding Arab states. The United States began in the 1960s to side closely with Israel, supporting its military operations in 1967 and especially 1973 and providing tremendous amounts of foreign aid—far more per capita than to any other nation. American leaders had several reasons to do so. Many Americans admired the Jewish state, founded in the ashes of the Nazi holocaust as a democracy in a neighborhood of dictatorships, and were keen to help it survive in that dangerous environment. Moreover, hawkish supporters of Israel in America's Jewish community had developed effective and powerful political organizations since the 1967 war that rallied votes for and channeled donations to politicians avidly committed to Israel. Because there was no equivalent Palestinian or Arab lobby, American politicians had strong incentives to vote for legislation that would benefit the Jewish state and to criticize any policy that might harm it. But there were also geopolitical reasons to ally with Israel in the Middle East. American strategists saw Israel as a surrogate willing to contend with Soviet client states in the region, such as Syria, while at the same time cooperating with U.S. officials in areas of regional military planning and intelligence gathering.

The OPEC boycott of 1973–74 revealed, however, that America's increased backing for Israel came with a cost. Seasoned observers were not surprised: wholesale support for any nation is likely sooner or later to antagonize that nation's adversaries. The United States had no interest in respecting the demand of Israel's more vituperative enemies, which was to drive it into the sea. But it did have reason to take seriously Israel's occupation of the Gaza Strip and the West Bank, home to hundreds of thousands of Palestinians and an increasing number of heavily defended Jewish settlements. Many right-wing figures in Israel were determined to assert Jewish dominion over Gaza and the West Bank, and their strategy was to gradually establish Jewish-only towns in the two regions and pressure the Palestinians there to leave.

In response, Palestinian groups, led by Yasser Arafat's Palestinian Liberation Organization (PLO), waged terrorist and paramilitary campaigns against the settlers and Israel itself. Arab states in the region, including moderate oil-rich states like Saudi Arabia, demanded that the United States pressure the Israelis to desist from the occupation and perhaps work to create an independent Palestinian state. Such a solution, these states argued, could temper Arab grievances and put an end to the violence without threatening Israeli security. Almost immediately upon taking office, Carter launched a series of diplomatic efforts to secure an Israel-Palestinian peace.[17] In 1977 he established direct relations with the new Israeli prime minister, Menachem Begin, and moderate Arab leaders, including Egypt's Anwar Sadat, for the purpose of convening a grand international conference—to be held in Vienna, perhaps, or Jerusalem—to sort out the conflict and arrive at a general peace.

Begin, however, adamantly opposed the idea of an international summit, particularly one involving the Soviet Union and the PLO, and he rebuffed Carter's initiative. Sadat then took matters into his own hands by announcing his interest in visiting Israel and normalizing Egypt's relations with the Jewish state. While such a venture did not speak directly to the Palestinian problem, it was a start, and in early 1978 the president sent American diplomats, including Secretary of State Vance, to the Middle East to facilitate an Israeli-Egyptian accord. These efforts failed, and in September Carter invited Sadat and Begin to the presidential retreat, Camp David, to work out a deal. On the table was an Egyptian promise to recognize Israel and to rally other moderate Arab states to do the same, in exchange for an Israeli agreement to evacuate the Sinai peninsula and provide some form of political autonomy to the beleaguered Palestinians in Gaza and the West Bank. Negotiations among the three sides were arduous, but eventually Carter convinced Begin to agree to an evacuation of Sinai and a vague commitment to return control of Gaza and the West Bank to the Palestinians.

It was an incomplete success, but arguably the crowning achievement of Carter's presidency. On September 18 the three men announced the agreement, for which all three would receive the Nobel Peace Prize (Begin and Sadat in 1978, Carter in 2002). Many observers noted that the terms on the occupied territories—the most contentious issue in Arab-Israeli relations—were hazy and unenforceable. Several Arab states denounced the agreement for not requiring Israel to give up all occupied territories and for not guaranteeing a Palestinian homeland. But perhaps a more comprehensive deal could be reached in Carter's second term, when he would be freer to pursue a tougher line. On March 26, 1979, Begin and Sadat signed the formal treaty on the White House lawn, with a beaming Carter looking on.

Recognizing China

A final feature of the administration's new strategy, one spearheaded by Brzezinski, was its decision in 1978 to secure full diplomatic relations with China. Nixon and Kissinger had initiated the process, but they lacked the political will—especially as Watergate took its toll and the Vietnam War still raged—to undertake the work necessary for full normalization.

The decision was not a simple one. For one thing, the pro-Taiwan lobby, adamantly opposed to recognition, still wielded power in Washington. Some thirty years after the Chinese revolution, many congressmen and senators, egged on by lobby groups, still supported the revanchist notions of Chiang Kai-Shek and still vowed undying opposition to the Beijing government's legitimacy. For another, recognition of China in the aftermath of the horrendous Cultural Revolution, in which millions suffered persecution (though the scope was not yet clear), hardly reflected a commitment to universal human rights. Furthermore, a conspicuous and formal recognition of China threatened to alienate the Soviet Union and damage the prospects for SALT II, a particular worry for Vance. At the same time the benefits were substantial. Recognizing China fit precisely within the strategy of redirecting American foreign policy away from bipolar power politics. Access to the China market, moreover, would bring tremendous wealth to American corporations eager to trade there, provide American consumers with access to cheap Chinese goods, and, most important, draw China into the capitalist world system.[18]

And so in the summer of 1977 Brzezinski met in Beijing with the new Chinese premier, Deng Xiaoping, in order to establish a framework for formal recognition. The Chinese insisted that Washington cease arms sales to Taiwan and cancel its defense treaty. Brzezinski demurred; such action would never be acceptable to Congress. More than a year of diplomatic negotiations followed. Then, in late 1978, Carter announced that China had dropped its demands and would now be formally recognized by the United States. The two sides stepped up trade relations and joined in rebuking their Soviet rival for its alleged adventurist policies.[19]

Viewed in hindsight, Carter's decision, coming in the aftermath of Nixon's extraordinary first steps, seems all but foreordained. At the time, though, it was another gamble for a beleaguered administration, certainly from a domestic political point of view. Rightwing critics of the administration, angered already by the Panama Canal "giveaway" and Carter's actions in Iran and Nicaragua, condemned the move. Republican elder statesman Barry Goldwater called it "cowardly." And, as Vance had anticipated, Moscow responded by adopting a more intransigent line in the SALT talks.[20]

Either Carter did not fully grasp the contradictions inherent in his China policy or he chose to overlook them. If the United States wished to adopt a "unified" foreign policy of human rights, then an overture to China not long after its grim Cultural Revolution was a sure way to undermine it. And if securing an arms control deal with Moscow was a strategic priority, then making an obvious bid to curry favor with Beijing and to appear to endorse the anti-Soviet utterances of Chinese leader Deng Xiaoping all but ensured failure.[21]

Cold War Renewed

But the big tests for the Carter administration were still to come. Soon after the normalization agreement, China launched an attack on Vietnam, a Soviet ally—a step for which Moscow had to assume Brzezinski had given the green light. Soviet-American relations had in fact been deteriorating for some months, and the Kremlin now took dramatic steps to show it would not be marginalized. It arrested dissidents, including Sakharov, escalated its tough talk at the arms control negotiations, and prepared to increase Soviet involvement in Angola and Nigeria. At a conference in mid-1979, the two nations did agree on a final SALT II treaty, as a result of the tireless efforts of lead U.S. negotiator Paul Warnke and the USSR's desire to link the treaty to American economic concessions. It capped strategic nuclear launchers at 2,400 (with a future reduction to 2,250), only 1,320 of which could be MIRVed. To help facilitate passage by the U.S. Senate, Brezhnev allowed 50,000 Jews to leave the USSR in 1979. The deal nevertheless came under scathing attack from conservatives in and out of Congress, and Senate leaders put the matter on the back burner.

And there it remained; there would be no formal Senate debate. For in late December came the shocking news: the Soviet Union had invaded Afghanistan in order to shore up a pro-Soviet regime there that was politically divided and under siege from Islamic radicals. The previous year, following a leftist military coup in Kabul, Moscow had stepped up its presence in Afghanistan in order to ensure stability on its southern border. But a power struggle soon arose between Afghani prime minister Nur Mohammad Taraki and his deputy Hafizullah Amin. When Taraki, who enjoyed Moscow's support, was murdered by forces under Amin's control, the Soviets struck. While its mechanized forces were crossing the border into Afghanistan, Soviet commandos killed Amin and set up Babrak Karmal, an Afghan communist, as the head of a puppet government. The Kremlin was determined to crush Islamic fundamentalism in Afghanistan as well as in various areas of the USSR, an objective that Brezhnev believed might temper American hostility. He also hoped to reassert Soviet hegemony over a country proximate to the oil-rich regions of Central Asia and the Middle East, and nearer to the warm-water ports that Russian statesmen had always coveted. Brezhnev and his colleagues hoped they could be in and out of Afghanistan before anyone really noticed, including the Americans.[22]

Carter not only noticed but, under intense pressure from the right, reacted firmly. "The most serious threat to peace since World War II," he called the invasion, perhaps unable to recall China's entry into the Korean War or the Cuban Missile Crisis.[23] The president secretly authorized the CIA to distribute aid, including weapons and military support, to the Mujahideen rebels fighting the communist government and sanctioned military assistance to their backer, Pakistan. In addition, Carter endorsed Brzezinski's demand that the United States move to establish a full rapprochement with China, knowing that this would invite a hostile response from Moscow. He also authorized an increase in defense spending, went ahead with a new land-based ICBM system (the MX), and in early 1980 announced the Carter Doctrine: the United States would regard any attempt by an outside power to seize control over the Persian Gulf region as a direct act of aggression against the United States. Echoing the language of Truman thirty years earlier, Carter hoped to demonstrate toughness to the American electorate and to fend off a challenge from Senator Ted Kennedy of Massachusetts, a likely contender for the Democratic nomination that fall. By designating the Persian Gulf—a region known not for its human rights and democracy but rather for its massive oil reserves—as a basic Cold War stake that America would defend just as it would its NATO allies, Carter also made clear that Western access to regular and cheap oil had become a strategic priority of the first order.[24]

Republicans were unimpressed. They charged that the administration's feckless foreign policy had emboldened the Soviets to launch the invasion—that Carter had "lost Afghanistan." Republican National Committee chairman Bill Brock went on television to assert that a "policy of patience" is a "policy of weakness." Former president Gerald Ford, smarting from Brzezinki's criticism of the Ford administration's foreign policy, asserted that Carter had lowered U.S. military capability, which "has contributed to the aggressiveness of the Soviet Union, resulting in the invasion of Afghanistan. So the Carter administration must be, and can be, blamed for what's happening in Afghanistan."[25]

Carter's forceful response to the Soviet invasion owed something to the fact that he simultaneously faced another difficult foreign policy challenge, this one in neighboring Iran. By early 1979 the Islamist radicals led by Ayatollah Khomeini had seized power from the hated and politically impotent shah, who fled into exile. Outraged by the White House's decision to allow the shah to travel to the United States for medical treatment—they demanded instead that he be returned to Iran to face justice—a mob of students and other rebels stormed the U.S. embassy in Tehran in November 1979, taking sixty-five hostages and demanding that the United States turn him over. The captors eventually released a few of the Americans, but fifty-two languished under Iranian guard.

The hostage crisis did not have the large geopolitical implications of the Soviet action in Afghanistan, but it was a far more humiliating setback for the Carter administration. Here was a band of radical students, apparently supported by a vociferously anti-American government, seizing U.S. citizens and parading them blindfolded before the cameras, while the world's most powerful nation could do nothing about it. It was a political nightmare, particularly for a president about to run for reelection and already vulnerable to right-wing accusations of weakness. Carter understood the problem. CIA director Stansfield Turner recalled that the president was "consumed" by the crisis and by the need to get the hostages out safely. In a meeting with congressional leaders, Carter—his emotion palpable—said that the safety and return of the hostages "is constantly a burden on my mind, no matter what I am thinking about. If I am worrying about an announcement that I am going to be a candidate for president or if I am worrying about the windfall profits tax or I am worrying about anything else, I am always concerned about the hostages." On another occasion he said he felt "the same kind of impotence that a powerful person feels when his child is kidnapped." He took steps to isolate Iran economically, freezing Iranian assets in the United States. In April 1980 he severed diplomatic relations with Tehran.[26]

The administration's initial response to the Soviet invasion did not sit well with all observers. George Kennan, dismayed by Carter's tough talk at a White House breakfast in early January, told a gathering at the Century Club in New York a few days later: "Everyone is rushing to define political and diplomatic problems in military terms and to insist on military responses . . . I have been involved in Soviet-American relations for fifty-two years, longer than anyone on either side. I have had my share of frustration and agony. I know what the Soviet leaders are like. But I have never been so depressed by the state of the relationship as I am today."[27]

Among the general public, however, the instinct to rally behind a president in a time of crisis temporarily increased Carter's popular support. In early 1980 his poll numbers shot up, both against Kennedy and also against the leading candidate for the Republican nomination, Ronald Reagan. But the uptick could not be sustained, due in part to bad luck. An attempted rescue operation to free the hostages failed ignominiously, as two U.S. helicopters collided in midair and the mission had to be aborted. Eight U.S. soldiers were killed, and Secretary of State Vance, who had opposed the operation, resigned in protest. Newspapers and magazines began to feature the hostages on a daily basis: "Day 200 of the hostage crisis." Even worse for Carter, the Middle East turmoil caused a spike in oil prices, damaging the American economy. By the last months of the year, inflation was rising without any corresponding economic growth, leading some economists to say the country now suffered from "stagflation."

All of it was further ammunition for the political right, who were already chomping at the bit as the 1980 election loomed. Echoing the missile gap alarmism unleashed by the Democrats twenty years earlier, right-wing political leaders and journalists, including several associated with the Team B study group, thundered that the Soviet Union was surging ahead in its race against the United States—a claim even more ridiculous than the charges of the late 1950s. Republicans in Washington, joined by several conservative Democrats, blasted the administration as ineffective and weak and hyped insignificant Soviet incursions into East Africa or Cuba as dire challenges to the American way of life. Senator Henry Jackson, staying true to the script, called administration attempts to improve relations with the USSR "appeasement in its purest form." One prominent group, the American Conservative Union, spent millions on a lobbying campaign to denounce the "giveaway" of the Panama Canal and the SALT II treaty.[28]

And there was a new player on the scene, the Committee on the Present Danger (CPD), a pressure group formed in 1975 to oppose détente. Made up of conservative intellectuals and former officials, and funded by David Packard of the military-industrial giant Hewlett-Packard, the CPD was co-chaired by veteran Cold Warriors Paul Nitze and Eugene Rostow. They enlisted numerous "new conservatives"—later called "neoconservatives"—such as Richard Perle (a long-time aide to Jackson and member of Team B), Paul Wolfowitz (another Team B participant), and Jeane Kirkpatrick to develop a thoroughgoing, moralistic attack on the Carter administration's foreign policy. Neoconservatism was a new kind of American political ideology, born not of the agrarian traditions of the Republican Midwest or the East Coast establishment of John Foster Dulles and Nelson Rockefeller but rather of disillusioned old progressives. Enchanted by the elitist political philosophy of the University of Chicago theorist Leo Strauss, and enraged by the perceived anti-Americanism that pervaded left-wing politics during the 1960s, neoconservative pioneers such as Norman Podhoretz and Irving Kristol saw in American foreign policy and especially the mentality of détente a moral relativism unworthy of the United States.

To neoconservatives, Jimmy Carter, with his liberal, "bleedingheart" concern for human rights, his unwillingness to brandish American power, and his disinclination to regard the Cold War as a titanic struggle between good and evil, personified this kind of weakness, and they went for the jugular. The committee accused the White House of grossly underestimating the Soviet threat, of undermining anti-Soviet leaders around the world, and of insufficiently trumpeting the superiority of the American system. In the pages of *Commentary* magazine, Podhoretz, Kristol, and other writers blamed "isolationism" and "the culture of appeasement" for producing SALT II, accused the president of being shackled by the legacy of Vietnam, and denounced Carter and Brzezinski for their supposed anti-Israel tendencies, even after the success at Camp David.[29]

The CPD developed three specific arguments that would become staples of neoconservative attitudes toward American foreign policy in the decades to come. The first, famously articulated by Kirkpatrick in an article in *Commentary* in 1979, justified continued American support for repressive right-wing regimes by drawing a distinction between "authoritarian" governments, such as Somoza's Nicaragua, that were friendly to the United States and capable of reform, and "totalitarian" ones such as the Soviet Union that were hostile to America and could never be reformed. Carter's human rights–oriented foreign policy was misguided and dangerous, Kirkpatrick charged, because it missed this crucial point: it undermined admittedly repressive regimes that could change, in the face of worse totalitarian nations that would never do so.[30]

The CPD's second argument stressed the importance of American preponderance throughout the world. The group rejected both the cooperative emphasis of the Trilateral Commission, which envisioned joint management of the world economy by the United States, Europe, and Japan, and the détente of Nixon and Kissinger, which implied a long-term management of world politics by the United States, the Soviet Union, and (perhaps) China. The CPD instead demanded that the United States, and only the United States, should dominate international affairs. Unilateralism was the name of the game, not trilateralism or multilateralism.

Finally, the committee argued that the United States must be willing to use military force to advance the cause of democracy and capitalism. Committee members could hardly argue with Carter's criticisms of Soviet human rights violations or with his view that capitalism, not communism, represented the destiny of mankind. But preaching was not enough. Leading by example was not always sufficient, not in a dangerous world with adversaries bent on America's destruction. The United States had to be pre-

pared to impose its fundamental aims on the rest of the world—
and if necessary, through power rather than persuasion. It had to
be prepared to stand up and fight for its way of life.[31]

Enter Reagan

The rise of the Committee on the Present Danger could not have
come at a better time for one of its founding members, Governor
Ronald Reagan of California, who by early spring of 1980 had secured the Republican Party's nomination for president. A longtime
Hollywood actor, Reagan in the 1940s had been a New Deal Democrat, but in the 1950s he moved steadily rightward, especially
after becoming a corporate spokesman for General Electric. He
gained national political attention with his televised speech in support of Barry Goldwater in 1964 and with his election to the California governorship two years later. In 1976 he battled Gerald Ford
for the GOP nomination; now, four years later, he was the party
standardbearer.[32]

Americans frustrated by the ability of a radical Islamist regime
to continue to hold U.S. hostages in Tehran, and thereby thumb its
nose at American power, were delighted by Reagan's full-throated
demand that the United States once again "stand tall." In the same
way, his promise to increase military spending massively appealed
to defense contractors and blue-collar workers in their factories, as
well as to those convinced that a major hike in military spending
would lift the nation out of its economic doldrums. Nor did it hurt
Reagan that, though more than a decade older than Carter, he
came off as younger and more energetic. He campaigned as a vigorous, optimistic alternative to his cautious, seemingly unimagi-
native opponent, as a leader who could, all by himself, make it
"Morning in America." It was, some noted, 1960 all over again.

Well, not exactly. While Eisenhower had refused to give in to
the Democrats' alarmism back then, Carter, prompted by Brzezin-

ski and other political advisers, including his pollster Pat Caddell, was not so resolute.[33] He had already declared the Carter Doctrine in response to Afghanistan; soon afterward, he announced that the United States would also boycott the summer Olympic Games, to be held that year in Moscow, and would suspend grain sales to the USSR. The president also gave up on securing congressional ratification of SALT II, recognizing that whatever its contribution to world peace and stability, an arms control deal with the Soviet Union would probably cost him, rather than help him, in the election that fall.

In July, Carter authorized Presidential Directive 59, a startling strategy statement that commissioned the building of new tactical nuclear weapons systems and seemed to endorse limited nuclear war. Carter's stunning affirmation of such a position is only one of the most vivid examples of how forays into nuclear strategy during the second half of the Cold War often represented political, rather than strategic, considerations. The president surely had not come around to the idea that a limited nuclear war was somehow "winnable"; rather, developing the kind of aggressive strategy articulated by PD 59 was a ready means of demonstrating his toughness to the electorate and to influential voices inside the Beltway.[34] As the November election neared, he threatened the Soviet Union with action should it invade Poland, where a new anti-communist Solidarity trade union movement was staging mass demonstrations.[35]

More and more, domestic political imperatives encroached on foreign policy. No longer could Brzezinski claim, as he once did, that "the worst thing you could say to President Carter was that 'it would be good for us politically.'" No longer could it be argued that Carter, determined to promulgate a moral and confident American foreign policy in a world passing the Soviet Union by, would disavow the game of alarmist Cold War politics. On the contrary, after the invasion of Afghanistan he played the game with relish. In the space of twelve months the president adopted one anti-Soviet policy after another, authorizing new weapons systems, isolating the USSR diplomatically, and outdoing his critics in exaggerating the dangers now facing the country.[36]

But Carter's move to the right was for naught, and may have played into Reagan's hands by seeming to substantiate the Republican's own alarmist claims. Aided by John Anderson's liberal third-party candidacy, which cut into Carter's support, Reagan won the election with considerable room to spare. To add insult to Carter's injury, mere minutes after Reagan was sworn in, the hostages were released into U.S. custody, the Khomeini government having concluded that it could gain nothing by continuing the standoff.

The new president arrived in office in early 1981 with set views on how the United States should contend with the Soviet Union and international communism. Fully in line with CPD thinking, he wanted to divide the world cleanly again into black and white, with the Soviet Union and its allies on one side, and the United States and its allies—no matter how distasteful some of them might be—on the other. His secretary of state, Alexander Haig, was a vociferous critic of Carter's and Brzezinski's belief that the bipolar Cold War should be de-emphasized in favor of managerial trilateralism. The confrontation with Moscow, Haig asserted, should return to the center stage of world politics. Haig rejected reports of Soviet decline and scoffed at the Kremlin's repeated demands for a new détente as so much subterfuge.[37] Other hardliners in the Reagan administration agreed. At a time when secret CIA and other estimates showed the Kremlin to be facing severe economic decline, to be losing support among its own people and the populations of eastern Europe, and to be falling farther and farther behind the United States in advanced military technologies, influential voices in the administration suggested with a straight face that the USSR in fact stood on the verge of Cold War supremacy.

Reagan bought these claims more or less down the line. He ad-

hered to a few core principles, the first being a deep and unyielding anti-communism that had dictated his political worldview for
decades and served as the bedrock of his campaign. A second
principle—and a main reason for his appeal to voters—was a basic
and essential optimism about the capacity of American power and
ideals to solve problems in the world and bring about positive
change. Even in the early months of his administration, he was
troubled by the continuing specter of Mutual Assured Destruction
and the widespread notion that the Cold War would last for many
more decades; surely, he thought, there had to be another way to
prevail. This in turn connects to another aspect of Reagan's temperament: his pragmatism. Little noticed by most critics as well as
many supporters at the time, it had in fact emerged with regularity
during his time as governor. For example, his conservative rhetoric
did not keep him from signing one of the nation's most liberal
abortion laws. Together, these elements of the new president's personality explain both his aggressive policies toward the Soviets
in his first term and his willingness in his second to respond af-
firmatively to Kremlin leader Mikhail Gorbachev's call for Soviet-
American conciliation and "new thinking" in global politics.[38]

Military Buildup

But that was later. Early on, the new team in Washington lived up
to its billing as the most anti-Soviet administration in decades,
perhaps ever. In a 1980 interview, Reagan declared that "the Soviet
Union underlies all the unrest that is going on. If they weren't engaged in this game of dominoes, there wouldn't be any hotspots in
the world." A few months later, in his first news conference as president, he denounced Soviet leaders as scoundrels who reserved the
right to "commit any crime, to lie, to cheat." On another occasion Reagan told an audience of evangelical Christians in Florida
that the Soviet Union was "the focus of evil in the modern world

. . . an evil empire." In 1981 when Moscow's client government in Warsaw again cracked down on the Solidarity labor movement, the administration condemned the action in vituperative language and placed restrictions on Soviet-American trade.[39] Two years later Reagan restricted commercial flights to the USSR after a Soviet pilot mistakenly shot down a Korean airliner that had strayed far off course and entered Russian airspace, killing 269 on board.

Reagan had campaigned on the need for massive new military spending, and with Secretary of Defense Casper Weinberger he moved quickly to make good on that claim.[40] The two men told military officials, soon after arriving in Washington: "Spend what you need." The Pentagon duly ordered scores of additional B-1 bombers, at roughly $280 million dollars per plane, and stepped up the development of the B-2 Stealth bomber ($44 billion for development plus the first twenty aircraft) as well as various missile systems. The navy initiated plans for a 600-ship "blue water" fleet, which entailed construction of 133 new ships at a total cost of $80 billion.

While embarking on this spending spree, Reagan moved at the same time to cut taxes, especially for higher-income Americans, taking the Keynesian logic of previous administrations to a new level. During the 1980 Republican primary campaign, George H. W. Bush, while running against Reagan for the party's nomination, had derided this supply-side approach as "voodoo economics." Although later, as vice president, he supported Reaganomics, Bush was right. Rather than balancing the nation's books, as "supply side" economists somehow claimed, Reagan's massive tax cuts and military expenditures would fasten more than a trillion dollars of debt on the country, creating a structural fiscal debt that remains to this day.[41]

Much like Kennedy two decades before, Reagan and his advisers combined their acquisition of new weapons systems with the development of strategies for waging a "winnable" nuclear war. The Pentagon commissioned new "counterforce" cruise and intermediate-range ballistic missiles, to be based in Europe, which were designed not to retaliate to a Soviet nuclear attack but to destroy Red Army forces in a potential first nuclear strike. In 1982 the State Department and the NSC produced a new national security policy which maintained that the United States military must be able to prevail in a war with the Soviet Union, not merely retaliate against a Soviet attack, and to "contain and reverse the expansion of Soviet control and military presence around the world."[42] The picture was hard to misinterpret, especially when one added in Reagan's rhetorical denunciations of the "evil empire," as well as the claim by the head of America's civil defense program that the public could survive a nuclear war as long as there were "enough shovels" for everyone to bury themselves underground. The United States seemed to be preparing to fight, and win, a nuclear war.

Postures are one thing, actions are another. Like every previous Cold War president, Reagan had no intention of instigating a war against the Soviet Union, and indeed throughout his presidency he was careful to avoid conflict that might cause the Kremlin to respond with force. He authorized one conventional military operation during his two terms, an invasion to overthrow the leftist government of tiny Grenada in late 1983—a military action about as unlikely to involve the Soviet Union as one can imagine. Never did he consider using military force in traditional Cold War hotspots or making a preemptive strike, even if some advisers did; indeed, the word he used in his memoirs to describe those Pentagon planners who seemed seriously to believe that a nuclear war was winnable was "crazy."[43]

But neither the aging Soviet leadership nor an alarmed Western public had any way to know this. Throughout the United States and western Europe, anti-nuclear movements focused on Reagan's incendiary rhetoric and provocative policies, and some senior Politburo members, including General Secretary Yuri Andropov, said they believed the Americans were seriously considering a first nuclear strike.[44] The dangers of a nuclear war were brought home to Americans in 1982 by Jonathan Schell's gripping anti-nuclear treatise *The Fate of the Earth,* and in early 1983 by the television drama "The Day After," which followed the fate of a Kansas community after an all-out nuclear war.

Other Americans were becoming alarmed as well. Four veteran American diplomats, led by George Kennan, published a thoroughgoing critique of the administration's nuclear strategy and demanded that the United States adopt a "no-first-use" policy instead. At about the same time Kennan published one of the most penetrating attacks ever written on the idea of winnable nuclear war, *The Nuclear Delusion,* which one academic reviewer in the *New York Times* praised as a book "replete with wisdom and learning." This in turn was followed by a path-breaking scholarly work on precisely the same subject, Robert Jervis's *The Illogic of American Nuclear Strategy.*[45] Throughout the world, the fear of nuclear war that many had put aside after the Cuban crisis returned. Sales of bomb shelters rose in 1983, as did emigrations to Australia and New Zealand. Around Europe, protesters marched wearing masks of Reagan, Andropov, and the grim reaper. And from popular artists like The Police, Nena, and Prince came sardonic songs about the absurdity of human nuclear suicide.

Star Wars

In 1985, when the military budget hit $294.7 billion (a doubling since 1980) and the Pentagon was burning through an average of $28 million per hour, defense spending finally slowed. But resources were being shifted to a high-cost project: the Strategic Defense Initiative (SDI or, to its critics, Star Wars). In a surprise presidential speech in March 1983—one not cleared with any senior foreign policy advisers—the president had announced that the United States would commence a major effort to deploy a space-based missile defense system. The idea was hardly new: for more than two decades scientists and policymakers had explored providing a defense against attack using missiles and associated radar and computer systems. The new initiative, set to cost hundreds of billions of dollars over the next decades, would be designed to shoot intercontinental ballistic missiles out of the sky, thereby protecting the United States from any kind of Soviet nuclear attack and depriving the Soviet state of its ability to retaliate against an American attack. SDI aimed to make Mutual Assured Destruction obsolete. This was Reagan's stated goal.[46]

Critics immediately denounced the plan. To many strategic thinkers, it threatened to undermine the stability of MAD and thus the long peace that had been sustained between the United States and the Soviet Union. The arms race would almost certainly speed up. Scientists, meanwhile, saw gaping technical holes: any space-based missile defense system would be highly vulnerable to inexpensive counter-measures, including launching sand bags or bits of metal into space before a missile attack, in order to damage sensors and confuse detection. Or, since the defensive shield could never provide total coverage, the enemy could simply build and fire off more missiles. Offense would always overwhelm defense. Other opponents pointed to the price tag: the United States, already running a large deficit as a consequence of the trifecta of major military spending, tax cuts, and a growing trade imbalance with Japan and other nations, could hardly afford to develop a scientifically questionable space system that might cost more than $1 trillion by the time it was completed.

The announcement of SDI, coming at the height of Reagan's remilitarization of the Cold War, was regarded by critics at home and abroad as merely the most extreme aspect of the administration's apparent attempt to destroy détente and revive the possibility of World War III. Not only was the system technologically questionable, but—more ominously—its development suggested that the White House might be seriously pursuing a first-strike capability. Without question, there were figures in the White House and the Pentagon who entertained such thoughts.[47]

Soviet scientists shared their American counterparts' skepticism that a workable system could be devised, but Kremlin officials were becoming nervous. Were the Americans really willing to abandon the stability of Mutual Assured Destruction? Did they actually believe that a nuclear war was winnable? Soviet leaders, schooled like all their predecessors in a world of unremitting power politics and feeling absolutely reliant on nuclear deterrence for their nation's security, had to take such questions seriously. The United States had been going on the offensive, it seemed, in various areas of the world. It was building up its military beyond any rational requirement. It was deploying offensive nuclear weaponry in Europe. And now it threatened to overturn the stable if brutal formula of MAD by proposing a defensive shield that could free American leaders to embark on the insanity of nuclear war. To the Soviet Politburo and to many independent observers of the international scene, it all pointed to an uncomfortable conclusion: not since the harrowing crisis period of the late 1950s and early 1960s had the Cold War been this dangerous.

Cold War by Proxy

If after the military buildup and the rhetorical broadsides people needed further proof that a new sheriff was in town, they got it with the swift demise of Carter's already-struggling human rights campaign. Determined to wage battle with international communism on every front and emboldened by the neoconservative distinction between authoritarian (acceptable) and totalitarian (very bad) regimes, the Reagan administration moved fast to extend support to tyrannical governments that promised to fight communists or other anti-American forces.

In Nicaragua, where Somoza had been ousted in 1979 by the leftist Sandinistas (who took their name from martyred Nicaraguan nationalist Augusto Sandino), the administration approved a plan immediately upon taking office to fund and train a rebel force—the Contras—operating in remote parts of the nation's hinterlands and in neighboring El Salvador. Over two years the administration funneled $1 billion to the Contras and provided them with bases in Honduras from which they could launch their attacks.[48] Reagan called them "freedom fighters" and compared them to America's founders, but reporters exposed the rebels' terrorist tactics, which included torture and the widespread killing of civilians.

The far-right government of El Salvador, meanwhile, accepted billions of dollars to suppress leftist movements in that small Central American country. The regime used (or could not control) paramilitary death squads, who by the end of the decade had killed tens of thousands, using the most brutal tactics. These forces expanded their operations beyond the nation's borders, waging irregular warfare in Guatemala (where the right-wing government, immediately following Reagan's election, had initiated a campaign of violent repression against indigenous rebels) and, with less success, in Nicaragua.[49]

Tyrannical regimes further afield also found themselves recipients of America's largesse. Iraq's leader Saddam Hussein, who had taken power in 1978, initiated a war against neighboring Iran in 1980 in a bid for regional supremacy. Though the Reagan administration had established contacts with the Iranian government through Israeli intermediaries, it concluded by 1982 that it could not accept the prospect of a victory for Iran's fundamentalist rulers. If Iran emerged victorious, it could mean Persian hegemony over much of the Middle East and, above all, control over the vast oil reserves of the two nations. This was anathema to an American government also committed to Israel's security and military dominance in the region. Quietly, the Reagan administration funneled funds and weaponry to Saddam Hussein's government, including materials for constructing chemical weapons, and at the same time removed Iraq from a State Department list of terrorism-sponsoring nations. The American aid gave Iraq the edge it needed to halt Iranian counter-attacks, and the resulting stalemate settled into a long war of attrition. By the end of Reagan's term, the United States had established full relations with Saddam's Iraq, with companies on both sides engaging in brisk trade, especially in American arms and Iraqi oil.[50]

If the meddling in the Iran-Iraq War was one sign of the Middle East's importance in U.S. foreign policy, the growing threat of terrorism against American targets was another. In 1982 Reagan had sent marines into Lebanon as part of a European-American peacekeeping force. Their purpose: to bring a measure of stability to an area torn by civil strife, longstanding religious rivalries, and the presence of PLO guerrillas on the run from Israel. Soon the American troops became embroiled in a war between Christian and Muslim factions, and the latter accused the marines of helping the Christian-dominated government rather than remaining impartial. In October 1983 terrorist bombs demolished a barracks, killing 241 U.S. servicemen. In 1985 terrorists took new hostages in Lebanon, while others hijacked American airline flights and bombed a nightclub frequented by U.S. soldiers in West Berlin. Of the 690 recorded terrorist acts around the world in 1985, 217 were targeted at Americans. Retaliation against these attacks proved difficult, however, as U.S. intelligence found it hard to collect reliable information on the various factions involved. Reagan sent bombers to attack sites in Libya, whose anti-American leader, Muammar Qaddafi, had links to terrorists. Qaddafi escaped injury, but the raid killed nearly thirty civilians.[51]

But all of these efforts paled in comparison with the adminis-tration's funneling of advanced weaponry to the Mujahideen reb-els in Afghanistan. Following the Soviet invasion in 1979 the war devolved into a ghastly struggle between Red Army conscripts and hardened Islamist fighters. Soviet forces were hampered from the beginning by poor-quality Afghan Army allies and a hostile population that aided the Mujahideen. As early as March 1980, some Moscow officials were looking for a way out. U.S. officials hoped to keep the Soviets bogged down and fighting, however, and therefore continued Carter's policy of providing covert assistance through Pakistan. As Russian casualties mounted, the Kremlin dug in, pouring more money and men into the struggle. Soviet aircraft pounded villages to bits, killing hundreds of thousands of Afghans and driving countless others across the border into Pakistan. Still, by early 1984 the Soviets had suffered 17,000 dead and wounded, according to CIA estimates.[52]

No one took more delight in the Soviet misery than CIA direc-tor William J. Casey. Journalist Steve Coll has referred to him as "among the most ardent of the jihad's true believers."[53] To Casey and other administration hawks, it mattered not at all that the Mujahideen (who counted among their number a wealthy Saudi named Osama bin Laden) were fighting to overthrow a secular cli-ent regime and establish a fundamentalist Islamic state. What mat-tered was that they were anti-Soviet. Casey made numerous trips to Pakistan to coordinate the flow of arms and other assistance. When the Soviets escalated the fighting in 1985, Washington re-sponded by sending more high-tech weapons. Particularly impor-tant were anti-aircraft Stingers—easily transportable, lightweight missiles manufactured by General Dynamics and fired from the shoulder by a single soldier. Their passive infrared seekers, which locked on to the heat generated by aircraft engines, made any Soviet jet or helicopters flying below 11,500 feet vulnerable. Red Army commanders had no effective response.[54]

Superpower relations, almost forty years into the Cold War, had seldom been this frosty. The conflict seemed set to last into perpetuity, and Ronald Reagan's aggressive Soviet policy appeared to be fully and firmly entrenched. The new president talked a more optimistic and assertive game than his predecessor, but he was stymied by the same problems: a Soviet Union that would not bend; divisions and wrangling among his advisers; the reality that all of the military spending and bravado in the world could not win the Cold War in an age of Mutual Assured Destruction.

But a change was coming. The president would soon embark on a new course, one wholly unexpected by many veteran observers of the man and by most foreign policy professionals. A new leader was about to arrive in the Kremlin, and together he and his American counterpart would set about changing history.

9

ENDGAME

During Ronald Reagan's first term, the United States appeared to be readying itself for a final military confrontation with the Soviet Union. His administration had poured hundreds of billions of dollars into new military projects, borrowing money to pay for this buildup at a staggering pace so as to avoid demanding sacrifices from the American taxpayer. The Pentagon was in the process of launching a massive new "blue water navy," increasing troop levels in Europe and Asia, and, most controversially, deploying new intermediate-range nuclear weapons systems in several NATO countries. President Reagan, together with some of his senior advisers, appeared to be actively considering the possibility of waging war against the Soviet Union—what else could explain the president's belligerent rhetoric, his deployment of war-winning "counterforce" weapons in Europe, his authorization of a beefed-up global conventional strike force, and, especially, his determination to push ahead with the Star Wars anti-missile defense program? Sober analysts throughout the West seriously feared that the Cold War was heading toward a nuclear showdown. Allies in Europe and Asia, with the notable exception of Margaret Thatcher's Tory government in Britain, urged American restraint. Anti-nuclear and peace movements flourished around the planet.

Yet by the end of Reagan's second term, the Cold War was coming to a peaceful end. Anyone who predicted this in 1984 would have been advised to seek psychiatric help. But it happened, and largely without violence—the consequence of extraordinary political reforms in Moscow, spectacular political upheaval and boldness in eastern Europe, and, most amazing of all, the establishment of warm relations between the two leaders of the United States and the Soviet Union. By the end of 1989, during the administration of Reagan's hand-picked successor, George H. W. Bush, governments in eastern Europe had fallen—like dominoes—and the Berlin Wall had tumbled down, signaling the end of the Cold War. The United States and the West had won. The drama was not over within the Soviet Union, however, as leader Mikhail Gorbachev, the central figure in all that had occurred, struggled in vain to right the ship of state and maintain his own position of authority. He failed in that endeavor, and by 1991 the USSR itself was consigned to history.

What could possibly explain such an astonishing and unexpected outcome? Historians and students of international relations have been conducting a sustained debate over this question for the better part of three decades. Much archival material that bears on the debate remains under lock and key, but enough information exists to fashion a reasonably complete answer. With respect to the direct, proximate causes of the Cold War's end, it is fairly clear that the United States played less of a role than did the revolutionary policies undertaken by a new government in Moscow, along with the bold actions of groups and individuals in eastern Europe. To a lesser but still important degree, however, American foreign policy also mattered in bringing the long superpower confrontation to a conclusion.[1]

The Rise of Gorbachev

In 1982 Leonid Brezhnev, who had ruled the Soviet Union for eighteen years, died. During that time, he had been content above all else to sustain his nation's military superpower status while ignoring the deterioration of its society. That he lasted as long as he did surprised many who had watched his declining health and his growing dependence on prescription drugs of various kinds. He was replaced by Yuri Andropov, an intelligent and capable veteran of the KGB who brought with him some ideas about domestic reform but who himself died after about two years in office, having accomplished little.

In stepped the octogenarian Konstantin Chernenko, from whom nobody expected much of anything. To most of the world the Soviet Union had become a sclerotic, reactionary state—unable to prevail in Afghanistan, stuck in a bitter rivalry with the People's Republic of China, reviled by ordinary citizens throughout its empire in eastern Europe, and, perhaps most important, seemingly incapable of reforming its tottering economy. Chernenko seemed to personify the nation's woes: aged and backward-looking, he mumbled vague ideas about reform that had no chance of realization. After only eleven months in office, he died too.[2]

The new American secretary of state, George Shultz, traveled to Moscow for Chernenko's funeral. While there, he met the newly installed Soviet premier. In his fifties and a good generation younger than his predecessors, Mikhail Gorbachev had not spent his politically formative years steeped in the Stalinist terror of the 1930s or battling the inferno of the Great Patriotic War. Rather, he rose through the ranks of the risk-averse Brezhnev regime, during a period when the intensity of politics, both domestic and international, eased considerably and when the Soviet superpower sought mostly to solidify the status quo. The new premier came from a provincial part of the Soviet Union and had been regarded as something of a hick by his more urbane Kremlin colleagues. But that was not at all how he appeared now. In stark contrast with his immediate predecessors, Gorbachev projected an air of confidence and generosity. His fashionable young wife, Raisa Gorbacheva—a professor of philosophy who seemed unwilling to assume the traditional Soviet role of the subservient, inconspicuous spouse—appeared at his side on state business and foreign journeys, favorably impressing all who met her. At least in terms of image, a new era had arrived in Soviet politics.

Was there substance to the perception? Many Kremlinologists in the West believed that Gorbachev's generation might adopt a different attitude toward the United States and world politics. The secretary of state concurred: "Ideology," Shultz had earlier suggested to Reagan, "will be less of a living force" for the new Soviet Union.[3] The historian Melvyn Leffler has argued that the communist dream lived on among the new generation of Soviet leaders during the 1980s, but it is doubtful whether this dream was still central to their political agenda.[4] To be sure, Gorbachev and his reformist colleagues believed in communism, but how could any politician in the Soviet Union not? It came with the territory, just as faith in capitalism was a given for Reagan, Truman, or any other modern-day American president. This had long been the view of George Kennan: Marxism-Leninism, he believed as early as 1950, was a "stale ritual" practiced by jaded Kremlin leaders who had long abandoned revolutionary fervor in favor of great-power statecraft. Whether this was exactly so with Gorbachev, it was undeniable that the new Soviet leader came into office motivated not by the mission of international working-class revolution but by a determination to repair his nation's broken society. At the Chernenko funeral, Canadian prime minister Brian Mulroney asked Shultz when he thought Gorbachev would begin the formidable process of reforming his country. "Today," Shultz replied.[5]

Gorbachev had reason to be impatient. The USSR had been in economic decline since the 1960s. Its factories were decrepit, its infrastructure crumbling, its consumer economy barren, its labor force cynical. Around the Soviet Union, ordinary citizens, trudging off to dismal jobs, muttered the slogan, "They pretend to pay us, and we pretend to work." "Soviet Man" got back at the system by engaging in absenteeism, alcoholism, and petty theft. Factories produced nothing of value for months at a time, while badly needed goods sat rotting or rusting along disused railroad tracks. The largest agricultural nation on earth was forced to import grain from the United States to feed its population.

The worst manifestation of Soviet decline was the disaster at the Chernobyl nuclear power plant, located in the northern Ukraine, shortly after midnight on April 26, 1986. The explosion of the reactor there, a result of years of neglect and political corruption, contaminated vast areas of the Ukraine and Byelorussia. Scores were killed and thousands sickened, with many more, to this day, suffering birth defects and other deformities. Much of the immense agricultural production of this area was deemed unusable. For months, little was done to address the destruction because the corrupt political system would not permit it. Local and regional bureaucrats pointed fingers at one another, while the Kremlin seemed more interested in covering up the explosion for international propaganda purposes than acting quickly to limit the suffering. Chernobyl had a powerful impact on Gorbachev, who himself was not blameless in Moscow's callous political damage control during the first week after the explosion. It demonstrated how dysfunctional the Soviet political system really was. Perhaps even more important, Chernobyl brought home the dangers of nuclear war in a way that only a catastrophe can. If the bursting of just one reactor could cause this much damage, what unimaginable destruction would a war waged with thousands of nuclear weapons do?[6]

Yet reforming Soviet society would not be easy. Stalin had demonstrated that enough repression could terrorize the population into productivity and obedience—but those days had long since passed. The emergence of new technologies and the globalization of Western culture made it increasingly difficult for the Kremlin to conceal from its restive population the vast discrepancies between

East and West. Perhaps a Soviet (or Polish, or Hungarian) citizen during the 1930s or the 1950s could believe that her economic situation was no worse than that of the oppressed masses of the West. By the 1980s, no one bought that line anymore. Irresistibly, over the decades, the West's "soft power" asserted itself, thanks to radio, television, movies, and fax machines. Young people wanted the rock 'n roll records, personal stereos, and American blue jeans that they knew their counterparts in the West could buy with ease. They wanted access to Western fiction and film. An underground trade in dissident *Samizdat* literature flourished, especially in the big cities. By the middle of the 1980s, Soviet youth seethed with frustration, as did their counterparts all over eastern Europe.[7]

Gorbachev understood the implications of this unrest, at least to a degree. He grasped that the Soviet Union could not remain a genuine superpower unless it reformed itself, and in short order. True, his country wielded a world-class military force, but how did its brute capabilities enhance the Soviet Union's international power? Invading western Europe or attacking the United States was a nonstarter; that would likely mean the end of the world. Meanwhile, the legendary Red Army, conqueror of the Nazi war machine, was bogged down in a catastrophic war in Afghanistan, in impoverished parts of East Africa, and in policing an eastern European empire simmering with resentment. Yes, the formidable arsenal built by Stalin, Khrushchev, and Brezhnev had protected the Soviet Union for four decades, and memories of the Second World War had led these Soviet leaders to value this achievement above all others. But Gorbachev understood that in doing so they had neglected positive aspects of national power—the economic, cultural, and political assets that ensure domestic support, sustain alliances, and attract clients. A new course would have to be charted.

Accordingly, Gorbachev announced a plan to restructure the Soviet economy and open it up to domestic innovation and foreign influences. His policy of *Perestroika* aimed at orienting the economy more toward consumer needs and eliminating the thick layers of useless bureaucracy. *Glasnost* was about easing government control over free speech and encouraging Soviet citizens to speak up about, rather than sullenly tolerate, the inefficiencies and dysfunction of their country. In the field of foreign policy, Gorbachev fired the ageless foreign minister Andrei Gromyko, who had been waging Cold War since the 1940s, through eight American administrations, and replaced him with a fellow reformer, Eduard Shevardnadze. In short order the two of them began to hint, and then to declare openly, that the USSR would not stop its allies in eastern Europe from pursuing socialism in their "own way." At least in terms of declared policies, there could be no doubt that the Soviet Union was bent on change. This presented the United States with an opportunity. But an opportunity to do what?

Iceland Summit

Reagan thought he knew. Having won reelection easily over the Democratic candidate—Carter's vice president, Walter Mondale—in 1984, he began his second term only a few months before Gorbachev assumed power in Moscow. At home, Reagan's political popularity was high, but he faced difficult problems abroad. Although he had a close ally in Britain's Margaret Thatcher, elsewhere in Europe, in Japan, and in other nations of the Western alliance, public opinion was becoming increasingly anti-American. Millions of young people in the West opposed Reagan's repressive policies in Latin America and the Middle East, and the antinuclear movement was going strong. From Norway to New Zealand, protestors demonstrated against America's nuclear arsenal and the talk of a winnable nuclear war emanating from Washington. To be sure, the administration's public relations problems were nothing compared with the economic woes and political sclerosis facing Gorbachev. But Reagan worried—as his predecessors had done off and on since the start of the Cold War—that an increasingly disaffected West might choose a third way between the United States and the USSR.

Soon after his rise to power, Gorbachev wrote to the president expressing his keen desire to improve Soviet-American relations. Reagan was happy to agree to meet him at a summit conference in Geneva, which took place in November 1985. In hindsight, we can compare this meeting to the summit in Tehran in 1943. During the Second World War, Roosevelt and Stalin had regarded their main business as personal diplomacy, as taking the "measure" of one another. Something similar happened at Geneva. Reagan, to the consternation of some of his advisers, was determined to pursue a lasting legacy during his second term, and his consultation with Shultz had persuaded him that it might be possible to secure a wide-ranging accord with the new Soviet leader.

What led Reagan to consider negotiations with the "evil empire"? For one thing, in a very real way, his thinking had evolved. Over the previous year—even before Gorbachev came to power —his public rhetoric had taken a less aggressive, less confrontational tone. In early 1984, during the primary campaign season, he spoke in terms scarcely conceivable even a few months before. "Our challenge is peaceful," he declared in a speech on January 16. "We do not threaten the Soviet Union . . . Our countries have never fought each other; there is no reason why we ever should." The superpowers must "rise to the challenges facing us," Reagan declared, "and seize opportunities for peace."[8] Too much should not be made of the changed rhetoric, but neither should it be dismissed. Reagan's domestic advisers hoped for a more conciliatory tone in advance of the upcoming election, and the president's wife, Nancy, her eye now on her husband's place in history as well as his reelection, also urged him to appear magnanimous.

But Reagan's change of heart came about not just for reasons of political expediency. He seemed to be genuinely worried about the massive nuclear arsenals on both sides and about the possibility that a crisis could trigger an uncontrollable escalation, which in turn fueled his single-minded promotion of the Strategic Defense Initiative.[9] The problem with SDI, however, was that it would become operational only in the distant future, long after Reagan had left office. And in the fall of 1983, two events forced him to confront the immediacy of nuclear danger. In late October, Reagan attended a Pentagon briefing on SIOP, the Single Integrated Operational Plan to wage total nuclear war. By all accounts, including those of his hawkish secretary of defense Caspar Weinberger, the president was deeply horrified by the world-ending plans that were part and parcel of America's nuclear strategy. Then, in early November, NATO undertook an elaborate exercise, code-named Able Archer, that spanned western Europe. The operation simulated a war between NATO and the Warsaw Pact that escalated to a nuclear exchange. Reagan, already troubled by the implications of the exercise, was horrified when he learned that Soviet leaders seriously believed it might be signaling the onset of a U.S. first nuclear strike.[10]

To many nuclear strategists on the right, such fears were nothing out of the ordinary. The Cold War, after all, was a nuclear showdown. But Reagan's understanding of world politics differed in a fundamental way from that of his more hawkish foreign policy aides. And notwithstanding his references to the "evil" Kremlin in the first term, it probably had always been different. The neoconservatives associated with his administration—Paul Nitze, Richard Perle, Caspar Weinberger—regarded the Soviet Union as a permanent enemy, and the practice of foreign relations as the art of incessant struggle. They sought to vanquish the USSR, nothing less, even as they also grossly exaggerated the Soviet system's strength. For them, conflict was inevitable. Thus, Weinberger told members of the Harvard class of 1938 meeting in November 1985 (the same month as the Geneva summit) that the Russians "are bent on world conquest." Not only that, the secretary of defense added, they were ahead in Star Wars research, ahead in military power.[11] Reagan knew better. The Soviet Union was moribund, not menacing. More than many of his close aides, he believed that international politics could change, that the Cold War was not immutable.

But if some of this shift in Reagan's outlook occurred even before the new regime arrived in Moscow, it took Gorbachev's rise to power and his expressed desire for serious reform to bring about genuine change. Fed a steady diet of Leonid Brezhnev since the mid-1960s, American leaders could be pardoned for concluding that meaningful diplomacy with the Soviet Union would never accomplish much. Gorbachev was a breath of fresh air, and he appealed to an American president who was not content with the status quo. At the Geneva talks, the two heads of state reached no firm agreements, and Reagan made clear his continuing commitment to SDI, much to Gorbachev's consternation. Each man discerned, however, that the other might really be ready for a substantial deal. They agreed that nuclear dangers must be lessened. Yet neither of them, it seems clear, had any idea of what was to come.

In early 1986 Gorbachev announced publicly his desire to see strategic nuclear weaponry outlawed by the year 2000. Regarding this assertion as standard Soviet propaganda, Weinberger, together with his chief assistant, Perle, devised a ploy that would have fit perfectly with America's diplomatic strategy during the early Cold War. Reviving the stratagems of the Baruch and Marshall plans, Weinberger and Perle suggested that Reagan see Gorbachev's bet and raise it, by urging him to agree to the immediate abolition of all strategic missiles. They were certain that the Kremlin would refuse, since the Soviets were so far behind in advanced conventional weaponry and so reliant on their nuclear deterrent to maintain their superpower status. And when Gorbachev rejected it, the United States could blame Moscow for the perpetuation of the Cold War arms race. This in turn would deflate anti-American disarmament movements in western Europe and elsewhere and redirect that protest toward the Soviet Union.[12]

The scene was set to play out along these lines when Gorbachev and Reagan met again, this time in Reykjavik, Iceland, in October 1986. The main item on the agenda was arms control, an objective that Gorbachev had described as "crucial" when he spoke to Shultz at Chernenko's funeral. During its first term the Reagan administration had offered a "zero option" plan whereby the USSR would dismantle intermediate-range missiles based in eastern Europe in exchange for a U.S. promise not to deploy comparable ones in western Europe. This odd proposal, born of America's strategic superiority, had not been taken seriously by Gorbachev's predecessors. He, however, was desperate to deal. Moreover, Reagan arrived in Iceland equipped with the Weinberger-Perle scheme to make the Soviets an offer they had to refuse. The stage seemed set for a summit characterized by American domination and Soviet conciliation.

Something different happened. When the two sides began negotiating on the intermediate missiles, Gorbachev, to the shock of the U.S. delegation, not only effectively accepted the American offer but proposed a fifty percent cut in *all* strategic nuclear weapons. Reagan countered with the plan to eliminate all strategic weapons as long as the United States (and any other nation) could deploy defense systems against remaining nuclear arms—a proposal that played wholly to American strengths and Soviet weaknesses. In previous years this notion, if offered at all, would have been rejected out of hand, or met with an unserious counterproposal designed a priori to be ignored.

In this high-stakes game of international poker, it was Gorbachev who called and raised the bet, urging that the two sides seek to eliminate *all* nuclear weaponry by 1996. And to the panicky disbelief of many in his delegation, Reagan seemed to take the Soviet leader's proposal seriously. Rather than use the proposal as a means of scoring yet another tactical Cold War victory, the American president appeared to have been impressed with Gorbachev's earnestness, which matched his own deepening fear of nuclear war. The two men warmly affirmed their desire to rid the world of the scourge of nuclear weapons, and they met privately, away from their anxious subordinates, to discuss this radical notion further.

Gorbachev had come to Iceland desperate for a deal, but he would not submit entirely. Nuclear weapons were pretty much the only bargaining chips the Soviet Union had left. So he demanded one concession: that the United States cease its work on SDI. Otherwise, the Soviet Union, having dismantled its nuclear missiles while Star Wars went forward, could be at the mercy of the United States. The military men in the Kremlin, Gorbachev implied, would never accept a deal that deprived Russia of its last vestige of superpower status and left the nation open to possible American blackmail. Gorbachev pleaded with Reagan to grant him this one concession. He added that he had no problem with basic laboratory research and testing; that could continue. But if Washington started to deploy weapons in space, violating the ABM treaty of 1972, then he would be unable to follow through on his proposal. The glorious opportunity to achieve a lasting peace would be gone.

Reagan balked. He was too committed to the promise of Star Wars to want to negotiate on this point, and the United States was in too commanding a position for him to feel the need to compromise. The president's reasoning, as he repeatedly expressed to Gorbachev, was that if the two sides dismantled their strategic weapons, then a strategic defense system would manifestly not threaten the USSR—it would no longer have Soviet ICBMs to shoot down and would be deployed only to deal with future nuclear threats from other nations. Indeed, Reagan assured Gorbachev that the

United States would willingly hand over its space defense technologies to the USSR if it succeeded in perfecting them.

Was the president sincere in making these assurances? Probably, though he may also have been conscious of the Weinberger-Perle ploy. But Reagan failed to perceive how such an offer would be regarded in Moscow. How could Soviet leaders be certain that the United States would not secretly build ICBMs and deploy them in tandem with Star Wars to fashion a first strike capability? Why should Kremlin leaders, given decades of Soviet-American hostility, and given U.S. secrecy over the atomic bomb project during World War II, believe his promise that the United States would share its technology? It was all too much to ask.

And so, the amazing initiative the two leaders conceived at Reykjavik fell through. They left the summit with grim faces and terse comments. Of course, even if Gorbachev had accepted Reagan's proposal, neither nation would likely have followed through on the deal. In the harsh light of history, it is difficult to imagine either side having enough confidence to dismantle every one of its strategic nuclear weapons when it could never be absolutely certain the other had done the same. Even less likely was the possibility of Moscow and Washington disarming while other nuclear powers kept their weapons. But this was not quite the point of Reykjavik; it was not what gave the summit its historical importance.

Reagan saw what he had begun to perceive in Geneva, namely, that he had in Gorbachev a Soviet counterpart who did not fit the old framework, who was not cynical and obstinate, who seemed to have no interest, not even for show, in revolutionary communist politics, who did not regard the United States as an ideological enemy destined for the dustbin of history. Gorbachev seemed to want what he wanted, what all sensible Americans wanted: an easing of nuclear danger, a more stable international order, and greater prosperity for his nation. If this was so, how much sense did it make for the Soviet Union and the United States to continue the Cold War? At Reykjavik, Reagan seemed to ponder this question himself.[13]

Others, too, were beginning to ponder it. Yet few predicted the dramatic developments that would soon bring about not merely the end of the superpower confrontation but the demise of the Soviet Union itself.

Reagan Stumbles

Gorbachev would be the leading individual in these unexpected events, though they depended crucially as well on courageous actions by many ordinary Russians, not to mention Poles, East Germans, Hungarians, Czechs, Slovaks, Romanians, Balts, and other east-central Europeans. Reagan's part was smaller. He and his senior arms control advisers worked with their Soviet counterparts to secure an agreement by both sides to reduce their intermediate nuclear forces in Europe and to begin substantial negotiated reductions on their strategic nuclear weapons as well. He invited Gorbachev to visit the United States, which the Russian did in late 1987, greeting enthusiastic crowds and eluding his security detail to shake outstretched hands, looking like any seasoned American pol. Reagan himself visited Russia soon afterward.

But Reagan's principal attention was on a scandal threatening to engulf his presidency. In November 1986 news leaked that Reagan's national security adviser, John M. Poindexter, and an aide, marine lieutenant colonel Oliver North, in collusion with CIA director William Casey, had covertly sold weapons to Iran as part of an attempt to win the release of several American hostages held by Islamic fundamentalist groups in Lebanon. Money from the arms deal had then been illegally diverted to fund the Contras doing America's Cold War bidding in Nicaragua.

The scheme was not wholly American in conception. Israeli officials and moderates in Iran, as Trita Parsi has shown, sought to forge a tacit alliance to prevent Iraq from winning the ongoing Iran-Iraq war, and U.S. planners cleverly used that opening for their own ends. In the immortal words of North, a key American participant in the scheme, it was "a neat idea." By selling arms to Iran, the United States could signal its willingness to work with Iran's more secular politicians, who were opposed to the Islamic radicalism of their leader, Ayatollah Khomeini. Further, by arming Iran, the United States could prevent Iraq from winning the war, which, as a result of its use of chemical-weapon attacks (produced partly with American materials), it was threatening to do. (The administration wanted neither side to score a clear-cut victory.) Then, by surreptitiously diverting the funds to the Contras, the White House could get around Congress and operate with an entirely free hand in the jungles of Central America, as the money was coming from unknown sources rather than officially from the U.S. government. And finally, in exchange for American arms, Iran would be obliged to pressure its allies in Lebanon to release American hostages held there—perhaps the most important factor of all for the sentimental president.[14]

The plan manifestly violated both a congressional ban on aiding the Contras and the official administration policy of not trading arms for hostages. The United States would be selling arms to a nation it was publicly condemning as a terrorist state, one it had pressured its allies not to do business with. Furthermore, Iran was at war with an Iraqi government the United States supposedly backed. Nevertheless, proponents of the plan, including both North and National Security Adviser Robert McFarlane (Poindexter's predecessor), together with many of the Israeli and Iranian agents involved, believed it could work—and go undetected. Reagan signed off on it in August 1985, though he would later deny the fact.

The operation did not go smoothly. The Iranians got their weapons, even though some of them came directly from the Israeli arsenal, still marked with the Star of David. Iranian officials persuaded Hezbollah, the Lebanese terrorist group holding the American hostages, to release a few of them, though not all of them, as the White House expected. The Contras got some money, $16 million, but much less than the arms sales should have produced; shady middlemen appear to have made off with the rest. The Irangate hearings, held during the summer of 1987, left the president's role unexplained—questions remained about what he knew and when he knew it—but eleven members of the administration were ultimately convicted or pleaded guilty. At the height of the public inquiry, McFarlane tried to commit suicide. Reagan's popularity took a beating, and he left office in early 1989 with relatively low poll ratings and a Cold War still in place. Many conservatives were by then deeply disillusioned, convinced that the second-term Reagan had turned into a naive and dangerous appeaser, taken in by a Soviet leader who, even if not quite as deceitful and wicked as all his predecessors, would soon enough be replaced by one who was. "To greet [the Soviet government] as if it were no longer evil," William F. Buckley charged a few months before, "is on the order of changing our entire position toward Adolf Hitler." Reagan's overtures to Gorbachev, right-wing columnist Charles Krauthammer bellowed, were "ignorant and pathetic."[15]

A World Transformed

The world was changing, but some things remained the same. Eastern Europe seemed to be on the verge of revolution; Gorbachev was offering concession after concession; and the two presidential candidates, George H. W. Bush and Michael Dukakis, former governor of Massachusetts, traded blows with one another over who would take the tougher line on the communist threat. A GOP pollster urged Bush to organize his campaign under the "thematic umbrella of anti-Communism. Anti-Communism is at the very core of the Republican Party. Ask Nixon, whose early career was defined and kept alive by anti-Communism." Bush followed the advice. In what the journalist Sidney Blumenthal called the "last campaign" of the Cold War, the vice president had no trouble painting his adversary as an out-of-touch endive-eating liberal who would go soft in a hard world. Bush won the election with room to spare.[16]

The new administration took office in January 1989 clearly undecided about how to deal with the shocking changes in eastern Europe. Bush, who had once served as director of the CIA and was by temperament a cautious realist, commissioned a general review of U.S. policy toward the Soviet Union and sat back to watch how events unfolded in the East. Gorbachev seemed to be doing everything he possibly could to demonstrate to the West that his nation no longer wished to engage in the Cold War, and in March George Kennan said at a congressional hearing that the USSR could simply no longer be seriously regarded as a military adversary. Still, many hawks in the White House refused to believe it. Deputy National Security Advisor Robert Gates had to be ordered not to give a series of anti-Soviet talks; Vice President Dan Quayle mocked Gorbachev as a Stalinist "in Gucci shoes."[17] Most mistrustful of all, perhaps, was Secretary of Defense Dick Cheney, who publicly predicted in April, while the review was still being written, that Gorbachev's reforms would fail and the USSR would return to a full Cold War footing.[18]

President Bush, together with his secretary of state, James A. Baker, recognized that Gorbachev's reforms were genuine and that it would be a tragic mistake for the United States to assume otherwise. The two men clamped down on the overheated rhetoric of Gates, Cheney, and others during the first few months of their administration, but they were also wary of supporting Gorbachev too enthusiastically too soon. They understood that first-term administrations can pay a high political price for adopting dovish positions, and they took a cautious, wait-and-see approach, one befitting their conservative, realist inclinations. Moreover, as the historian John Dumbrell has pointed out, Bush and Baker may have perceived that hearty support and encouragement from Washington could well hurt the reform movement in Moscow.[19] In their ongoing attempts to derail Gorbachev, the old Cold Warriors in the Kremlin might simply point to the fact that his most vocal supporters appeared to be the imperialists running Washington.

Bush and Gorbachev needed a dramatic event, something that would prove to skeptics and militarists in Washington and Moscow alike that the Cold War was approaching its end. In the fall of 1989 they got it, in the form of a cataclysmic upheaval in eastern Europe that shook the very foundation of world politics. The immediate impetus for this development was Gorbachev's determination, made in consultation with foreign minister Shevardnadze in the aftermath of Reykjavik, that the twin policies of *Glasnost* and *Perestroika* could not be sustained as long as the USSR continued to bleed in Afghanistan and to support and subsidize unpopular client regimes in eastern Europe. Though Gorbachev had initially stood firm in Afghanistan and had even escalated Soviet involvement somewhat in 1985, by the start of 1987 he came to accept arguments by senior civilian and military aides that withdrawal was the only answer. Soviet losses had continued to rise, and the Mujahideen, though taking enormous casualties, showed no signs of breaking. Gorbachev ordered a full disengagement. When the last Soviet solider left Afghanistan in February 1989, some 20,000 of his comrades (the exact number is still hidden) had perished, with perhaps five times that number seriously wounded. Hundreds of thousands of soldiers returned home to try to make their way in civilian life.[20]

Eastern Europe presented a more complex challenge. Gorbachev and Shevardnadze were acutely aware of the broad resentment simmering throughout the region, especially among young people and the intelligentsia. They recognized the cutting irony in the fact that the boldest political movement anywhere in the Eastern Bloc, Poland's Solidarity campaign, stemmed from working-class rebellion. They understood that the Soviet economy, slowed to a crawl by the Afghanistan quagmire, the Chernobyl disaster, declining oil revenues, and the general corruption of Soviet society, could no longer afford to pay the subsidies that client states in eastern Europe and elsewhere constantly demanded. To have any hope of repairing its society, the Kremlin had to free itself from policing an empire. At about the same time that Reagan left office, the two Soviet statesmen let it be known that they were withdrawing economic and political support from their client states and that Moscow—despite the Brezhnev Doctrine—would not intervene to prevent political change in the empire, even if this led to the ousting of communist governments.[21]

But the two men did not anticipate what happened next. In the space of a few months in 1989, one of the most astounding political upheavals in history took place throughout eastern Europe. In nation after nation, popular movements challenged communist regimes and brought them down, almost everywhere resorting to little or no violence. In Poland, the Solidarity labor movement, led by the dynamic Lech Walesa, seized political power in the main cities and demanded participation in the national government. Poles, inspired not only by Walesa but also the steadfast anti-Soviet position of a Polish pope, John Paul II, led the way in eastern Europe's rebellion against the Russian empire. By the summer of 1989, Poland's communist regime had succumbed and turned over the country to Walesa. In the Baltic states of Latvia, Estonia, and Lithuania, mass demonstrations mostly by young people demanded independence. In Czechoslovakia, an alliance of intellectuals and workers led by the playwright Vaclav Havel took power in the fall, as did a comparable movement in Hungary. Late in the year, the dictatorships of Bulgaria and Romania fell. In each case, Moscow did nothing.

The most dramatic episode in this "velvet revolution" occurred in East Germany that autumn. The East German communist regime had been one of the region's harshest, notorious for the pervasive social control exercised by its secret police (the STASI) and its brutal behavior at the Berlin Wall, where more than a hundred East Germans and others attempting to escape over the years were shot down and sometimes left to decompose in the no-man's land of central Berlin.[22] Emboldened by events in Poland, Czechoslovakia, and Hungary, East Germans began to rise up against the government headed by Erich Hoeneker, who stepped aside (on account of "ill health") in favor of a little-known bureaucrat, Egon Krenz.

Facing massive popular opposition, as well as a wave of emigration by East Germans to the West via Czechoslovakia and Hungary, Krenz apparently gave local authorities permission to open the gates of the Berlin Wall. The official on the scene, Gunter Schabowski, took this to mean an immediate opening, and once he announced this the floodgates opened. Berliners from both sides, along with dumbfounded tourists, began to smash at the wall, climbed and danced on it, and over the next several weeks knocked it down piece by piece. The most vivid symbol of the Cold War ceased to exist, as a result of popular contempt for Soviet communism and a decision by Moscow to let it happen.[23] By the end of 1989, the Soviet Union's eastern European empire had obviously collapsed. International politics would never be the same. In America, policymakers and scholars began to recognize that what to many of them had been unimaginable even a few years earlier was actually happening, at that very instant. On the day after Krenz opened the Berlin Wall, the historian John Lewis Gaddis, who had devoted his scholarly career to studying the U.S.-Soviet rivalry, walked into a graduate seminar a few minutes late. "Well," he said, "the Cold War ended yesterday."[24]

ENDGAME

Eight days later, Arthur M. Schlesinger Jr. captured the mood in his diary: "The pace of developments in Eastern Europe continues to astonish. So many things have happened in the last year, last month, last week, that I never expected to happen in my lifetime. The collapse of the Berlin Wall is followed by the upheaval in Bulgaria and now by the incipient rescue of Czechoslovakia. How right I have been to argue the inscrutability of history! Once again events defy all our expectations and history outwits all our certitudes."[25]

Unconditional Surrender

By November 1989, the Cold War no longer had much geopolitical meaning. The Soviet Union had stood by in silence while its last and most important allies expelled their communist governments, one after another, and put an effective end to the Warsaw Pact. President Bush and Secretary of State Baker remained cautious, however. They saw that Cold War victory was theirs for the taking, but they were determined to have it in a way that would neither give ammunition to the Cold War dead-enders in Washington nor make the White House appear weak to the American electorate. Perhaps most important, Bush and Baker wanted to ensure that the Soviet Union did not unravel, as its client states in eastern Europe had so rapidly done. The Soviet government still controlled a vast territory stretching over a major swath of Eurasia, and it still possessed a huge arsenal of nuclear weaponry whose security must be maintained.

Not long after the Berlin Wall fell, Bush and Gorbachev held a brief summit meeting in the Mediterranean, off the coast of Malta. Meeting on board both American and Soviet cruisers, buffeted by winter storms, the two leaders discussed the endgame. They agreed to pursue radical cuts in conventional and nuclear weapons systems, with the USSR once again bearing the brunt of the cuts. They quibbled pointlessly on desultory Soviet support for rebel groups in Latin America. But Bush induced the Russian to make the clearest statement of Soviet Cold War surrender that had yet been seen. The Soviet Union, Gorbachev declared, would move sharply toward economic cooperation with other nations. It would become, he said, "part and parcel of the world economic system."[26]

What a change from four and a half decades earlier, when Stalin's rejection of precisely such a course had helped bring on the Cold War. Stalin had reconfirmed this stance in 1947 by repudiating the Marshall Plan and forcing his client states in eastern Europe to do the same. Now, Gorbachev unambiguously declared that the USSR would join the capitalist world in the global marketplace. If the collapse of eastern Europe deprived the Cold War of real geopolitical purpose, Gorbachev's agreement at Malta signaled the end to the ideological contest between capitalism and communism.

Over the following year the Bush administration sought to solidify the deal. The United States, together with its allies in Europe and Asia, put together economic packages designed to incorporate eastern Europe and the Soviet Union into a new globalism led by American entrepreneurial initiatives. The Marshall Plan, it could be said, was complete, some forty years late. At the same time, Bush carefully avoided calling for further political upheaval. When Gorbachev cracked down on dissent in the Baltic states, the Ukraine, and Azerbaijan, the White House offered only muted criticism. Maintaining stability was paramount. The Soviet Union had already abandoned eastern Europe and autarkic communism. If it retained the rest of the empire and kept its nuclear weapons under central control, that was fine with Washington.[27]

The new Soviet-American relationship faced another test in the second half of 1990, following Iraq's invasion of neighboring Kuwait. Bush condemned the invasion and vowed to defend Kuwait. His motives were complex and included a desire to solidify his domestic political standing, to show Cold Warriors that he was not afraid to flex American muscle, and to foreclose any move by Iraqi leader Saddam Hussein to gain control of the region's petroleum supplies. The president called for an international coalition to turn back the invasion, and the Soviet response demonstrated, perhaps better than anything to date, just how much had changed in such a short time. During the Cold War, the Kremlin would have opposed American-led military action and in all likelihood would have provided support for Iraq; perhaps, in such an important region as the Persian Gulf, it might even have threatened major war. This time, though, Gorbachev acquiesced. Under pressure from hardliners in the Kremlin, he tried initially to forestall military action; when that effort failed, he backed off and declared Soviet support for an international force to be deployed to the Gulf. When the deadline for Saddam to leave Kuwait expired and Operation Desert Storm commenced, Gorbachev stayed mum. Any threat of war, which would have naturally occurred to his predecessors, was completely off the table. The United States initiated military action in a key region of the world to further its own interests, and the Soviet Union in effect went along.[28]

To indicate its unconditional Cold War surrender, there was only one more thing the Soviet Union could do. It could cease to be. In early 1991 old guard conservatives in the Kremlin plotted to overthrow Gorbachev and somehow restore the Soviet system of old. When the Soviet premier left Moscow for a vacation in August 1991, they acted, deposing Gorbachev and moving swiftly to seize executive power. A brash reformer, Boris Yeltsin, rallied opposition to the coup and succeeded in preventing the plotters from attaining serious political power and control over the armed forces. Gorbachev thus was able to return to Moscow as the head of state, but the political damage to the nation and to his own standing was irreparable.

In August the Soviet parliament banned the Communist Party —an event that, not long before, would have been akin to the Vatican banning the Catholic Church—and offered the three Baltic republics their independence. In the meantime, Yeltsin and his fellow radicals maneuvered to seize power from Gorbachev, who had always sought merely to reform the Soviet system, not eradicate it; he was not ready to accept the actual dissolution of the USSR. Increasingly isolated, he surrendered authority to his rival in December. On December 26, Yeltsin announced the termination of the Soviet Union. Employees at Kremlin Square lowered the red flag of the USSR, with its workingman's hammer and sickle, for the last time.

U.S. Foreign Policy and the End of the Cold War

How to assess these momentous developments of 1989–1991? Who was primarily responsible for ending the Cold War? Was it inevitable, or did it require the bold risk-taking of Gorbachev and his allies? Did it have more to do with internal Soviet politics or with international pressures? These questions are particularly interesting because the Cold War's sudden demise defied the predictions and logic of mainstream international relations theorists, who had suggested that the Cold War could not end peacefully—that great powers do not go down without a fight.[29] These questions also relate centrally to the larger issue of American power in the early and mid-1980s: was it instrumental, or even decisive, in forcing Gorbachev's hand, and if so, would the application of American pressure produce similar effects elsewhere? Or was the end of the Cold War largely a Russian and eastern European affair, conducted with disregard for, or even in spite of, the United States? Was Reagan correct when he said, modestly, that he had simply "been dropped into a grand historical moment"?

Scholars who study Soviet politics closely have put forward strong arguments and evidence that Gorbachev's decision to relax Soviet control over the other Eastern Bloc nations—the move that triggered the "velvet revolution," the fall of the Berlin Wall, and the collapse of the last bulwark of Soviet imperial power—derived primarily from domestic concerns and much less from direct American pressure. Gorbachev, desperate to reform the Soviet economy, which had been hit even harder by the disaster at Chernobyl and the drop in the price of oil, was forced to take radical steps to stop the hemorrhaging, and among these moves was the decision to stop subsidizing the corrupt communist regimes of eastern Europe. Moreover, Gorbachev felt a personal responsibility not to respond to the economic crisis in the usual Soviet way, by cracking down on political opponents, flaunting Soviet military power, and announcing another five-year plan to nowhere. He believed he could fashion a different response that would ease the tension of the Cold War and remake the USSR into a more progressive and attractive regime. What he did not anticipate was the rapid unraveling of eastern Europe and the acute political crisis this caused in Moscow. Such motivations were basically Gorbachev's own, put into action by bold individuals in eastern Europe, and were not dictated or even foreseen in Washington.

This argument is persuasive, more so than the claim by so-called Cold War triumphalists that the collapse of the Soviet Union was, in effect, engineered by the Reagan administration—that the massive military buildup, combined with Reagan's tough overall posture, "squeezed" the Soviet Union to the point that Gorbachev was forced to wave the white flag.[30] The weight of the evidence goes against this view, especially the fact that many of the hardliners in the Reagan administration who supported the military buildup most vociferously—Weinberger, Perle, Nitze, and others—did not believe in Gorbachev's sincerity and continued, throughout Reagan's second term, to trumpet the ongoing Soviet threat. Many of these individuals had spent their entire adult lives regarding Soviet communism as a static monolith, unchanged, unchanging, and unchangeable. Representative of their views was the statement of

Under-Secretary of State Lawrence Eagleburger, who argued in 1983 that "no one man—indeed no group of men—can affect, except at the very margins, the fundamentally competitive nature of our relationship."[31] The hardliners in Washington did not believe that they could end the Cold War peacefully; they thought it would go on forever, or resolve itself through military combat. It is difficult to imagine these advisers—if not Reagan himself—believing in any serious way that the Soviet Union could be vanquished in a matter of a few years by political maneuverings that stopped short of war.

Which is not to say that American actions and American actors had nothing to do with what occurred. Reagan was too modest in claiming he had merely been dropped into a momentous event. In particular, two policies undertaken by Reagan and George H. W. Bush contributed to the end of the Cold War and the subsequent disintegration of the Soviet Union. The first was simply the decision by both Reagan and Bush to reject the alarmist warnings of severe anti-Soviet advisers that the Gorbachev revolution was an inauthentic charade designed to weaken Western vigilance. It was hardly preordained that the two men would go this way. Throughout the Cold War, shrill rhetoric warning of Soviet superiority and mendacity repeatedly carried the day over more moderate views; the same thing could have happened here. Powerful voices in Washington and around the country, including spokesmen from the military-industrial complex, had a vested interest in the continuation of the superpower conflict. And the Soviets over the years had given reason for people to be distrustful.

Reagan and especially Bush felt considerable pressure to withdraw their public support for Gorbachev, to regard his reforms as bogus, and to return to an adversarial footing. Had either man done so, it is by no means impossible that the old guard in the Kremlin would have attracted much more support for their attempt to oust Gorbachev in 1991 and to resurrect the Soviet Union

as a Cold War superpower. Granted, the crumbling Soviet economy would have made it difficult for these conservatives to contend with the United States for very long.[32] But they could have
tried, and surely they could have cobbled together a Soviet state,
even minus its eastern European empire, that might have lingered
on for years. In that event, with conservative Cold Warriors back
in power at the Kremlin, a dangerous new era might have unfolded. Great empires, after all, seldom manage a "good death."
Many resort to war out of desperation. Reagan and Bush deserve
credit for not facilitating such an outcome.

A second American contribution to the end of the Cold War
grew out of Reagan's increasing fear of nuclear war. As the political
scientists Daniel Deudney and G. John Ikenberry have argued, by
agreeing with his Soviet counterpart that they must put an end
to the threat of nuclear holocaust, Reagan gave Gorbachev reason
to believe that he could pursue a more idealistic foreign policy
without worrying that Washington would immediately exploit it.[33]
Reagan's nuclear fear gave the Soviet premier a small reed to grab
onto when he had little else—it provided a base from which to radically reform and demilitarize the Soviet system without risking an
aggressive American response.

Ironically, Reagan's commitment to the Strategic Defense Initiative enhanced this process. The logic of Star Wars, so different from the more conventional American military buildup of the
1980s, put the Soviet Union in a uniquely difficult position. For
although Kremlin leaders had become accustomed over the decades to America's technological superiority, they had always been
able to counter it with the heavy club of nuclear deterrence. The
rich Americans could build all the ships and missiles they wanted,
but they would never be able to conquer the Soviet state as long as
it could threaten nuclear retaliation. Suddenly, however, and for
the first time in twenty years, the Soviet leadership had to face the
prospect that its retaliatory forces would not be enough. Everyone

knew, of course, that SDI would take a long time to develop and might never work perfectly. And to be sure, Gorbachev and his advisers did not seriously believe that the United States was about to initiate World War III. Nothing was imminent.

But the rapid deployment of SDI was not the issue. What Reagan succeeded in doing with Star Wars (wittingly or not) was to deal two blows to Gorbachev's hopes of staging a long-term reform of the Soviet Union. To begin with, the prospect of SDI informed Gorbachev that the United States would not be content to rely upon Mutual Assured Destruction forever: over the medium and long term the Soviet Union could expect a new technological race in which it was wholly unprepared to compete. When the nuclear status quo eventually came to an end, the Soviet Union would be facing an adversary much less intimidated by the Kremlin's one remaining source of power—its nuclear arsenal. The Americans had the money and the advanced technology to follow through with their project; the USSR was broke and hopelessly behind in advanced military capabilities, especially those related to burgeoning computer technologies. Reagan himself grasped this point: his membership in the hyper-alarmist Committee on the Present Danger did not keep him from asserting as early as 1976 that "the Russians know they can't match us industrially or technologically."[34]

True, many scientific experts termed SDI a pipedream, a technological impossibility. A reliable system of missile defense was a contradiction in terms, they said. Gorbachev was not unaware of these views, having heard such utterances from his own scientists. As leader of the Soviet Union, however, he could not afford be so sanguine. Maybe the American system would never work, but maybe it would work well enough. The Americans had shown plenty of wizardry before. And if it did work, the Soviet Union would be left defenseless. More important, Gorbachev knew that his military advisers would never go along with a policy of simply ignoring Star Wars and hoping that it failed. The Soviet Union would have to compete, and it just did not have the resources to do so.[35]

Thus, if the United States can be said to have squeezed the Soviet Union during the 1980s, the squeeze was felt between Reagan's nuclear idealism on one side and the prospect of SDI on the other. The American president's fear of nuclear war encouraged Gorbachev to believe that a grand reform—not an end—of the Soviet project might be possible. Star Wars helped to make that reform a political nightmare for him. Hence his determined attempt at Reykjavik to persuade Reagan to abandon SDI.

But Star Wars was influential, not decisive. The Cold War ended when it did because Gorbachev decided to withdraw support from the corrupt client states in eastern Europe, because many thousands of eastern Europeans took history into their own hands, and because reformers in the Kremlin saw no alternative than to give up their superpower status peacefully. It is not difficult to understand why some scholars, regarding the five-decade implementation of the Cold War as a great and peaceful victory for the United States, are inclined to give Washington full credit for its termination as well. But the historical record simply does not justify such a conclusion.[36]

During the amazing years of 1989–1991, Gorbachev and his successor, Boris Yeltsin, gravitated toward the conclusion that the Soviet Union could not, must not, fight for its superpower life in the nuclear age. Reagan's fears of war and his commitment to SDI may well have been influential in pushing the Soviet leaders toward this decision, but it was they who made it when others in Moscow would likely have followed a very different path. The specter of nuclear destruction gave the two statesmen yet another reason to leap over the edge, and when they did, presidents Reagan and Bush, defying pressure from the hawks in their midst, wisely stepped aside.

CONCLUSION

During the first half of the twentieth century, modern war brought misery and destruction to the peoples of the world's great powers. The leading nations of Europe saw tens of millions of their citizens killed, many of their great cities destroyed, their colonial empires endangered, and their domination over world politics swept away. Ethnic and religious minorities—particularly the Armenians of western Asia and the Jews of central Europe—were victims of extermination campaigns. In East Asia, millions of Chinese died during the Japanese conquest of the 1930s and 1940s, and millions more during the civil war of 1945–1949. Japan itself was physically devastated by American air attacks, with ancient Kyoto its only city to escape massive bombardment. Even that experience paled compared with what the Soviet Union endured—the loss of twenty-five million people in its ghastly war of attrition against Nazi Germany. In all of these places, for all of these societies, a bid for great international power entailed modern war, and modern war meant hardship, suffering, grief, and impoverishment for victors as well as vanquished.[1]

The American experience after 1941 could hardly have been more different. To be sure, in the war that elevated it to super-

CONCLUSION

power status, roughly half a million American soldiers lost their lives, and Korea and Vietnam together would claim almost 100,000. These sacrifices must not be minimized. But they can be contrasted. Not only did the United States lose a far smaller percentage of its population to foreign wars than did any other major power in the twentieth century, it also escaped the traumatic miseries of having war waged on its territory and against its civilian population. At the end of 1945, the great nations of Europe and Asia found themselves with ruined economies, ravaged countrysides, cities in rubble, and—especially in Germany, China, the Soviet Union, and Japan—millions of dead civilians. By the starkest contrast, the American homeland was pristine, unscathed since Pearl Harbor by the weapons of industrial war, and the U.S. economy was running on full steam. For the vast majority of Americans, World War II meant not starvation, terror, and desperation but prosperity and national pride.

This fortune persisted and intensified through the Cold War. Driven by America's preeminent position in the capitalist world system, the efficiency and innovativeness of its private sector, and the Keynesian engine of intensive government spending, the U.S. economy grew by leaps and bounds during the Cold War, giving its citizenry the highest standard of living in human history. Removed from the Eurasian mainland by two great oceans and deterred from fighting a third world war by the prospect of nuclear holocaust, the United States seized and wielded great power for fifty years without having to demand significant wartime sacrifices from its population. To be an average citizen of the United States during the Cold War was to enjoy abundant material comforts and to be only dimly aware of the hardship that a major war could bring.[2] The empires of Europe and Asia had sought hegemony for centuries, sacrificing untold millions of their citizens and bearing the brunt of fearsome combat, only to fail. By 1991, fifty years after joining the ranks of the great powers, the United States bestrode the world without having to ask the vast majority of its citizens to give up their everyday conveniences, much less their lives.

Not only did Cold War victory come easily to the majority of Americans; it also came complete. Few great-power rivalries in history have led to such a lopsided conclusion. The United States did not defeat the Soviet Union in battle, physically destroying and then occupying it as it had western Germany and Japan; it did not have to. The USSR gave up its empire, then gave up its own existence. The successor state, Russia, retreated more or less to its traditional borders, abandoned the ideology of Marxism-Leninism, and allowed itself, fundamentally, to be incorporated into the capitalist world system. The United States, meanwhile, continued after 1991 to spend vast sums on defense, to expand its geopolitical reach, and to maintain military installations all over the world. It even forged alliances with former Soviet client states. By anyone's definition, such an outcome must be regarded as a total defeat for the Soviet project and a clear victory for the United States and the West. As the new millennium dawned, America stood supreme in a unipolar world.

How to explain this remarkable outcome after four-plus decades of intense superpower competition? Most fundamentally, the U.S. victory came because of the systemic and ultimately fatal weaknesses of the Soviet system. These were manifest early, indeed from the start, as Stalin opted to seek full coequal superpower status with Washington (and to spend accordingly) and felt compelled to use coercion to maintain friendly regimes on Russia's borders. Winston Churchill spoke with perspicacity when he told French leader Charles de Gaulle in November 1944, with reference to Stalin's impending territorial acquisitions, that "after the meal comes the digestion period." Painful that digestion would be! In 1948 Tito's Yugoslavia broke away, and in 1949 Stalin thought it prudent to end the Berlin blockade. In 1950–1952 he allowed North Korea to go from being largely a Soviet satellite to being a

Chinese one. Uprisings in eastern Europe followed, as well as a split with Mao Zedong's China. In 1961 only the construction of a heavily patrolled wall could stop the drain of East Germans fleeing to the West. By then, millions of people behind the Iron Curtain had lost faith in the Soviet system. The ranks of unbelievers would continue to grow until, by the end, there were precious few defenders left.

The historian and native Hungarian John Lukacs made a trenchant observation in 1991:

> In 1945 many thousands of Germans committed suicide. Many of those who killed themselves were not National Socialist party leaders, some of them not even party members, but all of them believers. But I know not of a single instance, in or around 1989, when a believing Communist committed suicide because of the collapse of Communism, in Russia or elsewhere. Dogmatic believers in Communism had ceased to exist long before, even as dogmatic anti-Communists continued to flourish.[3]

Lukacs's observation reminds us of the Cold War mismatch. Anyone who experienced life in both a NATO country and a Warsaw Pact nation during the Cold War quickly grasped the wide chasm between the two. Next to the glitz and bustle and well-stocked store shelves of the former were the drab housing projects, polluted skies, and scarce consumer goods of the latter. Over time, the Soviet economy proved less and less able to compete with America's free market, less and less able to cope with the demands of its own citizenry and that of eastern Europe. A command economy could not produce both guns and butter, jet fighters and stereos, missiles and overseas holidays. Advances in communication technology only dramatized the differences between East and West (the CNN effect) and aided the efforts of dissident groups and other nongovernmental organizations working to reform the system if not bring it down.

American Successes

At the most basic level, then, the United States won the Cold War because it proved spectacularly better able than the Soviet Union to give more people more of what they wanted—in economic, social, and cultural terms. In an important sense, the Soviet collapse was less about U.S. government policies, less about the trillions of dollars spent on nuclear weapons, and more about what is nowadays called soft power—music, movies, consumer goods, and the prospect of a freer, more comfortable, more exciting life for ordinary Russians and eastern Europeans.[4]

But foreign policy mattered too. For at the end of the Second World War it was far from obvious that the West would achieve such levels of affluence, technological sophistication, or cultural appeal; nor was it self-evident that such soft power would prevail over austere and authoritarian political systems. The legacy of the 1930s, when combined with the near-victory of Nazi Germany and the awesome performance of the Red Army, as well as the widespread appeal of statism and communism to beleaguered Europeans and others after the war, inclined many to believe that the opposite was more likely. Such was the message of Orwell's *1984*.[5]

This is where American foreign policy proved decisive. Awesomely powerful though their nation may have been, in both economic and military terms, U.S. leaders still had to construct a political environment, in western Europe and East Asia, that would permit affluence and democracy to flourish while avoiding the third world war that might destroy civilization forever. Three aspects of this basic Cold War policy stand out.

First, American decisionmakers adhered to the general strategy of containing Soviet expansion. Every U.S. president from Harry

Truman to George H. W. Bush signed on to the basic imperative that the United States should reject both isolation from world politics, which entailed indifference to Soviet expansion, and the active initiation of war against the USSR. Perhaps such a general policy seems obvious and unremarkable today, but it is well to remember that in 1945–46 isolation and war were the only two approaches to power politics that most Americans understood. Containment was based on the core insight, articulated most famously by George Kennan, that the Kremlin did not seek immediate military conquest, and that if it were prevented from opportunistically expanding into key industrial areas, it would be effectively shackled. Over the long term, Kennan prophetically predicted, the USSR would be forced inward upon itself and eventually would implode. To facilitate such an outcome, the United States had to maintain an activist foreign policy and to provide basic security guarantees to its major allies, while at the same time resisting the temptation to hasten the decline by initiating war with the Soviet Union. Though some officials, such as John Foster Dulles and Ronald Reagan, at times flirted with going a step further—that is, rejecting the middle way of containment by seeking to win the Cold War now rather than waiting for the Soviet Union to lose it—no one ever seriously acted on such sentiments.

Nevertheless, and as Kennan himself lamented, after 1949 the United States radically expanded its containment project, transforming it eventually into a global campaign of anti-communism that went far beyond the spare geopolitical strategy he articulated at the outset of the Cold War. No more was it just about stopping Soviet power. Kennan's and Walter Lippmann's fear that the Truman Doctrine's sweeping scope could portend interventions in far-flung and nonvital corners of the world was to a significant extent realized. It bolstered what would become known as the domino theory and helped lead, most notably, to the disaster of Vietnam. Thus Truman expanded the war in Korea, when a much more limited intervention to preserve the status quo would have produced the same results. Thus Eisenhower undermined and helped topple legitimate regimes in Iran and Guatemala that posed no threat to the United States, sowing the seeds of long-term anti-American resentment. And thus successive administrations bankrolled cruel and repressive regimes on near and distant shores just because they were anti-communist.

But if containment was bent almost beyond recognition, it did not break, for the simple reason that the United States never initiated a major war—not over China in 1949, or Hungary in 1956, or Cuba in 1962, or successive crises in Berlin. In the broadest sense, containment meant rejecting both isolation and any provocation that risked World War III, and this was the policy that American leaders followed. They contained Soviet power for close to half a century and, when the great crises came, they stepped back from the precipice.

Herein lies the second successful policy undertaken by the United States during the Cold War: the decision by every administration from Eisenhower to George H. W. Bush to accept Ike's understanding that a nuclear war could not be won and must never be fought. To be sure, this understanding gave even greater weight to Kennan's demand that the United States should avoid situations that might trigger a major war against the Soviet Union. But the real risk of nuclear war, as Eisenhower realized, lay not in the possibility that one day one or the other superpower would decide to commence a third world war, but in a U.S-Soviet confrontation that escalated to total war, against the wishes of both sides. Despite the development of all sorts of nuclear strategies by every administration from Kennedy onward, no American president dissented from Eisenhower's logic. Indeed, after the Cuban Missile Crisis of October 1962, every American president—as well as every leader in Moscow—steered clear of the kind of chest-pounding confrontation that would raise the serious possibility of a nuclear holocaust.

CONCLUSION

U.S. analysts in 1946 could not have known that containment would necessitate not only the avoidance of all-out war between the United States and the Soviet Union but, in fact, *any* kind of war between them. It required real determination and political skill for Eisenhower to impose this understanding on American foreign policy at a time when a great many people in Washington opposed him. It required the common sense of his successors to maintain this policy in defiance of many in government, as well as in universities and think tanks, who believed that a nuclear war could be won and might well be fought.[6]

Finally, a third reason for America's Cold War success lay in the willingness of the United States to engage in diplomatic give-and-take both with its key allies, particularly in Europe, and also, after a considerable lag, with its adversaries. The great accomplishments of the late 1940s—the Marshall Plan, the Berlin Airlift, and the NATO alliance—were all based on the coordination of American foreign policy with the policies of its allies in western Europe, and above all on the willingness of Washington to negotiate with states like Britain, France, and West Germany to achieve mutually beneficial results rather than to impose American policy on them. Given the bipolar nature of the Cold War and the vast disparity of power between the United States and its close allies, U.S. leaders could have acted more unilaterally during this early period. They could have forced American policies on western Europe without consulting, without conciliating, without rewarding, much as the USSR did in eastern Europe. By choosing not to follow this imperious path, Washington avoided giving its European allies cause to drift toward neutralism, toward a third way—a development that almost certainly would have led to a very different kind of Cold War.

With its communist adversaries, the United States initially followed a very different course, with baleful effects. Early negotiations with the Kremlin were effectively ruled out until the regime transformed its foreign policy and abandoned its repressive communist ideology. By adopting this stance, the Truman and Eisenhower administrations ignored the possibility that diplomatic encounters with foes, even when they achieve no tangible outcome, can provide useful intelligence, allow for a deeper understanding of the adversary's *modus operandi,* and establish lines of communication that are useful when a crisis suddenly breaks out. Anxious at all times to project strength, these two administrations lost sight of the fact that talks display weakness only if one shows weakness in the talks. Chamberlain's mistake in 1938 was not that he went to Munich; it was what he did when he got there.

Little by little, however, the thinking changed. The concrete and quite extraordinary steps taken to improve Soviet-American relations following the Cuban Missile Crisis were a testimony to this. John F. Kennedy, defying charges of appeasement by the right wing, grasped the nettle, and both he and his country emerged in a stronger political position for it. Though some of the old thinking would be visible in the years to come, particularly in Lyndon Johnson's Vietnam initiatives, contacts with Moscow and Beijing were more frequent and more productive. Richard Nixon and Henry Kissinger used skillful triangular diplomacy in the early 1970s to reduce tensions between the United States and the two major communist states and to deepen the Sino-Soviet schism. Diplomacy, they understood, could be used to hasten rather than delay the goal of winning the Cold War peacefully. To be sure, détente had its limits: it could ease the superpower confrontation but it could not end it. Absent an American determination to negotiate, however, to engage in diplomacy with its adversaries, the USSR and the People's Republic of China might have overcome some of their differences, an event that could have rejuvenated Soviet power and ultimately prolonged the Cold War.

It was no accident, then, that all three of these American policies were in play during the last years of the conflict. Ronald Reagan, having staked out a hardline posture in his 1980 campaign and during much of his first term, shifted course—modestly before Mikhail Gorbachev assumed power in Moscow, and more radically thereafter. Grasping the logic of containment, Reagan combined a confidence in the ultimate demise of the Soviet Union with a determination to avoid warlike stances that could rally the militarists in Moscow. Grasping the logic of the nuclear revolution, he openly declared his determination to avoid nuclear war, and he fended off the extremists inside and outside his administration who advocated otherwise. Belatedly grasping the logic of diplomacy, he engaged Gorbachev on numerous occasions, using the age-old tactic of stick and carrot and the humanizing effect of direct and personal negotiation to give the Soviet leader reason to continue his policies of *Glasnost* and *Perestroika*. Neoconservatives in Washington thundered on about appeasement and surrender, and some of the president's aides, such as Secretary of Defense Caspar Weinberger and his deputy Richard Perle, urged a more belligerent stance. But Reagan, joined by his secretary of state George Shultz, stood his ground. That diplomatic determination helped make possible the astonishing scenes of jubilation in eastern Europe in 1989.

The Price To Be Paid

A triumphalist, largely self-congratulatory account might end right here. America contained communism and won the superpower struggle without blowing up the world and without obliterating freedom at home. End of story. But that will not do, because any historical account must reckon not only with benefits but also costs, and whether those costs were necessary. Even a cursory look at the balance sheet shows the cost of America's Cold War to have been enormously high, and, in terms of lives and limbs lost, paid primarily not by Americans but by others. Next to the U.S casualty figures in Korea and Vietnam must be placed the tremendously greater losses suffered by Korean and Vietnamese citizens (along with Cambodians and Laotians). Elsewhere in the world, successive U.S. administrations backed repressive anti-communist regimes in dozens of nations, many of them employing ruthless security services and death squads, some of them waging protracted counterinsurgencies supplied with American arms. Accurate numbers are hard to come by, but certainly U.S. policies in the Third World after 1945 led to the death or maiming of several million civilians who had never raised a hand against the United States.[7] If the vast majority of Americans emerged from the Cold War unharmed, the same cannot be said for a great many others in a great many places.

The economic costs were likewise vast. The United States spent trillions of dollars on Cold War interventions of dubious worth and on weapons systems that had little or no obvious utility in an era of Mutual Assured Destruction. When the Cold War began, Truman, Kennan, and other economic traditionalists hoped that it could be waged on the cheap. Eisenhower echoed their sentiments, especially when contending with representatives of the military-industrial complex who always demanded more. But their opposition was overwhelmed by a logic of bipolar overkill and Keynesian spending that perhaps no American politician could have resisted. Bipolarity incessantly pushed U.S. decisionmakers to rely exclusively on military power, no matter how redundant: since alliances could not decisively enhance American security, why not buy another weapons system?

Why not indeed, when doing so enriched rather than impoverished Americans? For unlike previous great powers, the United States managed to parlay its massive military spending into a series of economic booms. By borrowing money rather than raising taxes to pay for its new weapons and remote wars, and by pumping this borrowed money back into the domestic economy, Washington leaders discovered that high military spending need not entail the austerity, rationing, and confiscatory taxation it had required in the past but rather could fuel explosive economic growth and the political success that invariably came with it. Politicians, industrialists, and military leaders who benefited from this spending naturally found reasons to call for more and more weapons and to inflate Soviet capabilities and intentions, however dubious or wholly fabricated the claims.

But there is no such thing as a free lunch. Massive military expenditures year after year deprived Americans of large sums that might otherwise have gone into more productive investment. Moreover, by borrowing trillions of dollars (increasingly from foreign lenders), by subsidizing military industries to the point that entire regions of the country became economically dependent on them, by conditioning the American public to adopt a buy-now-pay-later mentality, the architects of America's Cold War set the United States on a precarious fiscal path. Just who shall pay down this mountain of debt is uncertain, but it will not be the generation of Americans who accumulated it.

A final cost of the Cold War is less easily measured. This was the militarization of American politics. Contrary to myth, foreign policy after 1945 was never uncontaminated by domestic politics. Throughout the era each new generation of politicians in Washington rediscovered the winning political formula of talking tough on communists, both foreign and domestic. Political parlance shifted to the right on foreign policy and stayed there, year after year, with only a modest tacking back during the last days of the Vietnam War. A dovish national campaign of the type waged by Henry Wallace and the Progressive Party, advocating Soviet-American conciliation, was still possible, barely, in the 1948 election; for twenty years thereafter it was a complete non-starter.

The anti-communist hysteria reached its absurd extreme during High McCarthyism (1950–1954), but in less virulent form it was a feature of congressional, senatorial, and presidential elections throughout the Cold War, often irrespective of what was happening overseas. Politicians who were accused of being insufficiently vigilant against the Reds were put on the defensive and often found it irresistible to call for a more militaristic waging of Cold War, whatever they actually thought about the merits of such a policy. This process culminated during the early and mid-1980s, when rabid anti-communism and chest-thumping militarism animated much of the capital's foreign policy discourse even as the Soviet Union was beginning to fall apart.

Did decisionmakers always make policy on the basis of partisan pressures and perceived electoral needs? No, but these concerns were usually part of the causal equation, shaping decisions in subtle and at times not so subtle ways. American political figures grasped the logic of the "intermestic." They came to understand that sizable political benefits could be accrued by characterizing international incidents or trends, no matter how minor, as dangerous threats to the nation, and that this process could substitute for the making of effective foreign policy. They grasped (consciously or not) that, as in earlier times of free security, the direct military threat to American territory was at most times quite low, which meant they could afford to play politics with national security. They ran little risk in erasing the distinction between politics and policy; and as a result, governing too often became the pursuit of partisan or careerist goals rather than the common good.

The militarization of American politics went beyond partisan one-upmanship. It manifested itself in the rise of interest groups such as the Taiwan, Israel, and Cuban émigré lobbies, who successfully pressured American politicians to back aggressive policies that often ran counter to America's Cold War interests. For example, in October 1976 Cyrus Vance, then a foreign policy adviser to Jimmy Carter's presidential campaign, argued that on Cuba "the time has come to move a way from our past policy of isolation. Our boycott has proved ineffective, and there has been a decline of Cuba's export of revolution in the region." Carter was sympathetic, but he acted cautiously in the campaign in order not to offend the Cuban-American community in south Florida and thereby lose that state and its sizable chunk of electoral votes in the November election. "There were no votes to be won, and many to be lost, by indicating friendliness toward Castro," the historian Gaddis Smith wrote of Carter's thinking.[8] Neither the Cuban lobby group nor any of the others were all-powerful—had they been so, America might well have gone to war over China in 1949, over Quemoy-Matsu in 1958, over Cuba in 1961–62, or over the Middle East in 1973. But it would be foolish to deny that they influenced policy to a significant degree.

Finally, the militarization manifested itself in the rise of the military-industrial complex, as Eisenhower anticipated in his farewell address of 1961. Satisfying the voracious appetite of this machine encouraged American leaders to pursue Cold War aims less by negotiation and alliance-building than by fabrication of ever more costly weapons systems and the massive export of armaments. Millions of people, many of them living in California and other states with burgeoning populations and lots of electoral votes, became accustomed to deriving their livelihood from local defense industries. A powerful bond developed between contractors, labor unions, and Washington politicians, who together created a huge military arms establishment in times of peace and had a great vested interest in the Cold War.

The end result of all this? A remarkable transformation of American political culture, whereby a people that before 1940 had been, on the whole, opposed to standing armies and suspicious of power politics now seemed tempted so often to choose the military option and revel in American power, to regard diplomacy, sophisticated debate, and consideration of the other side's position as policies of the timid. The distinguished scholar Hans Morgenthau, observing this phenomenon, worried that modern nationalism too often reflected the common man's desire to regard war as an instrument of his own power. Modern war, he wrote, had become a vehicle in which "individual egotisms and aggressive instincts find vicarious and morally expedient satisfaction."[9] Americans like Charles Beard once touted the fact that in the United States one did not need to talk tough and project bellicosity in the arena of foreign affairs in order to assert national pride. The disappearance of this noble sentiment in U.S. society must be counted as one of the Cold War's great casualties.

Yes, the skeptical reader may respond, some Cold War–related actions, especially Vietnam, were regrettable. Yes, there was too much military spending, too much addiction to short-term economic incentives, and too much pandering to interest groups. Yes, the militarization of American society had its unsavory elements. And yes, McCarthyism was an embarrassment, and the narrowing of political discourse after the late 1940s dealt a blow to free political expression. But this was a relatively small price to pay for a victory of such monumental scale, achieved without recourse to major war or the establishment of a garrison state, without Americans having to experience massive impoverishment, conscription, or repression. During World War II the United States spent vast sums, killed millions of people, and clamped down on political dissent at home—does that mean the war should not have been fought?

That would be a winning response if the excessive costs of America's Cold War could be shown to be merely the inevitable collateral damage of a necessary policy. They were not. On the contrary, not only were these costs fundamentally unnecessary, they probably prolonged the Cold War. As early as 1947, George Kennan argued in *Foreign Affairs* that Soviet power "bears within it the seeds of its own decay, and that the sprouting of these seeds is well advanced." He and fellow Soviet expert Charles Bohlen believed that Stalin had neither the intention nor the capability to embark on a Hitler-like plan for world conquest, which meant that Washington could afford to be patient. Even the "Twin Shocks" of 1949—the Soviets' production of an atomic bomb and the communist victory in China—did not prevent Harvard president James Conant from predicting, early in 1950, that by 1980 the USSR's "absurdities and static system would cause them to grind to a stop," and that "if we can hold what we have, especially the United Kingdom, and avoid war, then the competition between our dynamic free society and their static slave society should be all in our favor, or if not, we deserve to lose." In three decades, Conant guessed (and he was not far off!), "Russia may Balkanize or Byzantine itself."[10]

It is true that against these predictions could be placed more alarmist ones uttered by equally informed observers. But the weight of the evidence, together with Kennan's clear geopolitical reasoning, suggests strongly that the mission of containment as originally conceived was largely accomplished by about 1950. If one adds to it the task of dissuading the Soviet Union from ever imagining that it could win the Cold War by launching a nuclear attack, the mission was completed by 1960. The Soviets' "digestion" problems were by then chronic, while in western Europe the "miraculous fifties" had brought a robust economic recovery.[11]

If Kennan's formulation was right, then by this time the process of Soviet implosion should have been well on its way. The optimal American strategy, according to the logic of containment, should have been to restrain itself from foreign adventures and avoid superpower showdowns. But what the United States did was quite the opposite. It embroiled itself in conflicts in far-flung regions of the world, most notably Vietnam, that caused great self-damage and badly tarnished its anti-communist cause. Its continuing buildup of nuclear and conventional weapons systems—armaments that would have little or no purpose in an age of Mutual Assured Destruction—led the Soviet Union to doubt America's antiwar intentions and provoked a bipolar arms race that stoked the fires of the military-industrial complex in both Washington and Moscow.

It also fed the Kremlin's addiction to power politics. By exacerbating and globalizing the Cold War rather than confidently sticking with defensive containment, the United States gave Kremlin leaders an excuse to use American belligerence as a justification for its continued obsession with external threats. The arms race sustained the power and legitimacy of Soviet oligarchs, who were terrified by the prospect that the American bogeyman might recede and force them to attend to the deep structural problems of their domestic economy, not to mention the growing restiveness among eastern Europeans. They understood that the intrinsically dysfunctional Soviet system could battle only external challenges, and that any attempt to shift attention to domestic concerns would be the mechanism of their decline. By providing the USSR with such convenient foreign challenges, U.S. militarism bolstered the Soviet Union's own military-industrial complex and protracted the Cold War.[12]

History does not allow reruns. It is impossible to say with certainty what would have happened had different paths been followed. But if one accepts the logic of containment as originally conceived, it follows that the most costly aspects of America's Cold War—far from being the regrettable excesses of a necessary strategy—actually prolonged its rivalry with the Soviet Union. Apart from the task of establishing a nuclear deterrent, the United States was poised to initiate the Cold War's endgame in the early 1950s. Its economy was at its height, its population patriotic and self-confident, its worldwide reputation strong, its security almost absolute. Instead, the dangerous confrontation lasted another forty years.

CONCLUSION

Continuities

Nor did the demise of the Soviet Union bring an end to the power of the intermestic in U.S. foreign policy. The military-industrial complex remained a power within itself, largely insulated from public opinion, resistant to correction from the outside. Thousands of firms—and many labor unions—continued to be dependent upon military contracts, as did communities across the country. Interest groups favoring a hegemonic U.S. foreign policy retained outsized clout, while those arguing for a reduced global presence remained, as during the Cold War, mostly on the fringes. Neoconservatives, disillusioned with the latter-day Reagan's shift toward détente with Gorbachev and with what they saw as his and his successors' insufficient support of Israel, in the 1990s pressed for a return to the aggressive policies of the early Reagan. They derided Bill Clinton's foreign policy as feckless, and they lobbied obsessively for decisive U.S. action to oust Iraqi leader Saddam Hussein. Increasingly, as the decade wore on, these "neocons" framed the terms of the foreign policy debate in Washington; more and more, the political discourse took on a familiar refrain. Just as no Democrat or Republican after 1945 wanted to be tagged with the soft-on-communism label, so no politician around the turn of the twenty-first century was going to take the chance of being called weak-kneed on Saddam.[13]

Following the 9/11 terrorist attacks in 2001 the echoes became still louder, as public officials across the land resorted to language and tactics that would have made the staunchest Cold Warrior proud. All the familiar techniques were used, often by familiar faces—anti-Soviet stalwarts such as Richard Perle, Paul Wolfowitz, and Dick Cheney were now key players in George W. Bush's Washington. Diplomacy was for the weak, or the weak-willed: "terrorist" states were not to be negotiated with but rather attacked, as in the case of Iraq (which had nothing to do with the 9/11 attacks), or positioned on an "Axis of Evil." As during the Cold War, adversaries were to be demonized, and trivial dangers transformed into transcendent ones. "Keep elevating the threat," Secretary of Defense Donald Rumsfeld instructed his underlings after 9/11. "Make the American people realize they are surrounded in the world by violent extremists."[14] It was not a hard sell; in the months after the attacks, many commentators seriously compared the war on terror to World War II, a handful of stateless terrorists to Nazi Germany. Acceptable political discourse narrowed substantially, particularly during the run-up to the war in Iraq. Mainstream media outlets avoided challenging official justifications for the war, for fear of appearing insufficiently patriotic. Few were the print or television journalists who questioned administration claims regarding Saddam Hussein's intentions and capabilities; for the most part, editorial writers seconded White House talking points. On Capitol Hill, lawmakers, even those skeptical about the military option, loudly trumpeted their determination to be "tough on Saddam." Democrats, as in an earlier age, felt especially vulnerable. "The top Democrats were at their weakest when trying to show how tough they were," the lone GOP dove in the Senate, Lincoln Chafee of Rhode Island, stingingly recalled. "They were afraid that Republicans would label them soft in the post-September 11 world, and when they acted in political self-interest, they helped the president send thousands of Americans and uncounted innocent Iraqis to their doom."[15]

The rise of Barack Obama in 2008 demonstrated that much of the American public was fed up with this overseas adventurism and in particular with the war in Iraq, widely seen as a disaster of the first order. Obama appealed to that sentiment in his campaign, and his victory in the Democratic nomination fight and then in the November election owed much to the fact that he had opposed the Iraq War when his opponents had supported it.[16]

As president, however, Obama found it hard to escape the politics of insecurity. In the campaign he had pledged to stand firm in Afghanistan (he referred to it as the good war, as compared to the bad war in Iraq), and he faced pressure to show evidence of progress in the military campaign against the Taliban, lest Republicans in Congress and critics outside accuse him of weakness. In the fall of 2009, therefore, with the security situation deteriorating as the Taliban extended its control in major areas of the country, he expanded the U.S. commitment, and the struggle ground on. Military spending, even with Obama's drawdown in Iraq, continued to increase, outstripping that of the next seven to ten (depending on the metrics used) nations combined—in 2016, Obama's final year, the Pentagon spent $600 billion, not including supplemental appropriations for Iraq and Afghanistan. For hawks in both parties, claiming to see existential threats all over the globe, it was still not enough.

Are there signs of change? Perhaps. More than at any point since the Vietnam War, Americans are debating the nation's global commitments. From various quarters can be heard the argument that Washington can and should reduce its overseas commitments dramatically, shifting the burdens of regional security to friendly governments, thereby allowing more resources and time to be spent on improving the lives of Americans at home. Some, including President Donald J. Trump, have been openly skeptical of military intervention. Even so, Trump, despite his erratic opposition to "endless wars," pushed Pentagon spending past the $800 billion mark, authorized the continued bombing of several nations, and reveled in militaristic bombast to a degree seldom seen before in American presidential history.

Habits can be hard to break. The United States developed an addiction to insecurity during the Cold War, and many American politicians still find it hard to shake the easy benefits that come from exaggerating threats and demonizing adversaries. But from the Cold War as well come examples of American foresight, restraint, and diplomatic prowess. As more and more Americans search for a way to check interventionism abroad and militarization at home, they could do worse than take a lesson or two from the likes of Eisenhower, Kennedy, or the latter-day Reagan. These presidents understood that the politics of overreaction and threat inflation damaged the nation from within and ran risks of war that, in a nuclear age, threatened apocalypse. This remains as true today as it was then.

The great diplomat George Kennan viewed the policy of containment that he and others developed after World War II as a means to protect American security in a changing world. He had no illusions about Soviet beneficence, and he predicted hard times ahead. Isolationism was not an option, but in those early days, and at all points thereafter, Kennan called on U.S. leaders to remember that in the effort to prevent Soviet expansion American liberties must not be sacrificed—that the United States should never, in the course of its global struggle, sacrifice what it was purporting to protect. Over time his concern grew, as political demagoguery found an audience and as both foreign policy and national life became more and more intertwined with military affairs. "This great militarization of our view of the Cold War," he declared in 1984, "is not only an external danger for the country but an internal one as well, promoting pernicious habits to which great parts of our society become almost hopelessly committed."[17]

Kennan has now passed from the scene, but his cautionary words still resonate. It is true that containment has relatively little to say about the challenges facing American foreign policy today—our current problems are in vital respects different. But as the United States commences its fourth decade as the world's lone superpower—its global reach even greater than during the height of the Cold War, its politics of insecurity undimmed—one last warning from the late statesman seems particularly apt. Perhaps a strategy of containment, he once said, should now be targeted not so much at a foreign adversary but at an American political system that threatens to undermine a hard-fought Cold War victory from within. "It could in fact be said," Kennan concluded, "that the first thing we Americans need to learn to contain is, in some ways, ourselves."[18]

NOTES

Introduction

The epigraph is from Kenneth Waltz, "Structural Realism after the Cold War," in G. John Ikenberry, ed., *America Unrivaled: The Future of the Balance of Power* (Ithaca: Cornell University Press, 2003), 53.

1. George F. Kennan, "American Democracy and Foreign Policy," reprinted in *At a Century's Ending: Reflections, 1982–1995* (New York: W. W. Norton, 1996), quotation from 135. We thank Jacques Sandberg, Heather Hootman, and Kevin O'Prey, all Grinnell '86, for their recollections of this Kennan lecture.

2. Any study of Kennan should begin with John Lewis Gaddis's magisterial biography, *George F. Kennan: An American Life* (New York: Penguin, 2011). Our interpretation parts company with Gaddis's in some respects.

3. George F. Kennan, "Flashbacks," *The New Yorker*, Feb. 25, 1985, reprinted in *At a Century's Ending*, 30–43. Quotation is on p. 38.

4. On militarism in the Cold War and after, a powerful account is Andrew J. Bacevich, *The New American Militarism: How Americans Are Seduced by War* (New York: Oxford University Press, 2005).

5. The literature on the Cold War is large and growing, and much of it is cited in the chapters that follow. For works that cover the whole period

of the Cold War and give close attention to U.S. policy, see, e.g., John Lewis Gaddis, *Strategies of Containment: A Critical Appraisal of Postwar American National Security Policy* (Oxford: Oxford University Press, 1982; rev. and expanded ed. 2005); John Lewis Gaddis, *The Cold War: A New History* (New York: Penguin, 2005); Walter LaFeber, *America, Russia, and the Cold War, 1945–2006,* 10th ed. (Boston: McGraw Hill, 2007); Melvyn P. Leffler, *For the Soul of Mankind: The United States, the Soviet Union, and the Cold War* (New York: Hill and Wang, 2007); Thomas J. McCormick, *America's Half-Century: United States Foreign Policy in the Cold War* (Baltimore: Johns Hopkins University Press, 1995); and H. W. Brands, *The Devil We Knew: Americans and the Cold War* (New York: Oxford University Press, 1993). A perceptive early account is Louis J. Halle, *The Cold War as History* (New York: Harper and Row, 1967). Also insightful is Martin Walker, *The Cold War: A History* (New York: Henry Holt, 1993). But see also broader studies, e.g., David Reynolds, *One World Divisible: A Global History since 1945* (New York: W. W. Norton, 2000); Eric Hobsbawm, *The Age of Extremes: The Short Twentieth Century, 1914– 1991* (London: Michael Joseph, 1994); Geir Lundestad, *East, West, North, South: Major Developments in International Politics, 1945–1990* (Oslo: Norwegian University Press, 1991). And see the collections of essays in O. A. Westad, ed., *Reviewing the Cold War: Approaches, Interpretations, Theory* (London: Frank Cass, 2000). For the United States in a comparative perspective, see Thomas Bender, *A Nation among Nations: America's Place in World History* (New York: Hill and Wang, 2006); Charles Maier, *Among Empires: American Ascendancy and Its Predecessors* (Cambridge, Mass.: Harvard University Press, 2006); and Brian Loveman, *No Higher Law: American Foreign Policy and the Western Hemisphere since 1776* (Chapel Hill: University of North Carolina Press, 2012).

6. Samuel Flagg Bemis, *The Diplomacy of the American Revolution* (New York: D. Appleton-Century, 1935); Ernest R. May, *The World War and American Isolation, 1914–1917* (Cambridge, Mass.: Harvard University Press, 1959).

7. On the need for the Cold War to be studied as international history, see, e.g., John Lewis Gaddis, *We Now Know: Rethinking the Cold War* (New York: Oxford University Press, 1997), 282–283; Odd Arne Westad,

"Introduction: Reviewing the Cold War," in Westad, ed., *Reviewing the Cold War*, 1–23.

8. A major study, focusing in particular on superpower interventions in the 1970s, is Odd Arne Westad, *The Global Cold War: Third World Interventions and the Making of Our Times* (New York: Cambridge University Press, 2005). See also Piero Gleijeses, *Conflicting Missions: Havana, Washington, and Africa, 1959–1976* (Chapel Hill: University of North Carolina Press, 2002). A superb primer on how to research and write international history is Marc Trachtenberg, *The Craft of International History: A Guide to Method* (Princeton: Princeton University Press, 2006), and its companion website, http://www.sscnet.ucla.edu/polisci/faculty/trachtenberg/guide. A breathtakingly comprehensive international history of the Cold War is Odd Arne Westad, *The Cold War: A World History* (London: Allen Lane, 2017).

9. Thomas W. Zeiler, "The Diplomatic History Bandwagon: A State of the Field," *Journal of American History* 95 (March 2009), 1053–73. Zeiler also provides a useful overview of the important work being done by those examining the role of culture, ideology, gender, race, religion, and language.

10. On this point, see Walter LaFeber, "Response to Charles S. Maier, 'Marking Time: The Historiography of International Relations,'" *Diplomatic History* 5 (Fall 1981), 362; and Marilyn Young, "The Age of Global Power," in *Rethinking American History in a Global Age,* ed. Thomas Bender (Berkeley: University of California Press, 2002), 275.

11. Chen Jian, "Far Short of a Glorious Victory: Revisiting China's Changing Strategies to Manage the Korean War," *The Chinese Historical Review* 25 (Spring 2018).

12. Robert J. McMahon, "The Study of American Foreign Relations: National History or International History," in Michael J. Hogan and Thomas G. Paterson, eds, *Explaining the History of American Foreign Relations* (New York: Cambridge University Press, 1991), 15–16.

13. C. Vann Woodward, "The Age of Reinterpretation," *American Historical Review* 66 (October 1960), 2–8. See also Campbell Craig, "The Not-So-Strange Career of Charles Beard," *Diplomatic History* 25 (Spring 2001), esp. 253.

14. The recent literature is thin, but see, e.g., Gretchen Heefner, *The Missile Next Door: The Minuteman in the American Heartland* (Cambridge, Mass.: Harvard University Press, 2012); Alex Roland, *The Military-Industrial Complex* (Washington, DC: American Historical Association, 2001); and Walter L. Hixson, *The Myth of American Diplomacy: National Identity and U.S. Foreign Policy* (New Haven: Yale University Press, 2008), esp. 197–200. Also useful is Michael S. Sherry, *In the Shadow of War: The United States Since 1930* (New Haven: Yale University Press, 1995). For a different perspective, see Aaron L. Friedberg, *In the Shadow of the Garrison State: America's Anti-Statism and Its Cold War Grand Strategy* (Princeton: Princeton University Press, 2000).

15. The metaphor is Kennan's. See At a Century's Ending, 118.

16. On this point as it pertains to recent scholarship in U.S. foreign relations history generally, see Fredrik Logevall, "Politics and Foreign Relations," *Journal of American History* 95 (March 2009), 1074–78.

17. Fredrik Logevall, "Bernath Lecture: A Critique of Containment," *Diplomatic History* 28 (September 2004), 473–499.

18. A classic, highly influential revisionist account is William Appleman Williams, *The Tragedy of American Diplomacy*, 3rd ed. (New York: W. W. Norton, 1972). See also Gabriel Kolko and Joyce Kolko, *The Limits of Power: The World and United States Foreign Policy, 1945–1954* (New York: Harper and Row, 1972). An important recent revisionist treatment is Christopher Layne, *The Peace of Illusions: American Grand Strategy from 1940 to the Present* (Ithaca: Cornell University Press, 2006).

19. Robert David Johnson, "Congress and the Cold War," *Journal of Cold War Studies* 3 (Spring 2001), 76–78; Fredrik Logevall, "Party Politics," in Alexander DeConde, Richard D. Burns, and Fredrik Logevall, eds., *Encyclopedia of American Foreign Policy* (New York: Scribners, 2002), vol. 3, esp. 99–101. For an important corrective, see Julian E. Zelizer, *Arsenal of Democracy: The Politics of National Security from World War II to the War on Terrorism* (New York: Basic, 2009).

20. Fredrik Logevall, "Domestic Politics," in Frank Costigliola and Michael J. Hogan, eds., *Explaining the History of American Foreign Relations*, 3rd ed. (New York: Cambridge University Press, 2016).

21. On threat inflation in American political culture, see also Michael

A. Cohen and Micah Zenko, *Clear and Present Safety: The World has Never Been Better and Why That Matters to Americans* (New Haven: Yale University Press, 2019).

22. For varying interpretations of Kennan and his role, see, e.g., Anders Stephanson, *Kennan and the Art of Foreign Policy* (Cambridge, Mass.: Harvard University Press, 1989); Walter L. Hixson, *George F. Kennan, Cold War Iconoclast* (New York: Columbia University Press, 1989); John L. Harper, *American Visions of Europe: Franklin D. Roosevelt, George F. Kennan, and Dean G. Acheson* (New York: Cambridge University Press, 1994); Wilson D. Miscamble, *George F. Kennan and the Making of American Foreign Policy, 1947–1950* (Princeton: Princeton University Press, 1992); David Mayers, "Containment and the Primacy of Diplomacy: George Kennan's Views, 1947–1948," *International Security* 11 (Summer 1986); idem, *George Kennan and the Dilemmas of U.S. Foreign Policy* (New York: Oxford University Press, 1998).

23. Kennan, "American Democracy and Foreign Policy," 137.

1. The Demise of Free Security

1. Charles Beard, "A Reply to Mr. Browder," *New Republic* 83 (February 2, 1938), 357–359. For Beard's views on free security, see Campbell Craig, "The Not-So-Strange Career of Charles Beard," *Diplomatic History* 25 (Spring 2001), 251–274.

2. Adams's speech, dated July 4, 1821, and given to the House of Representatives, can be found at www.millercenter.virginia.edu/academic /americanpresidents/jqadams.

3. N. Gordon Levin, *Woodrow Wilson and World Politics* (New York: Oxford University Press, 1967), remains a trenchant analysis of Wilson's assessments of the Great War and the Bolshevik challenge. On the threat posed by Lenin, see also Arno J. Mayer, *The Political Origins of the New Diplomacy, 1917–1918* (New Haven: Yale University Press, 1959); Lloyd Gardner, *Safe for Democracy* (New York: Oxford University Press, 1984), 151–175; David Foglesong, *America's Secret War against Bolshevism: U.S. Intervention in the Russian Civil War, 1917–1920* (Chapel Hill: University of North Carolina Press, 1999), 24–46. On Wilson's larger visions, see

John A. Thompson, *Woodrow Wilson* (London: Longman, 2002), 141–187; and Thomas J. Knock, *To End All Wars: Woodrow Wilson and the Quest for a New World Order* (Princeton: Princeton University Press, 1992). On Wilsonianism and its legacy see Frank Ninkovich, *The Wilsonian Century: U.S. Foreign Policy since 1900* (Chicago: University of Chicago Press, 1999); and Tony Smith, *America's Mission: The United States and the Worldwide Struggle for Democracy in the Twentieth Century* (Princeton: Princeton University Press, 1994).

4. On the postwar peace conference and aftermath, see Margaret MacMillan, *Paris 1919: Six Months That Changed the World* (New York: Random House, 2002); John Milton Cooper Jr., *Breaking the Heart of the World: Woodrow Wilson and the Fight for the League of Nations* (New York: Cambridge University Press, 2002).

5. Robert Dallek, *Franklin D. Roosevelt and American Foreign Policy, 1932–1945* (New York: Oxford University Press, 1979), 129.

6. In January 1941, 40% of Americans surveyed believed it was a mistake to enter World War I, 44% that it was not. In comparison, in an October 1939 survey, 59% said it was a mistake, while 28% said no. Hadley Cantril, ed., *Public Opinion: 1935–1946* (Princeton: Princeton University Press, 1951), 201–202. In a September 1939 survey, Americans were asked, "Do you think there are any international questions affecting the United States so important to us in the long run that our government should take a stand on them now, even at the risk of our getting into war?" 54.8% of respondents said no.

7. Marvin R. Zahniser, "Rethinking the Significance of Disaster: The United States and the Fall of France," *International History Review* 14 (May 1992), 252–276.

8. David M. Kennedy, *Freedom from Fear: The American People in Depression and War, 1929–1945* (New York: Oxford University Press, 1999), 464.

9. Dallek, *Franklin D. Roosevelt and American Foreign Policy,* 156–157.

10. Charles A. Beard, *Giddy Minds and Foreign Quarrels: An Estimate of American Foreign Policy* (New York: Macmillan, 1939), 15, 27, 32.

11. Nicholas Spykman, *America's Strategy in World Politics: The United*

States and the Balance of World Power (New Brunswick: Transaction Publishers, 2007), 194–199.

12. Quoted in Richard Rhodes, *The Making of the Atomic Bomb* (New York: Simon and Schuster, 1986), 296.

13. Ibid., 314.

14. Niebuhr's most thorough expression of this point can be found in *The Children of Light and the Children of Darkness* (New York: Charles Scribner's Sons, 1944). For an account of his emerging interventionist position, see Campbell Craig, *Glimmer of a New Leviathan* (New York: Columbia University Press, 2003), 38–51, and Richard Wightman Fox, *Reinhold Niebuhr: A Biography* (New York: Harper and Row, 1985), 187–209. On Weber, see "The Nation-State and Economic Policy," inaugural lecture at University of Freiburg, in Peter Lassman and Ronald Speirs, eds., *Political Writings* (Cambridge: Cambridge University Press, 1994). See also Michael J. Smith, *Realist Thought from Weber to Kissinger* (Baton Rouge: Louisiana State University Press, 1986), ch. 2.

15. Justus D. Doenecke, *From Isolation to War, 1931–1941* (Wheeling: Harlan Davidson, 2003).

16. Quoted in James MacGregor Burns and Susan Dunn, *The Three Roosevelts: Patrician Leaders Who Transformed America* (New York: Grove Press, 2002), 416.

17. Herbert Feis, *The Road to Pearl Harbor: The Coming of the War between the United States and Japan* (Princeton, 1950), 244. For the broader history see Akira Iriye, *Across the Pacific: An Inner History of American-East Asian Relations* (New York: Harcourt Brace, 1967).

18. Elizabeth Borgwardt, *A New Deal for the World* (Cambridge, Mass.: Harvard University Press, 2007), 21–28.

19. Martin Gilbert, *Churchill: A Life* (New York: Henry Holt, 1991), 706; Kennedy, *Freedom from Fear,* 496.

20. For an account of the Norwegian sabotage operation, see Richard Rhodes, *The Making of the Atomic Bomb* (New York: Simon and Schuster, 1986), 455–457. And see Ole Kristian Grimnes, "The Allied Heavy Water Operations in Rjukan," in Olav Njølstad, Ole Kristian Grimnes, Joachim Rønneberg, and Betrand Goldschmidt, eds., *The Race for Norwegian*

Heavy Water, 1940–1945 (Olso: Norwegian Institute for Defense Studies, 1995).

21. See Thomas Powers, *Heisenberg's War: The Secret History of the German Bomb* (New York: Da Capo Press, 2000).

22. Fraser Harbutt, *The Iron Curtain: Churchill, America, and the Origins of the Cold War* (Oxford: Oxford University Press, 1986), 56–60.

23. Campbell Craig and Sergey Radchenko, *The Atomic Bomb and the Origins of the Cold War* (New Haven: Yale University Press, 2008), 8–12.

24. Dallek, *Franklin D. Roosevelt and American Foreign Policy,* 410.

25. Warren F. Kimball, *Forged in War: Roosevelt, Churchill, and the Second World War* (New York: W. Morrow, 1997), 158–159 and 197.

26. Ibid, 183–190.

27. Gerhard L. Weinberg, *A World at Arms: A Global History of World War II* (New York: Cambridge University Press, 1994), 433.

28. Mark A. Stoler, *The Politics of the Second Front: American Military Planning and Diplomacy in Coalition Warfare, 1941–1943* (Westport: Greenwood, 1977), 77.

29. See George C. Herring, *From Colony to Superpower* (New York: Oxford University Press, 2008), chapters 10, 13.

30. On Tehran, see Warren Kimball, *The Juggler: Franklin Roosevelt as Wartime Statesman* (Princeton: Princeton University Press, 1991), 63–82.

31. Harbutt, The Iron Curtain, 58.

32. Charles Kirkpatrick, *D-Day: 'Operation Overlord' from Its Planning to the Liberation of Paris* (London: Salamander Books, 1999), 8.

33. Thomas J. McCormick, *America's Half-Century: United States Foreign Policy in the Cold War and After* (Baltimore: Johns Hopkins University Press, 1995), 52–53.

34. See Steven Merritt Miner, *Stalin's Holy War: Religion, Nationalism, and Alliance Politics, 1941–1945* (Chapel Hill: University of North Carolina Press, 2003), part 2.

35. John Lewis Gaddis, *The United States and the Origins of the Cold War, 1941–1947* (New York: Columbia University Press, 2000), 23.

36. On the growing concerns about the "danger from the Soviet Union" among State Department officials in 1944–1945, see the recollection of

Louis Halle, a member during the war of the Policy Planning Staff, in Louis Halle, *The Cold War as History* (New York, 1967), 38.

37. Gaddis, *Origins,* 23.

38. George F. Kennan, *Memoirs* (Boston: Little, Brown, 1967), 503–531.

39. Vojtech Mastny, *Russia's Road to the Cold War* (New York: Columbia University Press, 1979), 183–186.

40. Gaddis, *Origins,* 158.

41. On this point, see Lloyd C. Gardner and Warren F. Kimball, "The United States: Democratic Diplomacy," in David Reynolds et al., eds., *Allies at War: The Soviet, American, and British Experience, 1939–1945* (New York: St. Martin's Press, 1994), 404–405.

42. Roosevelt's correspondence with Stalin on the veto question can be found in Susan Butler, ed., *My Dear Mr. Stalin: The Complete Correspondence between Franklin D. Roosevelt and Joseph V. Stalin* (New Haven: Yale University Press, 2005), 257–258.

43. Paul M. Kennedy, *The Parliament of Man: The Past, Present, and Future of the United Nations* (New York: Random House, 2006), 24–27.

44. Miscamble, *From Roosevelt to Truman,* 162–165.

45. Gaddis, *Origins,* 74.

46. On this possibility, see Campbell Craig, "The Atom Bomb as Policy Maker: FDR and the Road not Taken," in Michael D. Gordin and G. John Ikenberry, eds., *The Age of Hiroshima* (Princeton: Princeton University Press, 2020).

47. Mark Perry, *Partners in Command: George Marshall and Dwight Eisenhower in War and Peace* (New York: Penguin Press, 2007), 354–355, 369.

48. Arnold Offner, *Another Such Victory: President Truman and the Cold War, 1945–1953* (Stanford: Stanford University Press, 2002).

49. Alonzo L. Hamby, *Man of the People: A Life of Harry S. Truman* (Oxford: Oxford University Press, 1995), 315–318.

50. See Mary Glantz, *FDR and the Soviet Union: The President's Battles over Foreign Policy* (Lawrence: University Press of Kansas, 2005), 176.

51. See Geoffrey Roberts, *Stalin's Wars: From World War to Cold War,*

1939–1953 (New Haven: Yale University Press, 2006), 217–267. For an interpretation that stresses Stalin's ideological commitments somewhat more than does Roberts, see Vladislav Zubok and Constantine Pleshakov, *Inside the Kremlin's Cold War: From Stalin to Khrushchev* (Cambridge, Mass.: Harvard University Press, 1996), 275–276, and Vladislav Zubok, *A Failed Empire: The Soviet Union in the Cold War from Stalin to Gorbachev* (Chapel Hill: University of North Carolina Press, 2007), 1–93. Also see Gabriel Gorodetsky, *Grand Delusion: Stalin and the German Invasion of Russia* (New Haven: Yale University Press, 1999), a forceful argument for Stalin as a realist (who could nevertheless make major blunders); and Matthew Evangelista, "The 'Soviet Threat': Intentions, Capabilities, and Context," *Diplomatic History* 22 (Summer 1998), 439–449. For the case that Stalin was driven more by aggressive intentions, see John Lewis Gaddis, *We Now Know: Rethinking Cold War History* (Oxford: Clarendon Press, 1997), esp. 21–25, 292; Martin Malia, *The Soviet Tragedy: A History of Socialism in Russia, 1917–1991* (New York: The Free Press, 1994), esp. 297–298; and Georges-Henri Soutou, *La guerre de cinquante ans: les relations est-ouest, 1943–1990* (Paris: Fayard, 2001).

52. Robert L. Messer, *The End of an Alliance: James F. Byrnes, Roosevelt, Truman, and the Origins of the Cold War* (Chapel Hill: University of North Carolina Press, 1982), 82–83.

53. A powerful narrative account of the final months of the Pacific War is Max Hastings, *Retribution: The Battle for Japan, 1944–45* (New York: Knopf, 2008).

54. On Roosevelt's and Churchill's expansive interpretation of "unconditional surrender," see Tsuyoshi Hasegawa, Racing the Enemy: Stalin, Truman, and the Surrender of Japan (Cambridge, Mass.: Harvard University Press, 2005), 21–25.

55. A superb study of Stimson's thinking in this key period is Sean L. Malloy, *Atomic Tragedy: Henry L. Stimson and the Decision to Use the Bomb against Japan* (Ithaca: Cornell University Press, 2008), 96–124.

56. United States Department of State, "Briefing Book Paper," *Foreign Relations of the United States: Diplomatic Papers: The Conference of Berlin (the Potsdam Conference),* 1945, vol. 1. Doc. no. 590 (Washington, DC:

Government Printing Office), 885–887. On the Bard proposal, see Malloy, *Atomic Tragedy,* 120–121.

57. J. Samuel Walker, *Prompt and Utter Destruction: Truman and the Use of the Atomic Bomb against Japan* (Chapel Hill: University of North Carolina Press, 1997).

58. A fine account is Martin Sherwin, *A World Destroyed: The Atomic Bomb and the Grand Alliance* (New York: Knopf, 1975), chs. 8–9.

59. See Tsuyoshi Hasegawa, "Soviet Policy Toward Japan during World War Two," *Cahiers du Monde Russe* 52 (2011).

60. Craig and Radchenko, *Atomic Bomb,* 78–79.

61. The United States Strategic Bombing Survey estimated that between 70,000 and 80,000 Japanese were killed by the nuclear blast in Hiroshima. It also estimated that 130,000 total died from either the blast or acute radiation poisoning by the end of November 1945. Walker, *Prompt and Utter Destruction,* 77. More recent studies estimate 140,000 deaths up to the end of November 1945, reaching 200,000 deaths five years later. Rhodes, *Making,* 734.

62. The U.S. Strategic Bombing Survey estimated over 35,000 deaths from the blast in Nagasaki. Walker, *Prompt and Utter Destruction,* 80. A recent study estimates 70,000 deaths by the end of 1945. Rhodes, *Making,* 740.

63. See, e.g., Gar Alperovitz, *Atomic Diplomacy: Hiroshima and Potsdam: The Use of the Atomic Bomb and the American Confrontation with Soviet Power,* updated edition (New York: Penguin, 1985); Sherwin, *A World Destroyed;* Hasegawa, *Racing the Enemy;* Walker, *Prompt and Utter Destruction;* and Michael D. Gordin, *Five Days in August: How World War II Became a Nuclear War* (Princeton: Princeton University Press, 2007). Barton Bernstein has published a number of important articles on this topic, and a summary of his views may be found in his "Understanding the Atomic Bomb and the Japanese Surrender," *Diplomatic History* 19 (Spring 1995), 227–273. For "orthodox" perspectives that staunchly defend the use of the bombs, see, e.g., Robert James Maddox, *Weapons for Victory* (Columbia: University of Missouri Press, 1995); Robert Newman, *Truman and the Hiroshima Cult* (East Lansing: Michigan State University

Press, 1995); and Robert James Maddox, ed., *Hiroshima in History: The Myths of Revisionism* (Columbia: University of Missouri Press, 1997).

64. Walker, *Prompt and Utter Destruction*, 38–39, 102–103; Barton J. Bernstein, "The Atomic Bombings Reconsidered," *Foreign Affairs* Jan./ Feb. 1995, 135–152.

65. Hamby, *Man of the People*, 324–325.

66. See here also Craig and Radchenko, *Atomic Bomb*, ch. 3.

2. Confrontation

1. Harry S. Truman, "Address on Foreign Policy at the Navy Day Celebration in New York City," *Public Papers of the Presidents, Harry S. Truman, 1945–1953*, Oct. 1945.

2. Robert L. Messer, *The End of an Alliance: James F. Byrnes, Roosevelt, Truman, and the Origins of the Cold War* (Chapel Hill: University of North Carolina Press, 1982). Martin J. Sherwin, *A World Destroyed: Hiroshima and Its Legacies* (Stanford: Stanford University Press, 2003), ch. 7.

3. Gregg Herken, *The Winning Weapon: The Atomic Bomb in the Cold War, 1945–1950* (New York: Knopf, 1980), ch. 3.

4. For contrasting assessments of the late 1945–early 1946 period in general, and Truman's interaction with Byrnes in particular, see Arnold A. Offner, *Another Such Victory: President Truman and the Cold War, 1945–1953* (Stanford: Stanford University Press, 2000), 121–124; and Wilson Miscamble, *From Roosevelt to Truman: Potsdam, Hiroshima, and the Cold War* (Cambridge: Cambridge University Press, 2007), 273–275.

5. U.S. Department of State, "Memorandum by the Secretary of War (Stimson) to President Truman," *Foreign Relations of the United States: General Political and Economic Matters, 1945*, vol. 2, p. 42.

6. Sean L. Malloy, *Atomic Tragedy: Henry L. Stimson and the Decision to Use the Bomb against Japan* (Ithaca: Cornell University Press, 2008), ch. 7.

7. "That is our job. If they catch up with us on that, they will have to do it on their own hook, just as we did." Harry S. Truman, "The President's News Conference at Tiptonville, Tennessee," *Public Papers of the Presidents, Harry S. Truman, 1945–1953*, Oct. 8, 1945; Campbell Craig

and Sergey Radchenko, *The Atomic Bomb and the Origins of the Cold War* (New Haven: Yale University Press, 2008), 118.

8. John Lewis Gaddis, *The United States and the Origins of the Cold War, 1941–1947* (New York: Columbia University Press, 2000), 247–263.

9. Amy Knight, *How the Cold War Began: The Igor Gouzenko Affair and the Hunt for Soviet Spies* (New York: Carroll and Graf, 2005).

10. See Craig and Radchenko, *Atomic Bomb and the Origins,* 130–134, for further discussion of the effect of espionage on Truman.

11. Gaddis, *The United States and the Origins of the Cold War,* 290– 296.

12. Fredrik Logevall, "A Critique of Containment," *Diplomatic History* 28 (September 2004), 491.

13. Katherine Sibley, *Red Spies in America: Stolen Secrets and the Dawn of the Cold War* (Lawrence: University Press of Kansas, 2004), 169.

14. Herken, *The Winning Weapon,* 130.

15. On Roosevelt's promise, see Richard G. Hewlett and Oscar E. Anderson Jr., *The New World, 1939/1946: A History of the United States Atomic Energy Commission* (University Park: Pennsylvania State University Press, 1962), 274.

16. Joseph Stalin, "New Five-Year Plan for Russia: Election Address," *Vital Speeches of the Day* 12 (March 1, 1946), 300–304.

17. Milovan Djilas, *Conversations with Stalin* (New York: Harcourt, Brace & World, 1962), 114–115.

18. William O. Douglas told James Forrestal that Stalin's speech was "the Declaration of World War III." James Forrestal, *The Forrestal Diaries,* Feb. 17, 1947, ed. Walter Millis (New York: Viking Press, 1951), 134–135.

19. Geoffrey Roberts, *Stalin's Wars: From World War to Cold War, 1939–1953* (New Haven: Yale University Press, 2006); Craig and Radchenko, *The Atomic Bomb and the Origins of the Cold War,* ch. 6.

20. John Lewis Gaddis, Strategies of Containment: A Critical Appraisal of American National Security Policy during the Cold War (New York: Oxford University Press, 2005), ch. 2.

21. George F. Kennan, Memoirs: 1925–1950 (Boston: Little, Brown, 1967), 294–295.

22. For Truman's public denial, see Harry S. Truman, "The President's News Conference," *Public Papers of the Presidents, Harry S. Truman, 1945–*

1953, March 8, 1946. James Byrnes later claimed that after briefing Truman on the contents of the speech, Truman did not read the advance copy in order to truthfully deny Soviet charges of bullying the Soviets with the British. James F. Byrnes, *All in One Lifetime* (London: Museum Press, 1958), 349.

23. The speech, titled "The Sinews of Peace," is reprinted in *Winston S. Churchill: His Complete Speeches, 1897-1963,* ed. Robert Rhodes James (New York: Chelsea House, 1974), vol. 7, pp. 7285-93.

24. See, on this other part of the speech, Klaus Larres, *Churchill's Cold War: The Politics of Personal Diplomacy* (New Haven: Yale University Press, 2002), 124ff; John W. Young, *Churchill's Last Campaign: Britain and the Cold War, 1951-1955* (Oxford: Oxford University Press, 1996), 19-40; John Keegan, *Winston Churchill* (New York: Penguin, 2002), 178.

25. Alonzo L. Hamby, Man of the People: A Life of Harry S. Truman (Oxford: Oxford University Press, 1995), ch. 21.

26. James A. Bill, *The Eagle and the Lion: The Tragedy of American-Iranian Relations* (New Haven: Yale University Press, 1988), 33-37.

27. Melvyn P. Leffler, *A Proponderance of Power: National Security, the Truman Administration, and the Cold War* (Stanford: Stanford University Press, 1992), 62-63.

28. See Trachtenberg, *A Constructed Peace,* esp. chs. 2-3. We discuss the German question further later in this chapter.

29. On early U.S. involvement in Indochina, see Mark Atwood Lawrence, *Assuming the Burden: Europe and the American Commitment to War in Vietnam* (Berkeley: University of California Press, 2005); Mark Philip Bradley, *Imagining Vietnam and America: The Making of Postcolonial Vietnam, 1919-1950* (Chapel Hill: University of North Carolina Press, 2000).

30. Craig and Radchenko, *Atomic Bomb and the Origins,* ch. 5.

31. Michael S. Sherry, *In the Shadow of War: The United States in the 1930s* (New Haven: Yale University Press, 1995), 133.

32. J. Samuel Walker, *Henry A. Wallace and American Foreign Policy* (Westport: Greenwood, 1976); John C. Culver and John Hyde, *American Dreamer: A Life of Henry A. Wallace* (New York, 2000), 402-455. For a

critical assessment of Truman's handling of "L'Affaire Wallace," see Offner, *Another Such Victory*, 173–178.

33. Leffler, *Preponderance of Power*, 130–138

34. James Chace, *Acheson: The Secretary of State Who Created the American World* (New York: Simon and Schuster, 1998), 164–166.

35. Harry S. Truman, "Special Message to the Congress on Greece and Turkey: The Truman Doctrine," *Public Papers of the Presidents, Harry S. Truman, 1945–1953*, March 12, 1947.

36. Quoted in Small, *Democracy and Diplomacy*, 87.

37. Richard Fried, *Nightmare in Red: The McCarthy Era in Perspective* (New York: Oxford University Press, 1990), 63–64.

38. David Halberstam, *The Best and the Brightest*, 20th anniversary ed. (New York: Random House, 1992), 108–109.

39. Diplomatic historians have generally paid insufficient attention to this development, especially in recent years. But see Richard M. Freeland, *The Truman Doctrine and the Origins of McCarthyism: Foreign Policy, Domestic Politics, and Internal Security, 1946–1948* (New York: Knopf, 1972); Athan Theoharis and Robert Griffith, eds., *The Specter: Original Essays on the Cold War and the Origins of McCarthyism* (New York: New Viewpoints, 1974); and Robert M. Ubriaco Jr., "Harry S Truman, the Politics of Yalta, and the Domestic Origins of the Truman Doctrine" (PhD diss., University of Illinois at Urbana-Champaign, 1992).

40. "X" [George F. Kennan], "The Sources of Soviet Conduct," *Foreign Affairs* 25, no. 4 (July 1947).

41. Logevall, "A Critique of Containment," 477.

42. Walter Lippmann, *The Cold War: A Study in U.S. Foreign Policy* (New York: Harper and Row, 1947). There were fourteen columns in all, the first appearing on September 2, the last on October 2. A superb biography is Ronald Steel, *Walter Lippmann and the American Century* (Boston: Little, Brown, 1980).

43. Quoted in David Mayers, "Containment and the Primacy of Diplomacy: George Kennan's Views, 1947–1948," *International Security* 11 (Summer 1986), 134–135. See also George F. Kennan, *Memoirs, 1925–1950* (Boston: Little, Brown, 1967), 359–361.

44. For more on the desolation of postwar Europe, see Tony Judt, *Postwar: A History of Europe since 1945* (New York: Penguin Press, 2005), 13–40; and William I. Hitchcock, *The Bitter Road to Freedom: A New History of the Liberation of Europe* (New York: Free Press, 2008), 174–176, 182–192.

45. William I. Hitchcock, *The Struggle for Europe: The Turbulent History of a Divided Continent, 1945 to the Present* (New York: Doubleday, 2002), 14.

46. Hitchcock, *Bitter Road to Freedom*, 186–187.

47. See H. W. Brands, *The Devil We Knew: Americans and the Cold War* (New York: Oxford University Press, 1993), 14.

48. Walter Isaacson and Evan Thomas, *The Wise Men: Six Friends and the World They Made: Acheson, Bohlem, Harriman, Kennan, Lovett, McCloy* (New York: Simon and Schuster, 1986).

49. Leffler, *A Proponderance of Power*, 157–159. Several scholars assess the plan and its effects in "Special Forum: The Marshall Plan and the Origins of the Cold War Reassessed," *Journal of Cold War Studies* 7 (Winter 2005), 97–181. An authoritative recent treatment of the Marshall Plan, based upon sources from several nations, is Benn Steil, *The Marshall Plan: Dawn of the Cold War* (New York: Simon and Schuster Paperbacks, 2019).

50. Michael J. Hogan, *The Marshall Plan: America, Britain, and the Reconstruction of Western Europe, 1947–1952* (Cambridge: Cambridge University Press, 1987).

51. Kennan, *Memoirs*, 341–343.

52. Alan S. Milward, *The Reconstruction of Western Europe, 1945–1951* (Berkeley: University of California Press, 1984), argues that the Plan was relatively unimportant to Europe's recovery. A brief yet nuanced assessment is William I. Hitchcock, "The Marshall Plan," in Melvyn P. Leffler and Odd Arne Westad, *The Cambridge History of the Cold War* (New York: Cambridge University Press, 2009).

53. See Thomas McCormick, *America's Half-Century*, 80–81.

54. Marc Trachtenberg, *A Constructed Peace: The Making of the European Settlement, 1945–1963* (Princeton: Princeton University Press, 1999), ch. 3; Carolyn Eisenberg, *Drawing the Line: The American Decision to Divide Germany* (New York: Cambridge University Press, 1996).

55. Avi Shlaim, *The United States and the Berlin Blockade, 1948- 1949: A Study in Crisis Decision-making* (Berkeley: University of California Press, 1983).

56. Forrestal, *The Forrestal Diaries,* June 28, 1948, 454.

57. Hitchcock, *Struggle for Europe,* 93–96.

58. Shlaim, *The United States and the Berlin Blockade,* 150–159.

59. "Official discussion respecting the use of atomic weapons would reach the Soviets, who should in fact never be given the slightest reason to believe that the U.S. would even consider not to use atomic weapons against them if necessary . . . If Western Europe is to enjoy any feeling of security at the present time . . . it is in large degree because the atomic bomb, under American trusteeship, offers the present major counterbalance to the ever-present threat of the Soviet military power." U.S. Department of State, "Report to the National Security Council by the Executive Secretary (Souers)," *Foreign Relations of the United States, 1948: General; the United Nations,* vol. 1, part 2 (Washington, DC: Government Printing Office), 624.

60. Hitchcock, *Bitter Road to Freedom,* 19–43.

61. Lawrence Freedman, *The Evolution of Nuclear Strategy* (New York: Palgrave Macmillan, 2003), ch. 4.

62. Greece and Turkey joined NATO in 1952, while West Germany joined in 1955. On the origins, see Lawrence S. Kaplan, *The United States and NATO: The Formative Years* (Lexington: University Press of Kentucky, 1984).

63. Michael Creswell, *A Question of Balance: How France and the United States Created Cold War Europe* (Cambridge, Mass.: Harvard University Press, 2006).

64. See Andrew Preston, "The Little State Department: McGeorge Bundy and the National Security Council Staff, 1961-1965," *Presidential Studies Quarterly* 31, no. 4 (December 2001), 635–659.

3. To the Ends of the Earth

1. Richard Rhodes, *Dark Sun: The Making of the Hydrogen Bomb* (New York: Simon and Schuster, 1995), 363, 372–374.

2. Gordon H. Chang, *Friends and Enemies: The United States, China, and the Soviet Union, 1948–1972* (Stanford: Stanford University Press, 1990), 13; Marc S. Gallichio, *The Cold War Begins in Asia: American East Asia Policy and the Fall of the Japanese Empire* (New York: Columbia University Press, 1988), 73–112.

3. Quoted in David McCullough, *Truman* (New York: Simon and Schuster, 1992), 893.

4. Astute analysis can be found in Warren I. Cohen, "The China Lobby," in Alexander DeConde, Richard Dean Burns, and Fredrik Logevall, eds., *Encyclopedia of American Foreign Policy*, 2nd ed., vol. 1 (New York, 2002), 185–191. On Sino-American relations following Mao's victory and whether a "missed opportunity" existed for some kind of accord, see the roundtable discussion featuring several scholars in *Diplomatic History* 21, no. 1 (Winter 1997). On the domestic U.S. context, see also Thomas J. Christensen, *Grand Strategy, Domestic Mobilization, and Sino-American Conflict, 1947–1958* (Princeton: Princeton University Press, 1996).

5. See Vladislav Zubok, *A Failed Empire: The Soviet Union in the Cold War from Stalin to Gorbachev* (Chapel Hill: University of North Carolina Press, 2007), 79. The best overall study of Eisenhower's foreign policy is now William I. Hitchcock, *The Age of Eisenhower: America and the World in the 1950s* (New York: Simon and Schuster, 2018).

6. Campbell Craig, *Destroying the Village: Eisenhower and Thermonuclear War* (New York: Columbia University Press, 1998), ch. 2.

7. George F. Kennan, *Memoirs: 1925–1950* (Boston: Little, Brown, 1967), 473–476.

8. The Hiroshima blast was between 15–16 kilotons of TNT, whereas the first test of the hydrogen bomb was measured around 6–8 megatons of TNT. See the Nuclear Weapon Archive website, at nuclearweaponarchive.org/Usa/Weapons/Allbombs.html.

9. The most incisive discussion of the security dilemma remains Robert Jervis, "Cooperation under the Security Dilemma," *World Politics* 30 (January 1978). For a powerful discussion of its intellectual provenance and contemporary effects, see Ken Booth and Nicholas J. Wheeler, *The Security Dilemma* (London: Palgrave Macmillan, 2007).

10. Truman quoted by R. Gordon Arneson, "The H-Bomb Decision," *Foreign Service Journal* 46 (May 1969), 27.

11. Arnold A. Offner, *Another Such Victory: President Truman and the Cold War, 1945–1953* (Stanford: Stanford University Press, 2002), 364.

12. The text of NSC-68, along with numerous scholarly assessments of the document and its importance, is in Ernest R. May, *American Cold War Strategy: Interpreting NSC-68* (New York, 1993).

13. John Lewis Gaddis, "Was the Truman Doctrine a Real Turning Point?" *Foreign Affairs* 52 (Jan. 1974), 386–402.

14. U.S. Department of State, "A Report to the President Pursuant to the President's Directive of January 31, 1950," *Foreign Relations of the United States, 1950. National Security Affairs; foreign economic policy,* vol. 1, p. 238.

15. Ibid., 240.

16. Ibid., 244, 264.

17. Offner, *Another Such Victory,* 367.

18. See Michael Hogan, *A Cross of Iron: Harry S. Truman and the Origins of the National Security State* (New York: Cambridge University Press, 1998), 476.

19. John Lewis Gaddis, *Strategies of Containment: A Critical Appraisal of American National Security Policy during the Cold War* (New York: Oxford University Press, 2005).

20. Andrew J. Bacevich, *The Limits of Power: The End of American Exceptionalism* (New York: Metropolitan Books, 2008), 110.

21. Bruce Cumings, *The Origins of the Korean War,* vol. 2, *The Roaring of the Cataract* (Princeton: Princeton University Press, 1990).

22. William W. Stueck, *The Korean War: An International History* (Princeton: Princeton University Press, 1995), 17–19, 31–33; Chen Jian, *China's Road to the Korean War: The Making of the Sino-Soviet Confrontation* (New York: Columbia University Press, 1994), ch. 4; Sergei Goncharov, John Lewis, and Xue Litai, *Uncertain Partners: Stalin, Mao, and the Korean War* (Stanford: Stanford University Press, 1993), 136–137; Kathryn Weathersby, "New Evidence on the Korean War," *Cold War International History Project Bulletin* 6–7 (Winter 1995–96); Weathersby, "To Attack or Not to Attack? Stalin, Kim Il Sung, and the Prelude to War," *Cold War International History Project Bulletin* 5 (1995), 1–9.

23. Stueck, *The Korean War,* pp. 24–25.

24. Quoted in Offner, *Another Such Victory,* 399.

25. Small, *Democracy and Diplomacy,* 94.

26. All quotes are from Julian Zelizer, *Arsenal of Democracy: The Politics of National Security in America since World War II* (New York: Basic Books, 2009), ch. 3. On the domestic context of U.S. decision-making in Korea, see also Steven Casey, *Selling the Korean War: Propaganda, Politics, and Public Opinion, 1950–1953* (New York: Oxford University Press, 2008).

27. Stueck, *The Korean War,* 130–131, 239–240.

28. Bruce Cumings, "Korea: Forgotten Nuclear Threats," *Le Monde diplomatique* (December 2004); Conrad C. Crane, *American Airpower Strategy in Korea* (Lawrence: University Press of Kansas, 2008), 168–169.

29. See Hamby, *Man of the People,* 599–605. On the key to GOP chances in 1952, Robert Taft was clear: "We cannot possibly win the next election unless we point out the utter failure and incapacity of the present administration to conduct foreign policy." Quoted in Robert David Johnson, *Congress and the Cold War* (New York: Cambridge University Press, 2006), 55.

30. Rosemary Foot, *The Wrong War: American Policy and the Dimensions of the Korean Conflict, 1950–1953* (Ithaca: Cornell University Press, 1985), 158.

31. On the Truman administration's espionage investigations around 1950, see Katherine Sibley, *Red Spies in America: Stolen Secrets and the Dawn of the Cold War* (Lawrence: University Press of Kansas, 2004), 191–199.

32. John E. Haynes and Harvey Klehr, *In Denial: Historians, Communism, and Espionage* (San Francisco: Encounter Books, 2003).

33. Campbell Craig and Sergey Radchenko, *The Atomic Bomb and the Origins of the Cold War* (New Haven: Yale University Press, 2008), 115–123.

34. The Hiss case and the question of his guilt has generated a large literature and much scholarly controversy. See, e.g., Allen Weinstein, *Perjury: The Hiss-Chambers Case* (New York: Random House, 1997); Sam Tanenhaus, *Whittaker Chambers: A Biography* (New York: Random House, 1997); and Haynes and Klehr, In Denial. But see also Kai Bird and Svetlana Chervonnaya, "The Mystery of Ales," *American Scholar* (Summer 2007).

35. Reedy quoted in David Halberstam, *The Longest Winter: America and the Korean War* (New York: Hyperion, 2008), 384. See also Ellen Schrecker, *Many Are the Crimes: McCarthyism in America* (Boston: Little, Brown, 1997), 242.

36. A superb biography is David M. Oshinsky, *A Conspiracy So Immense: The World of Joe McCarthy* (New York: Free Press, 1983).

37. Quoted in Richard J. Barnet, *The Rockets' Red Glare: War, Politics, and the American Presidency* (New York: Simon and Schuster, 1990), 309.

38. See Michael Paul Rogin, *The Intellectuals and McCarthy: The Radical Specter* (Cambridge: MIT Press, 1969). On Taft's support of McCarthy, see James T. Patterson, *Mr. Republican: A Biography of Robert A. Taft* (Boston: Houghton Mifflin, 1972), 445–446. On the importance of the partisan dimension generally to McCarthy's success, see Sam Tanenhaus, "The Red Scare," *New York Review of Books*, Jan. 14, 1999.

39. On the CIO action, see Ellen Schrecker, *The Age of McCarthyism: A Brief History with Documents* (Boston: Bedford, 1994), 221ff.

40. Richard Rovere, *Senator Joe McCarthy* (Berkeley: University of California Press, 1959), 3.

41. Oshinsky, *Conspiracy So Immense*, 416ff.

42. For a very different interpretation of McCarthy and McCarthyism, one arguing that the senator was more right than wrong, see Arthur Herman, *Joseph McCarthy: Reexamining the Life and Legacy of America's Most Hated Senator* (New York: Free Press, 1999).

43. Christopher Andrew, "Intelligence in the Cold War," in Melvyn P. Leffler and Odd Arne Westad, *The Cambridge History of the Cold War* (New York: Cambridge University Press, 2009).

44. Melvyn Leffler, *A Preponderance of Power: National Security, the Truman Administration, and the Cold War* (Stanford: Stanford University Press, 1992), 355–360. Also see Leffler's more recent study of the Cold War, *For the Soul of Mankind*, 97.

45. See, e.g., Thomas J. McCormick, *America's Half-Century: United States Foreign Policy in the Cold War and After* (Baltimore: Johns Hopkins University Press, 1995), 99–103; Michael Schaller, "Securing the Great Crescent: Occupied Japan and the Origins of Containment in Southeast Asia," *Journal of American History* 69 (September 1982), 392–414; and

Andrew J. Rotter, *The Path to Vietnam: Origins of the American Commitment to Southeast Asia* (Ithaca: Cornell University Press, 1987).

46. Stueck, *The Korean War,* 134–145.

47. Robert L. Beisner, *Dean Acheson: A Life in the Cold War* (New York: Oxford University Press, 2006), 400–401.

48. Harry S. Truman, *Memoirs by Harry S. Truman,* vol. 2, *Years of Trial and Hope* (Garden City: Doubleday, 1955), 415–416.

49. Cumings, *The Origins of the Korean War,* 757–775. "The Americans, in turn, were deterred from the latter course by the positioning of formidable fleets of Soviet bombers in Manchuria, and settled for a barely digestible containment victory." Cumings, *Origins of the Korean War,* 757. For a description of U.S. willingness to start total war, see ibid., 746.

50. In his Farewell Address in January 1953, Truman stated that a nuclear war would destroy Western Civilization and must never be waged.

51. Only in the United States among the Western democracies, Eric Hobsbawm has written, was the "communist world conspiracy" a serious part of domestic politics. *The Age of Extremes: A History of the World, 1914–1991* (New York: Pantheon, 1994), 236–237. See also p. 234.

52. Logevall, "A Critique of Containment." See also the penetrating analysis in Barnet, *Rockets' Red Glare,* 285–307.

53. Michael S. Sherry, *In the Shadow of War: The United States in the 1930s* (New Haven: Yale University, 1995), 133–138.

54. On the staying power of this mode of thinking, and its contemporary resonance, see J. Peter Scoblic, *U.S. vs. Them: How a Half Century of Conservatism Has Undermined America's Security* (New York: Viking, 2008).

4. Leaner and Meaner

1. Stephen E. Ambrose, *Eisenhower: Soldier, General of the Army, President-Elect, 1890–1952* (New York: Simon and Schuster, 1983), 459–464, 489–490.

2. Forrest C. Pogue, *George C. Marshall: Organizer of Victory, 1943–1945* (New York: Viking Press, 1973), 268, 291–292, 522–523. On Eisenhower's timid approach to handling McCarthy, see Chester Pach, *The*

Presidency of Dwight D. Eisenhower, rev. ed. (Lawrence: University Press of Kansas, 1991), 25–26.

3. John Foster Dulles, "A Policy of Boldness," [Life, 19 May, 1952. On Dulles's early articulation of an alternative to containment, see Richard Immerman, *John Foster Dulles* (Wilmington: Scholarly Resources, 1995), ch. 3.

4. Hughes quoted in Lloyd C. Gardner, "Poisoned Apples: John Foster Dulles and the Peace Offensive," in Klaus Larres and Kenneth A. Osgood, eds., *The Cold War after Stalin's Death: A Missed Opportunity for Peace?* (Lanham: Rowman and Littlefield, 2006), 79.

5. Two important accounts include Robert R. Bowie and Richard H. Immerman, *Waging Peace: How Eisenhower Shaped an Enduring Cold War Strategy* (New York: Oxford University Press, 1998); Saki Dockrill, *Eisenhower's New-Look National Security Policy, 1953–1961* (New York: St. Martin's Press, 1996).

6. John W. Young, "Churchill and East-West Détente," *Transactions of the Royal Historical Society* 11, 6th series (2001), 378–379.

7. Dockrill, *Eisenhower's New Look*, 28.

8. Ambrose, *Eisenhower*, 530.

9. Ibid., 400–403; Dwight D. Eisenhower, *Crusade in Europe* (Garden City: Doubleday, 1948), 458.

10. Dwight D. Eisenhower, "Inaugural Address," Jan. 20, 1953, is available at http://www.presidency.ucsb.edu/ws/index.php?pid=9600.

11. Quoted in Ira Chernus, *Eisenhower's Atoms for Peace* (College Station: Texas A&M University Press, 2002), 94.

12. For consideration of the counterfactual question of whether there existed a genuine "missed opportunity" to ease the Cold War in the wake of Stalin's death and the armistice in Korea, see, in addition to the Larres and Osgood volume above, "Forum: Perspectives on The Cold War after Stalin's Death: A Missed Opportunity for Peace?" *Journal of Cold War Studies* 10, no. 2 (Spring 2008), 131–138, with essays by Robert L. Jervis, Thomas Maddux, and Bernd Greiner; Larres, *Churchill's Cold War*, 191, and n. 15 on p. 464; M. Steven Fish, "After Stalin's Death: The Anglo-American Debate Over a New Cold War," *Diplomatic History* 10 (Fall 1986), 333–355; James Richter, "Reexamining Soviet Policy Towards Ger-

many during the Beria Interregnum," *Cold War International History Project Working Paper* No.3 (June 1992). And see also Gunter Bischof and Saki Dockrill, eds., *Cold War Respite: The Geneva Summit of 1955* (Baton Rouge: Louisiana State University Press, 2000); Deborah Welch Larson, *Anatomy of Mistrust: U.S.-Soviet Relations During the Cold War* (Ithaca: Cornell University Press, 1997), 39–72.

13. In September 1953, Dulles suddenly urged Eisenhower to make "a spectacular effort to relax world tensions," a project that ought to include the demilitarization of Europe and the "control of weapons of mass destruction." The proposal was so totally at odds with what Dulles had argued up to that point and would claim over the next several years that it must be regarded with suspicion. In particular, it is almost impossible to believe that he genuinely thought in 1953 that the two superpowers could establish a serious regime of control over nuclear weaponry. For a different interpretation, see Melvyn P. Leffler, *For the Soul of Mankind: The United States, the Soviet Union, and the Cold War* (New York: Hill and Wang, 2007), 126–127.

14. Ambrose, *Eisenhower*, 468–469.

15. Gar Alperovitz, *The Decision to Use the Atomic Bomb* (New York: Knopf, 1995), 352–358. On Eisenhower's deep misgivings in the summer of 1945, see Mark Perry, *Partners in Command: George Marshall and Dwight Eisenhower in War and Peace* (New York: Penguin, 2007), 367–368.

16. Dockrill, *Eisenhower's New Look*, 52–53.

17. John Foster Dulles, "Policy for Security and Peace," *Foreign Affairs*, April 1954, 32.

18. Dockrill, *Eisenhower's New Look*, chs. 3–4, ably covers Solarium and NSC 162/2.

19. On the administration's deliberations concerning the potential use of nuclear weapons in East Asia in the period, see Matthew Jones, "Targeting China: U.S. Nuclear Planning and 'Massive Retaliation' in East Asia, 1953–1955," *Journal of Cold War Studies* 10 (Fall 2008), 37–65.

20. A good discussion of the atomic threat over Korea is in McGeorge Bundy, *Danger and Survival: Choices about the Bomb in the First Fifty Years* (New York: Random House, 1988), 238–242.

21. See Chen Jian's China and the Cold War (Chapel Hill: University of North Carolina Press, 2001), 111–112; Kathryn Weathersby, "New Findings on the Korean War," *Cold War International History Project Bulletin* 3 (Fall 1993).

22. Strauss meeting notes, Bermuda, 12/5/53, 711.5611/12–1153, Central Decimal Files, RG 59, USNA. We thank Matthew Jones for drawing this exchange to our attention.

23. Mark Atwood Lawrence, *Assuming the Burden: Europe and the American Commitment to War in Vietnam* (Berkeley: University of California Press, 2005), 233–275.

24. Julian Zelizer, *Arsenal of Democracy: The Politics of National Security in America since World War II* (New York: Basic Books, 2009), ch. 4; Robert E. Herzstein, *Henry R. Luce, Time, and the American Crusade in Asia* (New York: Cambridge University Press, 2005), 190.

25. For Dulles and Eisenhower quotes, see U.S. Department of State, "Editorial Note," *Foreign Relations of the United States: National Security Policy, 1955–57,* vol. 19, p. 61.

26. See Charles Alexander, *Holding the Line: The Eisenhower Era* (Bloomington: Indiana University Press, 1975).

27. Robert A. Divine, *Eisenhower and the Cold War* (New York: Oxford University Press, 1981).

28. A fine account can be found in Tim Weiner, *Legacy of Ashes: The History of the CIA* (London: Allen Lane, 2007), ch. 9. See also Mark J. Gasiorowski and Malcolm Byrne, eds., *Mohammad Mosaddeq and the 1953 Coup in Iran* (Syracuse: Syracuse University Press, 2004); and Trita Parsi, *Treacherous Alliance: The Secret Dealings of Israel, Iran, and the United States* (New Haven: Yale University Press, 2007), chs. 2–3.

29. Richard H. Immerman, *The CIA in Guatemala* (Austin: University of Texas Press, 1982); Piero Gleijeses, *Shattered Hope: The Guatemalan Revolution and the United States, 1944–1954* (Princeton: Princeton University Press, 1991).

30. Quoted in Gleijeses, *Shattered Hope,* 299.

31. Weiner, *Legacy of Ashes,* 101–104.

32. Dulles quoted in Walter LaFeber, *The American Age: United States Foreign Policy at Home and Abroad since 1750* (New York: Norton, 1988),

547. On the CIA's role, see Nick Cullather, *Secret History: The CIA's Classified Account of Its Operations in Guatemala, 1952-1954,* 2nd ed. (Stanford: Stanford University Press, 2006).

33. A penetrating assessment is by Robert J. McMahon, "Eisenhower and Third World Nationalism: A Critique of the Revisionists," *Political Science Quarterly* 101 (1986), 453-473.

34. See Jason C. Parker, "Small Victory, Missed Chance: The Eisenhower Administration, the Bandung Conference, and the Turning of the Cold War," in Andrew L. Johns, and Kathryn C. Statler, eds., *The Eisenhower Administration, the Third World, and the Globalization of the Cold War* (Lanham: Rowman and Littlefield, 2006), 154.

35. George M. Kahin and Audrey R. Kahin, *Subversion as Foreign Policy: The Secret Eisenhower and Dulles Debacle in Indonesia.* (New York: New Press, 1995), 78.

36. Behçet Yesilbursa, *The Baghdad Pact: Anglo-American Defence Policies in the Middle East, 1950-59,* Military History and Policy Series (New York: Routledge, 2005), 17.

37. Kenneth A. Osgood, *Total Cold War: Eisenhower's Secret Propaganda Battle at Home and Abroad* (Lawrence: University Press of Kansas, 2006). Two important studies of psychological warfare that look closely at the Eisenhower period are Scott Lucas, *Freedom's War: The American Crusade against the Soviet Union* (New York: New York University Press, 1999); and Gregory Mitrovich, *Undermining the Kremlin: America's Strategy to Subvert the Soviet Bloc, 1947-1956* (Ithaca: Cornell University Press, 2000).

38. Osgood, *Total Cold War,* ch. 7.

39. Mary L. Dudziak, *Cold War Civil Rights: Race and the Image of American Democracy* (Princeton: Princeton University Press, 2000); Thomas Borstelmann, *The Cold War and the Color Line: American Race Relations in the Global Arena* (Cambridge, Mass.: Harvard University Press, 2003).

40. Peter L. Hahn, *The United States, Great Britain, and Egypt, 1945-1956* (Chapel Hill: University of North Carolina Press, 1991). An illuminating history of the canal is Zachary Karabell, *Parting the Desert: The Creation of the Suez Canal* (New York: Knopf, 2003).

41. Steven Z. Freiberger, *Dawn over Suez: The Rise of American Power*

in the Middle East, 1953–1957 (Chicago: Ivan R. Dee, 2007), 159–209; Peter L. Hahn, *Caught in the Middle East: U.S. Policy toward the Arab-Israeli Conflict, 1945–1961* (Chapel Hill: University of North Carolina Press, 2006), 186–198.

42. See Douglas Little, *American Orientalism* (Chapel Hill: University of North Carolina Press, 2008), 93–94.

43. Salim Yaqub, *Containing Arab Nationalism: The Eisenhower Doctrine and the Middle East* (Chapel Hill: University of North Carolina Press, 2004), chs. 1–2.

44. Quoted in LaFeber, *The American Age,* vol. 2, 559. See Charles Gati, *Failed Illusions: Moscow, Washington, Budapest, and the 1956 Hungarian Revolt* (Stanford: Stanford University Press, 2006).

45. Mark Kramer, "New Evidence on Soviet Decision-Making and the 1956 Polish and Hungarian Crises," *Cold War International History Project Bulletin* 8/9 (Winter 1996), 358–384; Charles Gati, *Hungary and the Soviet Bloc* (Durham: Duke University Press, 1986), 153.

46. Richard H. Immerman, *John Foster Dulles and the Diplomacy of the Cold War* (Princeton: Princeton University Press, 1990).

47. Dockrill, *Eisenhower's New Look,* 135.

48. U.S. Department of State, "Memorandum of January 23, 1956 Meeting with Eisenhower," *FRUS, 1955–57,* vol. 19, 189.

49. Bernard Brodie et al., *The Absolute Weapon* (New York: Harcourt Brace, 1946), 76.

50. Campbell Craig, *Destroying the Village: Eisenhower and Thermonuclear War* (New York: Columbia University Press, 1998), 53–55.

51. See David A. Rosenberg, "The Origins of Overkill: Nuclear Weapons and American Strategy, 1945–1960," *International Security* 7 (Spring 1983), 3–71.

52. Quoted in Craig, *Destroying the Village,* 50.

53. At the U.S. Department of State, "Memorandum of May 24, 1956 White House Conference," *FRUS, 1955–57,* vol. 19, 312.

54. Craig, *Destroying the Village,* 55–70.

55. For a theoretical explanation of Eisenhower's logic, see Robert Jervis, *The Meaning of the Nuclear Revolution: Statecraft and the Prospect of Armageddon* (Ithaca: Cornell University Press, 1989).

56. An exceptionally fine study of Kahn is Sharon Ghamari-Tabrizi,

The Worlds of Herman Kahn (Cambridge: Harvard University Press, 2007). See also Fred Kaplan, *The Wizards of Armageddon* (New York: Simon and Schuster, 1983).

57. See Campbell Craig, "The Illogic of Henry Kissinger's Nuclear Strategy," *Armed Forces and Society* 29 (2003), 547–568; and Mario Del Pero, *The Eccentric Realist: Henry Kissinger and the Shaping of American Foreign Policy* (Ithaca: Cornell University Press, 2010), ch. 2.

58. Christopher Preble, *John F. Kennedy and the Missile Gap* (Dekalb: Northern Illinois University Press, 2004), ch. 1.

59. Martin Walker, *The Cold War: A History* (New York: Henry Holt, 1993), 117.

60. A perceptive study of Eisenhower's battles with the alarmists is Peter J. Roman, *Eisenhower and the Missile Gap* (Ithaca: Cornell University Press, 1995).

61. Quoted in Zelizer, *Arsenal of Democracy,* ch. 4.

62. Robert A. Divine, *The Sputnik Challenge* (New York: Oxford University Press, 1993), 68–83.

63. Kennan devoted one of his famous Reith lectures on the BBC to this topic. See George F. Kennan, *Memoirs* 1950–1963 (Boston: Little, Brown, 1972), 244–249.

5. The Nuclear Rubicon

1. On administration responses to Sputnik and the "missile gap" controversy, see David Snead, *The Gaither Committee, Eisenhower and the Cold War* (Columbus: Ohio State University Press, 1999); and Robert A. Divine, The Sputnik Challenge (New York: Oxford University Press, 1993). A powerful essay on the years covered by this chapter is James G. Hershberg, "The Crisis Years, 1958–1963," in Odd Arne Westad, ed., *Reviewing the Cold War: Approaches, Interpretations, Theory* (London: Frank Cass, 2000), 303–325.

2. Maxwell D. Taylor, *The Uncertain Trumpet* (New York: Harper, 1960).

3. Chen Jian, *Mao's China and the Cold War* (Chapel Hill: University of North Carolina Press, 2001), 171–173.

4. U.S. Department of State, "Memorandum of August 13, 1958 from Smith to Herter," *Foreign Relations of the United States,* 1958–60, vol. 19, microfiche supplement, pp. 1–2.

5. For recent documentation on Eisenhower's struggles against the military during this crisis, see "Air Force Histories Released through Archive Lawsuit Show Cautious Presidents Overruling Air Force Plans for Early Use of Nuclear Weapons," April 30, 2008 press release, National Security Archive Nuclear Vault, www.gwu.edu/nsarchiv/nukevault/ebb249/index.htm.

6. John Foster Dulles, "Challenge and Response in United States Policy," *Foreign Affairs* 36 (October 1957). On Dulles's growing antagonism toward Eisenhower's new policies, see Craig, *Destroying the Village,* 74– 78.

7. Aleksandr Fursenko and Timothy Naftali, *Khrushchev's Cold War: The Inside Story of an American Adversary* (New York: Norton, 2006). Sino-Soviet relations had begun to show signs of strain on several issues in recent months, and the Chinese resented Moscow's interference. The islands, Mao Zedong once complained to aides, "are two batons that keep Khrushchev and Eisenhower dancing." See Chen Jian, *Mao's China and the Cold War,* 64–67; Vladislav Zubok, *A Failed Empire: The Soviet Union in the Cold War from Stalin to Gorbachev* (Chapel Hill: University of North Carolina Press, 2007), 136–137. Mao quoted in Li Zhisui, *The Private Life of Chairman Mao: The Memoirs of Mao's Personal Physician* (New York: Random House, 1994), 270–271.

8. Qiang Zhai, *The Dragon, the Lion, and the Eagle: Chinese/British/American Relations, 1949–58* (Kent: Kent University Press, 1992), 194.

9. U.S. Department of State, "Memorandum of September 21, 1958 Conversation with the President," *FRUS, 1958–60,* vol. 19, pp. 244– 252.

10. Fursenko and Naftali, *Khrushchev's Cold War,* 211. See also Hope Harrison, *Driving the Soviets up the Wall: Soviet-East German Relations, 1953–1961* (Princeton: Princeton University Press, 2005), ch. 3; Zubok, *A Failed Empire,* 132–134.

11. Fursenko and Naftali, *Khrushchev's Cold War,* chs. 5–6, 10. Also see Campbell Craig and Sergey Radchenko, "MAD, not Marx: Khrushchev and the Nuclear Revolution," *Journal of Strategic Studies* 41 (2018), pp. 208–33.

12. U.S. Department of State, "Memorandum of March 20, 1959 Conversation," *FRUS, 1958–60,* vol. 8, 520–521.

13. See William Burr, "New Evidence on the Origins of Overkill," November 22, 2007, press release, National Security Archive Nuclear Vault, and Donald Steury, ed., *Intentions and Capabilities: Estimates on Soviet Strategic Forces 1950–1983* (Washington, DC: CIA Center for the Study of Intelligence, 1996), 109–113.

14. On the U-2 episode, see Tim Weiner, *Legacy of Ashes: The History of the CIA* (London: Allen Lane, 2007), 171–177; and Michael R. Beschloss, *Mayday: Eisenhower, Khrushchev, and the U-2 Affair* (New York: Harper and Row, 1988).

15. Chester Pach, *The Presidency of Dwight D. Eisenhower* (Lawrence: University Press of Kansas, 1991), 219. The perspective of both sides in the crisis is examined in Fursenko and Naftali, *Khrushchev's Cold War,* ch. 11. Powers, for his part, was sentenced to three years in prison plus an additional seven years of hard labor. In early 1962 he was exchanged for a Soviet spy, Vilyam Fischer, and released. A CIA board of inquiry subsequently determined that he had not acted disloyally. The board kept its findings secret, however, thereby preventing Powers from clearing his name.

16. Christopher A. Preble, *John F. Kennedy and the Missile Gap* (DeKalb: Northern Illinois University Press, 2004).

17. Ibid., 108–110. See also Richard Rhodes, *Arsenals of Folly: The Making of the Nuclear Arms Race* (New York, 2007), 85–86.

18. Soon after Kennedy took office, his secretary of defense Robert McNamara indiscreetly mentioned that the missile gap was of course a hoax.

19. Preble, *Missile Gap,* 146. Also see Rhodes, *Arsenals of Folly,* 110.

20. A few American personnel did die while on duty during the Eisenhower years, including, for example, a handful of military advisers in Vietnam. None, however, perished as part of a ground-force commitment.

21. Williams quoted in Robert Schlesinger, *White House Ghosts: Presidents and Their Speechwriters* (New York: Simon and Schuster, 2008), 98.

22. Dwight D. Eisenhower, "421-Farewell Radio and Television Ad-

dress to the American People," *Public Papers of the President, Dwight D. Eisenhower,* January 17, 1961.

23. See David Halberstam, *The Best and the Brightest* (New York: Random House, 1992).

24. Maxwell Taylor, "Security Will Not Wait," *Foreign Affairs* 39 (January 1961), 174–175.

25. On Castro and his rise to power, see Tad Szulc, *Fidel: A Critical Portrait* (New York: Avon Books, 1987).

26. James G. Blight and Peter Kornbluh, eds., *Politics of Illusion: The Bay of Pigs Invasion Reexamined* (Boulder: Lynne Rienner, 1998); Weiner, Legacy of Ashes, 171–177.

27. Quoted in Michael R. Beschloss, *The Crisis Years: Kennedy and Khrushchev, 1960–1963* (New York: HarperCollins, 1991), 225. See also James B. Reston, *Deadline: A Memoir* (New York, 1991), 290–292; and Richard Reeves, *President Kennedy: Profile in Power* (New York: Simon and Schuster, 1993), 172.

28. Craig, *Destroying the Village,* 132–135.

29. Ann Tusa, *The Last Division: A History of Berlin: 1945–1989* (Reading: Addison-Wesley, 1997), ch. 10; Harrison, Driving the Soviets Up the Wall, 205–207.

30. Beschloss, *Crisis Years,* 278. On the Berlin crisis, see also Frederick Kempe, *Berlin 1961: Kennedy, Khrushchev, and the Most Dangerous Place on Earth* (New York: Putnam, 2011).

31. The literature is huge. A superb recent account is Michael Dobbs, *One Minute to Midnight: Kennedy, Khrushchev, and Castro on the Brink of Nuclear War* (New York: Knopf 2008). See also Aleksandr Fursenko and Timothy Naftali, *"One Hell of a Gamble"*; Mark J. White, Missiles in Cuba (Chicago: Ivan R. Dee, 1997); Max Frankel, *High Noon in the Cold War* (New York: Presidio Press, 2004); Sheldon M. Stern, *The Week the World Stood Still* (Stanford: Stanford University Press, 2004); Graham Allison and Philip D. Zelikow, *Essence of Decision,* rev. ed. (Reading: Longman, 1999); and Len Scott and R. Gerald Hughes, eds., *The Cuban Missile Crisis: A Critical Reappraisal* (New York: Routledge, 2015). Two authoritative brief accounts are Don Munton and David A. Welch, *The Cuban Missile Crisis: A Concise History* (New York: Oxford University Press, 2007); and

James G. Hershberg, "The Cuban Missile Crisis," in Melvyn P. Leffler and Odd Arne Westad, *The Cambridge History of the Cold War* (New York: Cambridge University Press, 2009).

32. An excellent study is Lorenz M. Lüthi, *The Sino-Soviet Split: Cold War in the Communist World* (Princeton: Princeton University Press, 2008).

33. Khrushchev quoted in Dobbs, *One Minute to Midnight,* 45. See also James A. Blight and David A. Welch, *On the Brink: Americans and Soviets Reexamine Cuban Missile Crisis* (New York: Hill and Wang, 1989), 190. A penetrating overview of the crisis by one of our foremost experts is Sheldon M. Stern, *The Cuban Missile Crisis in American Memory: Myths versus Reality* (Stanford: Stanford University Press, 2012).

34. Fursenko and Naftali, *Khruschev's Cold War,* chs. 17–18. And see Rhodes, *Arsenals of Folly,* 93.

35. A young McNamara aide, William Kaufmann, analyzed the matter in the second week of the crisis and concluded the JCS and McNamara were both right. Deploying the missiles to Cuba improved Khrushchev's position, and compensated for his shortage of intercontinental missiles. But he could not deliver a knockout blow under any circumstances. Absent the Cuba missiles, Kaufmann estimated, a Soviet first strike would leave the U.S. with minimum retaliatory force of 841 nuclear weapons; if the Soviets fired missiles from Cuba as well, the number dropped, but only to 483 nukes. In either case, most of the hardened U.S. missile sites and nuclear-equipped Polaris submarines would survive. The end result: the U.S. could still inflict greater damage on the USSR than the Soviets had delivered on America. See Dobbs, *One Hour to Midnight,* 98–99.

36. On this factor, see Thomas G. Paterson and William Brophy, "October Missiles and November Elections: The Cuban Missile Crisis and American Politics, 1962," *Journal of American History* 73 (June 1986), 87–119.

37. All quotes are from Julian Zelizer, *Arsenal of Democracy: The Politics of National Security in America Since World War II* (New York: Basic Books, 2009), ch. 5.

38. See Alice L. George, *Awaiting Armageddon: How Americans Faced*

the Cuban Missile Crisis (Chapel Hill: University of North Carolina Press, 2003).

39. Dobbs, *One Hour to Midnight,* 350.

40. Ernest R. May and Philip D. Zelikow, eds., *The Kennedy Tapes: Inside the White House During the Cuban Missile Crisis* (Cambridge, Mass.: Belknap Press of Harvard University Press, 1997).

41. See, e.g., Thomas G. Paterson, *Contesting Castro: The United States and the Triumph of the Cuban Revolution* (New York: Oxford University Press, 1994), 260–261.

42. For a full treatment of the lessons of the crisis, see Len Scott, *The Cuban Missile Crisis and the Threat of Nuclear War: Lessons from History* (London: Continuum, 2008).

43. Scott D. Sagan and Kenneth N. Waltz, *The Spread of Nuclear Weapons: A Debate Renewed,* 2nd ed. (New York: Norton, 2003). ch. 1. For the original version, see Kenneth N. Waltz, "The Spread of Nuclear Weapons: More May be Better," Adelphi paper no. 171, International Institute for Strategic Studies, 1981. Also see John Mearsheimer, "The Case for a Ukrainian Nuclear Deterrent," *Foreign Affairs* 72 (Summer 1993), 50–66.

44. Dobbs, *One Hour to Midnight,* 336.

45. Recent work has only demonstrated further how precarious Mutual Assured Destruction was during the Cold War and how close we came to an accidental third world war. See David E. Hoffman, *The Dead Hand: The Untold Story of the Cold War Arms Race and Its Dangerous Legacy* (New York: Random House, 2010); Eric Schlosser, *Command and Control* (London: Penguin Books, 2013); and Daniel Ellsberg, *The Doomsday Machine: Confessions of a Nuclear War Planner* (London: Bloomsbury, 2017).

46. John Lewis Gaddis, *The Long Peace: Inquiries into the History of the Cold War* (Oxford: Oxford University Press, 1987), ch.7.

47. On the test ban treaty, see Lawrence Freedman, *Kennedy's Wars: Berlin, Cuba, Laos, and Vietnam* (New York: Oxford University Press, 2000), 261–275.

48. See Anders Stephanson, "Cold War Origins," in Alexander DeConde, Richard Dean Burns, and Fredrik Logevall, eds., *Encyclopedia of*

American Foreign Policy, 2nd ed., vol. 1 (New York: Scribner, 2002), 236–238; Jennifer W. See, "An Easy Truce: John F. Kennedy and Soviet-American Détente, 1963," *Cold War History* 2 (January 2002), 161–194.

49. Marc Trachtenberg, *A Constructed Peace: The Making of a European Settlement, 1945–1963* (Princeton: Princeton University Press, 1999).

6. Gulliver's Travails

1. Christopher Preble, *John F. Kennedy and the Missile Gap* (Dekalb: Northern Illinois University Press, 2004), 178–179.

2. On the growing dependence of regions in the American South and West on high military spending, see Ann Markusen, Peter Hall, Scott Campbell, and Sabina Deitrick, *The Rise of the Gunbelt* (New York: Oxford University Press, 1991).

3. Fredrik Logevall, *Choosing War: The Lost Chance for Peace and the Escalation of War in Vietnam* (Berkeley: University of California Press, 1999).

4. David W. P. Elliott, *The Vietnamese War: Revolution and Social Change in the Mekong Delta, 1930–1975*, concise edition (Armonk: M. E. Sharpe, 2003), 85–136; William Duiker, *Ho Chi Minh* (New York: Hyperion, 2000), 462–514; Jessica M. Chapman, *Cauldron of Resistance: Ngo Dinh Diem, the United States, and 1950s Southern Vietnam* (Ithaca: Cornell University Press, 2013).

5. Eisenhower's press conference is excerpted in William Appleman Williams, Lloyd C. Gardner, and Walter LaFeber, eds., *America in Vietnam: A Documentary History* (New York: Anchor, 1985), 156–157.

6. Edwin Moïse, "The Domino Theory," in Alexander DeConde, Richard D. Burns, and Fredrik Logevall, eds., *Encyclopedia of American Foreign Policy*, 2nd ed. (New York: Scribner, 2002), vol. 1, 554.

7. David Halberstam, *The Best and the Brightest*, 20th anniversary ed. (New York: Random House, 1992), xvii.

8. See the discussion in William P. Bundy, unpublished book manuscript, ch. 17, 9–26, Papers of William P. Bundy, Lyndon Baines Johnson Library, Austin, Texas. A superb study of McGeorge Bundy's role in

the escalation of the war is Andrew Preston, *The War Council: McGeorge Bundy, the NSC, and Vietnam* (Cambridge, Mass.: Harvard University Press, 2006).

9. Jonathan Schell, *The Time of Illusion* (New York: Knopf, 1976), 9. See here also the perceptive analysis in Robert J. McMahon, "Bernath Lecture: Credibility and World Power," *Diplomatic History* 15 (Fall 1991), 455–471.

10. Robert J. McMahon, ed., *The Cold War in the Third World* (New York: Oxford University Press, 2013).

11. Robert J. McMahon, *The Cold War: A Very Short Introduction* (New York: Oxford University Press, 2003), 85–88.

12. Elizabeth Cobbs Hoffman, *All You Need Is Love: The Peace Corps and the Spirit of the 1960s* (Cambridge, Mass.: Harvard University Press, 1998), 4–6. See also Molly Geidel, *Peace Corps Fantasies: How Development Shaped the Global Sixties* (Minneapolis: University of Minnesota Press, 2015).

13. Stephen G. Rabe, *The Most Dangerous Area of the World: John F. Kennedy Confronts Communist Revolution in Latin America* (Chapel Hill: University of North Carolina Press, 1999), 148–149.

14. W. W. Rostow, *The Stages of Economic Growth: A Non-Communist Manifesto* (Cambridge: Cambridge University Press, 1960). On Rostow's career in this period and later, see David Milne, *America's Rasputin: Walt Rostow and the Vietnam War* (New York: Hill and Wang, 2008). On modernization theory and U.S. foreign policy in the postwar era, see Nick Cullather, "Development: Its History," *Diplomatic History* 24 (Fall 2000), 641–653; and David C. Engerman, Nils Gilman, Mark H. Haefele, and Michael E. Latham, *Staging Growth: Modernization, Development, and the Global Cold War* (Amherst: University of Massachusetts Press, 2003).

15. On the Diem years in general, and the drama of his final months, see Edward Miller, *Misalliance: Ngo Dinh Diem, the United States, and the Fate of South Vietnam* (Cambridge, Mass.: Harvard University Press, 2013); and Philip Catton, *Diem's Final Failure: Prelude to America's War in Vietnam* (Lawrence: University Press of Kansas, 2003).

16. David Kaiser, *The Road to Dallas: The Assassination of John F. Kennedy* (Cambridge, Mass.: Harvard University Press, 2008). For a highly

detailed account which comes to the conclusion that Oswald acted completely alone, see Vincent Bugliosi, *Reclaiming History: The Assassination of President John F. Kennedy* (New York: W. W. Norton, 2007).

17. Fredrik Logevall, "Vietnam and the Question of What Might Have Been," in Mark J. White, ed., *Kennedy: The New Frontier Revisited* (London: Macmillan, 1998), 19–62.

18. See John M. Newman, *JFK and Vietnam: Deception, Intrigue, and the Struggle for Power* (New York: Warner Books, 1992); and Howard Jones, *Death of a Generation: How the Assassinations of Diem and JFK Prolonged the Vietnam War* (New York: Oxford University Press, 2003); James Galbraith, "Exit Strategy," *Boston Review,* January/February 2004.

19. Quoted in Michael R. Beschloss, ed., *Taking Charge: The Johnson White House Tapes, 1963–1964* (New York: Simon and Schuster, 1997), 248–249.

20. LBJ-McGeorge Bundy telcon, 27 May 1964, *FRUS, 1964–68,* vol. 27: *Mainland Southeast Asia: Regional Affairs* (Washington: Government Printing Office, 2000), doc. 53.

21. Pierre Asselin, *Hanoi's Road to the Vietnam War* (Berkeley: University of California Press, 2013).

22. Robert McNamara, with Brian VanDeMark, *In Retrospect: The Tragedy and Lessons of Vietnam* (New York, 1995), 141. On the Gulf of Tonkin incident, the standard account is Edwin Moïse, *Tonkin Gulf and the Escalation of the Vietnam War,* rev ed. (Annapolis: Naval Institute Press, 2019).

23. Barry Goldwater, *Why Not Victory? A Fresh Look at American Foreign Policy* (New York: McGraw-Hill, 1962), 44.

24. Logevall, *Choosing War.* Much of the analysis in this section is drawn from this book.

25. The memorandum is reprinted in full in Hubert H. Humphrey, *The Education of a Public Man: My Life and Politics* (Garden City: Doubleday, 1976), 320–324. For Johnson's response, see Carl Solberg, *Hubert Humphrey: A Biography* (New York: W. W. Norton, 1984), 287–288; and Humphrey, *Education,* 327.

26. Fredrik Logevall, *The Origins of the Vietnam War* (Essex, England: Longman, 2001), 77.

27. See, e.g., Arthur M. Schlesinger Jr., *The Bitter Heritage* (Boston: Little Brown, 1966).

28. See, e.g., "Inside LBJ's War: A Forum on Francis Bator's 'No Good Choices,'" *Diplomatic History* 32 (June 2008), 307–370.

29. Quoted in Charles E. Neu, *America's Lost War: Vietnam, 1945–1975* (Wheeling: Harlan Davidson, 2005), 86.

30. Fredrik Logevall, "There Ain't No Daylight: Lyndon Johnson and the Politics of Escalation," in Mark Philip Bradley and Marilyn B. Young, eds., *Making Sense of the Vietnam Wars: Local, National, and Transnational Perspectives* (New York: Oxford University Press, 2008), 91–108.

31. Quoted in Williams et al., *America in Vietnam*, 243.

32. Quoted in Marilyn Young, *The Vietnam Wars, 1945–1990* (New York: Harper Collins, 1991), 135.

33. Randall B. Woods, *Fulbright* (New York: Cambridge University Press, 1995), 382; Walter LaFeber, *America, Russia, and the Cold War*, 10th ed. (Boston: McGraw Hill, 2008), 256–257.

34. Joseph A. Fry, *Debating Vietnam: Fulbright, Stennis, and Their Senate Hearings* (Lanham: Rowman and Littlefield, 2006).

35. Rusk and LBJ quoted in Schulzinger, *U.S. Diplomacy since 1900*, 6th ed. (New York: Oxford University Press, 2008), 239–240. See also Joseph A. Fry, *Debating Vietnam: Fulbright, Stennis, and Their Senate Hearings* (Lanham: Rowman and Littlefield, 2006), 34–44.

36. On the Republican Party and the war, an important study is Andrew L. Johns, *Vietnam's Second Front: Domestic Politics, the Republican Party, and the War* (Lexington: University Press of Kentucky, 2012).

37. McNamara to LBJ, 19 May 1967, in Neil Sheehan, ed., *The Pentagon Papers* (New York: Bantam Books, 1971), 580. One of the curiousities about the latter-day McNamara is the degree to which he seemed to have forgotten how well informed he was in the key years of escalation, how well he understood the realities of the situation on the ground in Vietnam and in international and domestic U.S. opinion. In later years he would express astonishment at "revelations" that he knew of—and understood—then. See the McNamara-written sections in Robert McNamara, James G. Blight, and Robert Brigham (with Thomas J. Biersteker and Herbert Y. Schandler), *Argument without End: In Search of Answers to the Vietnam Tragedy* (New York: Public Affairs, 1999). See also Fredrik Logevall, "Bringing in the 'Other Side': New Scholarship on the Vietnam Wars," *Journal of Cold War Studies* 3, no. 3 (Fall 2001), 77–93.

38. Halberstam, *The Best and the Brightest,* 633.

39. George W. Ball, *The Past Has Another Pattern: Memoirs* (New York: W. W. Norton, 1982), 405.

40. Thomas Alan Schwartz, *Lyndon Johnson and Europe: In the Shadow of Vietnam* (Cambridge, Mass.: Harvard University Press, 2003); Frank Costigliola, "Lyndon B. Johnson, Germany, and 'the End of the Cold War,'" in Warren I. Cohen and Nancy Bernkopf Tucker, eds., *Lyndon Johnson Confronts the World: American Foreign Policy, 1969–1977* (New York: Cambridge University Press, 1994), 192–208; H. W. Brands, *The Wages of Globalism: Lyndon Johnson and the Limits of American Power* (New York: Oxford University Press, 1995), 119–120.

41. Warren Bass, *Support Any Friend: Kennedy's Middle East and the Making of the U.S.-Israel Alliance* (New York: Oxford University Press, 2003).

42. Ibid., 146. Badeau quoted on p. 146.

43. On the Six-Day War and U.S. policy, see Michael Oren, *Six Days of War: June 1967 and the Making of the Modern Middle East* (New York: Oxford University Press, 2002); and Tom Segev, *1967: Israel, the War, and the Year that Transformed the Middle East* (New York: Metropolitan Books, 2007). On the attack on the USS Liberty, see Oren, *Six Days of War,* 263–273. For the argument that the attack on the ship was deliberate, see James Bamford, *Body of Secrets: Anatomy of the Ultra-Secret National Security Agency* (New York: Doubleday, 2001).

44. The treaty's non-nuclear signatories agreed to forego pursuing a bomb in exchange for access to atomic energy technologies, and a promise by the nuclear states that they would commit in good faith to eventual disarmament. None of the nuclear signatories, fifty years on, have disarmed. On the larger purposes of U.S. nonproliferation policy from 1968 to the present, see Campbell Craig and Jan Ruzicka, *U.S. Unipolar Preponderance and Nuclear Nonproliferation* (Ithaca: Cornell University Press, forthcoming). Also see Nuno Monteiro and Alexandre Debs, *Nuclear Politics: The Strategic Causes of Proliferation* (Cambridge: Cambridge University Press, 2017).

45. J. Peter Scoblic, *U.S. vs. Them: How a Half Century of Conservatism Has Undermined America's Security* (New York: Viking, 2008), 60.

46. Mitchell Lerner, "Trying to Find the Guy Who Invited Them: Lyndon Johnson, Bridge Building, and the End of the Prague Spring," *Diplomatic History* 32 (January 2008), 77–104; Hal Brands, "Progress Unseen: U.S. Arms Control Policy and the Origins of Détente," *Diplomatic History* 30 (April 2006), 253–285.

47. On Soviet thinking, see Mark Kramer, "The Czechoslovak Crisis and the Brezhnev Doctrine," in Carole Fink, Phillip Gassert, and Detlef Junker, eds., 1968: *The World Transformed* (New York: Cambridge University Press, 1998), 121–151.

48. Quoted in Walter LaFeber, *Deadly Bet: LBJ, Vietnam, and the 1968 Election* (Lanham: Rowman and Littlefield, 2005), 30.

49. George C. Herring, *America's Longest War: The United States and Vietnam, 1950–1975*, 4th ed. (Boston: Houghton Mifflin, 2002), 248. On Westmoreland, see Gregory A. Daddis, *Westmoreland's War: Reassessing American Strategy in Vietnam* (New York: Oxford University Press, 2015).

50. Walter Isaacson and Evan Thomas, *Wise Men: Six Friends and the World They Made* (New York: Simon and Schuster, 1986), 684; Herring, *America's Longest War*, 249–250. On Acheson's shift, see Douglas Brinkley, *Dean Acheson: The Cold War Years, 1953–71* (New Haven: Yale University Press, 1994).

51. The complete text of the speech is in Marvin E. Gettleman, Jane Franklin, Marilyn B. Young, and H. Bruce Franklin, eds., *Vietnam and America: A Documentary History* (New York, 1995), 401–409. H. W. Brands makes the point that what made the speech meaningful regarding Vietnam was Johnson's withdrawal from the presidential race, his "declaration of lame-duckhood." Brands, *The Wages of Globalism*, 252. See also LaFeber, *Deadly Bet*, ch. 3.

52. Quoted in Mark Hamilton Lytle, *America's Uncivil Wars: The Sixties Era from Elvis to the Fall of Richard Nixon* (New York: Oxford University Press, 2006), 341.

7. Nixon's World

1. Major recent studies of the Nixon era in U.S. foreign policy include Gary J. Bass, *The Blood Telegram: Nixon, Kissinger, and a Forgotten Geno-*

cide (New York: Knopf, 2013); Jussi Hanhimaki, *The Flawed Architect: Henry Kissinger and American Foreign Policy* (New York: Oxford University Press, 2004); Robert Dallek, *Nixon and Kissinger: Partners in Power* (New York: Harper Collins, 2007); William P. Bundy, *A Tangled Web: The Making of Foreign Policy in the Nixon Presidency* (New York: Hill and Wang, 1998); Jeremi Suri, *Henry Kissinger and the American Century* (Cambridge, Mass.: Harvard University Press, 2007). See also Fredrik Logevall and Andrew Preston, eds., *Nixon in the World: American Foreign Relations, 1969–1977* (New York: Oxford University Press, 2008). The broader political context is ably handled in Rick Perlstein, *Nixonland: The Rise of a President and the Fracturing of America* (New York: Scribner, 2008). For a stimulating and important assessment of Nixon's legacy, see David Greenberg, *Nixon's Shadow: The History of an Image* (New York: W. W. Norton, 2003).

2. Nixon's speech, dated Jan. 20, 1969, is available at www.presidency.ucsb.edu/ws.

3. Henry Kissinger, *Diplomacy* (New York, 1994), 703. On the developments that flowed from these realities, see, in particular, Daniel Sargent, *A Superpower Transformed: The Remaking of American Foreign Relations in the 1970s* (New York: Oxford University Press, 2017).

4. Jussi Hanhimaki, "The Elusive Grand Design," in Logevall and Preston, eds., *Nixon in the World,* 25–44.

5. Quoted in Elizabeth Drew, *Richard M. Nixon* (New York: Times Books, 2007), 14.

6. Walter Isaacson, *Kissinger: A Biography* (New York: Simon and Schuster, 1992), 127–128.

7. Quoted in David Reynolds, *Summits: Six Meetings that Shaped the Twentieth Century* (New York: Basic Books, 2007), 230.

8. Kissinger quoted in Hanhimaki, *Flawed Architect,* 12; Nixon quoted in Margaret Macmillan, *Nixon and Mao: The Week That Changed the World* (New York: Random House, 2007), 59.

9. On this as on other policy issues, Kissinger could speak out of both sides of his mouth. In 1968, he told Hans Morgenthau that "in 1965 when I first visited Vietnam, I became convinced that what we were doing there

was hopeless. I decided to work *within* the government to attempt the get the war ended." Quoted in Suri, *Henry Kissinger,* 188.

10. See Fredrik Logevall, *Embers of War: The Fall of an Empire and the Making of America's Vietnam* (New York: Random House, 2014), 373–78, 491–94.

11. Richard J. Whalen, *Catch the Falling Flag: A Republican's Challenge to His Party* (Boston: Houghton Mifflin, 1972), 137.

12. On Nixon's Vietnam policy, see Jeffrey Kimball, *Nixon's Vietnam War* (Lawrence: University Press of Kansas, 1998); Jeffrey Kimball, *The Vietnam War Files: Uncovering the Secret History of Nixon-Era Strategy* (Lawrence: University Press of Kansas, 2004), 24–28, 121–198; Larry Berman, *No Peace, No Honor: Nixon, Kissinger, and Betrayal in Vietnam* (New York: Free Press, 2001); Daniel Ellsberg, *Secrets* (New York: Viking, 2005); and Robert K. Brigham, *Reckless: Henry Kissinger and the Tragedy of Vietnam* (New York: Public Affairs, 2018).

13. David L. Anderson, *Vietnamization: Politics, Strategy, Legacy* (Lanham: Rowman and Littlefield, 2019).

14. *Public Papers, Richard M. Nixon, 1970* (Washington, DC: Government Printing Office, 1971), 405–410.

15. George Herring, *From Colony to Superpower: U.S. Foreign Relations since 1776 (New York: Oxford University Press, 2008), 770.*

16. Conversation 471–2, 3/19/71, 7:03 pm–7:27 pm, Oval Office, as quoted in Ken Hughes, *"Fatal Politics: The Nixon Tapes, the Vietnam War, and the Casualties of Reelection* (Charlottesville: University of Virginia Press, 2015).

17. Robert S. Litwak, *Détente and the Nixon Doctrine: American Foreign Policy and the Pursuit of Stability* (Cambridge: Cambridge University Press, 1984); Hanhimaki, "Elusive Grand Design," 38–40.

18. Kissinger wrote his Harvard PhD dissertation on the nineteenth-century statesmen Metternich and Castlereagh. A revised version was published as *A World Restored: Metternich, Castlereagh, and the Problems of Peace, 1812–1822* (1957; rpt. London: Phoenix, 2000).

19. Quoted in Reynolds, *Summits,* 225.

20. Ibid.

21. Jeremi Suri, *Power and Protest: Global Revolution and the Rise of Détente* (Cambridge, Mass.: Harvard University Press, 2003); also see Sarah B. Snyder, *From Selma to Moscow: How Human Rights Activists Transformed U.S. Foreign Policy.* (New York: Columbia University Press, 2018).

22. Mary Sarotte, "The Frailties of Grand Strategies: A Comparison of Détente and Ostpolitik," in Logevall and Preston, eds., Nixon in the World, 146–163; Mary Sarotte, *Dealing with the Devil: East Germany, Détente, and Ostpolitik* (Chapel Hill: University of North Carolina Press, 2001).

23. Odd Arne Westad, *The Global Cold War: Third World Interventions and the Making of Our Times* (Cambridge: Cambridge University Press, 2005), 194–206; Raymond L. Garthoff, *Détente and Confrontation: American-Soviet Relations from Nixon to Reagan,* rev. ed. (Washington, DC: Brookings Institution, 1994), 588.

24. The authoritative study of the unfolding of the Sino-Soviet split in the 1960s is Sergey Radchenko, *Two Suns in the Heavens: The Sino-Soviet Struggle for Supremacy, 1962–1967* (Stanford: Stanford University Press, 2009).

25. Elizabeth Wishnick, *Mending Fences: The Evolution of Moscow's China Policy from Brezhnev to Yeltsin* (Seattle: University of Washington Press, 2001), ch. 2.

26. Hanhimaki, *Flawed Architect,* 129.

27. Henry Kissinger, *White House Years* (Boston: Little, Brown, 1979), 163–165; Macmillan, *Nixon and Mao,* 56–57.

28. Richard M. Nixon, "Asia after Vietnam," *Foreign Affairs,* Oct. 1967.

29. Quoted in Macmillan, *Nixon and Mao,* 56

30. Chen Jian, *China and the Cold War* (Chapel Hill: University of North Carolina Press, 2001), 238–249.

31. For the transcripts and summaries of these talks in 1971 and Nixon's session with Mao in 1972, see *Foreign Relations of the United States, 1969–1976,* vol. 27 (Washington, DC: Government Printing Office, 2007), 359–452, 498–558, 677–684.

32. A recent concise assessment of the U.S. response to the South Asian crisis is Robert J. McMahon, "The Danger of Geopolitical Fanta-

sies: Nixon, Kissinger, and the South Asia Crisis of 1971," in Logevall and Preston, eds., *Nixon in the World*, 249–268.

33. Drew, Richard M. Nixon, 89; David Greenberg, "Nixon as Statesman: The Failed Campaign," in Logevall and Preston, eds., *Nixon in the World*, 55–56.

34. Quoted in Richard Reeves, *President Nixon: Alone in the White House* (New York: Simon and Schuster, 2001), 455.

35. On this point, see Dominic Sandbrook, "Salesmanship and Substance: The Influence of Domestic Policy and Watergate," in Logevall and Preston, eds., *Nixon in the World*, 87; and Dallek, *Nixon and Kissinger*, 329.

36. Quoted in Greenberg, "Nixon as Statesman," 58.

37. William Burr, ed., *The Kissinger Transcripts: The Top Secret Talks with Beijing and Moscow* (New York: New Press, 1998), chap. 5; Walter LaFeber, *America, Russia, and the Cold War, 1945–2006*, 10th ed. (Boston: McGraw-Hill, 2008), 284.

38. Quoted in Greenberg, "Nixon as Statesman," 59.

39. An important account of this "Easter Offensive" and the U.S. response is Stephen P. Randolph, *Powerful and Brutal Weapons: Nixon, Kissinger, and the Easter Offensive* (Cambridge, Mass.: Harvard University Press, 2007). On North Vietnamese decisionmaking in the final years of the war, see Lien-Hang T. Nguyen, *Hanoi's War: An International History of the War for Peace in Vietnam* (Chapel Hill: University of North Carolina Press, 2012).

40. Nixon quoted in Herring, *America's Longest War*, 307.

41. Kimball, *Nixon's Vietnam War*, 328; Dallek, *Nixon and Kissinger*, 407–408; H. R. Haldeman, *The Haldeman Diaries: Inside the Nixon White House* (New York: G. P. Putnam's Sons, 1994), 500.

42. Pierre Asselin, *A Bitter Peace: Washington, Hanoi, and the Making of the Paris Agreement* (Chapel Hill: University of North Carolina Press, 2002). See also Robert K. Brigham, *Guerrilla Diplomacy: The NLF's Foreign Relations and the Viet Nam War* (Ithaca: Cornell University Press, 1999); Gregory A. Daddis, *Withdrawal: Reassessing America's Final Years in Vietnam* (New York: Oxford University Press, 2017).

43. A somewhat different version of the argument that follows is in Fredrik Logevall, "Vietnam's Place in the Cold War: Some Reflections on

the Domino Theory," in Malcolm Muir Jr. and Mark F. Wilkinson, eds., *The Most Dangerous Years: The Cold War, 1953–1973* (Lexington: VMI Press, 2005).

44. See, e.g., Michael Lind, *Vietnam: The Necessary War* (New York: Free Press, 1999); Mark Moyar, *Triumph Forsaken: The Vietnam War, 1954–1965* (New York: Cambridge University Press, 2006).

45. With respect to Johnson, see Logevall, *Choosing War,* 389–395

46. George Ball, "Cutting Our Losses in Vietnam," June 28, 1965, *FRUS, 1964–1968,* vol. 3, 222.

47. For the dubious argument that the major U.S. military intervention in Vietnam bought time for Southeast Asia to "stand on its own two feet," see, e.g., Walt W. Rostow, "The Case for the Vietnam War," *Parameters* (Winter 1996–1997), 39–50. On the Cambodian developments, and the role played by the U.S. in the rise of the murderous Pol Pot, see Ben Kiernan, *How Pol Pot Came to Power: Colonialism, Nationalism, and Communism in Cambodia,* 1930–1975, 2nd ed. (New Haven: Yale University Press, 2004).

48. Greenberg, "Nixon as Statesman," 46.

49. Isaacson, *Kissinger,* 511.

50. Dallek, *Nixon and Kissinger,* 276; see also 410. And see Craig Daigle, *The Limits of Détente: The United States, the Soviet Union, and the Arab-Israeli Conflict, 1969–1973* (New Haven: Yale University Press, 2012).

51. See Douglas Little, *American Orientalism: The United States and the Middle East since 1945* (Chapel Hill: University of North Carolina Press, 2002), 106–107.

52. Drew, *Nixon,* 94.

53. Quotes are from Mark Atwood Lawrence, "History from Below: The United States and Latin America in the Nixon Years," in Logevall and Preston, eds., *Nixon in the World,* 269; Seymour M. Hersh, *The Price of Power: Kissinger in the Nixon White House* (New York: Summit, 1983), 263; and Henry Kissinger, *Years of Renewal* (New York: Simon and Schuster, 1999), 706.

54. Tanya Harmer, *Allende's Chile and the Inter-American World* (Chapel Hill: University of North Carolina Press, 2014); Jonathan Haslam, *The Nixon Administration and the Death of Allende's Chile* (New York: Verso,

2005); Peter Kornbluh, ed., *The Pinochet File: A Declassified Dossier on Atrocity and Accountability* (New York: New Press, 2003). On Allende's death, see Tim Weiner, *Legacy of Ashes: The History of the CIA* (New York: Doubleday, 2007), 316.

55. Melvin Small, *The Presidency of Richard Nixon* (Lawrence: University Press of Kansas, 1999), 142; Haldeman, *Haldeman Diaries,* 53.

56. Richard Reeves, *A Ford, Not a Lincoln* (New York: Harcourt, Brace, Jovanovich, 1975), 200. For Ford's career, see also James Cannon, *Time and Chance: Gerald Ford's Appointment with History* (Ann Arbor: University of Michigan Press, 1994).

57. Fredrik Logevall and Andrew Preston, "The Adventurous Journey of Nixon in the World," in Logevall and Preston, eds., *Nixon in the World,* 3–4; Garthoff, *Détente and Confrontation,* 548.

58. Kissinger, *Years of Renewal,* 1064. On Congress in this period, see Robert David Johnson, *Congress and the Cold War* (New York: Cambridge University Press, 2006), xx–xxi, 190–241.

59. Herring, *From Colony to Superpower,* 811.

60. Kissinger quoted in Burr, ed., *Kissinger Transcripts,* 221.

61. Michael Cotey Morgan, *The Final Act: The Helsinki Accords and the Transformation of the Cold War* (Princeton: Princeton University Press, 2018).

62. CIA aid figures are from Weiner, *Legacy of Ashes,* 348–349. See also Piero Gleijeses, *Conflicting Missions: Havana, Washington, and Africa, 1959–1976* (Chapel Hill: University of North Carolina Press, 2002), 246ff; and Westad, *Global Cold War,* 220–227

63. LaFeber, *America, Russia,* 297

64. Ford quoted in Yanek Mieczkowski, *Gerald Ford and the Challenges of the 1970s* (Lexington: University Press of Kentucky, 2005), 288; Reagan quoted in Julian Zelizer, *Arsenal of Democracy: The Politics of National Security in America since World War II* (New York: Basic Books, 2009), ch. 7. For the argument that U.S. domestic political concerns were crucial in the breakdown of détente, see also Garthoff, *Détente and Confrontation,* 13

65. Albert Wohlstetter, "Is There a Strategic Arms Race? *Foreign Policy* 15 (Summer 1974), 3–20.

66. Anne Hessing Cahn, *Killing Detente: The Right Attacks the CIA* (University Park: Pennsylvania State University Press, 1998), chapters 6–9; James Mann, *Rise of the Vulcans: Inside Bush's War Cabinet* (New York: Viking, 2004), 74.

67. Gergen quoted in Zelizer, *Arsenal of Democracy*, ch.7.

68. The debate transcript can be found at: www.pbs.org/newshour /debatingourdestiny/1976.html.

8. A New Cold War

1. Jimmy Carter, "Human Rights and Foreign Policy," speech presented at the University of Notre Dame, South Bend, Ind., May 1977.

2. An older study that holds up very well is Gaddis Smith, *Morality, Reason, and Power: American Diplomacy in the Carter Years* (New York: Hill and Wang, 1986). See also Robert Strong, *Working in the World: Jimmy Carter and the Making of American Foreign Policy* (Baton Rouge: Louisiana State University Press, 2000); Olav Njølstad, *Peacekeeper and Troublemaker: The Containment Policy of Jimmy Carter, 1977–1978* (Oslo: Norwegian Institute for Defense Studies, 1995); John Dumbrell, *The Carter Presidency: A Re-Evaluation* (Manchester: Manchester University Press, 1993). Highly critical is Burton Kaufman and Scott Kaufman, *The Presidency of James Earl Carter, Jr.*, 2nd ed. (Lawrence: University Press of Kansas, 2006). Useful insight into Soviet thinking in the period can be gained from Anatoly Dobrynin, *In Confidence: Moscow's Ambassador to American's Six Cold War Presidents, 1962–1986* (New York: Random House, 1995).

3. Quoted in Walter LaFeber, *The American Age: U.S. Foreign Policy at Home and Abroad*, vol. 2 (New York: Norton, 1994), 681.

4. A revealing memoir is Jimmy Carter, *An Hour before Daylight: Memories of a Rural Boyhood* (New York: Simon and Schuster, 2001).

5. See their respective memoirs: Zbigniew Brzezinski, *Power and Principle: Memoirs of the National Security Adviser, 1977–1981* (New York: Farrar, Straus, Giroux, 1985); Cyrus Vance, *Hard Choices: Critical Years in America's Foreign Policy* (New York: Simon and Schuster, 1983); Jimmy Carter, *Keeping Faith: Memoirs of a President* (New York: Bantam, 1982).

6. See Chester Pach, "Top Gun, Toughness and Terrorism: Some Reflections on the Elections of 1980 and 2004," *Diplomatic History* 28 (September 2004), 549–562.

7. Stanley Hoffmann, *Primacy or World Order: American Foreign Policy since the Cold War* (New York: McGraw-Hill, 1978), 248–249.

8. Elizabeth Borgwardt, *A New Deal for the World: America's Vision for Human Rights* (Cambridge, Mass.: Harvard University Press, 2005). See also the insightful overview by Arthur M. Schlesinger Jr., "Human Rights and the American Tradition," *Foreign Affairs* 57 (1978–79).

9. Carter's human rights approach has spawned a large literature. See, e.g., Sarah Snyder, *From Selma to Moscow: How Human Rights Activists Transformed U.S. Foreign Policy* (New York: Columbia University Press, 2018); and Mark Philip Bradley, *The World Reimagined: Americans and Human Rights in the Twentieth Century* (New York: Cambridge University Press, 2016), part 2; Lars Schoultz, *Human Rights and United States Policy toward Latin America* (Princeton: Princeton University Press, 1981), looks at the application in the Western Hemisphere, as does William Michael Schmidli, *The Fate of Freedom Elsewhere: Human Rights and U.S. Cold War Policy Toward Argentina* (Ithaca: Cornell University Press, 2013). And see also David F. Schmitz and Vanessa Walker, "Jimmy Carter and the Foreign Policy of Human Rights: The Development of a Post Cold War Foreign Policy," *Diplomatic History* 28 (January 2004).

10. Jordan to Carter, December 3, 1977, quoted in Julian Zelizer, *Washington Warfare: The Politics of National Security in America since World War II* (New York: Basic Books, 2009), chap. 7.

11. Hess, Stephen. "Jimmy Carter: Why He Failed." Brookings. Brookings Institution, July 28, 2016. https://www.brookings.edu/opinions/jimmy-carter-why-he-failed/.

12. David Skidmore, *Reversing Course: Carter's Foreign Policy, Domestic Politics, and the Failure of Reform* (Nashville: Vanderbilt University Press, 1996), 115; J. Michael Hogan, *The Panama Canal in American Politics: Domestic Advocacy and the Evolution of Policy* (Carbondale: Southern Illinois University Press, 1986), 114–131

13. Trita Parsi, *Treacherous Alliance: The Secret Dealings of Israel, Iran, and the United States* (New Haven: Yale University Press, 2007), 66. See

also James Bill, *The Eagle and the Lion: The Tragedy of American-Iranian Relations* (New Haven: Yale University Press, 1988); and "The Iranian Revolution: An Oral History with Henry Precht, Then State Department Desk Officer," *The Middle East Journal* 58 (2004), 9–31.

14. Strobe Talbott, *Endgame: The Inside Story of SALT II* (New York: Harper and Row, 1979).

15. Piero Gleijeses, "Truth or Credibility: Castro, Carter, and the Invasions of Shaba," *International History Review* 28 (1996), 70–103; Melvyn Leffler, *For the Soul of Mankind: The United States, the Soviet Union, and the Cold War* (New York: Hill and Wang, 2007), 275–276; Nancy Mitchell, *Jimmy Carter in Africa: Race and the Cold War* (Stanford: Stanford University Press, 2016).

16. Vladislav Zubok, *Failed Empire: The Soviet Union in the Cold War From Stalin to Gorbachev* (Chapel Hill: University of North Carolina Press, 2007), 254–257.

17. William Quandt, *Camp David: Peacemaking and Politics* (Washington: Brookings, 1986). For Carter's own take, see his *Keeping Faith*.

18. Brzezinski, *Power and Principle*, 196–197.

19. James Mann, About Face: *A History of America's Curious Relationship with China, from Nixon to Clinton* (New York: Knopf, 1998).

20. Raymond Garthoff, *Détente and Confrontation: American-Soviet Relations From Nixon to Reagan* (Washington: Brookings, 1994), 701– 716.

21. Warren Cohen, *America in the Age of Soviet Power* (Cambridge: Cambridge University Press, 1993), 212.

22. Paul Thomas Chamberlin, *The Cold War's Killing Fields: Rethinking the Long Peace* (New York: Harper, 2018), 418–50; Zubok, *Failed Empire*, 227, 259–264.

23. Carter quoted in John Dumbrell, *American Foreign Policy from Carter to Clinton* (London: Palgrave, 1996), 48.

24. On the Carter Doctrine's affirmation of American policy on oil, see Michael Clare, *Rising Powers, Shrinking Planet* (New York: Metropolitan Books, 2008), 180.

25. Quoted in Zelizer, *Washington Warfare*, chap. 7.

26. David Farber, *Taken Hostage: The Iran Hostage Crisis and America's*

First Encounter with Radical Islam (Princeton: Princeton University Press, 2005), 164.

27. Quoted in Arthur M. Schlesinger Jr., *Journals, 1952–2000* (New York: Penguin, 2007), 486.

28. Jackson quoted in H. W. Brands, *The Devil We Knew* (New York: Oxford University Press, 1993), 159.

29. A fine study of neoconservativism is Stefan Halper and Jonathan Clarke, *America Alone* (Cambridge: Cambridge University Press, 2005). Also see James Mann, *Rise of the Vulcans: The History of Bush's War Cabinet,* (New York: Viking, 2004), and Jacob Heilbrunn, *They Knew They Were Right: The Rise of the Neocons* (New York: Anchor, 2009).

30. Jeanne Kirkpatrick, "Dictatorships and Double Standards," *Commentary* 68, no. 5 (1979), 34–45. On this piece also see Brands, *The Devil We Knew,* 157–159.

31. Heilbrunn, *They Knew They Were Right,* 145; Peter Steinfels, *The Neoconservatives: The Men Who Are Changing American Politics* (New York: Simon and Schuster, 1979).

32. On Reagan's evolving political views, see Kiron Skinner, Annelise Anderson, and Martin Anderson, eds., *Reagan: In His Own Hand* (New York: Free Press, 2001).

33. On Carter's difficult last year, as seen from the perspective of a top aide, see Hamilton Jordan, *Crisis: The Last Year of the Carter Presidency* (New York: Putnam, 1982).

34. Carter and Vance in their memoirs make no mention of PD 59, but Brzezinski expounds on it at length. According to him, this new limited nuclear war doctrine was in the making as early as 1977. Brzezinski explains the changes as a new strategy to deal with improved Soviet nuclear war-fighting capabilities. Brzezinski, *Power and Principle,* 454–459.

35. Douglas MacEachin, *U.S. Intelligence and the Confrontation in Poland, 1980–81* (University Park: Pennsylvania State University Press, 2002).

36. See the useful analysis in Kevin Embick, "The Triumph of Containment" (master's thesis, Florida Atlantic University, 2008), ch. 5. We thank Mr. Embick for making his study available to us.

37. Alexander M. Haig, *Caveat: Realism, Reagan, and Foreign Policy* (New York: MacMillan, 1984).

38. A major biography that gives much insight into Reagan's thinking on foreign policy is Lou Cannon, *President Reagan: The Role of a Lifetime* (New York: Simon and Schuster, 1991).

39. Reagan quoted in Strobe Talbott, *The Russians and Reagan* (New York: Vintage, 1982), 32–33.

40. For the defense secretary's perspective, see Caspar Weinberger, *Fighting for Peace: Seven Critical Years in the Pentagon* (New York: Warner, 1990).

41. Nick Kotz, *Wild Blue Yonder: Money, Politics, and the B-1 Bomber* (New York: Pantheon, 1988), 3; Congressional Budget Office, *Building a 600-Ship Navy: Costs, Timing, and Alternative Approaches* (Washington, DC: 1982), 62.

42. National Security Council May 20, 1982, "U.S. National Security Strategy," National Security Decision Directive No. 32.

43. Ronald Reagan, *An American Life* (New York: Simon and Schuster), 586.

44. See Christopher Andrew, "Intelligence in the Cold War," in Melvyn P. Leffler and Odd Arne Westad, *The Cambridge History of the Cold War* (New York: Cambridge University Press, 2009).

45. George F. Kennan, *The Nuclear Delusion: Soviet-American Relations in the Atomic Age* (New York: Pantheon, 1982); Robert Jervis, *The Illogic of American Nuclear Strategy* (Ithaca: Cornell University Press, 1984). The review, by historian Martin J. Sherwin, is quoted in Walter L. Hixson, *George F. Kennan: Cold War Iconoclast* (New York: Columbia University Press, 1989), 186.

46. Two very valuable studies are Francis FitzGerald, *Way Out There in the Blue: Reagan, Star Wars, and the End of the Cold War* (New York: Simon and Schuster, 2000); Paul Lettow, *Ronald Reagan and His Quest to Abolish Nuclear Weapons* (New York: Random House, 2005).

47. Zubok, *A Failed Empire*, 273.

48. William Leogrande, *Our Own Backyard: The United States in Central America, 1977–1992* (Chapel Hill: University of North Carolina Press, 1998), 104–124; Robert Pastor, *Condemned to Repetition: The United States*

and Nicaragua (Princeton: Princeton University Press, 1987), 230–247. On Reagan administration policy in the Third World more broadly, see James M. Scott, *Deciding to Intervene: The Reagan Doctrine and American Foreign Policy* (Durham: Duke University Press, 1996).

49. According to Greg Grandin, El Salvador received $6 billion in U.S. aid, and the fighting there caused 50,000–60,000 civilian deaths and 20,000–34,000 military deaths over twelve years. The Nicaraguan fighting, he finds, claimed 30,000 civilian lives, while the fighting in Guatemala killed 100,000 peasants killed in just two years (1981 and 1983). Greg Grandin, *Empire's Workshop: Latin America, the United States, and the Rise of the New Imperialism* (New York: Henry Holt, 2007), 108, 116, 90.

50. For a thorough account of U.S. aid to Iraq in the early 1980s, see National Security Archive report, "Shaking Hands with Saddam Hussein," National Security Archive Electronic Briefing Book No. 82, Joyce Battle, ed., www.gwu.edu/~nsarchiv/NSAEBB/NSAEBB82.

51. Brian Davis, *Qaddafi, Terrorism, and the Origins of the U.S. Attack on Libya* (New York: Praeger, 1990), 142.

52. Two revealing accounts are *The Soviet-Afghan War: How a Superpower Fought and Lost,* by the Russian General Staff, trans. and eds. Lester W. Grau and Michael A. Gress (Lawrence: University Press of Kansas, 2007); and Ali Ahmad Jalali and Lester W. Grau, *The Other Side of the Mountain: Mujahideen Tactics in the Soviet-Afghan War* (Quantico: US Marine Corps Studies, 1995).

53. Steve Coll, *Ghost Wars: The Secret History of the CIA, Afghanistan, and Bin Laden, from the Soviet Invasion to September 10, 2001* (New York: Penguin, 2004), 89.

54. Odd Arne Westad, *The Global Cold War: Third World Interventions and the Making of Our Times* (New York: Cambridge University Press, 2005), 348–357, 367–369, 372–378, 388.

9. Endgame

1. The Cold War International History Project (CWIHP) has been particularly invaluable on the end of the Cold War, facilitating the release

of a wealth of documentary evidence from various key archives. See, for example, Vladislav M. Zubok, "New Evidence on the 'Soviet Factor' in the Peaceful Revolutions of 1989," *CWIHP Bulletin* 12/13 (Fall/Winter 2001), 5–23.

2. On these developments, see, e.g., Vladislav M. Zubok, *A Failed Empire: The Soviet Union in the Cold War From Stalin to Gorbachev* (Chapel Hill: University of North Carolina Press, 2007), ch. 9.

3. George Shultz, *Turmoil and Triumph: My Years as Secretary of State* (New York: Macmillan, 1993), 478.

4. Melvyn Leffler, *For the Soul of Mankind: The United States, the Soviet Union, and the Cold War* (New York: Hill and Wang, 2007), 370.

5. Shultz, *Turmoil and Triumph*, 6.

6. On the deep structural problems, see Stephen Kotkin, *Armageddon Averted: The Soviet Collapse, 1970–2000* (New York: Oxford University Press, 2001).

7. Robert English, *Russia and the Idea of the West: Gorbachev, Intellectuals, and the End of the Cold War* (New York: Columbia University Press, 2000), 159–160; Matthew Evangelista, *Unarmed Forces: The Transnational Movement to End the Cold War* (Ithaca: Cornell University Press, 1999), 259.

8. Quoted in Beth A. Fischer, "U.S. Foreign Policy: From Reagan to Bush," in Melvyn P. Leffler and Odd Arne Westad, *The Cambridge History of the Cold War*, vol. 3 (New York: Cambridge University Press, 2009).

9. On the 1984 shift in US policy see Don Oberdorfer, *The Turn: From Cold War to a New Era, the United States and the Soviet Union, 1983–1991* (Baltimore: Johns Hopkins University Press, 1998); and Beth A. Fischer, *The Reagan Reversal: Foreign Policy and the End of the Cold War* (Columbia: University of Missouri Press, 1997). And on the era as a whole, see Raymond L. Garthoff, *The Great Transition: American-Soviet Relations and the End of the Cold War* (Washington, DC: Brookings Institution Press, 1994).

10. See Fischer, *The Reagan Reversal*, 120–131, and Richard Rhodes, *Arsenals of Folly: The Making of the Nuclear Arms Race* (New York: Knopf, 2007), 163–170. For a recent and thorough analysis of Able Archer, see

Arnav Manchanda, "When Truth is Stranger than Fiction: The Able Archer Incident," *Cold War History* 9 (February 2009), 111–133.

11. Arthur M. Schlesinger Jr., *Journals: 1952–2000* (New York: Penguin, 2007), 607.

12. Leffler, *For the Soul of Mankind,* 392; Rhodes, *Arsenals of Folly,* 231.

13. The preceding section is drawn from, among others, John Lewis Gaddis, *Strategies of Containment: A Critical Appraisal of American National Security Policy during the Cold War,* 2nd ed. (New York: Oxford University Press, 2005), 365–366; Leffler, *For the Soul of Mankind,* 392–395; Jack F. Matlock, *Reagan and Gorbachev: How the Cold War Ended* (New York: Random House, 2004), 217–242; Strobe Talbott, *The Master of the Game: Paul Nitze and the Nuclear Peace* (New York: Alfred A. Knopf, 1988), 322–326.

14. Parsi, *Treacherous Alliance,* ch. 11; Peter Kornbluh and Malcolm Byrne, eds., *The Iran-Contra Scandal: The Declassified History* (Washington, DC: National Security Archive, 1993).

15. The Buckley column, dated June 2, 1988, is reprinted in William F. Buckley Jr., *Happy Days Were Here Again: Reflections of a Libertarian Journalist* (New York: Perseus, 2008), 77. Krauthammer quoted in Dinesh D'Souza, *Ronald Reagan: How an Ordinary Man Became an Extraordinary Leader* (New York: Free Press, 1997), 185.

16. Sidney Blumenthal, *Pledging Allegiance: The Last Campaign of the Cold War* (New York: Harper Collins, 1990). GOP pollster quoted in Julian Zelizer, *Arsenal of Democracy: The Politics of National Security in America since World War II* (New York: Basic Books, 2009), ch. 9.

17. For contemporary accounts, see Bernard Weinraub, "Cheney Remarks on Soviet Future Ruffle the White House's Feathers," *New York Times,* May 2, 1989; and Thomas Friedman, "Handling Gorbachev: A Debate among Skeptics," *New York Times,* November 2, 1989. Quayle quoted in Oberdorfer, *The Turn,* 334.

18. On U.S. policy in 1989–1991, see George Bush and Brent Scowcroft, *A World Transformed* (New York: Alfred A. Knopf, 1998); Philip Zelikow and Condoleezza Rice, *Germany Unified and Europe Transformed: A Study in Statecraft* (Cambridge: Harvard University Press, 1995); Mi-

chael R. Beschloss and Strobe Talbott, *At the Highest Levels: The Inside Story of the End of the Cold War* (Boston: Little, Brown, 1993). For a broader perspective, see Olav Njolstad, ed., *The Last Decade of the Cold War: From Conflict Escalation to Conflict Transformation* (London: Frank Cass, 2004).

19. John Dumbrell, *American Foreign Policy: Carter to Clinton* (London: Palgrave, 1996), 147.

20. See Leffler, *For the Soul of Mankind*, 403–409.

21. Archie Brown, *The Gorbachev Factor* (New York: Oxford University Press, 1996), 247–257; English, *Russia and the Idea of the West*, 224.

22. Zentrum für Zeithistorische Forschung, "Victims of the Berlin Wall," Chronik der Mauer, 2007, www.chronik-der-mauer.de/index.php /de/Start/Index/id/593792

23. Mary Elise Sarotte, *The Collapse: The Accidental Opening of the Berlin Wall* (New York: Basic Books, 2014).

24. Campbell Craig was a member of the seminar.

25. Schlesinger, *Journals*, 681–682.

26. Quoted in Ronald E. Powaski, *The Cold War: The United States and the Soviet Union 1917–1991* (New York: Oxford University Press, 1998), 270.

27. On Bush's handling of the Soviet collapse, see Jeffrey A. Engel, *When the World Seemed New: George H. W. Bush and the End of the Cold War* (Boston: Houghton Mifflin, 2017).

28. On this point, see H. W. Brands, *Since Vietnam: The United States in World Affairs, 1973–1995* (New York: McGraw-Hill, 1996), 146–147.

29. The premise that great-power rivalries inevitably culminate in major war was a staple of Realist international relations theory. See Robert Gilpin, *War and Change in World Politics* (New York: Cambridge University Press, 1981), 187. Kenneth Waltz, *Man, the State, and War: A Theoretical Analysis* (New York: Columbia University Press, 1959), 182.

30. Authors who subscribe to this view would include, e.g., Peter Schweizer, *Victory: The Reagan Administration's Secret Strategy that Hastened the Collapse of the Cold War* (New York: Atlantic Monthly Press, 1994); Richard Pipes, "Misinterpreting the Cold War," *Foreign Affairs* 74 (January/February 1995), 154–161; Caspar Weinberger, *Fighting for Peace*

(New York: Warner Books, 1990); and Robert Gates, *From the Shadows: The Ultimate Inside Story of Five Presidents and How They Won the Cold War* (New York: Simon and Schuster, 1996). For perceptive analysis, see Vladislav M. Zubok, "Why did the Cold War End in 1989? Explanations of 'the Turn,'" in Odd Arne Westad, ed., *Reviewing the Cold War: Approaches, Interpretations, and Theory* (London: Frank Cass, 2000); and Jeremi Suri, "Explaining the End of the Cold War: A New Historical Consensus?" *Journal of Cold War Studies* 4 (Fall 2002), 60–92.

31. Quoted in Fischer, *The Reagan Reversal*, 19. Nitze, loyal to his new boss Shultz, supported Reagan's overtures to Gorbachev after Reykjavik.

32. The most compelling expression of this argument is Stephen G. Brooks and William C. Wohlforth, "Power, Globalization, and the End of the Cold War," *International Security* 25 (Spring 2000), 60–107. An illuminating forum on the end of the Cold War can be found in a special issue, "IR and the End of the Cold War," edited by G. John Ikenberry and Daniel Deudney, *International Politics* 48 (July/September 2011).

33. Daniel Deudney and G. John Ikenberry, "The International Sources of Soviet Change," *International Security* 16 (Winter 1991–92), 74–118. On Gorbachev's nuclear idealism, also see Archie Brown, *The Gorbachev Factor* (New York: Oxford University Press, 1996), 237–238.

34. John Mashek, "Where Reagan Stands," *U.S. News and World Report*, May 31, 1976, 20.

35. On the importance of Reagan's nuclear idealism, see G. John Ikenberry and Daniel Deudney, "The Logic of the West," *World Policy Journal* 10 (Winter 1993–1994), 17–25.

36. See Brooks and Wohlforth, "Power, Globalization, and the End of the Cold War"; William C. Wohlforth, "The End of the Cold War as a Hard Case for Ideas," *Journal of Cold War Studies* 7 (Spring 2005), 165–173.

Conclusion

1. A magnificent essay on modern war is Paul Fussell's introduction to Fussell, ed., *The Norton Book of Modern War* (New York, 1991).

2. Fussell, ed., *The Norton Book of Modern War* (New York, 1991). For

a compelling articulation of this point, see Andrew Bacevich, *The Limits of Power: The End of American Exceptionalism* (New York: Metropolitan, 2008), 25–27.

3. John Lukacs, "The Poverty of Anti-Communism," *The National Interest* 55 (Spring 1999).

4. Joseph S. Nye Jr. is credited with coining the term "soft power." An early articulation of it is in his *Bound to Lead: The Changing Nature of American Power* (New York: Basic, 1990).

5. See John Lewis Gaddis, *The Cold War: A New History* (New York, 2005), ch. 1.

6. On this point, see Robert Jervis, *The Illogic of American Nuclear Strategy* (Ithaca: Cornell University Press, 1984), 56–63.

7. An attempt at tabulating the number of casualties in wars and other conflicts in the epoch is Patrick Brogan, *The Fighting Never Stopped: A Comprehensive Guide to World Conflict since 1945* (New York: Vintage, 1990).

8. Gaddis Smith, *Morality, Reason, and Power: American Diplomacy in the Carter Years* (New York: Hill and Wang, 1986), 116.

9. Hans J. Morgenthau, *Scientific Man vs. Power Politics* (Chicago: University of Chicago Press, 1946), 174.

10. Quoted in James G. Hershberg, "Just Who Did Smash Communism?" *Washington Post,* June 27, 2004, p. B1 (draft version, in authors' possession).

11. William I. Hitchcock, *The Struggle for Europe: The Turbulent History of a Divided Continent, 1945 to the Present* (New York: Doubleday, 2002), ch. 5. "The Miraculous Fifties" is the title of the chapter.

12. See Vladislav Zubok, *A Failed Empire: The Soviet Union in the Cold War from Stalin to Gorbachev* (Chapel Hill: University of North Carolina Press, 2007), chs. 7–8.

13. Andrew Bacevich, *The New American Militarism: How Americans Are Seduced by War* (New York: Oxford University Press, 2005), 89–90.

14. Power, 112. On threat inflation after 9/11, see also John Mueller, *Overblown: How Politicians and the Terrorism Industry Inflate National Security Threats, and Why We Believe Them* (New York: Free Press, 2007).

15. Lincoln Chafee, *Against the Tide: How a Compliant Congress Empowered a Reckless President* (New York: Thomas Dunne), 93.

16. See Gary Jacobson, "George W. Bush, the Iraq War, and the Election of Barack Obama," *Presidential Studies Quarterly* 40 (June 2010).

17. "American Democracy and Foreign Policy," speech at Grinnell College, Grinnell, Iowa, February 1, 1984, rpt. in George F. Kennan, *At a Century's Ending: Reflections, 1982-1995* (New York, 1996), 127-137. This theme is powerfully explored in Bacevich, *New American Militarism*.

18. "Containment: Then and Now," based on a talk given at National Defense University, November 6, 1985, rpt. in Kennan, *At a Century's Ending*, 110-115. For a most penetrating analysis of how American foreign policy might be "contained" today, see Stephen M. Walt, *Taming American Power: The Global Response to U.S. Primacy* (New York: Norton, 2005), 110-115.

ACKNOWLEDGMENTS

We are deeply grateful to the numerous friends and colleagues who commented on all or portions of the manuscript in draft. Bob Jervis and Will Hitchcock read the entire work at an early stage and provided a range of useful suggestions. For penetrating critiques of individual chapters we thank John Dumbrell, Jim Hershberg, Mark Lawrence, Sean Malloy, Ken Osgood, Andrew Preston, John Thompson, and David Welch. Doug Gibbons, Justin Granstein, and Charity Tubalado provided important and timely research assistance. Others who helped in various ways, large and small, include Christine Nielsen-Craig, Danyel Logevall, Chen Jian, Matthew Jones, Tim Naftali, Olav Njølstad, David Owen, Ben Selwyn, Julie Simmons-Lynch, and Julian Zelizer. Campbell would also like to thank the International Security Studies program at Yale University, the Politics Department at the University of Southampton, and the Norwegian Nobel Institute in Oslo for generous financial and institutional support, and the Rai d'Or in Salisbury for continued sustenance. Fred is grateful for the support provided by the Department of History at Cornell University and by the Universities of Nottingham and Cambridge during a marvelous sabbatical year—and (on the topic of sustenance) by fellow mem-

Acknowledgments

bers of the Red Bull Seminar, who put up with the lightweight Swede. We also thank the Peace Studies Program at Cornell for providing a forum for us to test out some of our ideas. At Harvard University Press we received expert editorial supervision from Kathleen McDermott and Susan Boehmer, and we also thank their colleague Lisa LaPoint. We dedicate this book to our children, who were born after the Cold War but who will come of age in its shadow. Peace, now, to all.

INDEX

Index

Index

Index

Dewey, Thomas, 124

Diem, Ngo Dinh. *See* Ngo Dinh Diem

Dien Bien Phu, battle of, 149–150, 153

Dirksen, Everett, 203

Dobrynin, Anatoly, 205–206, 254, 261, 267

Domino theory, 218, 221, 226, 227–228

Dominican Republic, 238–239

Dubcek, Alexander, 246

Dulles, Allen, 156, 196

Dulles, John Foster, 135, 148, 153, 160–161, 166, 189, 219, 265, 304, 353, 392n13; initial foreign policy of, 140–141, 144–145; and massive retaliation, 145–147; and Quemoy-Matsu, 150–152, 180–182; and Guatemala, 155–156; and thermonuclear dilemma, 161–162, 167–170, 176, 180; and Berlin ultimatum crisis, 184; death of, 185

Dukakis, Michael, 334–335

Dumbarton Oaks Conference (1945), 40

Dumbrell, John, 336

Eagleburger, Lawrence, 344

Eden, Anthony, 164

Egypt, 162, 164, 221, 287, 296; and 1967 war, 242–245; and Camp David accords, 277–279

Einstein, Albert, 21

Eisenhower, Dwight D., 7, 123, 354; commander in World War II, 35, 43, 139, 143, 170; and McCarthy, 128; background, 139–140; 1952 presidential campaign of, 140–141; early Cold War policies, 141–143, 146–147, 153–154, 160–162, 177; and death of Stalin, 142, 144; and intermestic politics, 144; views of USSR, 144–145; and massive retaliation, 145–147; and Korean War, 147–148; atomic diplomacy of, 148–153; and Britain, 144, 148–149, 162, 166–165, 181–182, 184–185; and Vietnam, 149–150, 218, 227, 236; and first Quemoy-Matsu crisis, 151–152; coup in Iran, 154–155, 292; coup in Guatemala, 155–156; policy toward neutralism, 156–158, 177; and psychological warfare, 158–160; and Suez crisis, 162–165; and Hungarian uprising, 165–166; and thermonuclear dilemma, 167–175, 176–178, 180, 182, 193–194, 209, 354–355; development of MAD, 168–169; and *Sputnik,* 173–174; and second Quemoy-Matsu crisis, 179–182; and Berlin ultimatum crisis, 183–185; and U-2 affair, 187–188; Farewell Address, 191–194, 212, 358, 361; and Cuba, 196, 274

Eisenhower Doctrine (1957), 164

Elections: *1948,* 124; *1952,* 138–139; *1960,* 188–191; *1964,* 229–230; *1968,* 248–249; *1972,* 270; *1976,* 284–285; *1980,* 307–308; *1988,* 334–335

Ellsberg, Daniel, 241

El Salvador, 315, 419n49

Elsey, George, 78–79

Estonia, 38, 337

European Recovery Program. *See* Marshall Plan

Fate of the Earth (Schell), 312

"Flexible Response," 195–196, 197–198, 204

Index

Index

Index

358, 363; "long telegram" of, 70–73, 111; conception of Soviet foreign policy, 3–4, 70–72, 322, 335; Lippmann critique of, 84–86; and Marshall Plan, 89; NATO, 100; and hydrogen bomb, 108, 110; and thermonuclear dilemma, 175, 312; and Vietnam, 240; disillusionment with Carter, 302

Kennedy, John F., 6, 243, 244, 310, 354; and missile gap, 173–174, 176, 186, 190–191, 285; background, 189; election of 1960, 188–191; and "Flexible Response," 194–196, 199–200, 209; and thermonuclear dilemma, 197, 199, 208– 210; and Bay of Pigs fiasco, 196–197, 202; intervention in Indochina, 197, 217–221, 224–225, 226; at Vienna summit, 197–198; and Berlin Wall crisis, 197–199, 202; and Cuban Missile Crisis, 200–207, 208, 214; pursuit of détente, 211–212, 356; and Vietnam, 222, 225–226; assassination of, 225–226

Kennedy, Robert, 203, 205, 248–249
Kennedy, Ted, 301, 303
Kent State shootings (1970), 257
Keynesian economics, 134, 349, 358; as component of NSC-68, 115–116; under Reagan, 310; as component of contemporary U.S. foreign policy, 366
Keyserling, Leon, 115
Khan, Ayub, 265
Kirkpatrick, Jeane, 304–305
Kissinger, Henry, 290, 297, 305; as nuclear strategist, 172–173; initial foreign policy of, 251–253; background, 253–254; bureaucratic technique, 254, 262; and Vietnam

War, 255–258, 267–271, 274–275; and détente, 258–260, 356; and overture to China, 263–265; and Middle East, 277–279; and Chile, 279–280; under Ford, 280–284
Khmer Rouge, 275
Khomeini, Ayatollah Ruhollah, 154, 156, 293, 301, 308, 333
Khrushchev, Nikita, 6, 162, 163, 177, 214, 219, 222, 232, 243, 274, 324; intervention in Hungary, 163, 165–167; and Berlin ultimatum crisis, 183–185; visit to U.S., 185; at Paris summit, 187–188; at Vienna summit, 197–198; and Berlin Wall, 198–199; and Cuban Missile Crisis, 201–202, 205–207, 208
Kim Il Sung, 6, 117, 129, 147
Knowland, William, 120, 121, 151
Korean War, 111, 116–117, 138, 231, 300; origins of, 116–118; initial U.S. response, 118–120; and NSC-68, 122; and election of 1952, 123; and McCarthy, 126, 128; historiographical debate, 129–131, 134–135; and Eisenhower atomic diplomacy, 147–148
Kosygin, Alexei, 245–246, 261
Krauthammer, Charles, 334
Krenz, Egon, 338
Kristol, Irving, 304

Laird, Melvin, 256
Laos, 218–219, 226, 228, 257, 271, 275, 281
Latvia, 38, 238
Lawrence, Ernest, 108
League of Nations, 13, 15, 19
Le Duc Tho, 270–271
Leffler, Melvyn, 129, 322
Lend-Lease, 25, 47

Index

Index

Index

Index

Index

United States Information Agency (USIA), 159
USS *Liberty* incident (1967), 245
Ussuri River conflict (1969), 261

Vance, Cyrus, 288, 289, 293, 298, 303, 368
Vandenberg, Arthur, 79, 80, 81
Vienna summit (1961), 197–198, 202
Vietnam. *See* Vietnam War
Vietnam War, 349, 353, 356, 357, 359, 362, 363; origins, 112, 149–150; early U.S. involvement, 216–217; Kennedy and, 217–226; initial Johnson policy on, 215–217, 227–229, 247; escalation of, 229–238; early criticism of, 238–240, 242–243, 248–249; Tet Offensive in, 246–247; Nixon and, 255–258, 268–271, 281; Paris Peace Accords in, 271; fall of Saigon, 271; casualties caused by, 271; Cold War and, 271–276; Carter and, 286; and U.S. image abroad, 290; postwar Chinese attack on Vietnam, 299
Vladivostok summit (1974), 282
Voice of America, 160

Walesa, Lech, 337
Wallace, Henry A., 44, 67, 78, 83, 135, 359
Waltz, Kenneth, 1, 11, 209
Warnke, Paul, 299
Warsaw uprising (1944), 38
Watergate scandal, 276, 280
Weber, Max, 23
Weinberg, Gerhard, 32

Weinberger, Caspar, 310, 327, 328; suspicion of Gorbachev, 343, 357
Welch, Joseph, 128
Williams, Ralph, 192
Willkie, Wendell, 17
Wilson, Woodrow, 43, 289, 291; and U.S. intervention into World War I, 13–20; compared to Roosevelt, 24, 33, 36, 43
Wohlstetter, Albert, 284
Wolfowitz, Paul, 304, 365
Woodward, C. Vann, 7
World Bank, 37
World War I, 13, 14–16, 17, 24
World War II: systemic effects of, 7, 19–20, 23, 34–35, 57–58; U.S. neutrality in, 17–18; and Roosevelt interventionism, 18–19, 24–27; and race for atomic bomb, 21–22, 28–29; in Pacific, 27, 28, 44, 47–49, 51–53; in Europe, 27, 28–29, 30–31, 46; and U.S.-Britain relations, 29–36; Casablanca conference, 29, 31–32; Tehran conference, 33–34; and U.S.-Soviet relations, 36–43, 58–59, 60–61; Yalta conference, 41–42; Potsdam conference, 48–50

Yalta conference (1945), 41–42, 43, 44, 47
Yeltsin, Boris, 341–342, 345
Yom Kippur War (1973), 277–278
Yugoslavia, 101, 157, 350

Zhou Enlai, 181, 263–265
Zhukov, Grigori, 143, 144